MORE

WOODWORKERS'

ESSENTIAL

Facts, Formulas
& Short-Cuts

MORE Woodworkers' Essential

Facts, Formulas & Short-Cuts

Figure it out,
with or without math

Ken Horner

Fox
Chapel Publishing

CAMBIUM PRESS

MORE WOODWORKERS' ESSENTIAL
Facts, Formulas & Short-Cuts
© 2006 by Ken Horner

ISBN 1892836211
First printing: April 2006
Printed in the United States of America

Cambium Press
www.cambiumpress.com

Cambium Press books are published by
Fox Chapel Publishing
1970 Broad Street
East Petersburg PA 17520
www.FoxChapelPublishing.com

Library of Congress Cataloging-in-Publication Data

Horner, Ken, 1936-

MORE Woodworkers' Essential Facts, Formulas & Short-Cuts : figure it out, with or without math / Ken Horner.

p. cm.

Includes index.

ISBN 1-892836-21-1

1. Woodwork. 2. Wood. 3. Woodworking tools. I. Title.

TT180.H664 2006
684'.08—dc22

2006004112

Dedication

To Laura Lee. You urged me on.

Contents

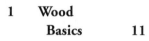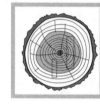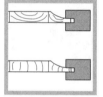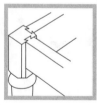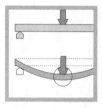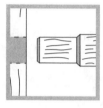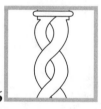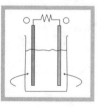
Rule of Thumb

Three coats of clear polyurethane provide the best protection against water vapor.

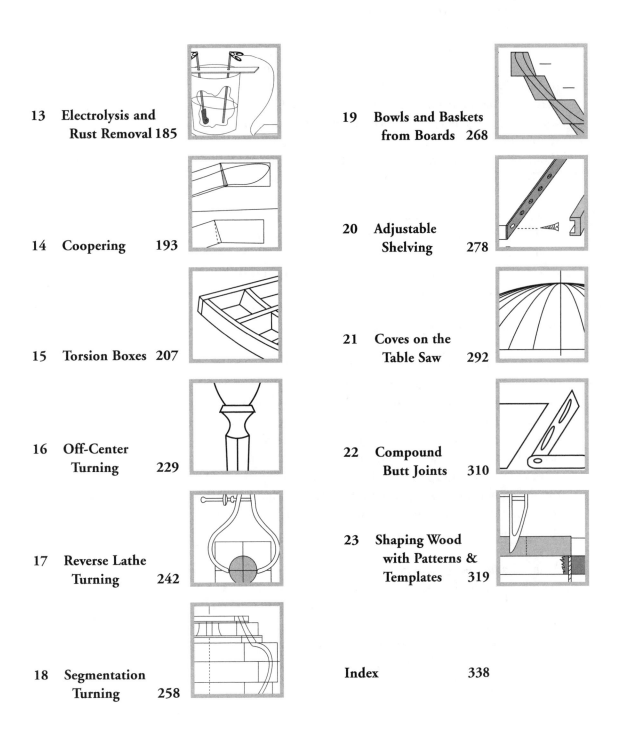

Preface

The first volume of this *Woodworkers' Essential* series grew from a collection of notes and math formulas I kept in a shoe box in my wood shop. I tossed in scraps of paper from time-to-time and as the collection grew it became apparent that there was enough data for a book. In 2003 *Woodworkers' Essential Facts, Formulas & Short-Cuts* was published with 30 chapters. For this *MORE Woodworkers' Essential* volume the shoe box was nearly empty. I thought a lot about what fundamental problems and solutions should be in a basic 2-volume set. How about the basics of wood — how a tree grows and how wood is cut and dried? Wood strength, wood movement and moisture protection should be there. I was also able to dig into more esoteric subjects such as the math of torsion box strength, cutting asymmetric coves on a table saw and the chemistry of why tools rust and rust removal with electrolysis. The 55 subjects covered in the two books are diverse and I think they span most of the workshop problems you're liable to encounter.

In the Preface to *Woodworkers' Essential,* I mentioned the math versus rule-of-thumb dilemma. Early on, my publisher, John Kelsey, was adamant that woodworkers would not buy a woodshop problem-solving book if it had only math solutions. He was insistent that each problem had to be solved, if at all possible, by a seat-of-the-pants method in addition to a math solution. So every chapter has rules-of-thumb answers; sometimes they are right-on, sometimes they are a close approximation – but they are there if you want to use them.

As in *Woodworkers' Essential*, there are only a few jigs mentioned in this book – on purpose. Both books would probably have doubled in size if I had included jigs, and there are already scads of books and articles about them. With the widespread use of the hand-held calculator, I've dispensed with trig tables. There are step-by-step directions in the use of a calculator scattered throughout the book.

Acknowledgements

The 23 chapters in this book cover a lot of complicated subjects — from *Column Strength and Entasis* to *Reverse Turning*. I'm fortunate to live in the center of Silicon Valley, an area replete with engineers, mathematicians and clever fellows — many who also are woodworkers. I relied heavily on some very smart friends in the South Bay Woodworkers Association who read and critiqued my efforts. Tom Kenyon read ***Wood Strength***. Jim Sweet read ***Marquetry***, ***Off-Center Turning***, and ***Shaping Wood with Patterns***. Fred Sotcher read ***Twists and Spirals***. Chuck Aring read ***Coopering***. Jay Perrine read ***Torsion Boxes***. Mike Wirth read ***Coves on the Table Saw*** and Syd Dunton read ***Compound Butt Joints***. Thanks a lot guys, the book is better because of you.

Linda Salter, the best segmented bowl turner I know, read the ***Segmented Turning*** chapter and helped to make a complicated subject understandable. She then went on to read and evaluate every chapter; she found errors and omissions, and offered valuable suggestions. Thanks a lot, Linda. My brother, Byron Horner, a mechanical engineer and math whiz, checked all the column- and beam-strength sections and kept me from straying. My nephew, Jeff Horner, a scientist at Lawrence Livermore Labs, showed me how to figure compound butt joints when the ends and the sides slope at different angles.

Ken Horner, Sunnyvale, CA, March 2006

CHAPTER 1

Wood Basics

A **tree starts when a seed first puts out roots** and a shoot emerges from the soil. At this point the nascent plant consists only of some inner pith, a surrounding layer of cells, a fragile bark covering and a bud on the tip. As the tree grows the roots extend, the trunk gets bigger and the branches develop to support the foliage. The leaves or needles absorb air containing carbon dioxide and the roots gather water and minerals. Elongated cells in the sapwood transport the water and minerals up the trunk to the leaves where a remarkable reaction takes place.

Photosynthesis is the process by which light energy is converted into chemical energy. This reaction, which takes place in all green plants, requires light, air, water, and minerals — all now present in the leaves. In its simplest form this reaction is:

Carbon dioxide plus water yields glucose plus oxygen

$$6CO_2 + 6H_2O \longrightarrow C_6H_{12}O_6 + 6O_2$$

Minerals, such as magnesium and calcium, also play a part in this complicated reaction.

The glucose produced in the leaves is converted into cellulose, the basic building block of all plants, and the cellulose is transported throughout the tree by a layer of cells called the cambium. The tree grows by continually

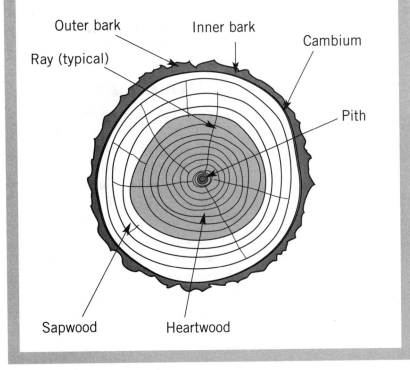

Figure 1 — Cross-Section of a Tree

The outer bark is dead and protects the inner bark; it often cracks as it expands. The inner bark is alive and protects the inner layers; it is impregnated with waxy substances and is waterproof. The sapwood is live wood that transports sap (water and minerals) from the roots to the leaves where photosynthesis takes place. The cambium layer moves the newly manufactured food (glucose) throughout the system, enabling the tree to grow. The heartwood is dead wood that provides structural support for the tree. The pith, the original tree stem, is also dead wood and very dense and hard. The rays radiate outward from the center (medulla) and connect all the layers; they transfer food from the sapwood to the isolated inner layers.

Outer bark   Inner bark   Cambium   Ray (typical)   Pith   Sapwood   Heartwood

Rule of Thumb

The tree grows in diameter by adding layers of wood to the outside.

A branch remains the same height off the ground as it was when it first began to grow.

adding sapwood and pushing the cambium and bark layers outward. Both height and girth are increased by addition of new wood to the existing tree structure thus the height of a branch from the ground doesn't change even though the top of the tree gets higher. This is the same with the girth; if a nail was pounded into the bark when a tree was 6 inches in diameter, then the nail will stay 3 inches from the center of the tree even if it grows to 3 feet in diameter. This embedment of a foreign object is common in back-yard wood, much to the consternation of sawyers who find horseshoes, wire, nails, and screws deep in logs when ripping them for lumber. The growing tree has outer bark, inner bark, cambium, sapwood, heartwood, rays, and pith. **Figure 1** shows the cross section of a tree.

Tree Growth

The cambium layer extends from the roots, up the trunk and out along all the branches and twigs. These cambium cells, wherever they are, divide and, as needed, become cells for food storage, for mechanical support, or for conduction of water, nutrients, or food. In a human, such multi-purpose cells are called stem cells: they can be used as needed throughout the body to produce bone, muscle, an eye, or a fingernail. In a tree, the cells divide longitudinally to produce growth in height, or tangentially to create growth in circumference.

When the cambium cells divide they arrange themselves around the tree in a circle. The rate of cell division depends on the type of tree and on external factors that encourage or discourage growth. In temperate climates, trees usually grow quickly in spring, slow over the summer, and are dormant in winter. Cells produced during the period of rapid growth are large in diameter with thin walls, while the cells produced during slow growth have smaller interiors and thicker walls. This difference in cell size results in a visible contrast between slow growth at the end of the year and rapid growth in the spring; producing a distinguishable layer that we call an annual ring.

The portion of the annual ring containing the fast growth is called the earlywood or springwood. The portion containing the slow growth is called the latewood or summerwood. The difference in density between the two, caused by the variation in thickness of the cell walls, results in the early wood being softer and wearing away more easily than the late wood. This effect can be observed in a weathered or sandblasted piece of wood that has a rippled surface.

In the roots, the cells have

thinner walls with large cavities to facilitate water movement. In branches, the opposite is true with smaller, thick-walled cells to provide extra strength. These cell walls, collectively, form the rigid structure of wood. In its early life, a cell is strong and flexible as needed for growth and support for the tree. Once the expansion growth of an annual ring is complete, the cell dies and is flooded with cellulose molecules that are very long polymers, with hundreds of glucose molecules strung end-to-end. These cellulose strings are cemented together by a glue-like substance called lignin, another long polymer, produced in the tree by enzymatic and microbial biosynthesis from basic amino acids. When the transformation of sapwood to heartwood is complete, although the heartwood cells are dead, the tree remains alive because of rays. Wood rays are horizontally oriented tissue extending through the radial plane of the tree. They connect the sapwood to the pith and heartwood and transport nutrients and extractives into the center of the tree.

Wood rays were once known as 'medullary rays' because they extend from the medulla or center of the tree outward in a radial plane to the sapwood. Modern usage is now wood rays.

Figure 2 — Chemical Composition of Wood

All woods are similar in that cellulose, hemicellulose and lignin form the cell walls. Cellulose is composed of long chains of glucose molecules; hemicellulose is composed of long chains of sugar molecules other than glucose, and lignin is made of complex organic compounds that help bond cells together. Extractives are compounds that are not an integral part of the cell wall but fill the heartwood cells to provide strength and resistance to biological degradation, and they also give color to hardwoods.

Chemical group	Wood volume (%)	
Cellulose	40-50	Glucose
Hemicellulose	25-30	Other sugars
Lignin	15-20	Vanillin-like compounds
Extractives	<5	Other chemicals

Chemical Composition

Wood consists of three main chemical groups: sugar, glue, and dyes. The cellulose and hemicellulose groups are the carbohydrates (sugar molecules) that make up the majority of the cell wall. Lignin acts as glue to bond cells together into a stiff and strong material. The extractives are chemicals that are deposited in the cells and provide unique properties to wood such as color and resistance to biological degradation. Woods with high natural resistance to decay contain a relatively high percentage of biocidal extractives, sometimes as high as 20% to 30% of the volume. Examples of naturally resistant woods include cedars and redwood. **Figure 2** shows the percentage by volume of the chemical groups in wood.

Wood Structure

Rule of Thumb

A flatsawn board typically moves twice as much in width as in thickness, while a quartersawn board typically moves half as much in width as in thickness. That's why quartersawn wood is considered the most stable.

Wood is composed of hollow, elongated, spindle-shaped cells arranged parallel to each other along the trunk of a tree. The characteristics of these fibrous cells and their arrangement affect such properties as strength and shrinkage, as well as the wood's grain pattern, or figure. Here are some elements of wood structure.

Tree Seeds — Tree seeds vary in size from quite large (27 seeds per pound, buckeye) to almost microscopic (300,000 seeds per pound, redwood). When conditions are right, seeds sprout and begin to grow in the soil.

Roots — The roots support the tree by penetrating the soil. They hold the soil in place and conduct water and minerals to the trunk.

Root Hairs — The root hairs absorb water plus dissolved minerals from the soil.

Outer Bark — The outer bark is corky and dead. Its thickness varies greatly with species and age. The growth in thickness of the outer bark is caused by the addition of new cells and by cell growth in the cambium. No wood or bark growth takes place outside the cambial zone. New wood cells are formed on the inside of the cambium and new bark cells on the outside. Thus, as new wood is added to the outside of old wood, the diameter of the trunk increases. The existing bark is pushed outward by the formation of new bark, causing the outer bark layers to become stretched, cracked, and ridged, and finally to drop off.

Inner or Live Bark — The inner bark is thin and alive and it carries some food from the leaves to growing parts of the tree. It contains a waxy substance that makes it impervious to water, insects, and disease. The existing live bark is pushed outward by the formation of new bark until it dies and becomes outer bark.

Cambium — The cambium layer, which is inside the inner bark, produces both wood (xylem) cells towards the center of the tree and bark (phloem) cells to the outside. This thin layer of cells can be seen only with a microscope. Each year the cambium produces new sapwood on the inner side and live bark on the outer side.

Sapwood — As cambium cells reproduce they form new sapwood. Old sapwood, laid down two or threes years ago, dies and becomes heartwood. Sapwood is located between the cambium and heartwood and comprises both living and dead tissue. The living cells carry sap (water plus minerals from the soil) from the roots to the leaves. The dead cells' function is primarily to store food. The sapwood layer, which sets itself apart with a light or tan color, varies in thickness and number of growth rings. In a fully grown tree, 24 to 36 inches in diameter, it commonly ranges from 1½ inches to 2 inches in radial thickness. As a rule, the more vigorously growing trees have wider sapwood, in fact second-growth trees of commercial size may consist mostly of sapwood. Sapwood is always susceptible to decay.

Heartwood — The function of heartwood is mainly structural and it is formed by a gradual change in the inner sapwood. In general, heartwood consists of inactive cells that do not function for either water transport or food storage. During the transition from sapwood to heartwood, no cells are added or taken away, nor do any cells change shape or size. The basic strength of the wood is not affected by the transition from sapwood to heartwood, though the cell walls do take on chemicals that provide unique properties to wood, such as its natural resistance to biological deterioration. These materials, transported by the wood rays, are called extractives. They darken the heartwood and give species their characteristic color (black for walnut, red for cherry) although in some species (hemlock, spruce, fir, basswood, cottonwood, and buckeye) the

Figure 3 — Heartwood Decay Resistance

Some heartwoods are very resistant to decay, others have only slight resistance.

Very Resistant	Resistant	Moderately Resistant	Slight Resistance
Black Locust	Catalpa	Douglas Fir	Alder
Azobe	Cedar (all)	Gum, Red	Ash (all)
Balata	Cherry	Larch	Aspen
Goncalo Alves	Chestnut	Locust, Honey	Beech
Greenheart	Cypress	Pine, Northern	Birch
Ipe (lapacho)	Juniper (all)		Butternut
Jarrah	Mahogany		Cottonwood
Lignum Vitae	Mesquite		Elm
Osage Orange	Oak (all)		Gum, Sweet
Pine, Southern Yellow	Redwood		Hackberry
Purpleheart	Walnut		Hickory
Teak			Linden
Yew			Maple (all)
			Pecan
			Persimmon
			Pine, Southern
			Poplar
			Spruce
			Tanoak
			Tupelo
			Willow

heartwood is lighter in color than the sapwood. As extractive chemicals fill the cell walls, the cells harden and the heartwood becomes stiffer, and the wood becomes resistant (more or less) to fungi, decay, and insect attack. In cedar and redwood, the extractives total 25% of the total weight and make the heartwood quite resistant to decay. In finished pieces of lumber the sapwood, having no extractives, is more susceptible to rot, decay, fungi, and invasion by insects. **Figure 3** compares the decay resistance of heart-woods.

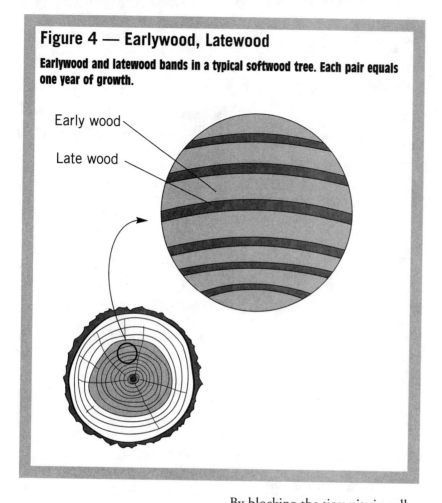

Figure 4 — Earlywood, Latewood

Earlywood and latewood bands in a typical softwood tree. Each pair equals one year of growth.

Early wood

Late wood

Heartwood is more resistant to dimensional change from moisture conditions and weighs slightly more than sapwood.

Pith — The pith is a small core of tissue located at the center of tree trunks, branches and twigs about which initial wood growth originally took place. Like the heartwood, pith is composed of dead cells. The pith is almost always cut away from a board and discarded during milling.

Knots — A knot is that portion of a branch that has been incorporated into the structure of a tree. Because all branches begin at the pith, so also do all knots radiate outward from the pith. As long as a limb remains alive, there is continuous growth at the junction of the limb and the trunk of the tree. This results in lumber with an inter-grown knot where fibers of the tree are continuous with the fibers of the knot. Once a branch dies, it stops growing and additional growth at the trunk encloses the dead limb. In time new wood fibers will cover the knot and the dead branch will not be visible. Lumber cut from this tree will have an encased knot where tree fibers are not interwoven with the knot fibers.

The shape of a knot on the sawn surface depends on the direction of the saw cut. A round knot is produced when the lumber and

By blocking the tiny pits in cell walls that normally allow liquid movement, extractives cause heartwood to resist absorption of liquids better than sapwood. Makers of treated lumber for outdoor use choose woods with a high percentage of sapwood because sapwood accepts the chemicals and heartwood does not. So, in this man-altered wood product, the heartwood becomes more susceptible to decay than the sapwood. Heartwood extractives also make the wood slower to dry and more difficult to impregnate with chemical preservatives.

Rule of Thumb

Knots in wood mark where branches grew from the trunk. All knots radiate from the center of the tree.

the branch are sawn through at right angles to the length. An oval knot is produced if the saw cut is diagonal to the length of the tree. See Chapter 5, *Wood Strength* for how knots affect wood strength.

Growth Rings — In temperate climates, the difference between wood that is formed early in a growing season and that formed later is sufficient to produce well-marked annual growth rings. The age of a tree at the stump or the age of any cross section of a limb may be determined by counting these rings (see **Figure 4**). However, if the tree's growth is interrupted by drought, disease, or defoliation by insects for example, more than one ring may be formed in the same season. Then the inner rings do not have sharp boundaries and are called false rings.

The inner part of a growth ring formed first in the growing season is called earlywood and the outer part formed later in the growing season is latewood. Earlywood cells have relatively large cavities and thin walls. Latewood cells have smaller cavities and thicker walls. If the growth rings are prominent, as in most softwoods, earlywood differs markedly from latewood in physical properties. Early-wood is lighter in weight, softer, and weaker than latewood.

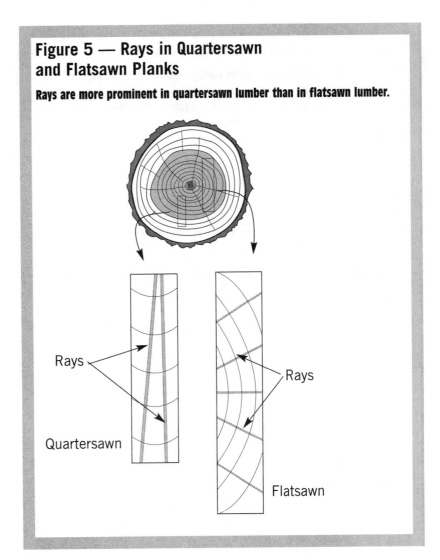

Figure 5 — Rays in Quartersawn and Flatsawn Planks

Rays are more prominent in quartersawn lumber than in flatsawn lumber.

Rays

Quartersawn

Rays

Flatsawn

Because latewood is denser, the proportion of latewood is used to judge the strength of a piece of wood, with more latewood indicating higher strength (and conversely, wide bands of earlywood may indicate weaker wood). **Figure 4** shows earlywood and latewood.

Wood Rays — Although the heartwood of the tree is essentially dead and its main function is physical support for

Figure 6 — Softwood Tracheids

Wood capillaries (tracheids) are dead, hollow cells in the sapwood about ¼ inch long. They are the main conduit for water as it travels up through the sapwood from the roots to the branches and leaves. A tracheid is about 100 times longer than it is in diameter. The hollow center is called the lumen, the openings through the side walls are pits.

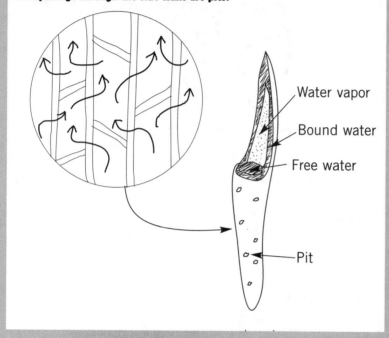

Water vapor

Bound water

Free water

Pit

and barely visible. In hardwoods, however, the rays can be quite large, up to ⅟₃₂ inch wide and 4 inches high. Ray cells radiate outward from the tree's center, so they only show up clearly in quartersawn lumber (see **Figure 5**). White oak is a good example of a tree with large rays. Ray tissue raises woodworking problems because it is cross-grain to the rest of the wood and is prone to tear-out. On the other hand, rays provide visual interest and have a restraining effect on radial shrinkage. Because the size of rays varies from species to species, they can be useful in identification. For example, the presence of large rays distinguishes white oak from ash.

Wood Cells — Softwoods have only one cell type which provides mechanical support for the tree and serves as a water conductor. These tracheids are closed at both ends and water moves from cell to cell through small openings (pits) in the cell walls. In hardwoods, there are two types of cells. The tracheids are open at both ends and water flows through from end to end through the hollow core (lumen). Mechanical support is by thick-walled cells with small lumens.

How Water Moves in Wood

Moisture in wood is either free

the branches and foliage, it still requires some nutrients. As the tree grows and the heartwood and pith are getting further from the sapwood, small connectors called rays develop. These ray cells radiate out from the pith like spokes in a wheel, and transfer nutrients from the sapwood to the inner parts of the tree. While most (95%) wood cells are arranged vertically to support the tree and to transport water and nutrients up and down, the ray cells (5%) are horizontal.

In softwoods the rays are small

or bound. A wood cell (tracheid) is mostly hollow and the water that sits in the cavity (lumen) is called free water. The water contained in the cell walls is called bound water. The movement of fluids through wood involves diffusion and pressure-driven flow. Gases and vapors can move through the cell walls as well as through the spaces in the wood by the diffusion of water molecules. Wood movement and wood drying are both the result of water movement.

Bound water moves by diffusion from wetter wood to drier wood. The molecules move from cellulose molecule to cellulose molecule within the cell walls and between adjacent cell walls.

Liquid water moves through an intricate pathway of interconnected capillaries (tracheids) in response to pressure gradients. In softwoods, the tracheids are closed at the ends, so all water flow between adjacent capillaries must go through small openings in the walls (pits) (see **Figure 6**). In hardwoods, the vessels are open at the ends and water flows freely between the capillaries; very little flow is through pits in hardwoods.

Height of a Tree

Water vapor leaves a tree by a process called transpiration, passing through the membranes of leaves. As one molecule of water evaporates, it pulls another molecule of water to the surface of the leaf. This creates a chain of water molecules moving from the roots of the tree to the top. A tree can grow in height until water can no longer reach from the roots to the topmost leaves.

In order for transpiration to work, the tree has to maintain an unbroken column of water from the roots up the entire height of the trunk in the sapwood. The taller a tree grows, the more tension builds in the water column and, if stretched too far, the column breaks, bubbles form, and the flow stops. Without water, the top parts of the tree will die. Right now the world's tallest tree is a California coast redwood, 370 feet tall. Scientists believe this is about as high as a tree can grow due to the way water is transported upward. To compare, the Statute of Liberty is 305 feet tall.

Water Content and Movement

While a tree is living it can have as much as two thirds of its total weight in the form of water. The water is prevented from evaporating (other than through the leaves) by the waterproof inner bark. Once a tree has been cut into boards, however, the high water content is no longer

Rule of Thumb

The tracheid **carries water** and provides mechanical support for the tree. It is about 100 times longer than it is in diameter.

Figure 7 — Wood Shrinkage

As the amount of bound water in the cell walls change, so also does the dimensions of the wood change. On average, tangential shrinkage is 8.2%, radial 4.5%, and longitudinal 0.1% when green wood with 30% moisture content dries to oven dry, 0% moisture content.

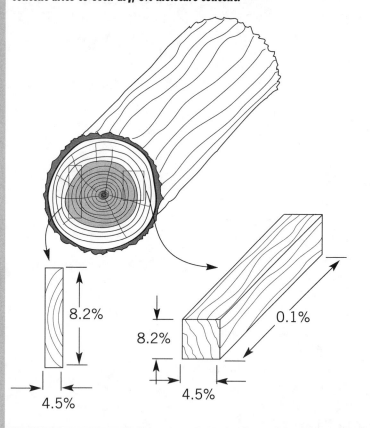

fluctuates because wood is hygroscopic, that is, it attracts and absorbs moisture from the air. Water molecules in the atmosphere are picked up by the wood until it reaches a balance with the surrounding air. Then the wood is said to have reached equilibrium moisture content (EMC).

Green wood, freshly cut from a live tree, has moisture content from 40% to 250%. The large variation depends on the wood species and whether the test sample is a piece of sapwood, heartwood, or pith. Because water is transported from the root system up through the sapwood to the leaves, the sapwood naturally has a higher moisture content than does the heartwood or the pith.

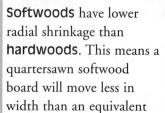

Rule of Thumb

Softwoods have lower radial shrinkage than **hardwoods**. This means a quartersawn softwood board will move less in width than an equivalent hardwood board.

maintained and the wood begins to dry out until its moisture content (MC) reaches a balance with the relative humidity (RH) of the surrounding air. This balance (MC versus RH) fluctuates as the relative humidity of the air changes, but the changes are measurable and predictable. For more on this see Chapter 2, ***Drying Wood***.

Wood is Hygroscopic

The moisture content of a board

How Wood Movement Occurs

Moisture in wood is either free or bound. A wood cell is mostly hollow and the water that sits in the cavity is called free water. When a log is cut into a board, the free water evaporates and escapes first. Water lost from the cell cavities does not cause the wood to shrink. Dimensional change occurs only after the cavities have been emptied and water begins to be lost from the cell walls. When all the free water is gone and only the bound water is left in the cell walls (fibers), the wood is said to have reached its fiber saturation point (FSP). The FSP of most woods is 25% to 35% moisture content, varying from species to species.

The bound water in the cell walls spreads and expands the wood. When this water is lost, the cell walls draw closer together. Because most of the long wood cells are oriented longitudinally in the tree, the greatest dimensional change occurs tangentially and radially (**Figure 7**).

To understand this, imagine the structure of wood to be like a bundle of straws made from absorbent paper. If the bundle was dropped into a pail of water, free water would fill the inside of the straws and bound water would be infused into the paper walls. When the bundle was

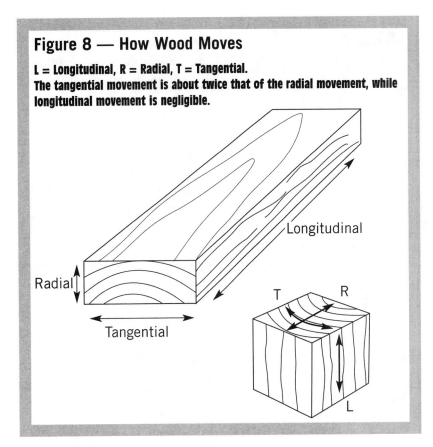

Figure 8 — How Wood Moves

L = Longitudinal, R = Radial, T = Tangential.
The tangential movement is about twice that of the radial movement, while longitudinal movement is negligible.

pulled from the pail, the free water would run out easily, just as when a tree is cut and the free water in the sapwood quickly escapes. However, the bound water, which is absorbed into the walls of the paper straws, takes longer to dissipate. Likewise, the bound water in the walls of the wood cells takes longer to escape. When the free water has left, the moisture content (MC) will be about 30% and the only water left (bound) will be in the walls of the cells. This is known as the fiber saturation point (FSP). Shrinkage begins with further drying, as the MC drops below the FSP.

Rule of Thumb

The **moisture content** (MC) of wood is rarely constant. It changes as the temperature and relative humidity (RH) of the surrounding air changes.

If the air conditions are kept constant then wood will eventually reach a MC in balance with its environment, the equilibrium moisture content (EMC).

The following approximations can be used to estimate the EMC.

Relative Humidity of the Air	EMC of the Wood
0%	0%
25%	5%
50%	10%
75%	15%

As the moisture content decreases below the fiber saturation point wood shrinks longitudinally, radially, and tangentially. **Figure 8** shows these directions.

Longitudinal Movement

Longitudinal or lengthwise movement is usually considered to be negligible, in the range of 0.1% to 0.2% as the wood dries from green (30% MC) to oven dry (0% MC). For most practical purposes, longitudinal movement can be ignored.

Radial Movement

Radial movement occurs perpendicular to, or across, the growth rings in the range of 4% as the wood dries from green (30% MC) to oven dry (0% MC). In all woods, radial movement is always less than tangential movement and more than longitudinal movement. In flatsawn wood, radial movement occurs primarily in the thickness of the board; in quartersawn wood it occurs primarily in the width.

Tangential Movement

The greatest movement will be in the tangential direction, that is, in the direction parallel to the growth rings, in the range of 8% as the wood dries from green (30% MC) to oven dry (0% MC). In flatsawn wood, tangential movement occurs primarily in the width of the board; in quartersawn wood it occurs primarily in the thickness. Because boards are wider than they are thick, quartersawn wood exhibits smaller dimensional change than flatsawn wood.

Tangential/Radial Movement

The tangential/radial (T/R) value is a ratio that compares tangential movement with radial movement. It is a good indication of whether the wood will distort during drying. The greater the difference between the two values, the higher the ratio and the greater is the tendency of the board to twist, cup, bow, wind, and warp during drying. The closer the two values, the closer the T/R ratio is to one, and the more stable the wood. See Chapter 4, *Wood Movement* for charts on T/R ratios and wood movement values.

Of the common woods, yellow birch has the lowest T/R ratio (closest to 1). Its T/R value of 1.3 means that yellow birch is the most stable wood during drying. The ratio is figured as follows:

Tangential Movement (yellow birch) = 0.0034

Radial Movement (yellow birch) = 0.0026

T/R Value (yellow birch) = 0.0034 ÷ 0.0026 = 1.3

Of the common woods, eastern white pine has the highest T/R ratio and thus should give a furniture builder the most problems while drying.

> Tangential Movement (white pine) = 0.0021
>
> Radial Movement (white pine) = 0.0007
>
> T/R Value (white pine) = $0.0021 \div 0.0007 = 3.0$

Dimension Change

The change in dimension due to changes in moisture content can be estimated by using the following equation:

$$\Delta D = D_I [C_T (M_F - M_I)]$$

Where ΔD = Change in dimension, D_I = initial dimension, C_T = the dimensional change coefficient in the tangential direction (for radial direction use C_R), M_F = final moisture content and M_I = initial moisture content.

Problem 1: Assume the width of a flat-grained piece of madrone is 11½ inches at 6% moisture content (MC). Estimate the width of the board as the MC rises to 12%. **Figure 23** on page 48 gives dimensional coefficients for tangential, radial and rift sawn lumber.

Solution 1: The tangential coefficient for pacific madrone is 0.0041.

$$\Delta D = D_I [C_T (M_F - M_I)]$$

$$\Delta D = 11.5 [0.0041(12 - 6)]$$

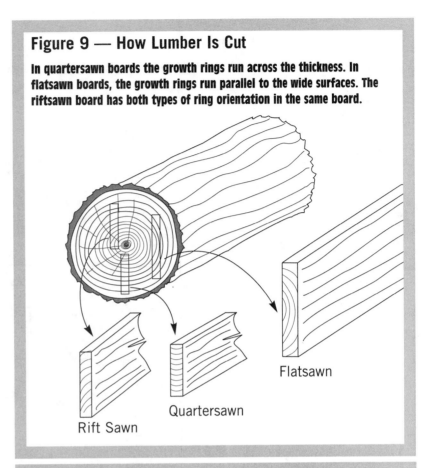

Figure 9 — How Lumber Is Cut

In quartersawn boards the growth rings run across the thickness. In flatsawn boards, the growth rings run parallel to the wide surfaces. The riftsawn board has both types of ring orientation in the same board.

Flatsawn

Quartersawn

Rift Sawn

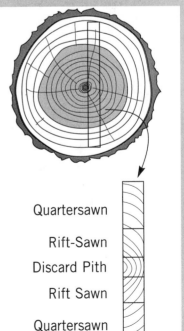

Figure 10 — Making Quartersawn Lumber from Flatsawn Pieces

A flatsawn board sawn from near the pith of the tree is not as stable as boards that are quartersawn or rift-sawn. Cut two narrow quartersawn pieces and two rift-sawn pieces from the flatsawn board. Box and discard the pith.

Quartersawn

Rift-Sawn

Discard Pith

Rift Sawn

Quartersawn

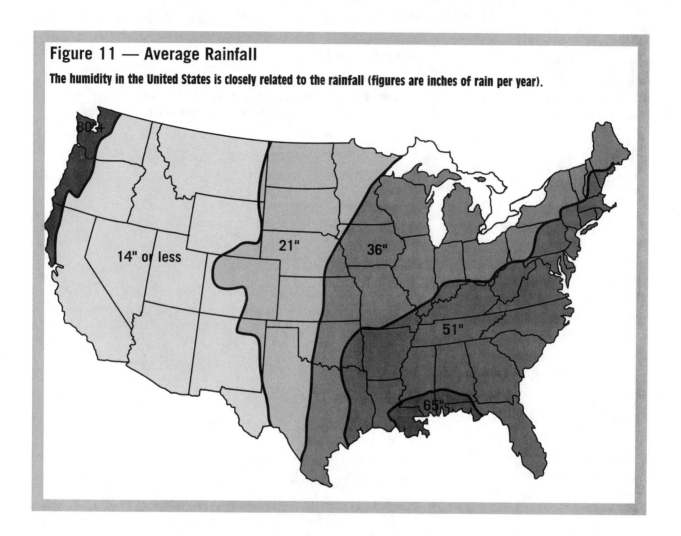

Figure 11 — Average Rainfall

The humidity in the United States is closely related to the rainfall (figures are inches of rain per year).

80"+

14" or less

21"

36"

51"

65"

CHAPTER 2

Drying Wood

When a log is freshly cut it's full of water; sometimes the trapped moisture weighs more than the wood itself. After milling, the green lumber still has about 30% moisture content (MC) and before the wet, heavy, and unstable boards can be used in construction they have to be dried. Wood dries naturally and will eventually reach moisture content that is in equilibrium with the humidity of the surrounding air, a condition called equilibrium moisture content (EMC). In most locations, air-drying will result in a MC no lower than 18% while for interior uses, woodworkers like a MC of 6-8%. To reach these lower values, it is necessary to dry the wood in a kiln. Under ideal conditions, one inch thick white pine boards in an outside stack will dry to 20% MC in three to four months (see **Figure 17**). A kiln will do the same job in four days and if the drying is carried out correctly, the boards will show only a little cracking on the ends but otherwise will remain straight and flat.

Wood used outdoors or for construction does not need to be as dry as lumber used for interior use — 12% to 16% MC is sufficient. This can be achieved by air-drying, but woodworkers also kiln-dry wood to save time, and to kill wood-boring insects and fungi.

Drying has always been a problem for the lumber industry because of losses due to checking, cracking, insects, stain, mold, and other misfortunes. During the 1800s when lumber was a relatively cheap raw material, losses of 50% were common and not considered important. After World War II, a building boom with the accompanying surge in furniture production strained the timber industry and it became necessary to sustain fewer losses, dry lumber faster, and produce higher quality material. In 1940 66% of U.S. lumber sold for building purposes was kiln-dried. Today nearly all lumber is dried in a kiln.

Rule of Thumb
You can dry small pieces of wood in the microwave oven

To dry small pieces of wood in a microwave, set the timer on 1 minute and the power on Defrost. After 1 minute, remove the wood and feel it with your fingers. If it feels cool, then heat on Defrost for another minute. Continue this until the wood feels warm to the touch then let the wood cool for 10 minutes. Nuke it again on defrost; this time for 30 seconds. Continue until the wood feels warm after 30 seconds of radiation. This procedure dries the wood without warps or cracks, and as a side benefit, kills insects, bugs and larvae – and fries insect eggs.

Figure 12 — Average Moisture Content of Newly Cut Wood

The average heartwood moisture content (MC) of newly cut wood is 73%, the average sapwood MC is 113%. In most cases the sapwood has a higher MC but in a significant number (15) of the wood species, the heartwood has the higher MC.

Wood Species	Heartwood Percent	Sapwood Percent	Wood Species	Heartwood Percent	Sapwood Percent
Alder, Red	-	97	Magnolia	80	104
Apple	81	74	Maple, Silver	58	97
Ash, Black	95	-	Maple, Sugar	65	72
Ash, White	46	44	Oak, California Black	76	75
Aspen	95	113	Oak, Northern Red	80	69
Baldcypress	121	171	Oak, Southern Red	83	75
Basswood, American	81	133	Oak, Water	81	81
Beech, American	55	72	Oak, White	64	78
Birch, Paper	89	72	Pine, Loblolly	33	110
Birch, Yellow	74	72	Pine, Lodgepole	41	120
Cedar, Port-Orford	50	98	Pine, Longleaf	31	106
Cedar, Eastern Red	33	-	Pine, Ponderosa	40	148
Cedar, Incense	40	213	Pine, Red	32	134
Cedar, West. Red	58	249	Pine, Shortleaf	32	122
Cherry, Black	58	-	Pine, Sugar	98	219
Chestnut, American	120	-	Pine, Western White	62	148
Cottonwood	162	146	Poplar, Yellow	83	106
Douglas Fir (Coastal)	37	115	Redwood, Old Growth	86	210
Elm, American	95	92	Spruce, Black	52	113
Elm, Cedar	66	61	Spruce, Sitka	41	142
Elm, Rock	44	57	Sweetgum	79	137
Fir, Balsam	88	173	Sycamore, American	114	130
Fir, White	98	160	Tupelo, Black	87	115
Hackberry	61	65	Tupelo, Water	150	116
Hemlock, Eastern	97	119	Walnut, Black	90	73
Hemlock, Western	85	170			
Hickory, Bitternut	80	54	**Average**	**73**	**113**
Hickory, Red	69	52	**Maximum**	**162**	**249**
Hickory, Water	97	62	**Minimum**	**31**	**44**
Larch, Western	54	119			

Removing Moisture from Wood

All wood is wet when it is cut from the log and most of this moisture must be removed before the wood can be used. When a plank dries, water follows the cell walls from inside to the surface according to the laws of physics, in which a substance seeks its own level and tries to distribute itself evenly throughout a material. Because evaporation occurs at the surface, the outer portions of the board dry first. This upsets the equilibrium and moisture from within begins to migrate toward the dry areas. If the surface evaporation is faster than the internal water movement, the surface drops to a low moisture content (MC) and drying quickens. If the surface moisture evaporates too quickly, however, the outer shell contracts and cracks. The evaporation process must be carefully controlled.

Water also moves toward the surface lengthwise through connecting cells called tracheids. This capillary action moves water and water vapor whenever the wood is sufficiently porous to permit it. Most of the tracheids are in the sapwood, which always dries faster than heartwood. **Figure 12** shows the moisture content of some common woods when newly cut.

Influence of Relative Humidity

Air is hygroscopic, that is it attracts and holds moisture, and the amount of water vapor in air is measured as humidity. Absolute humidity is the amount air can hold when fully saturated. Relative humidity is the amount of moisture actually in the air. The difference in moisture content between absolute humidity and relative humidity is the drying power of the air — how much more water this volume of air can absorb until it is saturated.

When air is fully saturated with water, it contains 778 mg per cubic meter (at 85°F.). If that same air contains only 194 mg it is said to be 25% saturated, or to be at 25% relative humidity. This air has the ability to take on three times more moisture. This is referred to as its drying power. As the temperature of air increases, it has a greater capacity for holding water vapor. At 170° F. the same volume of air can hold 7,300 mg (7.3 g.) of water. Therefore, at 170° F. and 25% saturation, it contains 1.8 grams of water but it can continue to absorb 5.5 grams more; this is its drying power.

Because wood is a hygroscopic material it will absorb and give up moisture according to its surroundings. If wood is immersed in water or in saturated air, it will absorb moisture until it is saturated and near to the moisture content (MC) of its surroundings. If placed in dry air it will give up some of its water to the air until both air and wood are nearly equal in MC. **Figure 22** on page 46 shows how dry lumber should be for use in woodworking. Wood for interior use in the south Atlantic and the Gulf Coast states should be 11% moisture content. For Arizona, Utah and Nevada and the hot interior area west of the Rockies, wood should be dried to 6%. The rest of the United States requires wood to be dried to 8% for interior use.

Rule of Thumb
Dense woods (specific gravity of 0.5 or greater) are harder to dry. They take more time, warp and twist more, and are less stable dimensionally.

Figure 13 — Distribution of Moisture in an Air-Dried Board

The average moisture content (MC) in the center sections of a board tested after six weeks of air drying show the effect of end drying and also the difference between end and side drying. The MC varies from 14% to 44%.

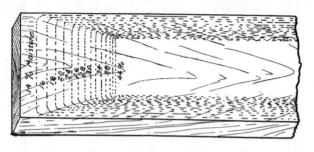

Figure 14 — Drying Rates of White Pine Boards in Different Parts of the Pile

The 1-inch boards were stacked and stickered during April, with spacing of two inches between the boards. The pile is 12 feet wide and 16 feet high. Boards in section 'A' dry to 25% MC in 2 weeks, those in 'B' dry to 25% MC in 3 weeks, those in 'C' in 4 weeks, 'D' in 8 weeks and the boards in section 'E' take 20 weeks to dry to 25% MC.

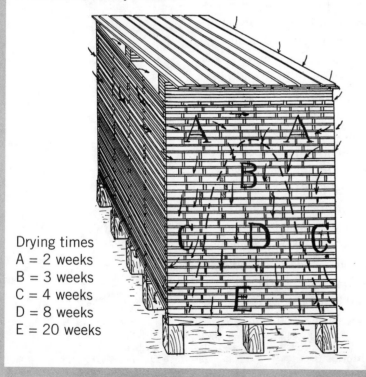

Drying times
A = 2 weeks
B = 3 weeks
C = 4 weeks
D = 8 weeks
E = 20 weeks

Rain influences humidity, which is highest where rainfall is highest. **Figure 11** shows the average rainfall in the United States. The Gulf States have the most rainfall, averaging 80 to 86 inches annually. The Atlantic and South Atlantic states average 65 inches. The Rocky Mountain states and the Southwest are fairly dry with 14 to 21 inches of annual rainfall.

Uneven Drying

The outside of a board dries faster than the inside, the ends of a board dry faster than the middle and sapwood dries faster than heartwood. One end of a board in the sun dries differently than the other end laying in the shade. Warm air circulates over the top of a board while the underside lies in dead air. For all these reasons, a freshly cut board left unattended dries unevenly. **Figure 13** shows a piece of wood air-dried for six weeks. The outside of the board has dried faster than the inside. The end of the board and the sides are at 14% moisture content (MC), while the center of the board is still at 44% MC. Because the end of the plank is porous, the dryness extends deeper than at the sides of the plank.

Figure 14 shows a pile of white pine at 30% MC, stacked and stickered for air drying. The 1 inch planks have 2 inch horizontal spaces between boards and ¾ inch vertical stickers. The pile was marked and taken apart so the moisture content (MC) of different sections could be tested. The boards at the top of the pile (A) dried to 25% moisture content in just two weeks while boards at the bottom interior of the pile (E) required 20 weeks. Shuffling a pile like this every week or so will result in faster and more uniform drying.

How Wood Dries

For wood to dry, both the free water held in the cavities of the cells and the bound water in the walls of the cells must be expelled. The free water is mostly in the sapwood and evaporates readily, leaving the wood with 30-35% MC. The bound water moves slowly to the surface of the wood and evaporates into the air. If the wood is stickered and stacked and left in the air to dry this process may take 3 months to a year, after which the moisture content (MC) will be from 20% to 25 %. Artificial heat must be used to dry wood to the 6% to 8 % MC necessary for interior woodworking.

Ninety percent of the losses that occur in drying lumber are due to uneven drying and uneven shrinkage whether the process is carried out in the yard or in a kiln. A kiln supplies artificial

heat and humidity — the heat to hasten the drying rate of the inside of the boards and the humidity to prevent too-rapid evaporation from the surface. By keeping the air in the kiln warm and moist, the drying is more uniform. The hot, humid air must be circulated over the surfaces of the boards at a regular rate and the conditions kept the same for all parts of the kiln so uniform drying can take place. Each wood species and thickness of lumber requires different kiln conditions.

Figure 15 shows the difference in weights for green wood with 30% moisture content (MC),

Figure 15 — Average Weights of Green Wood and Dried Wood

Green wood at 30% moisture content (MC) can be air dried to about 12% MC but then must be kiln dried to 6% MC. Air-dried wood weighs 31% less than green wood and kiln-dried wood is 42% lighter.

Wood	Green Weight 30% Water	Air Dry Weight 12% Water	Kiln Dry Weight 6% Water
Oak	5,000	3,909	3364
Ash	5,000	4,130	3533
Basswood	5,000	2,976	2619
Cottonwood	5,000	3,043	2717
Chestnut	5,000	2,800	2350
Elm	5,000	3,704	2685
Gum	5,000	3,056	2870
Hickory	5,000	4,000	3750
Maple	5,000	3,611	2778
Poplar	5,000	3,590	2821
Sycamore	5,000	3,158	2895
Tupelo	5,000	3,846	3333
Pine	5,000	0	2333
Redwood	5,000	3,375	2875
Average Wt.	**5,000**	**3,477**	**2,923**
Percent Diff.		**30.46%**	**41.54%**

Rule of Thumb

When you are **air-drying** a stack of wood, shuffle the stack every week for faster and more even drying.

Why Dry Wood?

There are several reasons why lumber should be dried before use:

1. **Dry lumber** is more stable and does not shrink or change shape as much as wet lumber while it is being worked or in use as furniture.

2. **Green wood** is heavy and drying will facilitate handling and reduce shipping charges.

3. **Wet lumber** is more susceptible to stain and mold.

4. **Boring insects** attack wet but not dry wood.

5. **Poles, posts, and ties** will not take preservative treatments until the sapwood has lost all of its free water.

6. Wood that is to be **painted or stained** must be dried first, otherwise the internal moisture will cause the finish to blister and peel.

7. **Proper drying** prevents wood from splitting and distorting.

air dried wood at 12% MC, and kiln dried wood at 6% MC. In general the air-dried wood weighs 31% less and the kiln dried wood weighs 42% less than the green wood. Shipping rates are figured on both volume and weight. A load of green redwood weighing 5,000 pounds drops to 3,477 pounds after air drying and to about 2,900 pounds after kiln drying.

The Drying Process

It is important for woodworkers to understand the drying process for two reasons. First, woodworkers need to recognize the difference between poorly dried and properly dried lumber. Second, most woodworkers eventually attempt their own drying on some scale, either for economy or to acquire otherwise unavailable material.

One might be tempted to simply place lumber in a hot environment and drive off the moisture. This would certainly dry the wood, but the stress of uneven shrinking would result in checks, honeycombing, casehardening, warps, and other defects. There are three stages that a piece of wood passes through if drying is not controlled. This illustrates how stress and defects develop.

Stage 1: Assume we take a plank of green wood (85% MC) and dry it under drastic

conditions, for example, place it on the ground in the hot sun for a week or two. The cross-section of the initial plank is shown in **Figure 16a**. During this stage, the plank is stress-free and defect-free. Although free water is escaping from the surface, no shrinkage will take place until the MC gets below 30% which is the fiber saturation point (FSP). Shrinkage will happen only when the bound water begins to escape.

Stage 2: Eventually the surface MC drops below the fiber saturation point (usually about 30%), and the wood near the surface, referred to as the shell (in contrast to the interior zone referred to as the core) begins to shrink. At the same time, the fully swollen core, at a much higher MC, is pushing outwards. The shell is now in tension around the outside of the board, and surface checks develop to relieve this stress. Because the shell is contracting, it places the core in compression, causing the cells in the core to buckle and collapse.

In Stage 2, the shell is shrinking around the core. Surface checks have appeared in the shell while the core begins to crush (see **Figure 16b**).

Stage 3: As the shell continues to dry, moisture moves from the core outward; the core begins to

Figure 16 — How Stress Develops During Three Stages of Wood Drying

A. In Stage 1 the moisture content (85% MC) is above the fiber saturation point (30% MC) throughout and drying begins with loss of free water from the surfaces and the ends. The board is stress-free and has no defects.

B. In Stage 2 the MC of the shell is below 30% while the MC of the core is above the 30%. Stress has developed with the shell shrinking around the core. To relieve the pressure, surface checks are starting to develop and the core is beginning to collapse.

C. In Stage 3 the MC of both the shell and the core are below the FSP (30% MC) and the core is shrinking away from the oversized shell which pulls the shell into compression. The interior stress has produced cupping, casehardening, honeycombing, and surface checks.

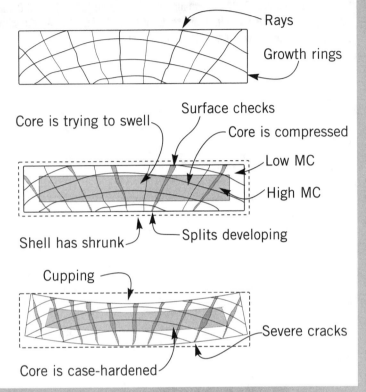

shrink and draws the shell inward. At this point the core is now in tension while the shell is in compression; this condition is known as casehardening and any surface checks that developed in Stage 2 now close up while splits develop inside the wood. The internal splits are known as honeycombing.

In Stage 3, the core has shrunk away from the shell and has pulled the shell into compression. The interior is casehardened (cell walls crushed) and beginning to honeycomb. The MC of the whole board is below the FSP (30%) but the board has

developed cups, honeycombs, casehardening, and surface checks. The plank is unfit for use (see **Figure 16c**).

Proper Drying

The woodworker is faced with a problem in drying wood: moisture will not move except from areas of higher moisture content (MC) to areas of lower MC, so to dry a piece of lumber a moisture gradient must be created, that is, a condition where the outside of the plank is drier than the inside. Also the MC of the surrounding air must be lower than the MC of the

Figure 17 — Drying Periods for One Inch Lumber

It takes an average of 127 days to air-dry green wood (30% MC) to 20% MC, and then seven days more in a kiln to dry it to 6%. A kiln will do the whole job, drying green wood from 30% MC to 6%, in 14 days.

Wood	Air Dry Green to 20% (Days)	Kiln Dry 20% to 6%. (Days)	Kiln Dry Green to 6% (Days)
Ash, White	90	6	15
Basswood	45	4	9
Beech	175	7	13
Birch	175	7	13
Cedar, Red	85	6	12
Cherry	175	6	11
Chestnut	105	6	10
Cocobolo	-	20	28
Cypress	240	5	8
Douglas Fir	55	3	6
Elm	105	5	12
Hickory	175	11	30
Mahogany	90	6	15
Maple	175	6	12
Oak, Red	210	6	21
Oak, White	270	9	33
Pine, Sugar	68	4	5
Pine, Western	68	4	4
Pine, White	105	4	6
Pine, Yellow	55	3	4
Poplar, Yellow	55	5	11
Redwood	120	6	8
Rosewood	-	17	26
Walnut	145	7	15
Average	**127**	**7**	**14**

Air Drying

Figure 17 shows that it takes an average of 127 days to air-dry lumber from green (30% MC) to 20% MC. Another 7 days in a kiln is needed to dry the wood to 6% MC. Lumber in a kiln can be brought from green (30% MC) to 6% MC in only 14 days.

Stacked lumber will only begin to dry from April to October when the temperature is high enough and the humidity sufficiently low. Lumber should be stacked at least 18 inches off the ground out of direct sun and in a well-ventilated, dry place. Temperature extremes such as hot, poorly ventilated attics should be avoided. Green wood generally requires two summers of air drying for every inch of thickness. The old rule of one year per inch applies only to ideal air-drying conditions.

Doubling the thickness of a board at least triples the drying time.

Figure 18 shows how flatsawn and quartersawn boards react to a change of MC from 12% to 6%. Also see Chapter 3, *Wood Movement* for more on this. As flatsawn lumber dries, it cups as though the growth rings were trying to straighten themselves out. The quartersawn boards will move proportionally more in thickness but less across the

wood to be dried. If this difference is too much, the wood dries overly fast and defects in the dried wood appear. If the difference in MC is too low, the wood takes overly long to dry and mold and mildew might develop. Thus the wood drier must settle for a compromise between speed and possible drying defects.

width and will also distort less. While drying causes the fibers to shrink, reintroduction of moisture will swell the fibers.

Air drying is only effective if a MC of more than 15% is needed, if long drying times are not a concern, and if exposure to extreme temperatures and low humidity can be avoided during the critical stage of drying from fresh cut to 25% MC. The best results are achieved when the air temperature is kept below 90°F and the humidity above 80% during the critical stage. In most parts of the U.S. these conditions cannot be expected especially during the summer months, though in some regions this would be considered normal summer weather. Some control over nature's drying conditions can be attained by taking the following steps:

1. **Avoid exposing** the wood to direct sunlight.

2. **Position the lumber** stacks in line with the prevailing winds; use a tarp to increase or decrease the amount of air that passes through.

3. **To increase the humidity** of the air surrounding the wood partially cover the stack with a tarp, or stack the wood inside a shed. This will capture some of the released moisture.

Recommendations for Quality Air-Drying

1. **Segregate lumber** by species and thickness. A rule of thumb is that doubling the thickness of a board at least triples the drying time.

2. **Stack the lumber** with strong, dry stickers of a uniform thickness (¾ inch or 1 inch by 1¼ inches wide). Lumber dries faster with thicker stickers and more air flow.

3. **Place stickers** 12 inches to 16 inches apart and align them vertically so that the weight of each board is carried down to the load supports.

4. **Add weight** at the top to help keep the lumber flat. Up to 150 pounds per square foot may be required to keep warp-prone species flat.

5. **Seal the end-grain** of each board with a wax-based end sealant to reduce end checking.

6. **Monitor** the moisture content of sample boards during drying.

7. **Control the drying conditions** according to the moisture content of the lumber. Be conservative as the MC nears 25% — the critical drying stage. As you gain experience with a particular species, thickness, and drying method, you can gradually alter the drying schedule to shorten drying time. Beware: most drying defects don't become visible until it is too late to do anything about them.

8. **Dry to a target** moisture content suitable for your needs.

9. **Check for casehardening** and condition the lumber if necessary by reintroducing moisture back to the stack with steam, water or higher humidity.

10. **Check for honeycomb** and collapse and try to counter by reintroducing moisture back to the stack with steam, water or higher humidity.

11. **Store dried lumber** in flat, solid stacks (no stickers) in a closed condition. A heated shed is ideal.

12. **Re-check the moisture content** before you use the lumber. Lumber with original 8% MC will slowly increase to 14% EMC in an unheated storage area.

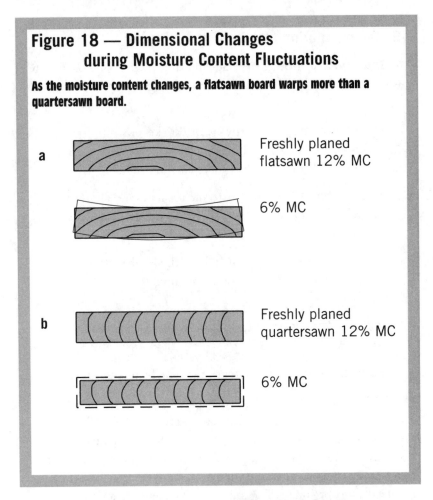

Figure 18 — Dimensional Changes during Moisture Content Fluctuations

As the moisture content changes, a flatsawn board warps more than a quartersawn board.

a — Freshly planed flatsawn 12% MC

6% MC

b — Freshly planed quartersawn 12% MC

6% MC

Kiln Drying

Ideally, the drying method should be capable of drying wood to 8% MC, be able to attain a temperature sufficient to kill insects and be capable of reintroducing moisture. A temperature of 160°F. will sterilize insect-infested wood. Reintroduction of moisture to the kiln is necessary to control drying and to condition casehardened lumber. Only a kiln will accomplish these goals.

Kiln temperatures typically range from 110°F to 200°F and the relative humidity ranges from 25% to nearly 100%. Drying times are much shorter when using a kiln. For example, 1 inch thick pine dries from 120% moisture content (MC) to about 8% in about one month. In an air-dried stack this would probably require two years and the results would be unpredictable. Also the lowest MC possible would be 20-25%. Kiln types include solar, steam-heated, hot water-heated, vacuum, radio frequency, microwave and, dehumidification.

Solar Kiln

A solar kiln can be the least expensive kiln to build and operate. Numerous design plans are available, and some companies sell a complete package of materials and design. The simplest solar kiln is a greenhouse that passively collects solar heat and distributes it through the lumber with a fan. It is important to monitor temperature and humidity, and to provide venting as a means of regulating the drying conditions. The major limitations of a solar kiln are the lack of complete control of drying conditions — the sun doesn't always shine and the heat varies from day-to-day. Also, the inability to achieve 160° F. for killing insects is a drawback. Solar kilns can be improved by adding auxiliary heat and humidification equipment.

Steam-Heated Kiln

The workhorse of the lumber drying industry is the steam-heated kiln, sometimes referred to as a conventional kiln. A gas- or wood-fired boiler delivers steam to fin-tube heat exchangers inside an insulated drying chamber. Kiln manufacturers provide continuous recorder/controllers to monitor and regulate the drying conditions according to pre-determined drying schedules. Excellent control can be achieved by regulating the amount of heat delivered by the steam system, venting the chamber to discharge excess heat or to bring in drier outside air to lower the humidity, or increasing the humidity by spraying steam into the chamber. High temperatures (185°F) are possible. A major disadvantage of steam kilns is the high cost of the equipment. If a steam boiler is available, then a steam kiln can be quite economical for the small operator.

Hot Water Kiln

This type of kiln is similar to a small steam-heated kiln except that hot water delivers the heat to the drying chamber instead of steam. The maximum temperature is about 150°F — just about the minimum to kill insects. They have the capability of adding humidity to the chamber to condition lumber and because a steam boiler is not required, these units are less expensive than steam-heated units.

Dehumidification Kiln

Dehumidification kilns are popular with small producers and woodworkers because of their low initial cost compared to all other lumber kilns except solar. These kilns use a dehumidifier to both remove moisture and to supply the heat needed to dry the wood. A dehumidifier operates on the same thermodynamic heat-pump principle as a refrigerator or air conditioner. When moist air from the drying lumber passes over a cold refrigeration coil (heat exchanger), the moisture in the air condenses onto the surface of the coil and is led off in a hose and measured as a gauge to drying. The condensing water gives off heat (latent heat of vaporization) that is recycled by the refrigerant cycle back into the air stream that conducts the heat to the lumber. This makes dehumidification drying very energy efficient. In all other convection lumber-drying methods, this latent heat held by the water molecules in air is lost when the moist air is vented from the kiln.

Some dehumidification units have a maximum operating

Rule of Thumb

Green wood generally requires **two summers of air drying** for every inch of thickness. Doubling the thickness of a board at least triples the drying time.

temperature of only 120°F but units are available that can reach 160°F. These kilns do not normally come from the manufacturer with a method of humidifying the air but they can be modified by adding a small steam generator to condition and minimize casehardening.

Vacuum Kiln

Wood can be successfully dried in a partial-vacuum chamber. Because water vaporizes at a lower temperature in a partial vacuum than it does at atmospheric pressure, wood can be dried faster at lower temperatures than by other drying methods. Because wood loses strength as its temperature increases, wood dried in a vacuum will have few drying defects because the critical stage of drying occurs at lower temperatures.

Vacuum kilns can reduce drying times by as much as 70%, depending on the species. In practice, the best results are obtained when drying short pieces of lumber (up to 2 feet in length) because the water vapor travels lengthwise along the grain of the wood faster than it does across the grain. In longer boards it is common to have a great deal of moisture content variation because moisture is trapped within the wood. Compared to the convection drying methods, capital, operating, and mainte-nance costs are high, but the

reduced drying times offset these costs. For a small operator, the economic analysis will be more favorable when drying expensive lumber than grade lumber.

Radio Frequency and Microwave Kilns

Wood can be dried using radio frequency or microwave energy. In these kilns the energy waves heat the water in the wood by exciting the hydrogen bonds. These methods will dry most species of wood two times faster than the convection kiln methods. The capital, operating, and maintenance costs are very high and the same problem of non-uniform wet pockets that is found in vacuum drying also occurs here. This method can be justified only in special circumstances. Wood turners often dry rough-turned bowls in a kitchen microwave oven. Uniform drying occurs because the wood is heated inside, outside, and through the center and very little cracking occurs.

The Critical Stage

The critical stage in drying occurs when the free water is gone and the bound water in the fibers is starting to leave the wood. Drying defects begin to occur as moisture leaves the outer shell faster than it leaves the inner core. The shell shrinks around the still swollen core. This stress causes checks in the shell along with honeycomb, casehardening, and collapse in the core. Most of these defects are not apparent until the wood is nearly dry, but they actually begin to develop very early in the process.

On fresh cut wood, this critical stage is from about 30% MC to about 25% MC. During this critical stage, the drying rate for 1 inch thick lumber should not exceed 1% to 2% MC decrease per day for most dense woods. Lower density woods can be safely dried at rates of 3% to 5% decrease per day. Once the stack reaches 25% MC more severe drying conditions can be used.

Biological Defects

Under proper conditions, wood will last for centuries. However, if conditions exist that permit the development of wood-degrading organisms, protection must be provided during drying and use. The principal organisms that can degrade wood are fungi, insects, and bacteria.

Fungus Damage

Fungus damage can be traced to four general causes:

1. Lack of suitable protective measures when storing lumber.

2. Improper seasoning of the lumber.

3. Improper storing of the lumber.

4. Failure to take precautions in use of the final product.

Molds, stains, and decay are caused by fungi, which are microscopic, thread-like microorganisms that must consume organic material to live. Wood offers the food supply for most of them and growth depends on mild temperatures, moisture, and oxygen from the air. By keeping the lumber dry (MC less than 20%), warm (above 60° F.), and covered by a protective coating of paint or wood preservative, most problems with fungi can be avoided.

Bacteria Damage

Most wood that has been wet for any length of time contains bacteria; the sour smell is indicative. Bacteria have little effect on wood properties although you might notice that infected areas absorb more paint or stain. Paint, oil, wax, or varnish will protect lumber that will be used in wet, cool conditions conducive to bacterial infestation.

Insect Damage

The list of insects that cause damage to lumber is long and includes beetles, worms, weevils, borers, wasps, bees, ants, termites, maggots, and grubs. In most cases these insects are in the tree when it is felled and the best way to get rid of them is to get the log to the mill quickly and cut into boards, then either apply an insecticide in water

Rule of Thumb

To control molds and stains:

1. Minimize oxygen available by keeping wood at a high moisture content until it can be dried, for example by constantly sprinkling the logs with water.

2. Once a tree has been cut, mill it quickly and stack it so the lumber can begin to dry.

3. Have adequate air circulation to remove moisture from the surface during drying.

4. Treat wood with fungicides but consider all fungicides as toxic.

Insects and eggs present in lumber will be killed during a normal dry kiln schedule with internal wood temperature above 160°F for at least 2 hours. Decay fungi will also be killed at this temperature.

emulsion to the green lumber or quickly move the boards to a kiln. Most insects will be killed by the high temperatures (160° F.) in a drying kiln.

Insects

Two categories of insects can attack or infest softwood lumber: forest insects, namely wood borers, ambrosia beetles, and horn-tailed wasps; and wood-in-service insects such as termites, carpenter ants, and powder-post beetles. The forest insects are of most concern to the lumber producer, while the wood-in-service insects are of most concern to the woodworker and homeowner.

You know you have an insect problem when you see insects emerge from the wood, though what you usually see is a tiny, tell-tale mound of dust (called frass). It is important to be able to tell the difference between a forest insect, which rarely poses a threat, and a wood-in-service insect, which can threaten the structural integrity of lumber. Both types of insect can be controlled, but the treatments are different.

Forest Insects – These insects do not reinfest seasoned wood and are best eliminated with kiln drying. These insects develop from eggs deposited in the bark of dead or dying trees. Upon hatching, the larvae bore into

the inner bark, forage there for several weeks, and then enter the wood. They slowly tunnel along the sapwood and ingest the soluble sugars. This larval stage lasts for several months to several years and is the only cycle of these insects when wood is used for food.

Following the larval stage, the insect pupates and emerges as an adult to mate and fly away in search of susceptible trees or barky logs on which to deposit eggs. Round- and flat-headed borers and horn-tailed wasps are the main members of this group. These insects require an environment provided by a weakened, dead or dying tree or log, complete with bark to carry on their life cycle.

Because these wood-boring insects are deep within a board and their tunnels are usually tightly packed with frass, surface applications of insecticides or fungicides are not effective. Fumigation is usually ineffective also. The most effective way to eliminate activity is with heat. Lumber kiln-dried at temperatures in excess of 150°F is considered safe from insect activity. Temperatures of 170°F are recommended to provide additional safety. The time required for treatment depends mainly on the thickness and moisture content of the wood (the higher the MC, the faster the heat transfer). Two hours at 170ºF will kill these insects.

Wood-In-Service Insects –

This second group of wood-boring insect attacks wood or lumber once it is in place. For the most part, they are not introduced into the structure by infested lumber, but rather as a result of construction deficiencies such as leaving pieces of wood scattered under a house. However, once in a structure, they can live and multiply in the dry softwood. Termites are the best known of the wood-in-service borers. Powder-post beetles, certain ants, moths, and bees will also bore into wood. Apart from termites and powder-post beetles, these insects attack wood for nesting purposes and not for food.

These dry-wood insects can be killed by elevated temperatures during the drying process but they often appear after the lumber is in use. A surface treatment of insecticide applied by a licensed pest controller will keep the pests away; however, these treatments rarely penetrate more that a few fractions of an inch into the wood. When an insect colony is well established and deep within the wood, insecticides injected by pressure needles or by boring holes or treating under pressure may be necessary.

There are three categories of termites: subterranean, drywood, and dampwood. They live in colonies composed of winged and wingless workers, nymphs, and soldiers.

Subterranean termites span the distance between ground and wood by building shelter tubes made of dirt, fecal material, and secretions. Because the nest is always below ground and the food source (your wood) is above ground, a tracking powder insecticide usually will eradicate the colony.

Drywood termites establish colonies in sound, very dry wood and never require contact with the ground. The first evidence of drywood termites is usually piles of brownish fecal pellets. Check with a licensed pest control agent for treatment.

Dampwood termites do not require contact with the ground but do need wood with a high moisture content. They are usually found under the bark of fallen trees, in forest cabins, or in beach houses where moist soil and high humidity conditions combine to make a structure vulnerable to attack. Check with a licensed pest control agent for treatment.

There are pest control agents advertising freezing and electrical zapping techniques for

Rule of Thumb

Decayed wood is difficult to dry and is already of poor quality because of fungi attacks to the cell walls of the wood. It's best to saw it off before beginning the drying process.

Rule of Thumb

When measuring the moisture content of wood with an **electronic meter**, take the measurement at least 2 feet from the board ends and 2 inches away from knots. Take at least three measurements per board — at both ends and in the middle. Apply correction factors provided by the manufacturer for the type of wood, as well as for temperature.

eradication of termites. I've seen no scientific data on the success of either technique.

Carpenter Bees – These bees are larger than a honey bee and they burrow into wood, not to feed, but to make nests. They are often found on unpainted rafters and posts on out buildings. They cut holes up to ½ inch in diameter and 3 to 4 inches deep. When I notice one crawling into such a hole, I squirt insect spray into the hole and tap in a wooden plug.

Marine-Boring Organisms

Damage by marine-boring organisms to wood structures in salt or brackish waters is a worldwide problem even in flowing rivers. Along the Pacific, Gulf and South Atlantic Coasts, attack is rapid, and untreated pilings may be completely destroyed in a year or less. Along the New England and the Northern Pacific Coast the rate of attack is slower because of cold water temperatures but it is still sufficiently rapid to require protection of the wood.

No wood is immune to marine-borer attack but jarrah, greenheart, azobe, and manbarklak have shown some resistance. Control is by heavy treatment with coal-tar creosote or a dual treatment with a creosote coal-tar solution and

copper-arsenate preservatives. Records show well-treated Douglas fir piles in San Francisco Bay waters have lasted from 22 to 48 years.

Moisture Meters

Many woodworking problems involve moisture: finishes that won't adhere, joints that break apart, and boards that change dimensionally. The easiest way to check if lumber has been properly dried is with a moisture meter. Meters are of two kinds. One type is a resistance meter that measures the electrical conductance between two pins that are stuck into the wood. The other type is pin-less and measures the dielectric constant of an electromagnetic field produced by a surface electrode. Both are based on the good correlation between electrical properties of wood and the moisture content below the fiber saturation point — about 30% MC. Manufacturers claim the accuracy of both types of meter is +/- 1.5%. The pin-type resistance meter is generally considered the more accurate of the two.

Both types of meter measure electrical or electromagnetic fields to estimate moisture content. Because different wood species differ in density, use the manufacturer's correction sheet for best results. In a test last summer on tanoak samples in

Mendocino County in Northern California, both types of meters were off by nearly 3% when compared to the conventional (and more accurate) weigh-and-heat method (Chapter 3).

Pin-Style Meters

These moisture meters have two pins that are pushed or driven into the wood. An electrical charge is emitted by one pin and travels through the wood to the other pin, using the wet wood as the conductor. The more moisture in the wood, the better is the electrical conductance. The meter measures electrical resistance within the board and converts it to a moisture reading. As wood dries, the electrical conductivity decreases. The meter takes a reading at a specific spot and the pins can penetrate anywhere from ⅛ inch to more than 1 inch deep. Some meters come with a hammer-probe attachment that allows you to pound larger pins deeper into the wood. The pins should be parallel to the grain, that is, placed lengthwise in the board. Follow the corrections for temperature closely because these meters are affected more by temperature than by wood species.

Procedures for pin-type meters:

1. Drive the pins into the wood so they are parallel to the grain direction.

2. Use insulated pins if surface moisture is present.

3. Drive the pins to a depth one forth the thickness of the lumber.

4. Most meters are calibrated for Douglas fir at 70° F. Correct for different species and temperature.

Pin-less Meters

Instead of an electrical charge, a pin-less meter uses radio waves to penetrate the wood and create an electromagnetic field. The waves bounce back from the surface of the board and the meter measures their reaction which differs depending on the moisture in the wood. The meter translates this behavior into moisture content. The main advantage of this type meter is that it leaves no marks in the wood. A disadvantage is that the top ⅛ inch of wood overly influences the result.

Procedures for pin-less meters:

1. The board being measured should not be in contact with any other material within 3 inches of the measuring zone.

2. Apply corrections for density and wood species.

Reference: ***Wood Handbook,*** Forest Products Laboratory, USDA, (2002) (Figure 12).

Reference: ***The Air Seasoning and Kiln Drying of Wood,*** Hiram Henderson, Albany, NY 1939 (Figures 13, 14, 15, 17).

Reference: John Shelly, University of California Forest Products Laboratory.

CHAPTER 3

Wood Movement

Wood movement is driven by changes in humidity because wood is hygroscopic. Wood attracts and absorbs moisture from the air and swells when the humidity is high, then when the humidity drops, it releases moisture back into the air and shrinks. In woodworking terms, this means joints that were tight today might be loose next week, the round table you made last winter may be elliptical now, and a table top may have pulled loose from its aprons. Wood movement is one of the biggest problems a woodworker faces.

Moisture from the air (water vapor) penetrates dry wood by diffusion until the wood eventually reaches a moisture content (MC) in equilibrium with its environment, a condition referred to as the equilibrium moisture content (EMC). This means unprotected furniture stored in a humid environment will absorb moisture as bound water (see Chapter 1, **Wood Basics** for a discussion of bound and free water). Understanding why wood moves is important, but in the workshop it is more important that we know how much it moves. We could just estimate and leave a little slack here and there but if we are not careless with our cuts and joints, why should we be sloppy about wood movement?

Actually wood movement is a double problem. Green lumber has to be dried so it is suitable for the intended end use and the drying conditions must be carefully controlled to avoid splits, cracks, warps and twists. For more on this see Chapter 2, **Drying Wood**. In California, where I live, we shoot for final moisture content of 6% to 8% and at this level the wood is relatively stable, reacts well with glue, and takes a good finish. Once the wood has been incorporated into a

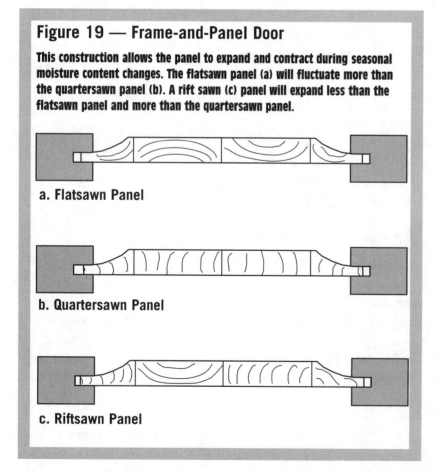

Figure 19 — Frame-and-Panel Door

This construction allows the panel to expand and contract during seasonal moisture content changes. The flatsawn panel (a) will fluctuate more than the quartersawn panel (b). A rift sawn (c) panel will expand less than the flatsawn panel and more than the quartersawn panel.

a. Flatsawn Panel

b. Quartersawn Panel

c. Riftsawn Panel

project the second problem appears: if the furniture piece is subjected to a humid atmosphere, the wood will swell as moisture is reabsorbed into the cells. The wood must be kept in the same 6% to 8% MC range to avoid buckles, cracks, and loose joints. A thorough knowledge of why wood moves will allow the savvy woodworker to build with wood movement in mind. For more on this, see Chapter 4, **Building with Wood Movement.**

Relative Humidity

The amount of water vapor that wood can absorb depends on the relative humidity (RH) of the surrounding air. Wood will absorb moisture until it is in balance with ambient humidity and at this point it will be stable and will not move. However, this stable state is not long-term because the relative humidity is constantly changing, cycling through daily and seasonal variations — and driving the moisture content of the wood through the same cycles.

Equilibrium Moisture Content (EMC)

When wood is exposed to outdoor humidity, its moisture content changes as it absorbs water vapor or as moisture evaporates. The average exterior relative humidity in the United

States is 12.5% and ranges from 4.0% RH to 18.1% RH. Unprotected furniture manufactured in the southeast, where the maximum equilibrium moisture content (EMC) is near 15% (for example Raleigh, NC), then moved to a southwestern state where equilibrium moisture content drops to 4% (for example Las Vegas, NV), will experience splitting, delamination of joints, or other noticeable defects.

Some parts of the country are easier on furniture because the humidity is relatively constant, for example Cheyenne, WY and Little Rock, AR have moisture content changes of only 1.1% over a twelve month period. Other parts of the United States have great swings in humidity, for example Pendleton, OR has a 9.1% MC variation from a high of 16.5% MC in December to a low of 7.4% MC in July.

Figure 20 shows the moisture content of wood stored outside and subject to humidity. As the relative humidity from January through December changes, so also does the equilibrium moisture content (EMC) of the stored wood. The annual maximum and minimum EMC are shown along with the monthly changes for 43 states. These values were measured by the National Climatic Data Center and are an average of 30 or more years of relative

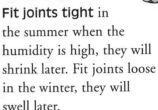

Rule of Thumb

Fit joints tight in the summer when the humidity is high, they will shrink later. Fit joints loose in the winter, they will swell later.

Figure 20 — Percent Equilibrium Moisture Content of Wood in the United States

State	City	Jan.	Feb.	Mar.	Apr.	May	Jun.	Jul.	Aug.	Sep.	Oct.	Nov.	Dec.	Max.	Min.	Diff.	Hi/Lo Avg.	12 Mo. Mean
AK	Juneau	16.5	16.0	15.1	13.9	13.6	13.9	15.1	16.5	18.1	18.0	17.7	18.1	18.1	13.6	4.5	15.9	16.0
AL	Mobile	13.8	13.1	13.3	13.3	13.4	13.3	14.2	14.4	13.9	13.0	13.7	14.0	14.4	13.0	1.4	13.7	13.6
AZ	Flagstaff	11.8	11.4	10.8	9.3	8.8	7.5	9.7	11.1	10.3	10.1	10.8	11.8	11.8	7.5	4.3	9.7	10.3
AZ	Phoenix	9.4	8.4	7.9	6.1	5.1	4.6	6.2	6.9	6.9	7.0	8.2	9.5	9.5	4.6	4.9	7.1	7.2
AR	Little Rock	13.8	13.2	12.8	13.1	13.7	13.1	13.3	13.5	13.9	13.1	13.5	13.9	13.9	12.8	1.1	13.4	13.4
CA	Fresno	16.4	14.1	12.6	10.6	9.1	8.2	7.8	8.4	9.2	10.3	13.4	16.6	16.6	7.8	8.8	12.2	11.4
CA	Los Angeles	12.2	13.0	13.8	13.8	14.4	14.8	15.0	15.1	14.5	13.8	12.4	12.1	15.1	12.1	3.0	13.6	13.7
CA	San Francisco	15.2	14.3	14.0	12.9	12.4	12.0	11.7	12.0	12.5	13.6	14.7	15.7	15.7	11.7	4.0	13.7	13.4
CO	Denver	10.7	10.5	10.2	9.6	10.2	9.6	9.4	9.6	9.5	9.5	11.0	11.0	11.0	9.4	1.6	10.2	10.1
CO	La Junta	12.3	12.0	11.3	11.0	11.7	11.1	10.5	10.7	11.1	11.0	12.1	12.5	12.5	10.5	2.0	11.5	11.4
DC	Washington	11.8	11.5	11.3	11.1	11.6	11.7	11.7	12.3	12.6	12.5	12.2	12.2	12.6	11.1	1.5	11.9	11.9
FL	Miami	13.5	13.1	12.8	12.3	12.7	14.0	13.7	14.1	14.5	13.5	13.9	13.4	14.5	12.3	2.2	13.4	13.5
GA	Atlanta	13.3	12.3	12.0	11.8	12.5	13.0	13.8	14.2	13.9	13.0	12.9	13.2	14.2	11.8	2.4	13.0	13.0
HI	Honolulu	13.3	12.8	11.9	11.3	10.8	10.6	10.6	10.7	10.8	11.3	12.1	12.9	13.3	10.6	2.7	12.0	11.6
ID	Boise	15.2	13.5	11.1	10.0	9.7	9.0	7.3	7.3	8.4	10.0	13.3	15.2	15.2	7.3	7.9	11.3	10.8
IL	Chicago	14.2	14.6	13.8	12.8	13.0	12.8	13.9	14.5	14.2	13.7	14.8	15.7	15.7	12.8	2.9	14.3	14.0
IN	Indianapolis	15.1	14.6	13.8	12.8	13.0	12.8	13.9	14.5	14.2	13.7	14.8	15.7	15.7	12.8	2.9	14.3	14.1
IA	Des Moines	14.0	13.9	13.3	12.6	12.4	12.6	13.1	13.4	13.7	12.7	13.9	14.9	14.9	12.4	2.5	13.7	13.4
KS	Wichita	13.8	13.4	12.4	12.4	13.2	12.5	11.5	11.8	12.6	12.4	13.2	13.9	13.9	11.5	2.4	12.7	12.8
KY	Louisville	13.7	13.3	12.6	12.0	12.8	13.0	13.3	13.7	14.1	13.3	13.5	13.9	14.1	12.0	2.1	13.1	13.3
LA	New Orleans	14.9	14.3	14.0	14.2	14.1	14.6	15.2	15.3	14.8	14.0	14.2	15.0	15.3	14.0	1.3	14.7	14.6
ME	Portland	13.1	12.7	12.7	12.1	12.6	13.0	13.0	13.4	13.9	13.8	14.0	13.5	14.0	12.1	1.9	13.1	13.2
MA	Boston	11.8	11.6	11.9	11.7	12.2	12.1	12.6	12.5	13.1	12.8	12.6	12.2	13.1	11.6	1.5	12.4	12.3
MI	Detroit	14.7	14.1	13.5	12.6	12.3	12.3	12.6	13.3	13.7	13.5	14.4	15.1	15.1	12.3	2.8	13.7	13.5
MN	St. Paul	13.7	13.6	13.3	12.0	11.9	12.3	12.5	13.2	13.8	13.3	14.3	14.6	14.6	11.9	2.7	13.3	13.2
MS	Jackson	15.1	14.4	13.7	13.8	14.1	13.9	14.6	14.6	14.6	14.1	14.3	14.9	15.1	13.7	1.4	14.4	14.3
MO	St. Louis	14.5	14.1	13.2	12.4	12.8	12.6	12.9	13.3	13.7	13.1	14.0	14.9	14.9	12.4	2.5	13.7	13.5
MT	Missoula	16.7	15.1	12.8	11.4	11.6	11.7	10.1	9.8	11.3	12.9	16.2	17.6	17.6	9.8	7.8	13.7	13.1
NE	Omaha	14.0	13.8	13.0	12.1	12.6	12.9	13.3	13.8	14.0	13.0	13.9	14.8	14.8	12.1	2.7	13.5	13.4
NV	Las Vegas	8.5	7.7	7.0	5.5	5.0	4.0	4.5	5.2	5.3	5.9	7.2	8.4	8.5	4.0	4.5	6.3	6.2
NV	Reno	12.3	10.7	9.7	8.8	8.8	8.2	7.7	7.9	8.4	9.4	10.9	12.3	12.3	7.7	4.6	10.0	9.6
NM	Albuquerque	10.4	9.3	8.0	6.9	6.8	6.4	8.0	8.9	8.7	8.6	9.6	10.7	10.7	6.4	4.3	8.6	8.5
NY	New York	12.2	11.9	11.5	11.0	11.5	11.8	11.8	12.4	12.6	12.3	12.5	12.3	12.6	11.0	1.6	11.8	12.0
NC	Raleigh	12.8	12.1	12.2	11.7	13.1	13.4	13.8	14.5	14.5	13.7	12.9	12.8	14.5	11.7	2.8	13.1	13.1
ND	Fargo	14.2	14.6	15.2	12.9	11.9	12.9	13.2	13.2	13.7	13.5	15.2	15.2	15.2	11.9	3.3	13.6	13.8
OH	Cleveland	14.6	14.2	13.7	12.6	12.7	12.7	12.8	13.7	13.8	13.3	13.8	14.6	14.6	12.6	2.0	13.6	13.5
OK	Oklahoma City	13.2	12.9	12.2	12.1	13.4	13.1	11.7	11.8	12.9	12.3	12.8	13.2	13.4	11.7	1.7	12.6	12.6
OR	Pendleton	15.8	14.0	11.6	10.6	9.9	9.1	7.4	7.7	8.8	11.0	14.6	16.5	16.5	7.4	9.1	12.0	11.4
OR	Portland	16.5	15.3	14.2	13.5	13.1	12.4	11.7	11.9	12.6	15.0	16.8	17.4	17.4	11.7	5.7	14.6	14.2
PA	Philadelphia	12.6	11.9	11.7	11.2	11.8	13.5	14.1	14.6	14.5	13.7	13.2	13.2	14.6	11.2	3.4	12.9	13.0
SC	Charleston	13.3	12.6	12.5	12.4	12.8	13.5	14.1	14.6	14.5	13.7	13.2	13.2	14.6	12.4	2.2	13.5	13.4
SD	Souix Falls	14.2	14.6	14.2	12.9	12.6	12.8	12.6	13.3	13.6	13.0	14.6	15.3	15.3	12.6	2.7	14.0	13.6
TN	Memphis	13.8	13.1	12.4	12.2	12.7	12.8	13.0	13.1	13.2	12.5	12.9	13.6	13.8	12.2	1.6	13.0	12.9
TX	Dallas	13.6	13.1	12.9	13.2	13.9	13.0	11.6	11.7	12.9	12.8	13.1	13.5	13.9	11.6	2.3	12.8	12.9
TX	El Paso	9.6	8.2	7.0	5.8	6.1	6.3	8.3	9.1	9.3	8.8	9.0	9.8	9.8	5.8	4.0	7.8	8.1
UT	Salt Lake City	14.6	13.2	11.1	10.0	9.4	8.2	7.1	7.4	8.5	10.3	12.8	14.9	14.9	7.1	7.8	11.0	10.6
VA	Richmond	13.2	12.5	12.0	11.3	12.1	12.4	13.0	13.7	13.8	13.5	12.8	13.0	13.8	11.3	2.5	12.6	12.8
WA	Seattle	15.6	14.6	15.4	13.7	13.0	12.7	12.2	12.5	13.5	15.3	16.3	16.5	16.5	12.2	4.3	14.4	14.3
WI	Madison	14.5	14.3	14.1	12.8	12.5	12.8	13.4	14.4	14.9	14.1	15.2	15.7	15.7	12.5	3.2	14.1	14.1
WV	Charleston	13.7	13.0	12.1	11.4	12.5	13.3	14.1	14.3	14.0	13.6	13.0	13.5	14.3	11.4	2.9	12.9	13.2
WY	Cheyenne	10.2	10.4	10.7	10.4	10.8	10.5	9.9	9.9	9.7	9.7	10.6	10.6	10.8	9.7	1.1	10.3	10.3
Avg.														14.1	10.9	3.3	12.5	12.4

Figure 21 — Moisture Content of Wood in Equilibrium with Humidity

Temp. Moisture Content (%) at various relative humidity values

Deg. F	5%	10%	15%	20%	25%	30%	35%	40%	45%	50%	55%	60%	65%	70%	75%	80%	85%	90%	95%
30	1.4	2.6	3.7	4.6	5.5	6.3	7.1	7.9	8.7	9.5	10.4	11.3	12.4	13.5	14.9	16.5	18.5	21.0	24.3
40	1.4	2.6	3.7	4.6	5.5	6.3	7.1	7.9	8.7	9.5	10.4	11.3	12.3	13.5	14.9	16.5	18.5	21.0	24.3
50	1.4	2.6	3.6	4.6	5.5	6.3	7.1	7.9	8.7	9.5	10.3	11.2	12.3	13.4	14.8	16.4	18.4	20.9	24.3
60	1.3	2.5	3.6	4.6	5.4	6.2	7.0	7.8	8.6	9.4	10.2	11.1	12.1	13.3	14.6	16.2	18.2	20.7	24.1
70	1.3	2.5	3.5	4.5	5.4	6.2	6.9	7.7	8.5	9.2	10.1	11.0	12.0	13.1	14.4	16.0	17.9	20.5	23.9
80	1.3	2.4	3.5	4.4	5.3	6.1	6.8	7.6	8.3	9.1	9.9	10.8	11.7	12.9	14.2	15.7	17.7	20.2	23.6
90	1.2	2.3	3.4	4.3	5.1	5.9	6.7	7.4	8.1	8.9	9.7	10.5	11.5	12.6	13.9	15.4	17.3	19.8	23.3
100	1.2	2.3	3.3	4.2	5.0	5.8	6.5	7.2	7.9	8.7	9.5	10.3	11.2	12.3	13.6	15.1	17.0	19.5	22.9
110	1.1	2.2	3.2	4.0	4.9	5.6	6.3	7.0	7.7	8.4	9.2	10.0	11.0	12.0	13.2	14.7	16.6	19.1	22.4
120	1.1	2.1	3.0	3.9	4.7	5.4	6.1	6.8	7.5	8.2	8.9	9.7	10.6	11.7	12.9	14.4	16.2	18.6	22.0
140	0.9	1.9	2.8	3.6	4.3	5.0	5.7	6.3	7.0	7.7	8.4	9.1	10.0	11.0	12.1	13.6	15.3	17.7	21.0
160	0.8	1.6	2.4	3.2	3.9	4.6	5.2	5.8	6.4	7.1	7.8	8.5	9.3	10.3	11.4	12.7	14.4	16.7	19.9
180	0.7	1.4	2.1	2.8	3.5	4.1	4.7	5.3	5.9	6.5	7.1	7.8	8.6	9.5	10.5	11.8	13.5	15.7	18.7
200	0.5	1.1	1.7	2.4	3.0	3.5	4.1	4.6	5.2	5.8	6.4	7.1	7.8	8.7	9.7	10.9	12.5	14.6	17.5

humidity and temperature data.

As shown in **Figure 20**, wood exposed to outdoor atmosphere will attain equilibrium moisture content (EMC) consistent with the relative humidity, for example a high of 18.1% MC (Juneau, AK) to a low of 4.0% MC (Las Vegas, NV). Furniture moved between areas of differing humidity will be subject to wood movement and must be protected. The states are listed month by month with the equilibrium moisture content of wood when exposed to outdoor atmosphere. The relative humidity, which drives the equilibrium moisture content, will be higher in all cases.

Wood Stored Outdoors

The moisture content of wood that is stored outdoors will come to equilibrium with the relative humidity (RH) that exists. **Figure 21** shows the moisture content of wood stored at different temperatures and relative humidity. For example, untreated lumber stored at 80°F at 80% RH will reach 15.7% MC. Wood that will be subjected to high humidity should be protected with a finish suitable to the situation; for more on this see Chapter 6, *Moisture Protection*.

Wood Stored Indoors

The moisture content (MC) of the wood in a project should be targeted to the equilibrium moisture content (EMC) that the finished piece will see. These conditions vary in the United States; regional average values of wood in building interiors are shown in **Figure 22**. The average

Figure 22 — Average Equilibrium Moisture Content (EMC) for Wood in Building Interiors.

The equilibrium moisture content for most of the United States is 8%, while the Atlantic and Gulf coasts are about 11% EMC and Arizona, Nevada and Utah average about 6% EMC.

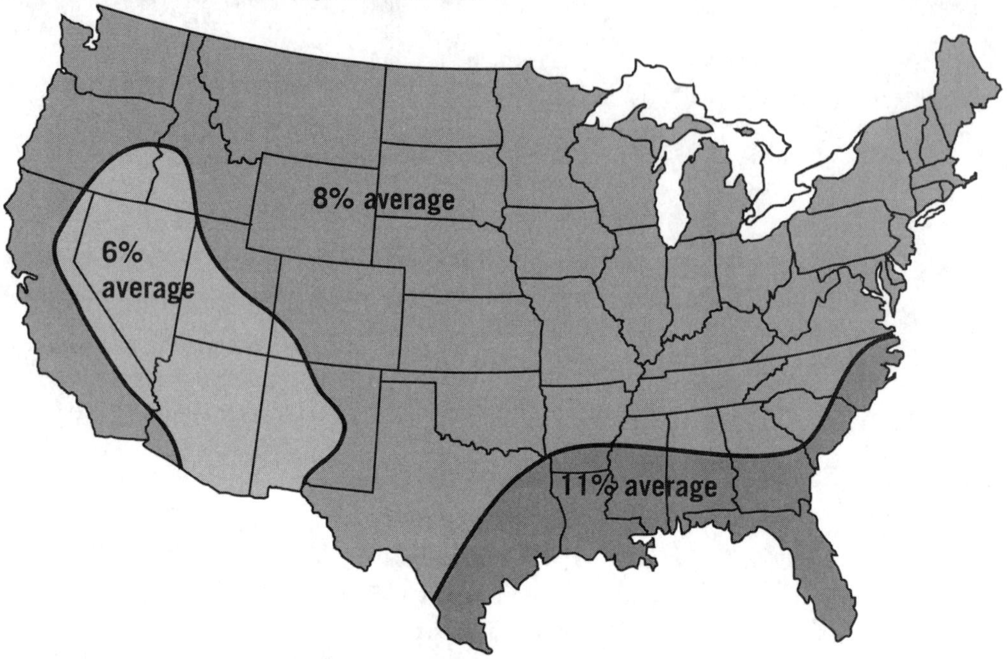

interior moisture content for most of the United States is 8%. The average increases to 11% MC along the southern Atlantic and Gulf coasts; in the arid Southwest, the EMC is relatively low at 6%.

Measuring Moisture Content

The moisture content of wood is defined as the ratio of the weight of water in a given piece of wood to the weight of the wood when it is completely dry. While you can measure moisture content with a moisture meter (see Chapter 2, **Wood Drying** for more on moisture meters), you can also do it by weighing and oven-drying samples. To find the moisture content of a stack of wood, proceed as follows:

Finding Moisture Content of a Stack of Lumber

a. **Select** two boards from different parts of the load.

b. **Cut** a 13-inch long piece from one end of each board.

c. **Cut** 1 inch off the end of each piece and discard.

d. **Cut** a 12-inch piece from the center of each board.

e. **Weigh** the four pieces

together. This is the initial weight.

f. Put the four specimens in an oven at 215ºF. Leave the door ajar and heat for 24 hours.

g. Weigh the four specimens and return to the oven for 1 hour.

h. Weigh the four specimens again and repeat step 'g.' until constant weight is reached. This is the oven-dried weight.

i. Calculate moisture content (MC) from the following equation:

MC = [(initial weight – oven-dry weight) ÷ oven-dry weight] x 100

Problem 1: We have just bought a load of green walnut lumber. The pieces are mostly 2 inch by 8 inch rough sawn planks, 10 to 12 feet long. What is the average moisture content of the pile?

Solution 1: Using the oven-drying procedure above we determine the four test pieces initially weigh 25 pounds. After drying, the pieces weigh 18 pounds.

MC = [(initial weight – oven-dry weight) ÷ oven-dry weight] x 100

Where initial weight = 25 pounds, oven-dry weight = 18 pounds.

MC = [(25 – 18) ÷ 18] x 100 = (7 ÷ 18) x 100 = 39%

Thus the load of walnut is at 39% MC.

Problem 2: If the four pieces of green walnut initially had weighed 55 pounds and after oven-drying weighed 20 pounds, what is the moisture content?

Solution 2:

MC = [(initial weight – oven-dry weight) ÷ oven-dry weight] x 100

Where initial weight = 55 pounds, oven-dry weight = 20 pounds.

MC = [(55 – 20) ÷ 20] x 100 = (35 ÷ 20) x 100 = 175%

The moisture content of the wood is 175%. This may seem strange. Can a piece of wood have more than 100% water? It can if the free and bound water together weigh more than the dry wood. Green wood can have a moisture content of anywhere from 30% to 200%.

Wood Movement

All wood contains moisture and when the amount of moisture changes, the wood will expand or shrink. This movement depends on five factors:

1. The species of wood.

2. How the wood was cut (flatsawn, quartersawn, or riftsawn). See Figure 24.

3. The width of the boards.

Rule of Thumb

The **average moisture content** for wood used indoors in most of the United States is 8%. The average increases to 11% MC along the southern Atlantic and Gulf coastal regions; in the arid southwest, the equilibrium moisture content is relatively low at 6%.

Figure 23 — Wood Movement per Inch of Width

Wood Species	Tangential (Flatsawn) Cut	Radial (Quartersawn) Cut	Rift Cut	Wood Species	Tangential (Flatsawn) Cut	Radial (Quartersawn) Cut	Rift Cut
Alder, Red	0.0024	0.0015	0.0020	Oak, Live	0.0032	0.0022	0.0027
Apple	0.0034	0.0019	0.0026	Oak, Northern Red	0.0029	0.0013	0.0021
Ash, Black	0.0026	0.0017	0.0021	Oak, Red	0.0030	0.0014	0.0022
Ash, White	0.0026	0.0016	0.0021	Oak, Southern Red	0.0038	0.0016	0.0027
Aspen, Quaking	0.0022	0.0012	0.0017	Oak, White	0.0035	0.0019	0.0027
Balsa	0.0025	0.0010	0.0018	Obeche	0.0018	0.0010	0.0014
Basswood, American	0.0031	0.0022	0.0027	Padauk	0.0019	0.0011	0.0015
Beech, American	0.0040	0.0018	0.0029	Pine, Eastern White	0.0020	0.0007	0.0014
Birch, Paper	0.0029	0.0021	0.0025	Pine, Loblolly	0.0025	0.0016	0.0020
Birch, Yellow	0.0031	0.0024	0.0027	Pine, Lodgepole	0.0022	0.0014	0.0018
Buckeye, Yellow	0.0027	0.0012	0.0020	Pine, Longleaf	0.0025	0.0017	0.0021
Butternut	0.0021	0.0011	0.0016	Pine, Pitch	0.0024	0.0013	0.0019
Cedar, Alaska	0.0020	0.0009	0.0015	Pine, Ponderosa	0.0021	0.0013	0.0017
Cedar, Eastern Red	0.0016	0.0010	0.0013	Pine, Red	0.0024	0.0013	0.0018
Cedar, Incense	0.0017	0.0011	0.0014	Pine, Shortleaf	0.0026	0.0015	0.0021
Cedar, North. White	0.0016	0.0007	0.0012	Pine, Slash	0.0025	0.0018	0.0022
Cedar, Spanish	0.0021	0.0014	0.0017	Pine, Sugar	0.0019	0.0010	0.0014
Cedar, West. Red	0.0017	0.0008	0.0012	Pine, Western White	0.0025	0.0014	0.0019
Cherry, Black	0.0024	0.0012	0.0018	Poplar, Yellow	0.0027	0.0015	0.0021
Chestnut	0.0022	0.0011	0.0017	Redwood, Old Growth	0.0015	0.0009	0.0012
Cocobolo	0.0014	0.0009	0.0012	Redwood, New Growth	0.0016	0.0007	0.0012
Cottonwood	0.0031	0.0013	0.0022	Rosewood, Indian	0.0019	0.0009	0.0014
Cypress	0.0021	0.0013	0.0017	Spruce, Red	0.0026	0.0013	0.0019
Dogwood	0.0039	0.0025	0.0032	Spruce, Sitka	0.0025	0.0014	0.0020
Douglas Fir (Coastal)	0.0026	0.0017	0.0021	Sycamore, American	0.0028	0.0017	0.0022
Douglas Fir (Inland)	0.0025	0.0014	0.0020	Teak	0.0013	0.0007	0.0010
Elm, American	0.0032	0.0014	0.0023	Walnut, Black	0.0026	0.0018	0.0022
Elm, Rock	0.0027	0.0016	0.0022	Walnut, European	0.0021	0.0014	0.0018
Fir, Balsam	0.0023	0.0010	0.0016	Wenge	0.0019	0.0010	0.0015
Fir, White	0.0024	0.0011	0.0017	Willow, Black	0.0029	0.0011	0.0020
Hackberry	0.0030	0.0016	0.0023	Yew, Pacific	0.0018	0.0013	0.0016
Hemlock, Eastern	0.0023	0.0010	0.0016				
Hemlock, Western	0.0026	0.0014	0.0020	**Average**	**0.0027**	**0.0015**	**0.0020**
Hickory, Pecan	0.0030	0.0016	0.0023	**High**	**0.0041**	**0.0025**	**0.0032**
Hickory, Shagbark	0.0035	0.0023	0.0029	**Low**	**0.0013**	**0.0007**	**0.0010**
Holly, American	0.0033	0.0016	0.0025				
Larch, Western	0.0030	0.0015	0.0023				
Lauan	0.0027	0.0013	0.0020				
Locust, Black	0.0024	0.0015	0.0020				
Locust, Honey	0.0022	0.0014	0.0018				
Madrone, Pacific	0.0041	0.0019	0.0030				
Magnolia, Southern	0.0022	0.0018	0.0020				
Mahogany	0.0014	0.0010	0.0012				
Mahogany, African	0.0015	0.0008	0.0012				
Maple, Red	0.0027	0.0013	0.0020				
Maple, Sugar	0.0033	0.0016	0.0025				
Oak, Black	0.0037	0.0015	0.0026				

Shrinkage or expansion per inch of width is shown for each percent moisture content change. Flatsawn lumber moves twice as much as quartersawn lumber.

4. The moisture content of the wood.

5. The equilibrium moisture content of the usage area.

Wood Species

Various wood species expand or contract differently when subjected to moisture. **Figure 23** shows wood movement per inch of width for each percent moisture content change for common woods. Values are given for sawn flatsawn (tangential), quartersawn (radial), and rift-sawn boards.

Wood Cut

A log can be cut to produce boards with the width parallel to the growth rings (flatsawn), with the width perpendicular to the rings (quartersawn) or a combination of the two (riftsawn). See Chapter 1, *Wood Basics* for more on this. The movement in width of flatsawn lumber is about double that of quartersawn boards.

Width

Wide boards and glued up pieces of furniture expand and contract more than narrow boards. The movement of a 12-inch cabinet door might be insignificant, while the swelling of a 32-inch door might be enough to cause it to stick.

Moisture Content

The exact moisture content of the wood that is used for the project can be found by weighing or with a moisture meter. For more on moisture meters see Chapter 2, *Drying Wood*. You can estimate moisture content by using **Figure 20** or **Figure 21**.

Equilibrium Moisture Content of Usage Area

Once the furniture piece has been moved into the usage area it begins to assume the ambient moisture content and in time will reach equilibrium moisture content. If a door or drawer is constructed during the winter when the humidity is low, it will swell and stick during the wet, highly humid summer months. Conversely, a door or drawer constructed when the humidity is high will shrink when the humidity drops.

Calculating Wood Movement

To find wood's dimensional change in width use the following formula:

Seasonal Movement = Panel Width x Chart Value x MC Change

To illustrate how this works:

Problem 3: Calculate the change in width for a 32-inch solid wood door made of flatsawn red oak as in **Figure 24**. It will be constructed in Phoenix in June, then installed in a cabin in

Figure 24 — Solid Wood Door

A solid wood door made of flatsawn (a) boards will shrink and swell twice as much as one made of quartersawn boards (b). A door of mixed flatsawn and quartersawn boards (c) and riftsawn boards (d) will move less than the flatsawn and more than the quartersawn door.

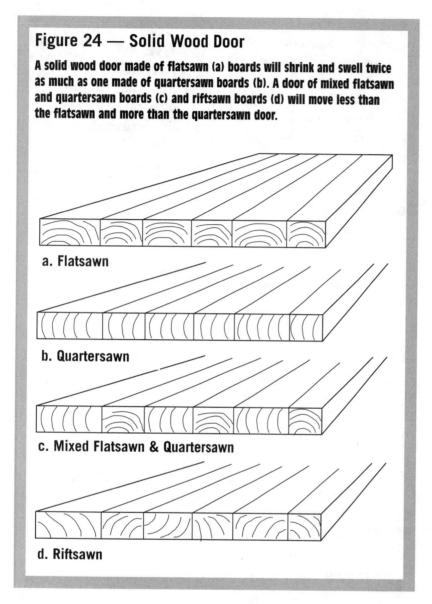

a. Flatsawn

b. Quartersawn

c. Mixed Flatsawn & Quartersawn

d. Riftsawn

Flagstaff soon after. How much wood movement may we expect?

Solution 3: Find the wood movement for flatsawn red oak in **Figure 23** and the equilibrium moisture content for Phoenix and Flagstaff (**Figure 20**).

The movement for flatsawn red oak is 0.003 inch per inch of

width, for each percentage point of moisture change. The moisture difference from Phoenix in June (4.6% MC) to Flagstaff in June (7.5% MC) is 2.9 percentage points.

> Seasonal Movement = Panel Width x Chart Value x MC Change
>
> Where width = 32 inches, value = 0.003 and MC change = 2.9%.
>
> Seasonal movement = 32 x 0.003 x 2.9 = 0.28 or ¼ in.

When the 32 inch wide door is constructed in Phoenix at 4.6% MC and moved to Flagstaff at 7.5% MC, it will swell to 32¼ inches in width.

Problem 4: How much will the door change dimensionally over the next 12 months after it is installed in Flagstaff?

Solution 4: Figure 20 shows Flagstaff has an annual moisture content fluctuation of 4.3 percentage points (11.8% MC in December and January to 7.5% MC in June).

> Seasonal Movement = Panel Width x Chart Value x MC Change
>
> Where width = 32 inches, value = 0.003 and MC change = 4.3%.
>
> Seasonal movement = 32 x 0.003 x 4.3 = 0.41 or ⅜ in.

The door will swell and shrink ⅜ inch over the 12-month period. Note that if the door had been constructed of quartersawn red oak with a chart value of 0.0014, the changes in width would have been one-half as great.

Frame-and-Panel Door

A frame-and-panel door (see **Figure 19, page 42**) allows the panel to expand and contract during seasonal wood movement. Trapping a wide panel inside a frame made of relatively narrow rails and stiles is a fundamental strategy for coping with wood movement. The question is, how much movement allowance should be built into the construction?

Problem 5: Given the following conditions: The panel width is 13¾ inches in the frame and panel door in **Figure 19**. The material is a mixture of flatsawn (tangential) and quartersawn (radial) black walnut. The moisture content fluctuation is 8 percentage points (from 6% MC in winter to 14% MC in the summer). Time of construction is winter. Find the seasonal movement.

Solution 5: Because the panel is a mixture of flatsawn and quartersawn, we can use the riftsawn column in **Figure 23**, which is 0.0022 inches of movement per inch of width for each percentage point of moisture content change.

Seasonal Movement = Panel Width x Chart Value x MC Change

Where width = 13.75 inches, value = 0.0022 and MC change = 8.0%.

Seasonal movement = 13.75 x 0.0022 x 8.0 = 0.24 or ¼ in.

Experts suggest adding a safety margin of 25% to guard against greater than normal fluctuation:

0.24 x 1.25 = 0.30 or ≈ ⁵⁄₁₆

The expansion allowance for the panel should be ⁵⁄₁₆ inch.

Drawers

Wood expansion is not only a problem with doors. Drawer sides are usually fit to close tolerances between the guides and are seldom protected with a finish. This makes wooden drawer sides especially susceptible to wood movement. We've all tried to open a drawer only to have it be firmly stuck in place.

Problem 6: We have a solid wood drawer side sliding between fixed runners in a solid wood or plywood case as in **Figure 25**. The drawer expands as the moisture content changes; the case does not change dimensions in length (height). How much clearance do we need to avoid the drawer being stuck shut in the humid months? The drawer side is made of flatsawn poplar and is 9½ inches high. We live in Fresno, California.

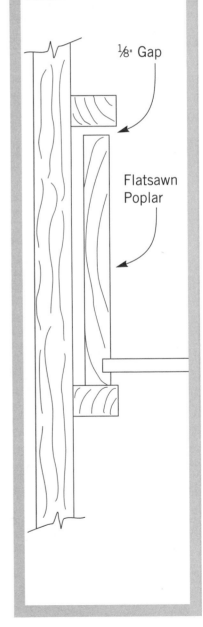

Figure 25 – Drawer Sides and Wood Movement

Solid drawer sides are usually unfinished and fit to close tolerances with the drawer runners. An ⅛ inch gap might not be enough to prevent the drawer from binding in humid weather.

⅛" Gap

Flatsawn Poplar

Solution 6:

Seasonal Movement = Panel Width x Chart Value x MC Change

Where width = 9.5 inches, value = 0.0027 (**Figure 23**, poplar, flatsawn) and MC change = 8.8% (**Figure 20**, Fresno, CA, Annual EMC Difference).

Seasonal movement = 9.5 x 0.0027 x 8.8 = 0.23 or ¼ in.

To figure in a 25% safety factor:

0.25 x 1.25 = 0.31 in. or ⁵⁄₁₆ inch.

The 9½ inch drawer sides should be set into drawer runners 9¹³⁄₁₆ inches apart to make sure the drawers don't bind due to wood movement.

Wood Movement by Percent

The chart in **Figure 26** lists the movement of 72 common woods as green wood at 30% MC is dried to 0% MC. Both tangential (flatsawn) and radial (quartersawn) movements are listed. The woods with the largest numbers (beech 11.9% MC, dogwood 11.8% MC and madrone 12.4% MC) are woods with the most tangential movement.

Problem 7: We have a piece of beech 1 inch thick by 14 inches wide by 48 inches long. The board is green and we plan to dry it in a home-made kiln to 6% MC. The board is flatsawn (tangential). What will be the final dimensions of the dried lumber?

Solution 7: Figure 26 shows that beech will shrink 11.9% tangentially (across the width) and will shrink 5.5% radially (across the thickness) when dried from 30% MC (green) to 0% (oven dried). We plan to only dry the wood to 6% or 24/30 as much; therefore we will use 24/30 or 80% of the table values.

New width = old width - change

Where old width = 14 inches, value = 11.9%

New width = 14 − (0.119 x 14 x 0.8) = 14 − 1.33 = 12.67 ≈ 12-5/8

New thickness = old thickness − change

Where old thickness = 1 inch, value = 5.5%

New thickness = 1 − (0.055 x 1 x 0.8) = 1 − 0.044 = 0.956 or ¹⁵⁄₁₆

Wood will shrink lengthwise about 0.1%.

New length = old length − change

Where old length = 48 inches, value = 0.001

New length = 48 − (0.001 x 48) = 48 − 0.048 = 47.95 or ≈ 48

Original size: 1" thick x 14" wide x 48" long

Figure 26 — Potential Wood Movement by Percent

The figures are given as percent movement as green wood (30% MC) dries to oven-dry (0% MC).

Wood Species	Tangential	Radial	Rift	T/R Ratio	Wood Species	Tangential	Radial	Rift	T/R Ratio
Alder, Red	7.3	4.4	5.9	1.7	Madrone, Pacific	12.4	5.6	9.0	2.2
Apple	10.1	5.6	7.9	1.8	Magnolia, Southern	6.6	5.4	6.0	1.2
Ash, Black	7.8	5.0	6.4	1.6	Mahogany	4.1	3.0	3.6	1.4
Ash, White	7.8	4.9	6.4	1.6	Mahogany, African	4.5	2.5	3.5	1.8
Aspen, Quaking	6.7	3.5	5.1	1.9	Maple, Red	8.2	4.0	6.1	2.1
Baldcypress	6.2	3.9	5.1	1.6	Maple, Sugar	9.9	4.8	7.4	2.1
Balsa	7.6	3.0	5.3	2.5	Oak, Black	11.1	4.4	7.8	2.5
Basswood, American	9.3	6.6	8.0	1.4	Oak, Live	9.5	6.6	8.1	1.4
Beech, American	11.9	5.5	8.7	2.2	Oak, Northern Red	8.6	4.0	6.3	2.2
Birch, Paper	8.6	6.3	7.5	1.4	Oak, Red	8.9	4.2	6.6	2.1
Birch, Yellow	9.2	7.2	8.2	1.3	Oak, Southern Red	11.3	4.7	8.0	2.4
Buckeye, Yellow	8.1	3.6	5.9	2.3	Oak, White	10.5	5.6	8.1	1.9
Butternut	6.4	3.4	4.9	1.9	Obeche	5.3	3.1	4.2	1.7
Cedar, Alaska	6.0	2.8	4.4	2.1	Padauk	5.8	3.4	4.6	1.7
Cedar, Eastern Red	4.7	3.1	3.9	1.5	Pine, Eastern White	6.1	2.1	4.1	2.9
Cedar, Incense	5.2	3.3	4.3	1.6	Pine, Loblolly	7.4	4.8	6.1	1.5
Cedar, North. White	4.9	2.2	3.6	2.2	Pine, Lodgepole	6.7	4.3	5.5	1.6
Cedar, Spanish	6.3	4.1	5.2	1.5	Pine, Longleaf	7.5	5.1	6.3	1.5
Cedar, West. Red	5.0	2.4	3.7	2.1	Pine, Pitch	7.1	4.0	5.6	1.8
Cherry, Black	7.1	3.7	5.4	1.9	Pine, Ponderosa	6.2	3.9	5.1	1.6
Chestnut	6.7	3.4	5.1	2.0	Pine, Red	7.2	3.8	5.5	1.9
Cocobolo	4.3	2.7	3.5	1.6	Pine, Shortleaf	7.7	4.6	6.2	1.7
Cottonwood	9.2	3.9	6.6	2.4	Pine, Slash	7.6	5.4	6.5	1.4
Dogwood	11.8	7.4	9.6	1.6	Pine, Sugar	5.6	2.9	4.3	1.9
Douglas Fir (Coastal)	7.8	5.0	6.4	1.6	Pine, Western White	7.4	4.1	5.8	1.8
Douglas Fir (Inland)	7.6	4.1	5.9	1.9	Poplar, Yellow	8.2	4.6	6.4	1.8
Elm, American	9.5	4.2	6.9	2.3	Redwood, Old Growth	4.4	2.6	3.5	1.7
Elm, Rock	8.1	4.8	6.5	1.7	Redwood, New Growth	4.9	2.2	3.6	2.2
Fir, Balsam	6.9	2.9	4.9	2.4	Rosewood, Indian	5.8	2.7	4.3	2.1
Fir, White	7.1	3.2	5.2	2.2	Spruce, Red	7.8	3.8	5.8	2.1
Hackberry	8.9	4.8	6.9	1.9	Spruce, Sitka	7.5	4.3	5.9	1.7
Hemlock, Eastern	6.8	3.0	4.9	2.3	Sycamore, American	8.4	5.0	6.7	1.7
Hemlock, Western	7.9	4.3	6.1	1.8	Teak	4.0	2.2	3.1	1.8
Hickory, Pecan	8.9	4.9	6.9	1.8	Walnut, Black	7.8	5.5	6.7	1.4
Hickory, Shagbark	10.5	7.0	8.8	1.5	Walnut, European	6.4	4.3	5.4	1.5
Holly, American	9.9	4.8	7.4	2.1	Wenge	5.8	3.1	4.5	1.9
Larch, Western	9.1	4.5	6.8	2.0	Willow, Black	8.7	3.3	6.0	2.6
Lauan	8.0	3.8	5.9	2.1	Yew, Pacific	5.4	4.0	4.7	1.4
Locust, Black	7.2	4.6	5.9	1.6					
Locust, Honey	6.6	4.2	5.4	1.6	**Average**	**8.2**	**4.5**	**5.9**	**2.0**

Dried size: $^{15}\!/_{16}$" thick x 12⅝" wide x 48" long

Wood Movement per Foot

Another way to figure wood movement is by the foot. **Figure 27** lists 72 woods with the size of a 12 inch board at 15% MC and its width at 6% MC. This corresponds to putting air-dried wood into a kiln.. To use this chart, you have to know three things: (1) the type of wood, (2) the width of the piece, and (3) its annual ring orientation.

Problem 8: We have a 29½ inch piece of flatsawn mahogany. What will be the change as the piece goes from air dry to kiln dry?

Solution 8: In **Figure 27,** a 12 inch piece of mahogany will shrink to 11.85 inches. Our piece is 29.5 inches wide.

New width = panel width x 11.85 ÷ 12

New width = 29.5 x 0.9875 = 29.13 or 29⅛ inches.

Reference: Figures 20, 21 and 23 are from *Wood Handbook,* Forest Products Laboratory, USDA. Reprinted 2002.

Figure 27 — Wood Movement by Board Width

Shrinkage or expansion for each 12 inches as the moisture content of the wood changes from air-dry to kiln-dry (15% MC to 6% MC).

Wood Species	15% MC Flatsawn Inches	6% MC Flatsawn Inches	15% MC Qtrsawn Inches	6% MC Qtrsawn Inches	Wood Species	15% MC Flatsawn Inches	6% MC Flatsawn Inches	15% MC Qtrsawn Inches	6% MC Qtrsawn Inches
Alder, Red	12.00	11.74	12.00	11.84	Locust, Honey	12.00	11.76	12.00	11.85
Apple	12.00	11.64	12.00	11.80	Madrone, Pacific	12.00	11.55	12.00	11.80
Ash, Black	12.00	11.72	12.00	11.82	Magnolia, Southern	12.00	11.76	12.00	11.81
Ash, White	12.00	11.72	12.00	11.82	Mahogany	12.00	11.85	12.00	11.89
Aspen, Quaking	12.00	11.76	12.00	11.87	Mahogany, African	12.00	11.84	12.00	11.91
Balsa	12.00	11.73	12.00	11.89	Maple, Red	12.00	11.70	12.00	11.86
Basswood, American	12.00	11.67	12.00	11.76	Maple, Sugar	12.00	11.64	12.00	11.83
Beech, American	12.00	11.57	12.00	11.80	Oak, Black	12.00	11.60	12.00	11.84
Birch, Paper	12.00	11.69	12.00	11.77	Oak, Live	12.00	11.66	12.00	11.76
Birch, Yellow	12.00	11.67	12.00	11.74	Oak, Northern Red	12.00	11.69	12.00	11.86
Buckeye, Yellow	12.00	11.71	12.00	11.87	Oak, Red	12.00	11.68	12.00	11.85
Butternut	12.00	11.77	12.00	11.88	Oak, Southern Red	12.00	11.59	12.00	11.83
Cedar, Alaska	12.00	11.78	12.00	11.90	Oak, White	12.00	11.62	12.00	11.80
Cedar, Eastern Red	12.00	11.83	12.00	11.89	Obeche	12.00	11.81	12.00	11.89
Cedar, Incense	12.00	11.81	12.00	11.88	Padauk	12.00	11.79	12.00	11.88
Cedar, North. White	12.00	11.82	12.00	11.92	Pine, Eastern White	12.00	11.78	12.00	11.92
Cedar, Spanish	12.00	11.77	12.00	11.85	Pine, Loblolly	12.00	11.73	12.00	11.83
Cedar, West. Red	12.00	11.82	12.00	11.91	Pine, Lodgepole	12.00	11.76	12.00	11.85
Cherry, Black	12.00	11.74	12.00	11.87	Pine, Longleaf	12.00	11.73	12.00	11.82
Chestnut	12.00	11.76	12.00	11.88	Pine, Pitch	12.00	11.74	12.00	11.86
Cocobolo	12.00	11.85	12.00	11.90	Pine, Ponderosa	12.00	11.78	12.00	11.86
Cottonwood	12.00	11.67	12.00	11.86	Pine, Red	12.00	11.74	12.00	11.86
Cypress	12.00	11.78	12.00	11.86	Pine, Shortleaf	12.00	11.72	12.00	11.83
Dogwood	12.00	11.58	12.00	11.73	Pine, Slash	12.00	11.73	12.00	11.81
Douglas Fir (Coastal)	12.00	11.72	12.00	11.82	Pine, Sugar	12.00	11.80	12.00	11.90
Douglas Fir (Inland)	12.00	11.73	12.00	11.85	Pine, Western White	12.00	11.73	12.00	11.85
Elm, American	12.00	11.66	12.00	11.85	Poplar, Yellow	12.00	11.70	12.00	11.83
Elm, Rock	12.00	11.71	12.00	11.83	Redwood, Old Growth	12.00	11.84	12.00	11.91
Fir, Balsam	12.00	11.75	12.00	11.90	Redwood, New Growth	12.00	11.82	12.00	11.92
Fir, White	12.00	11.74	12.00	11.88	Rosewood, Indian	12.00	11.79	12.00	11.90
Hackberry	12.00	11.68	12.00	11.83	Spruce, Red	12.00	11.72	12.00	11.86
Hemlock, Eastern	12.00	11.76	12.00	11.89	Spruce, Sitka	12.00	11.73	12.00	11.85
Hemlock, Western	12.00	11.72	12.00	11.85	Sycamore, American	12.00	11.70	12.00	11.82
Hickory, Pecan	12.00	11.68	12.00	11.82	Teak	12.00	11.86	12.00	11.92
Hickory, Shagbark	12.00	11.62	12.00	11.75	Walnut, Black	12.00	11.72	12.00	11.80
Holly, American	12.00	11.64	12.00	11.83	Walnut, European	12.00	11.77	12.00	11.85
Larch, Western	12.00	11.67	12.00	11.84	Wenge	12.00	11.79	12.00	11.89
Lauan	12.00	11.71	12.00	11.86	Willow, Black	12.00	11.69	12.00	11.88
Locust, Black	12.00	11.74	12.00	11.83	Yew, Pacific	12.00	11.81	12.00	11.86

CHAPTER 4

Building with Wood Movement

At one time I repaired a lot of antiques and the usual problems were tables or cabinets with cracked tops — and the reason for the split was always the same: the top had been attached to the base without any allowance for the wood to move. Wood is hygroscopic and as the humidity in the surrounding air changes, so also does the moisture content (MC) change in a piece of furniture. Under humid conditions, such as during the summer, wood cells absorb moisture, swell and the wood expands. As conditions dry during the winter, the wood cells release moisture, shrink and the wood contracts. This expansion and contraction goes on season after season and the dimensional changes cause glue lines to fail, joints to open, finishes to crack, and table tops to split.

Building to Cope with Wood Movement

There are a number of steps you can take to minimize the effects of wood movement by using methods that allow for seasonal dimensional movement:

1. **Buy kiln-dried wood** at a MC close to that of the usage area.

2. **Store the rough boards** for 10-14 days in the area where the furniture piece will be used to let the boards acclimate to the temperature and humidity.

3. **If you have a choice**, use quartersawn or rift-sawn boards; they move about 50% less than flatsawn boards.

4. **Plan joinery** so adjacent boards are the same MC and milled the same (flatsawn or quartersawn).

5. **Use glues that work well** in the conditions (MC, wood species, temperature, inside-outside) you've chosen.

6. **Design the piece** with wood movement in mind.

7. **Use a finish** that will seal the wood to the degree that you need. See Chapter 6, *Moisture Protection* for more on this.

Why Antiques Crack

Antiques over seventy-five years old are especially vulnerable to wood movement for three reasons — humidity, finish, and adhesives.

Humidity — Wood in a piece of furniture moves as a result of changes in moisture content (MC) in the cells; and MC is driven by humidity in the room. Older houses did not have central heat, were not heavily insulated and the construction methods left them somewhat drafty thus the humidity was pretty much the same both inside the house and outside. A table that was built by a local woodworker began at equivalent 14% MC and didn't move much over the years as the furniture piece sat inside the house.

In contrast, a modern house is air-tight with thick insulation in the walls, ceiling and under the floor. Central heating and air conditioning keep the temperature and relative humidity inside the house constant regardless of how cold or wet it is outdoors. When a Chippendale table is purchased from a soggy London antique store and shipped to a Denver home, the wood will slowly change from the 14% MC it has been at for 200 years to 7% MC. A 48-inch European walnut table will shrink nearly ¾ inch under these conditions. The first indication of a problem will be a loud crack during the night with the damage found the next morning. See Chapter 3, *Wood Movement*, for more on this.

Finish — Present day finishes can repel up to 70% water vapor. This protection along with the constant humidity maintained inside a modern house with central heating and air-conditioning, means the moisture content of a piece of wood furniture will remain fairly constant from season to season. The older finishes, like oil and varnish, gave little protection to wood from water vapor. See Chapter 6, *Moisture Protection*, for more on this.

Adhesive — An adhesive should hold the adjoining pieces firmly, be impervious to water and water vapor and remain strong for the life of the piece. A joint subjected to wood movement is more likely to fail if the adhesive does not have any give to it. Modern PVA glues have a certain amount of creep and will save a joint unless the movement is extreme. See Woodworkers' Essential Chapter 28, *All About Glues* for more on adhesives.

Hide glue was the most common adhesive for furniture up until World War II. It is not a good glue when furniture is subjected to wood movement because it forms an extremely hard joint and softens when subjected to hot or warm water. Hide glue was prepared by the wood worker from flakes of dubious purity and left in the double boiler for weeks at a time. The resulting mixture gave irregular results. Some hide glue joinery is as hard and firm today as it was the year it was made. Other hide glue joints have turned to a brown powder.

Wood Movement

Woodworkers should learn about these dimensional changes and be able to anticipate seasonal movement when working with solid wood as opposed to plywood, MDF or other composites. Most wood movement that will affect your work will occur across the width of a board and that amount will vary depending on wood species,

Rule of Thumb

Buy kiln-dried wood whose moisture content is close to equilibrium for the usage location. To bring the wood to equilibrium moisture content, store it in the house for a couple of weeks before working with it, and turn the stack so the air can get at all surfaces.

Rule of Thumb

To minimize wood movement, choose and apply a suitable film finish. Of the finishes available to amateur woodworkers, three coats of polyurethane varnish provide the most protection against moisture exchange.

panel width, humidity, moisture content and whether the boards are flatsawn or quartersawn. Some wood movement in thickness is troublesome though most problems are widthwise.

There are a number of things you can do to counter wood movement; use ship-lap boards for the back of a case, frame-and-panel joinery for a door, breadboard ends for keeping a large panel flat, attach table tops and other cross-grain pieces with methods that allow for movement, and use dovetails to attach long mouldings.

Follow these suggestions and you'll never have to tell your client or spouse that a tablecloth is the best way to fix that crack in the beautiful old table.

Tabletops

Solid wood tabletops can grow ½ inch or more across the width of the boards, so rigidly fastening such a top to its supporting aprons can cause all sorts of problems. Properly attached, a tabletop can expand and contract with changes in humidity while staying flat and being firmly connected to its base. Tables that are properly connected gain strength from their connections, the top lending rigidity to the base and the base reinforcing the top. If you attach a tabletop to the apron solidly with screws or

glue, one or more of these things will happen:

1. The tabletop will split along the grain or at a joint line.

2. It will bow upwards at the center.

3. It will force the apron to bow outward.

To prevent this, attach tabletops in one of the ways shown in **Figure 28**.

Whichever method you choose, attach the top to the rails every 4 to 8 inches, starting close to the leg. For the end rails, use solid sticks with slots (see **Figure 28j**).

Wooden Button

Buttons are small blocks of wood tenoned on one end, creating a half-lap joint that engages a slot cut into the rail (see **Figure 28a**). In use, these notched blocks hold the top securely and also allow it to move and slide along grooves sawn into the inside face of the aprons. Fasten the clips where the tabletop meets the supports that run perpendicular to the tabletop grain — usually the side aprons. Do not fasten buttons to the tabletop where it meets apron pieces that run parallel to the grain. The usual button size is ¾ inch thick x ⅞ inch wide x 1¼ inches long.

Buttons look nice, are easy to

make and allow for a lot of wood movement. To ensure they won't break, make sure the grain runs lengthwise. Avoid using buttons when the space is cramped such as where a drawer uses the back rail as its stop.

Longer buttons can be used to flatten a warped top (see **Figure 28k**). Make the button at least 3 inches long and locate the screw close to the apron. Tightening the screw applies pressure but the top can still expand and contract.

Z-Clip

Metal Z-clips are thinner than wooden buttons and need smaller grooves cut into the inner face of the aprons (see **Figure 28b**). The Z-clip functions exactly like a wooden button, with one offset let into a saw kerf near the top of the rail and the other screwed to the top. These clips permit a great deal of wood movement but they shouldn't be used on fine furniture or period pieces.

Metal Clip from L-Bracket

Metal tabletop fasteners can be made from steel corner-irons or L-brackets. First bend one leg of the iron at a right angle (see **Figure 28c**). Then cut a thin kerf in the table apron that this bend will fit into. The bracket is strong and these clips can be made quickly as needed.

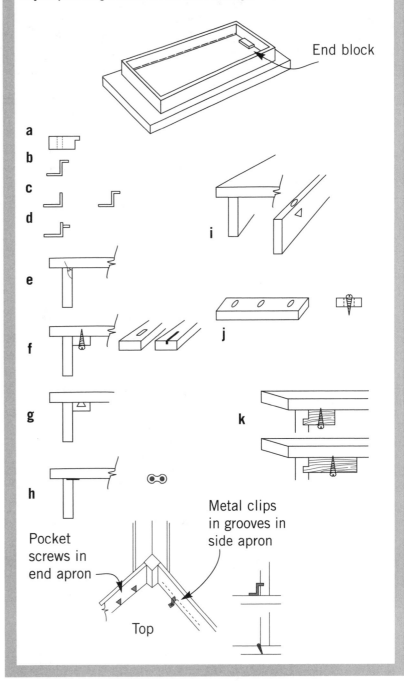

Figure 28 — Tabletop Fasteners

Remember that tables are picked up and moved by their tops so be sure that the reinforcers are strong enough to hold the weight of large tables. Shown here: wood button (a), metal clip (b), metal clip made from an L-bracket (c), shelf bracket (d), slotted screw (e), screw block (f), dovetail block (g), figure-8 clip (h), V-cut (i), and end block(j). To hold a warped top in place, use long buttons (k) for more leverage.

End block

a
b
c
d
e
f
g
h
i
j
k

Pocket screws in end apron

Metal clips in grooves in side apron

Top

Rule of Thumb

To minimize wood movement, choose quartersawn wood and rift-sawn wood, both of which move about half as much as flatsawn boards.

Metal Clip from Shelf Bracket

In a pinch, a metal shelf bracket can be used to fasten a tabletop (see **Figure 28d**). Drill a hole in the tongue of each bracket for a screw. The bracket's pin fits in a hole drilled in the apron. To accommodate wood movement, leave a little space between the bracket and the apron and elongate the hole in the apron.

Screw in Slot

Two holes are bored, one a pocket hole through the rail at a 10° angle for a screw that connects the base and the top (see **Figure 28e**). The other, a pilot hole, prevents the screw from splitting the rail. Make the top hole oval in the direction of wood movement by wiggling the drill bit a little. If the movement is to be equal on either side of the center of the top, fix the top securely in the middle and make the holes progressively bigger the further away from the center point. Let half the movement be toward the front and half toward the back.

Screw Block

Screw blocks are small blocks of wood glued to the rails, flush with the upper edge, and then screwed to the table top through slotted holes (see **Figure 28f**). They work like pocket holes, so on wider tabletops, the hole through the blocks should be oval on the side of the block against the top. Screw blocks make very secure connections.

To allow greater movement, cut a slot in the top in the direction of wood movement. Use a round head screw and steel washer to fasten the top to the apron. Start with 24 inch long stock ripped to 1 inch width. Set the blade to 3/8 inch and rip a groove lengthwise. Cut 2 inch blocks and drill a hole from the top.

Dovetail Block

Dovetail blocks are two-part connectors. A dovetail-shaped piece is screwed to the top, and a block with a corresponding slot is glued to the rail (see **Figure 28g**). Their primary advantage over other methods is that they allow for a great deal of wood movement, making them best-suited to wide tops on tables with straight rails. They're fairly time-consuming to cut, fit and install but they work well and make a good connection.

Figure-8 Clip

Figure-8 clips can be installed after the base is complete. With these clips, drill one shallow, flat-bottomed hole in the rail and attach the clip. Position the tabletop on the base and screw the other half of the "8" to the underside of the top, see **Figure 28h**. The clip rotates through a small arc to accommodate wood movement. One advantage of using these connectors is that you can install them late in the construction process. They are best suited to small tables because of their limited range of movement.

V-Cut

For a nice touch, especially on a period piece, the seat for the screw head can be cut with a chisel by making a V-shaped cut into the apron at an angle and leaving a small flat at the bottom for the screw head (see **Figure 28i**). Drill a pilot hole and elongate it on the edge next to the table.

End Block

To connect the table top to a rail when the grain of the top is parallel to the rail, use a solid piece of wood as an end block. Figure the wood movement and cut slots in the block long enough to accommodate this seasonal movement (see Chapter 3, **Wood Movement**). Screw the strips to the apron rails, and then attach the top with pan-head, sheet-metal screws inserted in the midpoint of the slot. Don't cinch these screws down; they should be loose enough to move when the top expands and contracts (see **Figure 28j**).

Breadboards

To help keep a solid wood tabletop flat, while hiding the end grain, you can add a breadboard end to the top. This type of end is made by attaching a board to the end of a panel in a cross-grain manner. The end

batten can be attached with a spline, a tongue and groove or a dovetail joint (see **Figure 29**). If you are making the breadboard ends during the humid summer months, cut them a little shorter than the width of the tabletop. During the dry periods (winter) make the ends longer than the width of the table. Gauge the difference by the species and width of the tabletop. See Chapter 3, **Wood Movement** for more on this.

Splined

The batten groove is cut to take advantage of long-grained strength. A groove is also cut along the ends of the boards making up the panel. The spline should be strong with long grain running with the panel. Use at least two pegs on either side of the glued center, one of them a few inches from each edge and one more centered on each side between the outboard pegs and the inner pair (see **Figure 29a**). The outer pegs should have elongated holes to allow for at least $\frac{1}{8}$ inch of movement. For the pegs closer to the center, drill slightly oversize holes.

Tongue and Groove

Grooving the batten and rabbeting the panel on both sides to create a tongue takes a little more effort, but the joint is stronger and looks nicer (see **Figure 29b**).

Rule of Thumb

When building a **box**, for example a drawer, jewelry box or toy chest, if the pieces measure more than 3 inches wide, design joints so the grain runs around the box. Cross grain assemblies constantly pull in different directions, weakening the joints.

Figure 29 — Breadboard Connections

The trick is to fasten the breadboard ends to the table while still allowing the top to move. To do this, use a spline (a), tongue and groove (b), or dovetail (c) joint. Apply glue only to the middle 3 or 4 inches of the joint then attach the ends with slotted holes and pegs. The ends will stay in place and the tabletop will move on both sides of the glued area.

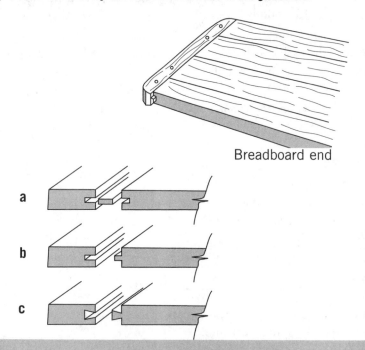

Breadboard end

a

b

c

Figure 30 — Mortise-and-Tenon Breadboard

Use a series of tenons connected by a continuous tongue for alignment. Apply glue only to the center tenon and use pegs in elongated holes to allow for movement.

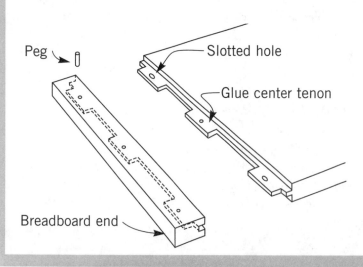

Peg

Slotted hole

Glue center tenon

Breadboard end

Dovetailed

Dovetailing the panel and routing a corresponding groove in the batten provides mechanical strength to the construction. This joint looks nice (**Figure 29c**), but the process requires greater precision. A sliding dovetail between batten and top works best on narrow panels such as cutting boards because to be effective, the joint should be tight but move when needed. This doesn't work over wide expanses as panels tend to cup and warp and the joint tightens. Also the batten is weakened by the dovetail: the dovetail flares in thickness, requiring the walls of the batten around the dovetail slot to be thinner than they would be for a tongue-and-groove batten. Keep the batten narrow, making it less liable to be broken off.

Mortise-and-Tenon

The strongest and most durable way of bread-boarding is with a mortise-and-tenon joint (see **Figure 30**). This method uses separate tenons for strength and a tongue for alignment. The center tenon is glued and pinned. The two end tenons have elongated holes and are pegged and not glued. This allows unrestricted movement of the table top. The stub tenons ensure alignment of batten and panel and keeps the tabletop from warping between the three separate tenons.

By making the breadboard end bigger than the panel (thicker and longer than the table is wide), shadow lines are created. By overhanging the ends and using a difference in stock thickness, an interesting design is created and any wood movement will be indiscernible. The ends are pinned into elongated holes then plugged.

Moulding

When moulding is applied to a face frame, it can be nailed or glued without considering wood movement because the moulding is attached to a rail whose grain runs in the same direction. But moulding attached across the grain of a solid wood side has to allow the wood to move and slide beneath it (**Figure 31**). Just as it is necessary to make allowance for solid wood sides to move against internal frames, one must also make provision for the sides to move against external attachments such as mouldings.

Dovetails

The side moulding is attached with a series of dovetailed keys (see **Figure 31a**). A dovetailed slot is cut in the back of the moulding that allows it to slide onto the short dovetailed keys attached to the case. The connection keeps the moulding snugged up tight to the carcass. Because the moulding is not glued to the carcass or to the

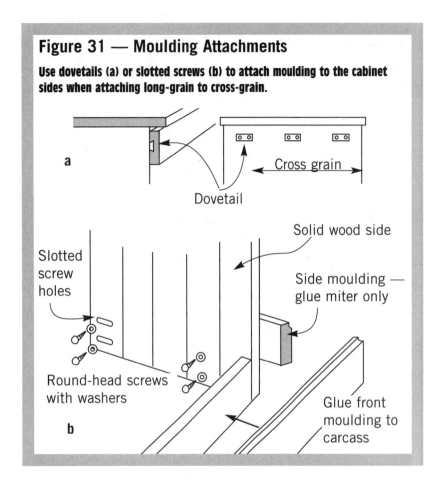

Figure 31 — Moulding Attachments

Use dovetails (a) or slotted screws (b) to attach moulding to the cabinet sides when attaching long-grain to cross-grain.

keys, the case sides are free to move. This technique has been used for centuries and is still found on high caliber work.

The dovetail tenon should be cut to a length 1 inch less than the cabinet width. Mark it into 3 inch sections and drill and countersink two holes in every other section. With a miter saw, cut halfway through each of the section lines from the narrow face (backside) of the tenon.

The easiest way to install the dovetail tenon on the carcass is to insert the tenon into the groove in the moulding, leaving one end

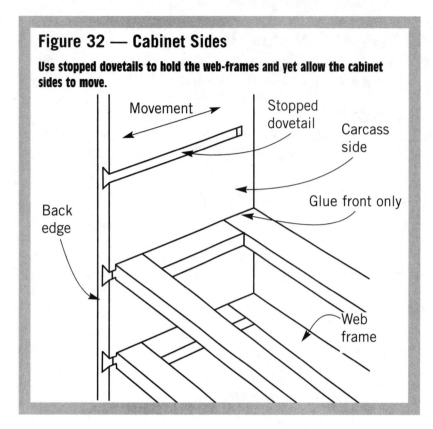

Figure 32 — Cabinet Sides

Use stopped dovetails to hold the web-frames and yet allow the cabinet sides to move.

Movement

Stopped dovetail

Carcass side

Glue front only

Back edge

Web frame

To attach the side mouldings, rout ½ inch long slots into the side, behind the position where the mouldings will be applied. Then attach (brads and glue) the front of the side moulding to the carcass and attach the rest with screws and washers that slide freely in the slots as the wood moves, (see **Figure 31b**).

Cabinet Sides

With projects such as a chest-of-drawers that have drawer web-frames attached to solid-wood chest sides, the web frames must not restrain the sides. To accomplish this, join the frames to the sides with sliding dovetail joints like those in **Figure 32**.

Plan the web frames so they align flush with the front of the carcass. To do this, stop the dovetail grooves about ⅜ inch from the front of the sides. The dovetail tongues should stop ½ inch short of the front of the web frames.

To assemble the joint, apply glue only to the front 3 inches of the groove, and slide the web frame into position from the back of the carcass. Because the dovetail tenon is captured, no other attachment is needed. There should be ⅜ inch of clearance between the frame and the carcass back. This also works with two small stub tenons instead of the dovetail.

exposed. With the tenon held back about 1 inch from the front of the cabinet, clamp the moulding in place and drive flathead screws through the front section and into the cabinet side. Unclamp the moulding, slide it back to expose the next screw-hole, reclamp, and add those screws. Now, with a small miter saw, cut the rest of the way through the section lines and remove the sections that contain no screws. Glue the front section only and slide the moulding into place from the rear.

Slotted Screws

The front moulding, going the same direction as the front of the carcass, can be fastened securely.

Aprons

Extra-wide aprons offer another example of design problems that require different solutions. Wood movement over such a wide apron must be a consideration. Also, a real concern is that a deep mortise can weaken the leg as the long sides of the mortise flex easily.

Mortise with Stub Tenon

One solution is two deep mortises with a groove for a tongue in between. The two mortises still have plenty of glue surfaces and lock the apron along its full height. If the apron is more than 3 inches, glue only the top part of the tenon, then pin the lower part with elongated holes, (see **Figure 33b**).

Sliding Dovetail

A sliding dovetail joint also works well for joining table aprons to legs, (see **Figure 33a**). If the aprons are 3 inches, or more wide, glue the dovetail only at the top.

Cleats

Attach cleats to solid wood panels such as to a tabletop or chest lid with slotted holes. The cleats help reinforce the panel and keep it flat.

Screw Slots

Similar to the breadboard end, you can permanently fix a cleat at its center with a screw and use

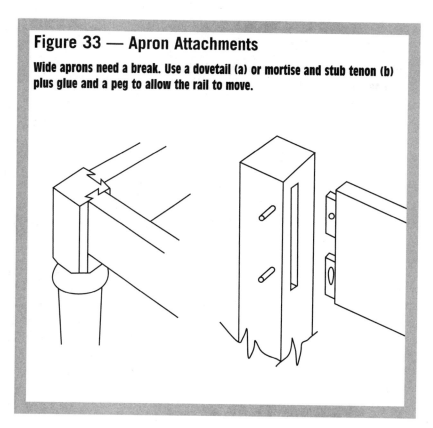

Figure 33 — Apron Attachments

Wide aprons need a break. Use a dovetail (a) or mortise and stub tenon (b) plus glue and a peg to allow the rail to move.

slotted holes for the ends. This arrangement still allows the panel to shrink and expand from the center (see **Figure 34a**).

Biscuit Joiner

Use a biscuit joiner to make concealed screw slots that will allow wood movement. The screws will swing in the slots allowing a solid wood lid panel to expand or contract with humidity changes (see **Figure 34b**).

Drawer Faces

If the face of the drawer fits outside of the carcass opening, then seasonal movement won't be a problem. However, when the drawer face fits inside the carcass, wood movement must

Figure 34 — Cleats

Use a cleat with slotted holes (a) or biscuit holes (b) to reinforce a panel and keep it flat.

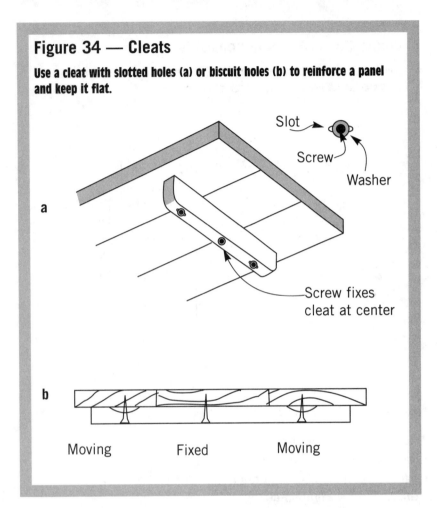

Slot
Screw
Washer

a

Screw fixes cleat at center

b

Moving   Fixed   Moving

expansion will be towards the back and won't force the sides apart. The bottom should slide easily but not be so loose that it rattles. Make the panel with $\frac{1}{16}$ inch to spare on each side. Seat it in the drawer front groove and mark it flush with the back end of the drawer side. Cut the bottom and saw a $\frac{3}{4}$ inch slot at the back edge (see **Figure 35**).

Slide the rabbeted panel (or flat piece) in from the back of the drawer, snug it to the drawer front, and secure it with a dab of hide glue at the front center so it can be softened and removed for repair. Secure the bottom to the drawer back with a single pan-head screw in an elongated hole or a slot. Tighten the screw and then back it off one-quarter turn.

If you don't glue the bottom to the drawer front (and there is reason not to when there is an expansion screw and slot at the back) it will probably work its way backwards as it expands and contracts, opening a gap at the drawer front. By securing the bottom with glue at the front, seasonal movement will be forced towards the back of the drawer. The bottom rarely needs to be removed — the most common drawer repair is worn runners.

be taken into consideration. Drawers three to four inches high (long grain running across the chest) will move only $\frac{1}{16}$ inch or less. The movement can be accommodated by making the drawer a little smaller. When the drawer is higher, consider making a frame-and-panel drawer front.

Drawer Bottoms

A solid wood bottom is a traditional feature of a well-made drawer but it must be designed correctly. Plan for the grain to run from side-to-side so wood

Frame and Panel Doors

The simple genius of the frame-and-panel system is in making a dimensionally stable frame from narrow members and allowing a large solid panel to expand and contract freely inside it. The panel may be large or small, elaborate or plain, but as long as it is made of solid wood it must be free to move so that it will not split or buckle with changes in humidity and at the same time be securely held so it cannot warp. Panels are typically held by their edges in grooves formed in the surrounding frame, and they are pinned or glued only at the center. Occasionally, the grooves are formed by adding a strip of moulding to a rabbet, but most often the groove is integral.

Because most panels are oriented with the grain running vertically, the rails have the most work to do in preventing the panel from warping. Therefore, the rails are usually the widest parts of the frame. So the frame does not appear top-heavy, the top rail is made a little narrower than the bottom rail. The stiles are generally made narrower than the bottom rail to give a pleasing appearance and minimizing the seasonal change in the width of the door.

When planning the size of panels that fit within frames you need to keep several things in mind. First, allow room for solid wood panels to expand widthwise. Refer to the charts in Chapter 3, *Wood Movement* to

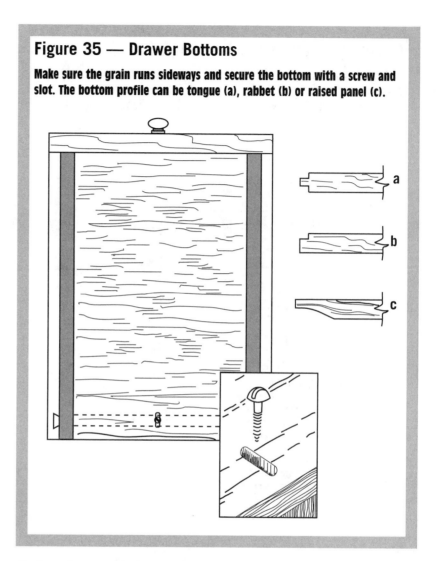

Figure 35 — Drawer Bottoms

Make sure the grain runs sideways and secure the bottom with a screw and slot. The bottom profile can be tongue (a), rabbet (b) or raised panel (c).

find out how much the panel will move. Panels won't expand lengthwise, but fit them with a hair of clearance or else the panel may interfere with the rail-stile joint (see **Figure 36**).

In the frame and panel door, the panel is free to expand and contract within the frame. Consequently, the overall seasonal movement of the panel is contained in the frame. The outside frame will move but because it is so narrow (3 inches

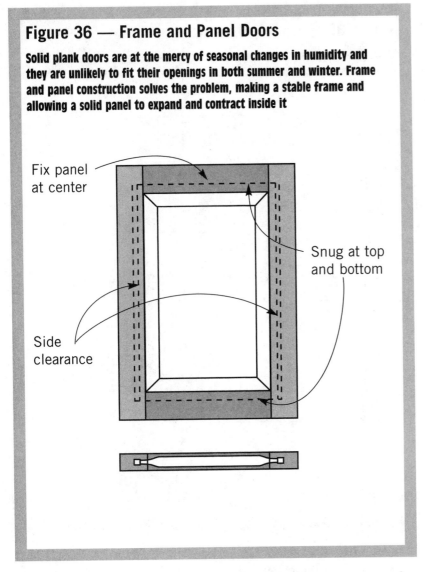

Figure 36 — Frame and Panel Doors

Solid plank doors are at the mercy of seasonal changes in humidity and they are unlikely to fit their openings in both summer and winter. Frame and panel construction solves the problem, making a stable frame and allowing a solid panel to expand and contract inside it

Fix panel at center

Snug at top and bottom

Side clearance

versus 32 inches), the movement will be much less.

The advantages of frame and panel construction are not limited to dealing with dimensional variations. As explained in Chapter 3, *Wood Movement*, wood also undergoes cyclical distortion as moisture content fluctuates. The plank door shown in **Figure 37a** will show the same kind of distortion

as a flatsawn board. The door panel in **Figure 37b** will distort in the same fashion as the plank door, but the panel is thin and any cupping will be restrained by the thicker frame. The frame-and-panel door will remain quite stable, unlike the plank door.

Double Panels

When making a raised panel door, the trick is to get the joint between each frame and panel tight enough to keep out cold air and moisture. But not too tight — the wood still has to be able to expand and contract. The traditional panel has a beveled edge. When the door is first built, the beveled panel will fit tight in the frame. But as the panel shrinks, a gap can develop. I've started making the panel out as two back-to-back layers of wood instead of as a single piece. Back-to-back panels can shrink at different rates and even after shrinking, they'll still fit tight. On an outside door rather than using a 1½ inch thick panel, use two ¾ inch panels set back-to-back. This allows the panels to move independently of each other. This also allows you to finish each panel front and back for less moisture absorption, and because they are thinner, the two panels will warp less.

Rails and Stiles

In a typical full-size frame-and-panel door, the stiles run through from bottom to top, and the grain in the panels is vertical. The rails are generally wider than the stiles, providing wider tenons and better resistance to warping of the panels. Minimal clearance is needed in rail groves; more clearance is needed in the stile grooves for cross-grain movement.

Typically rails and stiles on a cabinet door are 2-3 inches wide (see **Figure 38**). The wood movement in such narrow pieces usually won't cause any trouble as far as the door swelling in the cabinet opening. In cross-grain glue-ups, rail and stile assemblies of cabinet doors also won't cause problems. In addition, yellow glue has some 'give' in it even after curing that allows for a bit of movement. Remember that a plain-sawn board will move about twice as much as a quartersawn board of the same species. See Chapter 3, *Wood Movement* for more on this.

Inlay

Furniture builders who want to inlay thin veneer strips to a solid table face problems. Most border inlay pieces are made with the wood grain running lengthwise and, once glued in, may pull loose and buckle. Even 20 inches with some wood species is too great a distance to inlay across the grain. Because the flat panel moves across the grain, the best method is to make the grain of the inlay band match the grain

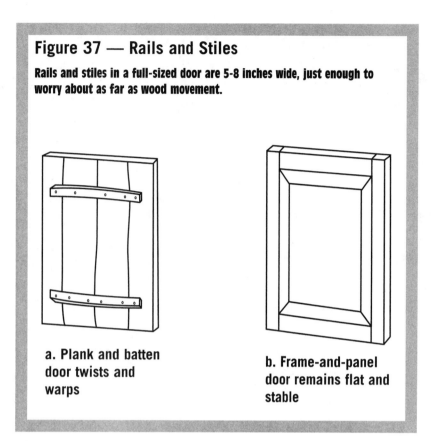

Figure 37 — Rails and Stiles

Rails and stiles in a full-sized door are 5-8 inches wide, just enough to worry about as far as wood movement.

a. Plank and batten door twists and warps

b. Frame-and-panel door remains flat and stable

of the wood that you are inlaying into. Crosscut pieces from a wide board so the grain of the inlay runs crosswise.

Marquetarians recommend preparing a separate veneer sheet that includes the inlay and then gluing the veneer sheet to a piece of MDF.

Directing Movement

Sometimes it is important to direct wood movement: on a demilune table (see **Figure 39b**) that will be placed against a wall or locked to a larger section of a table, the top should be secured at the rear so the wood expands

Figure 38 — Frame-and-Panel Door

The stiles run from top to bottom and the grain in the panels is vertical. Only minimal clearance is needed in the rail grooves; more clearance is needed in the stile grooves for cross-grain movement.

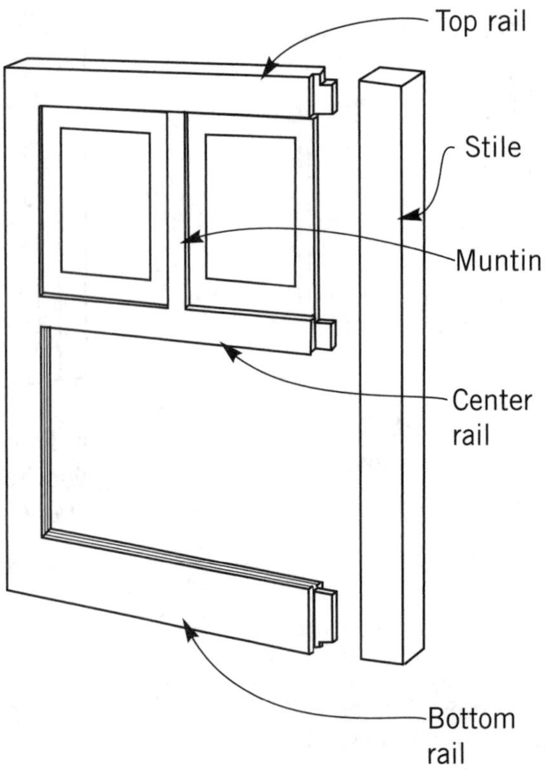

Top rail

Stile

Muntin

Center rail

Bottom rail

Rule of Thumb

On a **frame-and-panel** door, the rails are wider than the stiles and the bottom rail is wider than the top rail. Make the bottom rail three units wide, the top rail two units wide and the stiles one and one-half units wide.

towards the front. On a drop lid for a desk, the joint should be fixed on the hinge side so wood movement will be directed away from the hinges (see **Figure 39c**). This way the lid will operate without binding. On a table with an overhang that will be seen from and used on all sides, pin the tabletop at the center of both end rails (**Figure 39a**). Secure the top to the long side rails in a way that allows for seasonal movement. On a wide

apron (see **Figure 39d**) the top should be aligned with the top of the leg but allow movement towards the bottom.

House Construction

In house construction we rarely consider the potential for movement in joists and plates. But when you consider the total cross-grain width of lumber in the wall of a typical house, and the fact that framing lumber often sits out in the rain before being installed, you can see there is a lot of room to shrink, which we usually interpret as "the house is settling."

Framing

House frame lumber and interior wood should be dried to the moisture content that it will reach in use, thus minimizing future dimensional changes. This may be difficult, though usually you can stack it out of the rain. Some drying and shrinking of the frame may take place without visible defects appearing. Usually if the framing timbers are no more than 5% MC above that of the final interior moisture content of the house interior, there will be no problems. The most common sign of excessive shrinking are cracks in plastered walls, open joints and nail heads popping. Other problems include door opening distortions and uneven floors.

Figure 39 — Directing Wood Movement

The table with overhang, (a), the semi-circular (demilune) table (b), the drop lid desk (c), and the wide apron (d) all require that the wood movement be directed.

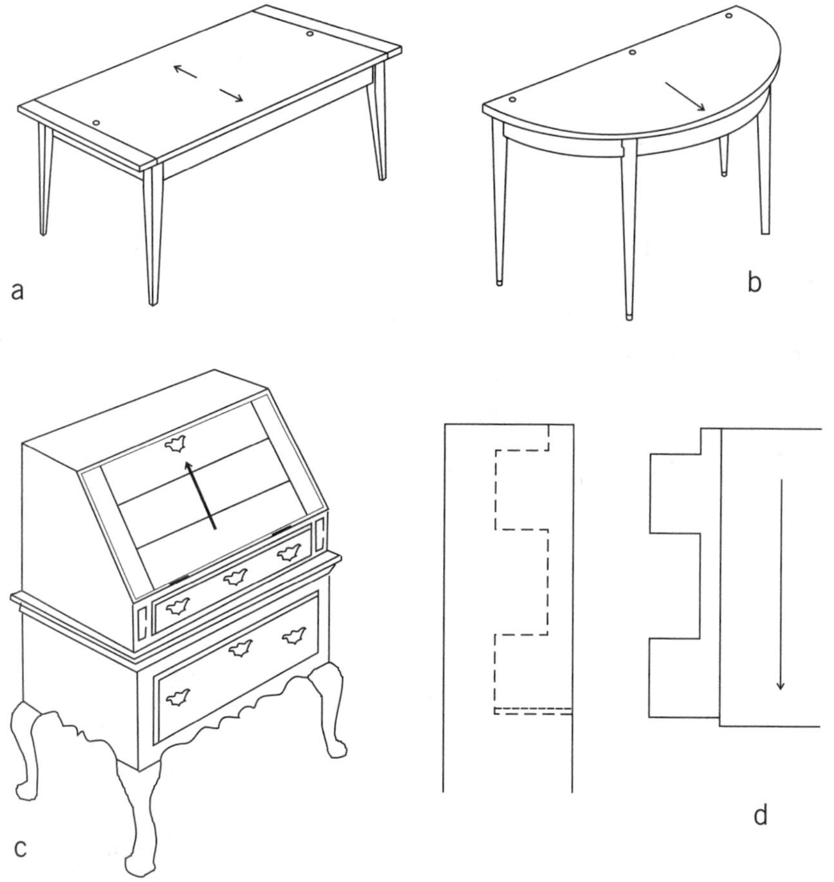

a

b

c

d

Interior Finish

Large interior beams, cornices, stair stringers and handrails should be made of kiln-dried wood or should be built up from smaller pieces. Wide baseboards and mouldings should be hollow backed. Wide door and window mouldings should be butt jointed. Large panels should be made of plywood or if solid, designed to move across the grain.

Flooring

Flooring is usually kiln dried to 6-8% MC and should not present a problem in swelling and buckling. For basement or large rooms, leave enough room around the edges for expansion.

CHAPTER 5

Wood Strength

The strength of a piece of wood is its ability to resist stress. When someone asks if a certain wood is strong, it's a tough question because all wood has some strength — however stress can come from any and all directions. Does the person mean, "I plan to use it as a shelf, so will it sag in the middle?" In this case he really means, "Will the wood have stiffness strength?" Or will he use the wood to make a bow and the question should be, "Does the wood have bending strength and will

Figure 40 — Stresses on Wood

The strength of wood is its ability to resist stress. Compressive stress results when force (weight) is applied either parallel or perpendicular to the grain (a). Tension stress occurs when a force is applied so the wood must resist being pulled apart (b). When shear stress is applied, the wood must resist being split (c). The stiffness of wood is how it resists both bending and deflection (d).

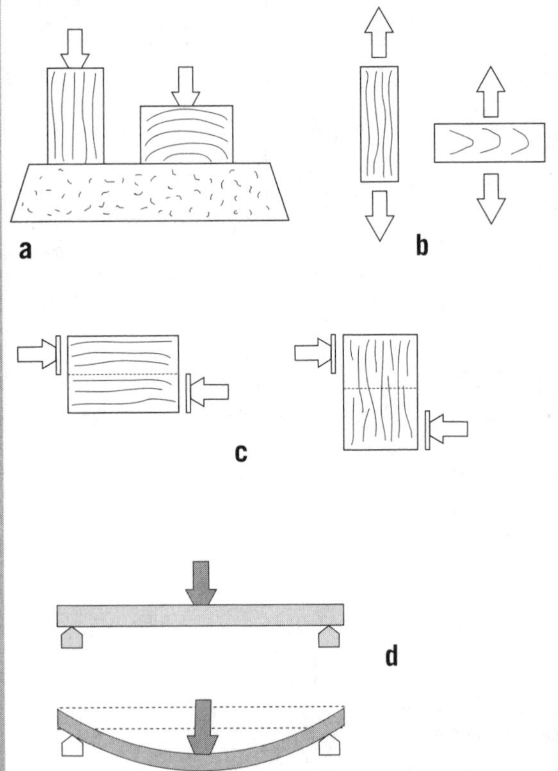

it flex and not break?" Or maybe the wood is for a column and the appropriate question is, "Can the wood withstand compression parallel to the grain?" If the wood is for a new floor and he is worried about heavy furniture denting it, then the question will be, "Can the wood withstand compression perpendicular to the grain?" **Figure 40** shows the different types of stress.

Assessing the strength of a piece of steel is easy because it is homogenous, that is, uniform in composition, and it has the same properties in compression or tension in any direction. If you try to compress, stretch, or bend a piece of steel, the direction of the force is mostly immaterial. While steel is made in different grades, these mixtures of iron, carbon, and other metals are uniform and can be reproduced. One load of steel beams of a certain grade is indistinguishable from any other batch.

Not so with wood. Wood is heterogeneous, it's made up of many unlike parts. It is not uniform in composition nor does it have the same strength in all directions. The different orders and families of trees differ widely both biologically and in strength. Even within the same genus there are wide species variations, for example, between red oak, black oak, northern red oak, southern red oak, and white oak. Even within the same wood species there are variations depending on where the tree grew — 2x4 studs from a Douglas fir that grew in Oregon are stronger (compressive strength both parallel and perpendicular to the grain) than 2x4 studs from a Utah tree. Cold climates promote tighter growth rings and denser wood.

Even in a single piece of wood there are different strengths because of growth ring placement, grain direction, physical defects, and whether the wood is wet or dry. Wood also reacts differently depending on whether the force is applied longitudinally, radially, or tangentially. **Figure 41** shows the tangential, radial, and transverse or cross-section parts of a piece of wood. Wood is very complicated and determining its exact strength is probably impossible. The best we can do is approximate from data gathered in testing similar pieces.

Definition of Terms

In discussing wood strength, it's important to understand standard terms.

Force. Force is the applied weight, whether it is from the

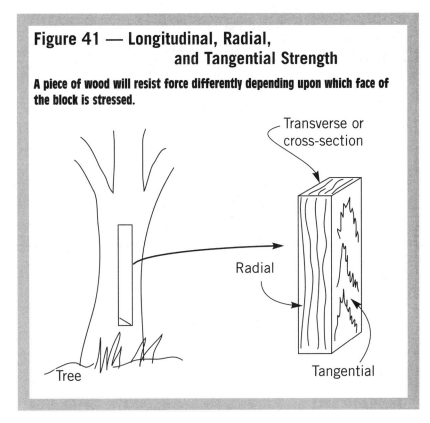

Figure 41 — Longitudinal, Radial, and Tangential Strength

A piece of wood will resist force differently depending upon which face of the block is stressed.

load of a roof to the top of a column, or the weight of a man distributed to the legs of a chair. Force is measured in pounds.

Stress. Stress is the amount of force that is applied per unit area. Stress is measured by dividing the force by the area. In the United States the units are pounds per square inch. For example:

Problem 1: We want to put our 50 gallon aquarium on wooden blocks. We plan to cut pieces of 2x4 and put one block under each leg. What is the stress applied to each block?

Solution 1: Water weighs 8¼ pounds per gallon so the 50

Rule of Thumb

Why does wood float in water? The density of water is 62 pounds per cubic foot, so any substance that weighs more will sink. Conversely, any substance that is lighter than 62 pounds per cubic foot will float. Only three common species are denser than water: ebony, 67 pounds per cubic foot; cocobolo, 68 pounds; lignum vitae, 77 pounds. Two more come close, so they'll also sink when fresh-cut: rosewood, 57 pounds per cubic foot, and wenge, 55 pounds.

gallon tank weighs about 415 pounds. Add in the glass and metal frame and the weight is about 500 pounds.

Stress is measured per square inch and the area of the bottom of each leg of the aquarium is ¾ x ¾ inch. The area of each leg is 0.75 x 0.75 = 0.56 sq. in.

The applied weight to each leg is 125 pounds. The stress or unit force is:

Stress = force ÷ area

Stress = 125 lbs. ÷ 0.56 in.^{2} = 223 lb. /in.^{2} (psi)

Deformation. Deformation is the change in size that a material experiences while under a force. This can be the shortening of a column if the force is applied at the top, or a change in thickness if the force is applied to the flat side of a plank. If the block of wood is measured in inches, then the deformation is also measured in inches.

Strain. Strain is the unit deformation or the amount of change per unit of original length. If a 10-inch pine block was subjected to 2,000 pounds of weight and the deformation was measured, we could find the strain. Strain is measured as inches per inch.

Problem 2: What is the strain on a 10-inch pine block if a force of 2,000 pounds causes a

deformation of 0.0035 inch?

Solution 2: Strain is found by dividing the deformation by the original length.

Strain = deformation ÷ original length

Strain = 0.0035" ÷ 10" = 0.00035 in. / in.

Proportional limit. Proportional limit is the weight a material can bear before failure. Wood is elastic and when a weight is applied, the fibers compress. When the force is removed the piece returns to its original shape. At some point, however, the increasing force is such that when the force is removed, the wood does not return to its original shape but remains in a permanent set. The proportional limit is defined as that point where, should the force be removed, the piece will spring back but if additional force is added, a permanent set will occur. By measuring different woods, the average proportional limit of each can be determined and this value can be used to measure the compressive strength, both parallel and perpendicular to the grain. The data can also be used to calculate the modulus of elasticity (MOE), that is, the stiffness of the wood.

Modulus of elasticity. The Modulus of elasticity (MOE) measures the ability of wood to resist deformation. It is defined as stress divided by strain. It is usually written as 'E' and referred to as the 'E Value'. **Figure 42** shows a list of the E Values of various woods. The E Values range from 1.24 million psi (pounds per square inch) for eastern white pine to 2.01 million psi for yellow birch. The E Value is often abbreviated, for example 1,800,000 psi is written as E1.8. The higher the E Value of the wood, the more resistant it is to stress.

Problem 3: We have a 2 inch by 2 inch pine block 10 inches long. We put it upright in a press and add weight to the top. As force increases, so too does compression. We reach the proportional limit at 3,500 pounds and the change in length is 0.0021 inches. What is the MOE?

Solution 3: The modulus of elasticity is equal to force applied per unit area divided by the amount of change per original length or:

MOE = stress ÷ strain

Where stress = 3,500 pounds, strain = 0.0021 inches/inch

MOE = 3,500 psi ÷ 0.0021-in. / in. = 1,666,666 psi

MOE = 1.67×10^6 psi.

E = 1.67

Deflection. Deflection in a horizontal beam is sag or droop. The strength to resist deflection depends upon the stiffness of the wood. Most woods are similar in stiffness as measured by the modulus of elasticity, see **Figure 42**. The highest MOE (yellow birch 2.01) is 62% higher than the lowest (eastern white pine 1.24). If a shelf made of yellow birch deflects 0.5 inch under a load, then a similar shelf made of eastern white pine will deflect 0.81 inch.

2.01 ÷ 1.24 = 1.62

0.5 in. x 1.62 = 0.81 in.

Resistance. The resistance of a material, in our case wood, is its ability to oppose applied stress. In some cases, resistance is the same as strength, but often we also want to know how much deflection results from applied stress or how much compression results from a unit force. Resistance is measured in pounds per square inch (psi).

Moment of inertia. The moment of inertia (I) of a piece of wood is a measure of its resistance to rotation about the end axis. The I Value of a beam depends on its cross section and because the cross section of most wood planks is rectangular, the I Value is the horizontal width times the vertical thickness cubed and divided by 12. Width and thickness are measured in inches.

I = (width x thickness^3) ÷ 12

Huge gains in the I Value are achieved when we increase the

Figure 42 — Stiffness Strength of Wood (E Value)

Wood Type	Modulus of Elasticity (x 100,000) (in psi)
Alder	1.38
Ash	1.77
Beech	1.72
Birch, Paper	1.59
Birch, Yellow	2.01
Cherry	1.49
Douglas Fir	1.95
Elm	1.34
Hickory	1.73
Maple, Sugar	1.83
Oak, Red	1.82
Oak, White	1.78
Pine, Eastern White	1.24
Pine, Western White	1.51
Poplar	1.58
Walnut, Black	1.68
Average	**1.65**

Rule of Thumb

In terms of strength there is little difference between the heartwood and sapwood of most wood species.

Rule of Thumb

To estimate the **stiffness** of different sizes of wood:

2x2 = 1

2x3 = 3

2x4 = 8

2x5 = 16

2x6 = 27

2x7 = 43

2x8 = 64

2x9 = 91

2x10 = 125

For example if you replace a 2x4 beam with a 2x6 beam the stiffness will increase by three: 27 ÷ 8 = 3.4

By using a 2x8 joist instead of a 2x6, you will gain 2½ times the stiffness:

64 ÷ 27 = 2.4

thickness (vertical) number. This is why a small increase in the width of an on-edge piece of wood such as a table apron, yields a large increase in its stiffness. This is also why a 2x8 floor joist is so much stiffer on edge than when laid flat.

Problem 4: What is the 'I Value' for an upright 2x8 floor joist?

Solution 4:

I = (width x thickness^3) ÷ 12

Where width = 2, thickness=8

I = 2 x (8^3) ÷ 12

I = (2 x 512) ÷ 12 = 85.3 (on edge)

Problem 5: What is the I Value for a 2x8 floor joist laying flat?

Solution 5:

I = (width x thickness^3) ÷ 12

Where width = 8, thickness = 2

I = 8 x (2^3) ÷ 12

I = (8 x 8) ÷ 12 = 5.3 (flat)

This means the beam on edge is about 16 times stiffer than the same beam laid flat.

85.3 ÷ 5.3 = 16

Be sure to add diagonal bracing to any beam so it can't twist — twisting in effect reduces the beam height.

Stiffness. The stiffness of a beam is defined as the amount of deflection under an applied force perpendicular to the grain. As the equation below shows, deflection (Y) depends on the weight applied (Wt.), the length of the beam (L), the modulus of elasticity (E), and the moment of inertia (I). The moment of inertia depends on the cross sectional area.

$$Y = (0.013 \times Wt. \times L^3) \div (E \times I)$$

Where Y = maximum deflection at mid-span measured in inches

Wt. = load weight measured in pounds

L = beam length measured in inches

E = modulus of elasticity in psi

I = moment of inertia

where I = (W x T^3) ÷ 12

Because L is cubed in the equation, doubling the length of a beam under load means the deflection will increase eight-fold.

Compression Strength

Compression can be applied to a piece of wood either parallel or perpendicular to the grain. See **Figure 43**.

Compression Parallel to the Grain

When wood is stressed in a way that shortens its fibers lengthwise, it is under compression parallel to the grain. Columns, furniture legs, and an old man's cane are examples of compression parallel to the grain. For its weight, wood is very strong in this direction.

In a standard test, a block of wood is placed upright in a press and force is applied to the top end. Weight and compression figures are charted until the proportional limit (see page 74) is reached, that is the point where the wood permanently deforms and does not spring back. Using the data from the experiment we can calculate the Modulus of Elasticity (MOE) for the wood. **Figure 44** shows that a piece of western white pine can withstand almost 4,500 psi without failure due to fiber crush or permanent set.

For more on the strength of wood when the load is parallel to the grain, see Chapter 8, *Column Strength and Entasis.*

Compression Perpendicular to the Grain

Fiber Stress at Proportional Limit (FSPL) is the amount of load (weight) the material can withstand and still spring back that is, retain its elasticity. Beyond this point the wood will be permanently deformed and is in danger of failure. The data in **Figure 44** are in pounds per square inch (psi).

A piece of Douglas fir can withstand about 870 pounds per

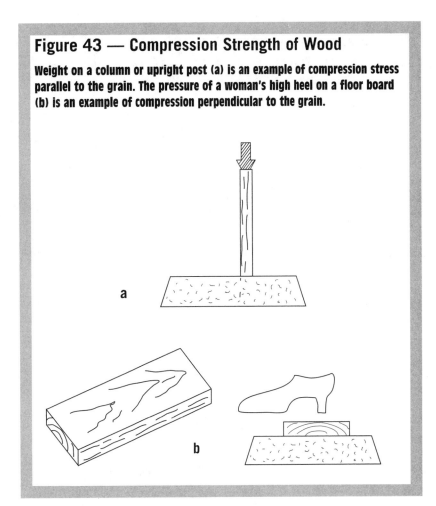

Figure 43 — Compression Strength of Wood

Weight on a column or upright post (a) is an example of compression stress parallel to the grain. The pressure of a woman's high heel on a floor board (b) is an example of compression perpendicular to the grain.

a

b

square inch perpendicular to the grain before the fibers deform and will no longer spring back. Weight on a floor board is a good example of compression perpendicular to the grain.

A 6-inch x 36-inch Douglas fir shelf is in little danger of failure by compression because the board can withstand about 90 tons of compressive weight.

6" x 36" = 216 sq. in.

216 x 870 psi = 187,920 lbs.

There are instances when

Figure 44 — Compression Strength of Wood, Parallel and Perpendicular to the Grain

Wood Type	Parallel To The Grain FSPL (1)	Perpendicular To The Grain FSPL (2)
Alder	4530	540
Ash	5790	1410
Beech	4880	1250
Birch, Paper	3610	740
Birch, Yellow	6130	1190
Cherry	5960	850
Douglas Fir	5850	870
Elm	4030	850
Hickory	5180	2130
Maple, Sugar	5390	1810
Oak, Red	4580	1250
Oak, White	4760	1070
Pine, Eastern White	3670	440
Pine, Western White	4480	540
Poplar	3730	560
Walnut, Black	5780	1250
Average	**4897**	**1047**

(1) Fiber Stress at Proportional Limit (parallel to the grain)
(2) Fiber Stress at Proportional Limit (perpendicular to the grain)

Rule of Thumb

Fast-grown wood with widely spaced annual rings usually is weaker than slow-grown wood with closely spaced annual rings.

compression perpendicular to the grain is a concern. A grand piano might weigh 1,500 pounds and be supported on only three legs.

Problem 6: Is there any danger of denting the maple floor on the high school stage when a grand piano is brought in for a concert? The piano weighs 1,500 pounds and has three 2 inch diameter casters. The casters are 1 inch wide.

Solution 6: The compression strength of maple perpendicular to the grain (from **Figure 44**) is

1810 psi. The round caster touches the floor about $3/16$ inch x 1 inch.

Area = 0.1875 x 1 = 0.1875 sq. in. per wheel

There are three casters:

3 x 0.1875 = 0.56 sq. in. total

The total piano weight of 1,500 pounds is spread over 0.56 sq. in. thus the weight per square inch is:

1,500 ÷ 0.56 = 2679 psi

This is more than the compressive strength of maple (1810 psi) so the weight will damage the floor.

Tension Strength

The ability to resist tension under load is a function of the wood itself — species, quality, and cut. With compression, the fibers of wood are compressed. Under tension, the fibers are pulled apart. See **Figure 40b** and **Figure 45**.

Tension strength is the ability to oppose stress designed to split a piece of wood crosswise.

Tension Parallel to the Grain

Wood will easily split under tension parallel to the grain. Examples are pounding a wedge into the end of a log, or driving a nail too close to the end of a flat board. In each case the split results from tension parallel to the grain. **Figure 45** shows perpendicular tension figures. The figures range from 310 psi for western white pine to 1150 psi for sugar maple.

Tension Perpendicular to the Grain

An example of tension perpendicular to the grain is when a wedge is driven into a piece of wood in an attempt to split it across the grain instead of lengthwise. Another example is when stress is applied to a piece of wood and it is pulled at each end, that is, it is stretched lengthwise. Wood is very strong in both these cases. Steel can withstand some 60,000 psi before it pulls apart. The same size piece of hickory can withstand about 30,000 psi in the same test. It can be argued therefore that on a weight-to-weight basis, wood is stronger than steel in tension perpendicular to the grain.

Shear Strength
Perpendicular Shear

Because of the way the wood fibers align, wood is extremely resistant to shearing perpendicular to, or across, the grain. Thin veneer (⅟₅₀ in.) can sometimes be cut cross-wise with scissors, but with any thicker material, the wood crushes or tears. There are no data on perpendicular shear. See **Figure 46**.

Parallel Shear

A force at the end of the block tries to force the block apart lengthwise (see **Figure 46**). **Figure 47** shows figures for parallel shear.

Bending Strength

Bending strength is important in the design of furniture and buildings but especially in beams. In our case, a simple beam is a piece of wood loaded perpendicular to its long axis. Examples are floor joists, stair treads, and shelves. A force on the face of a beam leads to bending which compresses fibers on the upper surface and stretches those on the lower surface. This is called compression along the top and tension along the bottom surface. Both stresses are at the maximum at the top and bottom surfaces and diminish to zero near the center of the beam — an area called the neutral axis.

Steam benders use a steel strap on the outside of the curve with end blocks that prevent the wood fibers at the top surface from stretching; in effect the neutral axis is moved from the center to the top surface and all stress of the bend becomes compression on the inside surface not tension on the outside.

Wood that is steamed, microwaved or soaked in boiling

Figure 45 — Tension Strength of Wood Parallel to the Grain

Wood Type	Tension psi (1)
Alder	420
Ash	940
Beech	1010
Birch, Paper	640
Birch, Yellow	920
Cherry	560
Douglas Fir	340
Elm	660
Hickory	1020
Maple, Sugar	1150
Oak, Red	800
Oak, White	800
Pine, Eastern White	310
Pine, Western White	310
Poplar	540
Walnut, Black	690
Average	**694**

(1) Fiber Stress at Proportional Limit

Figure 46 — Perpendicular and Parallel Shear

In tests, a force is applied in an effort to force the block apart. Wood separates in shear more readily along the grain. There are no data for perpendicular shear.

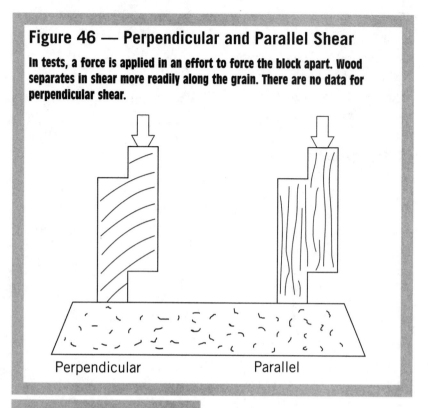

Perpendicular   Parallel

Figure 47 —

Shear Strength of Wood Parallel to the Grain

Wood Type	Shear psi
Alder	1080
Ash	1950
Beech	2010
Birch, Paper	1210
Birch, Yellow	1880
Cherry	1700
Douglas Fir	1160
Elm	1510
Hickory	2080
Maple, Sugar	2330
Oak, Red	1780
Oak, White	2000
Pine, Eastern White	900
Pine, Western White	850
Poplar	1190
Walnut, Black	1370
Average	**694**

water can be compressed as much as 30% parallel to the grain. The same wood can be stretched only 2%. To bend wood most of the deformation must be compression on the inner side of the bend. The outer side must experience only slight tension and zero strain. To accomplish this, a metal strap equipped with end fittings is used. **Figure 48** shows such a bending strap.

In homogeneous materials such as steel, the strength at the upper and lower surfaces are the same. This is not so in wood. See **Figure 49**.

For the woodworker, it is important to know how much a piece of wood will bend under a certain load. **Figure 50** shows bending strength for some domestic woods. The Stress at Proportional Limit is the force the beam will withstand and still spring back when the weight is removed. The Modulus of Rupture is the point where the beam fails.

Factors affecting Strength

The strength of a piece of wood or a beam depends on the moisture content, density, time, temperature, grain orientation, species, growth rate, sapwood versus heart wood and physical defects.

Moisture

Wet wood is not as strong as dry wood and engineers have separate strength tables for wet and dry beams. **Figure 51** shows wet and dry strength for compression. Wet wood has approximately 67% the compressive strength of dry wood perpendicular to the grain and 81% of the compressive strength parallel to the grain. In practice a wet beam will get stiffer as it dries.

The 21 woods listed average 347 psi wet and 520 psi dry in compression tests perpendicular to the grain before the fibers are crushed.

$$347 \div 520 = 67\%$$

The 21 woods average 920 psi wet and 1204 psi dry in compression tests parallel to the grain before the fibers are crushed.

970 ÷ 1204 = 81%

Density

Density is the weight per unit of volume. In **Figure 52** the density of balsa is 10 pounds per cubic foot while the density of lignum vitae is 77 pounds. Of all the properties of wood — growth ring spacing and width, early wood/late wood contrast, relative pore size, etc. — density is the best indicator of wood strength. Density predicts hardness, how difficult the piece will be to machine, nailing resistance, compressibility, and stiffness. Density is expressed as pounds per cubic foot or grams per cubic centimeter. Water has a density of 1 g/cm^3 or 62.4 lb./ft.^{3} Any wood with a density less than that of water will float in water, and any wood with a higher density will sink.

Time

A beam under a load for a long time slowly develops creep, a time-dependent deformation. At low to moderate loads, creep is imperceptible. Over long periods, when loads approach maximum, creep may result in objectionable amounts of bending or failure. Sagging timbers in old buildings are an example. Wood performs well

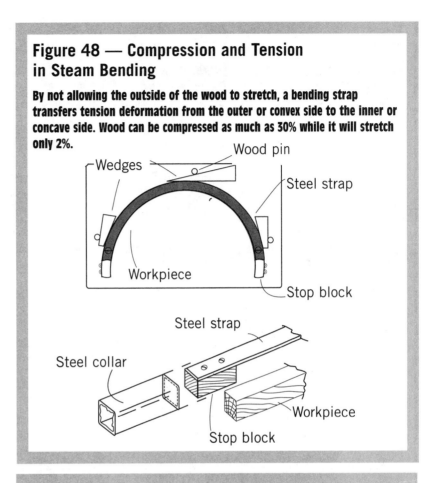

Figure 48 — Compression and Tension in Steam Bending

By not allowing the outside of the wood to stretch, a bending strap transfers tension deformation from the outer or convex side to the inner or concave side. Wood can be compressed as much as 30% while it will stretch only 2%.

Wedges — Wood pin — Steel strap — Workpiece — Stop block

Steel strap — Steel collar — Workpiece — Stop block

Figure 49 — Compression and Tension

When a piece of wood bends, the top is under compression and the bottom surface is under tension. The center of the beam (neutral axis) remains in the center and is under neither compression nor tension.

Neutral axis — Compression — Tension

Figure 50 — Bending Strength of Wood

The Stress at Proportional Limit is the maximum weight the beam will withstand and still spring back when the weight is removed. The Modulus of Rupture is the weight that will break the wood fibers and cause the beam to fail.

Wood Species	Stress at Proportional Limit (psi)	Modulus of Rupture (psi)
Alder	6,900	9,800
Ash	8,900	15,400
Beech	8,700	14,900
Birch, Paper	6,900	12,300
Birch, Yellow	10,100	16,600
Cherry	9,000	12,300
Douglas Fir	7,800	12,200
Elm	7,600	11,800
Hickory	9,100	13,700
Maple, Sugar	9,500	15,800
Oak, Red	8,500	14,300
Oak, White	8,200	15,200
Pine, Eastern White	5,700	8,600
Pine, Western White	6,200	9,500
Poplar	6,200	10,100
Walnut, Black	10,500	14,600
Average	**8113**	**12,944**

chamber no longer than necessary — usually about one hour per inch of thickness of the air-dried wood. This short heat period may still result in 20% permanent loss of strength.

Cross Grain
In most planks and beams the grain direction is parallel to the long axis of the piece and the piece is said to be straight-grained. When some grain goes crosswise on the beam, this portion is said to be cross-grained. Any cross-grain makes the beam subject to failure when bent, or to splitting when under stress. Compressive strength is not affected.

Species Variability
Within the same wood species, there is considerable variation in density and strength. Planks cut from the same tree will show compressive strengths varying from 3,000 psi to 6,000 psi before the fibers crush. Much of the difference in strength can be predicted by density and therefore can be sensed by the weight of the piece. Denser pieces are stronger.

Growth Rate
Growth rate and the spacing of growth rings are good indicators of wood strength. A faster growing tree has a greater proportion of early wood compared to late wood or summer growth compared to winter growth. Because early

under repeated short-term loads without failing or becoming brittle, unlike some metals and concrete.

Temperature
Wood gets stronger as the temperature lowers. In the natural state, lumber increases in strength by 2% to 5% for every 10°F decrease in temperature. When the temperature rises again, the wood returns to its original strength. Sustained heating can result in permanent loss of strength. Woodworkers who bend wood with steam try to keep the wood in the steam

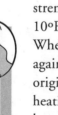

Rule of Thumb

A knot has the same effect on the strength of a board as a hole of the same size and placement.

wood is weaker, a board comprised of mostly early wood will be weaker.

A measure of rings per inch will indicate wood strength. Old-growth redwood harvested 1850-1900 can have 50 rings per inch and was strong enough (stiffness, compression, and tension) to be used for beams and joists in churches and fine homes. The faster growing redwood of today has five or six rings per inch and is good only for backyard fencing.

Mahogany grown today on managed tree farms is ready for harvest after 10 to 15 years. Many old-growth trees were harvested after 100 years. The difference in hardness is apparent.

Sapwood versus Heartwood

There is little difference between the strength of sapwood and heartwood. Heartwood is more decay resistant, has more extractives, and essentially is dead. Sapwood has more free and bound water, takes preservatives better and can be treated to retain its strength longer. When sapwood and heartwood are at the same moisture content, they are equal in strength.

Physical Defects

Bending and stiffness are most affected by physical defects. All

Figure 51 — Strength of Wet and Dry Wood

Above these weights the wood fibers crush and the beam fails. All strength ratings decrease dramatically when the wood is wet.

Wood Type	Compression Perpendicular (psi)		Compression Parallel (psi)	
	Wet	Dry	Wet	Dry
Aspen	177	265	725	725
Beech	477	715	960	1200
Birch, Sweet	477	715	960	1200
Birch, Yellow	477	715	960	1200
Cedar, Port Orford	283	425	800	1000
Cottonwood	213	320	620	775
Fir, Balsam	283	425	1120	1400
Fir, Calif. Red	270	405	1200	1500
Fir, Douglas	417	625	1360	1700
Hemlock, Western	247	370	1320	1650
Hickory	477	715	960	1200
Maple, Sugar	413	620	700	875
Oak, Red	590	885	880	1100
Oak, White	533	800	880	1100
Pine, Eastern White	223	335	960	1200
Pine, Ponderosa	223	335	840	1050
Poplar, Yellow	280	420	720	900
Redwood	433	650	1200	1500
Spruce, Red	283	425	1120	1400
Spruce, Sitka	223	335	960	1200
Spruce, White	283	425	1120	1400
Average	**347**	**520**	**970**	**1204**

of the defects — knots, checks, splits, and decay — concentrate strain and cause failure. Use only straight-grained wood for steam bending and for beams that must be stiff.

Knots are the most common defect because all trees have some type of branching system. Knots reduce strength in two ways. First, the knot itself is not connected to the surrounding tissue and second, some of the area around a knot is cross grain. Both of these result in severe strength reduction. Small, tight

Rule of Thumb

Wet wood bends about twice as much as dry wood.

Figure 52 — Density of Woods

The higher density woods are heavier, harder and stronger. Dense woods shrink and swell more during humidity changes and temperature fluctuations, take longer to dry and require more care to prevent splitting. Wood densities range from balsa (10 lb./ft.^{3}) to lignum vitae at 77 4 lb./ft.^{3}

Wood Type	gms/cm^3	lbs./ft.^{3}
Alder	0.48	30
Ash	0.61	38
Balsa	0.16	10
Beech	0.74	46
Birch, Paper	0.61	38
Birch, Yellow	0.67	42
Cedar	0.37	23
Cherry	0.58	36
Chestnut	0.48	30
Cocobolo	1.09	68
Cypress	0.50	31
Douglas Fir, Coast	0.53	33
Douglas Fir, Mountain	0.45	28
Ebony	1.07	67
Elm	0.56	35
Hickory	0.82	51
Koa	0.66	41
Lignum Vitae	1.23	77
Madrone	0.77	48
Mahogany, African	0.56	35
Mahogany, Sou. Amer.	0.59	37
Maple, Sugar	0.67	42
Oak, Red	0.66	41
Oak, White	0.75	47
Padauk	0.72	45
Pine, Eastern White	0.37	23
Pine, Ponderosa	0.51	32
Pine, Western White	0.35	22
Poplar, Yellow	0.53	33
Redwood, Calif.	0.42	26
Rosewood	0.91	57
Spruce	0.45	28
Sycamore	0.56	35
Teak	0.64	40
Walnut, Black	0.64	40
Wenge	0.88	55
Zebrawood	0.75	47
Average	**0.63**	**39**

Note: 1 gm/cm^3 = 62.4 lbs./ft.^{3}

knots might be a negligible problem while a large loose knot might cause the board to fall apart.

Put any knots on the top of a beam — a defect is less affected by compression than by tension.

Decay has a seriously harmful effect on the impact strength of a beam. If untreated, decay will progress and total loss will result. A stain fungus does not reduce strength but indicates that a condition once existed that favored decay. Any wood showing evidence of decay should be suspect.

Reference.: The wood strength figures come from Hoadley's **Understanding Wood**, Taunton Press, 1980 and from the USDA Forest Products Laboratory **Wood Handbook**, 2002.

CHAPTER 6

Moisture Protection

When woodworkers talk about a finish they are describing a final treatment that protects wood or enhances its appearance. A wood surface that is not protected in some manner is susceptible to damage from water, natural aging, abrasion, and dirt. A wide range of coatings is available and each has its good and bad points. Some finishes are more durable and protect against abrasion or indentation, some enhance the beauty of the wood and prevent changes in color due to light or atmospheric pollutants, and some possess qualities that adapt them for special purposes. In the home it is desirable to protect furniture from accumulating dirt and to create a surface that can be easily cleaned. But of all the reasons to apply a finish, the most important is to impede the exchange of moisture with the atmosphere, thus helping avoid the consequences of wood movement. For more on this see Chapter 3, *Wood Movement.*

Furniture kept indoors will seldom be subjected to prolonged exposure to liquid water — people usually clean up water spills immediately — and only a small part of the top surface is involved. However, water vapor in the form of humidity affects the whole furniture piece and can persist for weeks at a time. A good moisture-excluding finish, therefore, should be selected because of its ability to protect against water vapor rather than for its ability to protect against liquid water. Moisture protection basically should be a measure of the permeability of a coating to water vapor, not a measure of water repellency. Finishes differ in their ability to protect against the two.

Excluding Water Vapor

Some finishes, such as penetrating oils, protect wood from liquid water fairly well but are ineffective against water vapor. Other finishes, such as shellac, offer good protection from water vapor but are less protective against liquid water.

The protection afforded by coatings in excluding water vapor from wood depends on at least four variables:

1. The thickness of the coating film –
Usually three coats of an oil or varnish will give near maximum protection. Shellac goes on in thinner coats, so six coats gives maximum protection. In both cases use a wash coat, a sealer or a thinned finish first. A thick coating will cover the pores without penetrating and as it dries it will contract, leaving pin holes around the pores.

2. Defects and voids in the film – Fill cracks and voids before applying a finish. The object of a filler is to make a wood surface as smooth as possible and to seal exposed interior portions of wood.

3. The chemical composition of the oil or polymer – Manufacturers formulate finishes specifically to repel water vapor. The polyurethane exterior varnishes are excellent for water and vapor repellency.

4. The length of exposure to moisture –
Extended exposure to sun and water will degrade a finish. If the wood absorbs water and expands and contracts, the surface film will crack.

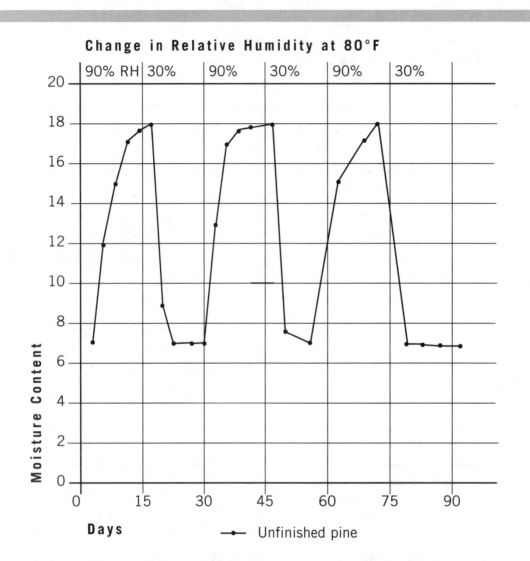

Figure 53 — Change in Moisture Content of Pine Wood

As the relative humidity cycles from 30% to 90% over 90 days, the moisture content of the untreated pine sample jumped from 6.5% to 18% and back down again every time the humidity changed.

Relative Humidity

The amount of water vapor that may be absorbed by a piece of unfinished wood depends primarily on the relative humidity of the surrounding air. If an unprotected furniture piece is stored at 0% relative humidity, eventually the moisture content of the wood will reach 0%. If the piece is stored at 100% relative humidity, in time it will reach maximum moisture content of 30% which is the fiber saturation point of wood. For more on this see Chapter 3, *Wood Movement*. When the relative humidity is between these two extremes, the wood will reach moisture content somewhere between 0% and 30%. The moisture content of wood is controlled by humidity, and when the two are in balance the wood is at its equilibrium moisture content. This balance rarely happens because atmospheric relative humidity is always in flux and as the humidity changes so also does the moisture content of the wood change. Daily and seasonal changes in humidity drive the moisture content of wood through the same cycles and to prevent this, a protective coating is needed. See Chapters 3, *Wood Movement* and 2, *Wood Drying,* for a more detailed discussion of these problems.

A Three-Month Experiment

The United States Forest Products Laboratory in Madison, Wisconsin devised a test to determine the effectiveness of commercial wood finishes. To find a baseline, unfinished pine samples at 6.5% MC were placed in a chamber where humidity could be varied while the temperature was kept constant at 80% F. The experiment lasted 90 days and the MC of the unfinished pine was measured approximately every other day. On the first day, humidity in the test chamber was raised to 90% and kept there for 15 days; the MC in the wood rose slowly to 18%. The humidity was then lowered to 30% and kept there for 15 days; the MC of the uncoated pine boards dropped to 7%. Humidity was raised and lowered this way every 15 days until the tests were completed three months later. **Figure 53** shows the results for the untreated pine; the MC climbed to 18% every time the relative humidity rose then dropped back near 7% when the humidity was lowered. This clearly demonstrates the need for a vapor-resisting finish to protect wood.

This test was extreme in that the humidity was kept constant (unusually high and unusually low) for long periods of time.

> ## Rule of Thumb
> Select a good finish based on its ability to protect against water vapor rather than its ability to protect against liquid water.

Rule of Thumb

Film finishes such as varnish and lacquer require three coats for moisture protection. Shellac is thinner and may require five or six coats.

Under normal conditions both temperature and humidity vary but not to these extremes nor for this length of time.

Kinds of Finishes

Moisture protective coatings can be classified into five general types:

1. Waxes
2. Oils
3. Lacquer
4. Shellac
5 Varnishes

The Tests

The Forest Products Lab tested these five types of finishes to determine their ability to protect wood from water vapor. The tests used single pieces of wood covered on all sides with 1-6 coats — though in normal construction, furniture is seldom coated on all sides.

As wood is exposed to water vapor, it absorbs or desorbs moisture depending on the surrounding humidity. A 30% relative humidity will generate 6% MC in unfinished wood and 90% relative humidity will generate 18% MC. See **Wood Basics**, Chapter 1 for more on this. The coated samples were first conditioned at 80° F. and 30% relative humidity then exposed to 90% humidity for 14 days at 80° F. Moisture vapor protection was determined by comparing the MC of the coated specimen with that of the uncoated control. A coating that blocked all vapor would be rated at 100%, however no coating was this effective. The results are given in the order of least water vapor protection to best in **Figure 54**.

Waxes

In the tests three coats of paste furniture wax gave zero moisture exclusion after 14 days. While wax can be used as the primary finish on a piece of furniture, its usual use is on top of another finish. A well-buffed wax coating imparts a soft, pleasing luster to a finish that accentuates both the wood's color and figure. Only a thin coat of wax is ever laid down. While multiple coats help ensure complete coverage and perhaps pack into open pores, there is no useful buildup beyond three coats because each new coat merely softens the ones below, then all the excess gets buffed off.

Waxes are insoluble in water, they bond to almost any surface and can be dissolved in most solvents, including mineral spirits or paint thinner. A thin film of wax creates a low-friction surface that can withstand minimal wear. Woodworkers can choose from many natural and synthetic waxes. A simple finish can be made with a sealer coat of shellac, varnish or lacquer followed by several coats of wax.

Wax alone is too soft for a table top but is fine for low-contact items.

In the tests, paraffin wax, melted and brushed on to form a thick coating gave 69% protection at 14 days. When furniture legs were dipped into molten paraffin wax, 95% protection resulted. This is useful for patio pieces though not for house furniture.

Beeswax is a soft wax secreted by bees for comb building and was historically the primary wax for woodwork.

Carnauba wax comes from palm leaves and is the hardest of the natural waxes.

Candelilla wax comes from a desert plant found in northern Mexico and the southwestern United States. It is often used in blends because of its low cost and its compatibility in mixing with other waxes.

Paraffin refined from petroleum is a very soft wax that's often blended with harder waxes to make them easier to apply. A thick coat of paraffin wax offers a great amount of water and water vapor protection. Note that dipping creates a more effective barrier than brushing.

Paste and spray wax are used in the home to reduce friction, add shine, and make furniture easier to dust. Three coats of paste wax provide minimal (17%) water protection for 1 day but none after a week. Spray furniture wax was of no use at repelling water.

Oils

Oils are easy to apply and give good protection against dirt and dust. They are marketed under several names: Danish oil, penetrating oil, boiled linseed and tung oil. Oil finishes soak into the wood, semi-harden and seal the top surface to form a protective barrier. The ability to penetrate into the wood surface gives these finishes three inherent advantages:

1. **A penetrating finish** will not chip or flake off the surface.

2. **Scratches and dents** are not as apparent because the finish extends under the top surface of the wood.

3. **The finish semi-hardens** the wood, making it less susceptible to damage.

Penetrating oil finishes are useful mainly to exclude dust and dirt and to enhance the looks of a piece. They offer only limited protection from liquid water and very little protection from water vapor, see **Figure 54**. Both linseed oil and tung oil gave zero protection from water vapor after 14 days.

Figure 54 — Moisture-Excluding Effectiveness of Woodworking Finishes, 3 Coats after 14 days

	Percent Moisture Exclusion
Paste furniture wax	0
50% Linseed oil	0
100% Linseed oil	0
100% Tung oil	2
Water repellent	11
Nitrocellulose lacquer	19
Spar varnish	30
Urethane varnish (with oil)	37
Shellac (3 coats)	39
Polyurethane varnish (clear finish)	66
Paraffin wax (brushed)	69
Paraffin wax (dipped)	95
Shellac (6 coats)	95

Rule of Thumb

Finishes protect

the wood from damage, and make it possible to clean the surface, but the main reason for applying a finish is to slow down the exchange of moisture between the wood and the surrounding air, and thus to minimize swelling and shrinkage.

Lacquer

Lacquer is composed of nitrocellulose plus a resin, a plasticizer, and a carrier. It is versatile, tough, and dries to a transparent shine. A lacquer coating is hard and durable and it will wear far longer than any other form of finish and still maintain a lasting luster. It resists both heat and water, will give a shiny surface that requires no special polish and it can cleaned with a damp cloth. Lacquer cures by the evaporation of the solvent. The drawbacks: traditional lacquers dry quickly, are best applied with a spray gun, and a damaged surface is difficult to repair or touch up. Newly formulated brushing lacquers can be applied with a brush and have a longer drying time.

Three coats of lacquer gave only 19% water vapor protection after 14 days. This finish is not as protective against water vapor as shellac or varnishes.

Shellac

Shellac is the classic evaporative finish and also the most forgiving, being very easy to repair. It is hard, clear, and glossy, and among the most attractive of all finishes. It has excellent resistance to ultraviolet deterioration and darkening, and is the most stable of all natural resins. It is tough enough to be used as a floor finish and is a superb sealer and undercoat for most other finishes. Dissolved in alcohol, it can seal over knots, oils, and waxes. It has low toxicity: in fact dry shellac is used to coat pills and is sprayed on fruit to retard over-ripening.

In use, dry shellac flakes are dissolved in alcohol where they form chemical compounds called esters, which then react with cellulose molecules in the wood to form very strong bonds. The clear solution can be applied by brush, spray, or with a rag. On the down side, a shellac finish has poor resistance to liquid water, heat, and alcohol. Spilled liquor will soften the finish, a wet drink glass will leave a white water ring, and a hot dish will soften the finish. Shellac cures by evaporation of the alcohol and the film can be redissolved by another application of the solvent. For this reason additional coats can be applied directly over a previous coat before the first has fully cured.

Three coats of shellac gave excellent resistance to vapor transmission — 39%. It's superior to waxes, lacquer and oils and on a par with most interior varnishes. Six coats of shellac gave 95% protection.

Varnish

Varnish and wax are the oldest finishes used for protection of furniture. Craftsmen four hundred years ago made a crude varnish by cooking grease, tallow, and alcohol. By 1815 woodworkers could buy varnish ready-made from oil heated with a natural resin such as tree sap or amber. The better varnishes were made from copal — a hard, lustrous resin obtained from various tropical trees. Today varnish is made by reacting man-made resins (alkyds, polyurethanes and phenols) with linseed oil at high temperature where partial polymerization occurs. The mixture is cooled and diluted with mineral spirits (paint thinner, naphtha, turpentine, or alcohol) and sealed into cans. Different resins and oil-to-resin ratios impart different properties to the varnish — UV protection, hard surface, non-yellowing, satin finish, flexibility, clarity, flow, leveling excellence, heat resistance, etc.

Varnish is a surface-coating material that builds up layers on top of the wood instead of penetrating deeply, and it is highly regarded for its durability and ease of application. Most varnishes use slow-evaporating solvents that allow it to be brushed on with more success than faster drying products such as lacquer. In contrast to evaporative finishes like shellac and lacquer, varnish hardens because of a chemical reaction. The resins join together (polymerize) to form a new and hard, plastic-like material bonded with the cellulose molecules in the wood. These strong bonds make the repair of a varnish finish difficult unless all the old coating is removed.

Spar varnish gave 30% protection after 14 days and urethane varnish with oil gave 37%. Three coats of polyurethane varnish (66% protection) was the best varnish finish tested to exclude water vapor.

Water Repellents

Water repellents advertised for protection of wooden decks are effective at repelling liquid water but were of little use in repelling water vapor (11%).

Conclusion

Woodworking finishes such as lacquer, shellac and varnishes show vastly different properties when tested against water vapor. The natural oils are ineffective. The urethane and polyurethane based varnishes are the best of the lot. Shellac is quite effective beating out the waxes, oils, lacquer, water repellents and interior varnishes.

The best protection for furniture or wood that must be subjected

Rule of Thumb

If you want some protection for the wood with the **thinnest possible finish,** use wax.

Three coats of polyurethane varnish provides excellent protection against water and water vapor.

The **best protection** against water vapor is six coats of shellac.

to water and water vapor is polyurethane varnish.

Although a primary objective of finishing treatments is to prevent moisture exchange, no finish is totally effective. Given enough time in a humid atmosphere, moisture will be deposited onto the surface and ultimately absorbed through any finish into wood. Moisture in the wood will also escape to a dry atmosphere. The role of a finish is to retard the rate of exchange enough so as to buffer the temporary extremes of high and low humidity and some finishes are better than others in this respect.

Multiple Coats

In all cases, multiple coats made a tremendous improvement in moisture protection. The US Forest Products Laboratory rated single coats of spar varnish as having only 6% effectiveness after 7 days, but three coats being 53% effective. Other finishes were equally more effective with multiple coats.

Waxes – To protect the legs of outdoor furniture from water wicking, paraffin wax will create a 95% barrier.

Oils – Pure tung oil was only 2% effective after 14 days or about 1/33 as effective as polyurethane varnish. Oils are not a good finish if the purpose is to exclude water vapor. Tung oil is about

twice as effective as linseed oil (three coats each after one day) but even three coats of tung oil are less effective than one coat of shellac.

Lacquer – Lacquer is about two-thirds as effective as spar varnish and three coats of nitrocellulose lacquer was only 19% effective after 14 days of exposure to high humidity (**Figure 54**). It was about one-third as effective as the best finish, the clear polyurethane varnish. Lacquer is not a good choice as a moisture barrier finish.

Shellac - Shellac provides an excellent barrier to water vapor but it is a poor choice for repelling liquid water. For a fine piece of furniture that will be in conditions of extreme humidity changes, three coats gave 39% protection after 14 days (see **Figure 54**). Six coats gave 95% protection after 14 days.

Varnishes – For furniture that must endure extreme humidity changes and the occasional water spill, varnishes are a good choice. Spar varnish (30%), sealing varnish (35%) and urethane resin varnishes (37%) offer good protection. Of the varnishes, polyurethane is the best (66%).

References: Figures 53 and 54 are from **Wood Handbook**, Forest Products Laboratory, USDA Forest Service, Madison, WI. (2002).

CHAPTER 7

Post-and-Rung Joints

Earlier in this book I discussed the problems woodworkers face because of expansion and contraction of wood. As the relative humidity in a room changes so also does the moisture content change in a piece of furniture causing glue lines to fail, joints to open, finishes to crack and wide panels to split. Another chapter showed ways to construct furniture so the inevitable shifting can be controlled. Wood movement, however, doesn't always mean making adjustments to avoid problems — sometimes the swelling and shrinking can be used to advantage, for example in building post-and-rung chairs, making a water-tight cask, constructing a Japanese wooden bath, or assembling redwood hot tubs. In all these cases, the success of the project actually depends on wood movement.

Using Wood Movement to Advantage

At the College of the Redwoods in Ft. Bragg, California a few summers ago, I joined twelve students and together, we spent six days converting newly felled tanoak trees into post-and-rung chairs. We depended upon wood movement to make these chairs — in fact, without the shrinking and expanding of the different parts, the project would have been a lot harder and the chairs not as sturdy.

A post-and-rung chair is one where rungs and spindles fit into legs and posts using mortise- and-tenon joints. European craftsmen have been making this type of chair for hundreds of years

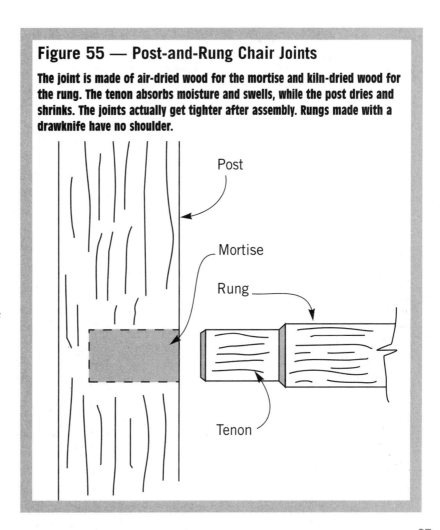

Figure 55 — Post-and-Rung Chair Joints

The joint is made of air-dried wood for the mortise and kiln-dried wood for the rung. The tenon absorbs moisture and swells, while the post dries and shrinks. The joints actually get tighter after assembly. Rungs made with a drawknife have no shoulder.

Post

Mortise

Rung

Tenon

Rule of Thumb

If you want to make the **strongest possible chair**, construct it using split or riven wood from a straight-grained log, so the wood grain runs from end to end in each part.

Rule of Thumb

If you want to figure out the effect of **wood movement on a hole** drilled in green wood, just consider what would have happened to the wood that formerly was in the hole. The hole behaves the same as the wood you excavated to create it.

— the British Windsor chair, Irish hedge chair, Welsh stick chair, and Swedish pinnar chair. In the 1800s English bodgers camped out in forests where they cut and split logs and then used primitive pole lathes to turn posts and rungs. The wood's extreme tendency to shrink and swell proved to be an advantage, because the spindles could be thoroughly seasoned and then tapped into the moist backs and posts. The spindles swelled while the backs and posts shrank, providing extremely tight joints often without the need for adhesives. Many of these rugged and inexpensive chairs are still in use today.

In the United States, the post-and-rung joining technique is the most common method of building wooden chairs — but today the posts and rungs are usually sawed from planks. This results in weak pieces, because the strength of a well-constructed post-and-rung chair depends on the wood grain running from end-to-end through both parts. All of the chair parts are best made from split sections of a straight-grained log, instead of from milled lumber. This splitting process is called riving.

Post-and-Rung Joints

The chair design and the moisture content of the different pieces of wood make tight-fitting joints. The theory is simple:

1. **A chair leg** is air-dried to about 15% moisture content and a mortise (a cavity that the end of the rung fits into) is drilled.

2. **The rungs** are dried to 3% to 5% moisture content and a tenon (a projection on the end of a piece of wood that fits into the mortise) is formed.

3. **Water-based PVA glue** is applied and the slightly oversized, dry tenon is forced into the slightly smaller, wet mortise.

4. **The wet leg** shrinks as it dries, causing the mortise to squeeze the tenon.

5. **The dry tenon** expands as it takes on moisture from the mortise, the glue and the air.

6. **Both pieces** soon attain equilibrium moisture content with the room (about 8%), locking the joint in place. **Figure 55** shows the joint.

Making a Post-and-Rung Chair

Here's the way we made our chairs.

Splitting Logs

We started with logs 6 feet to 8 feet long and 16 inches to 20 inches in diameter — any bigger and we couldn't have wrestled them around. The end of every log showed some radial cracks that crossed the middle, so that's where we started. We drove a

Figure 56 — Splitting the Log

Drive wedges into the natural splits in the log for the first division. Keep splitting the pieces in half until you have eight manageable bolts.

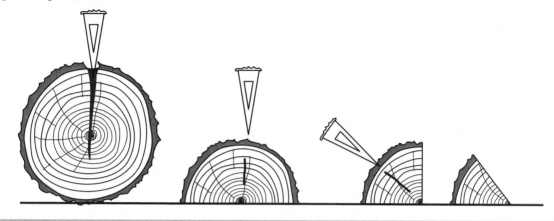

metal wedge into an end-crack and as the fissure opened, we pounded more metal and wooden wedges along the length until the log split apart. We laid the two halves face down and split them in half in much the same way as before. Most of the splits we made were divisions into approximate halves. We continued to spit the pieces until we had eight bolts from the log. See **Figure 56**.

Cutting to Length

The actual lengths we needed for the chair were: back legs 33 inches, front legs 18½ inches and rungs 13½ inches and 16½ inches. We cut some of the bolts into four foot lengths for the back legs and into two foot lengths for the front legs and spindles — all approximate lengths.

Riving

Rived parts are superior to similar parts made by sawing because the split pieces follow the natural grain of the wood, whereas sawing often severs the fibers at an angle. Rived parts are stronger and bend easier. Using a froe or a hatchet, we trimmed off and discarded the hard pith, the bark and the sapwood. Then we started cutting out the billets for the chair parts (**Figure 57**).

We made approximate 2 inch squares for the legs (1½ inches final) and 1 inch squares for the rungs (⅝ inch final).

The order of riving was:

1. **Split the bolts** in half.

2. **Remove** and discard the pith.

Rule of Thumb

For a really **tight post-and-rung joint** in a chair frame, make the posts out of air-dried wood around 15% moisture content, but dry the rungs as much as you can. After you assemble the joint, the post will continue to dry and shrink, while the rung takes on moisture and swells, locking the two parts together.

Figure 57 — Splitting Billets from Bolts

Split off and discard the pith, sapwood and bark. Use a froe to split the bolt and to rive out billets of a useful size.

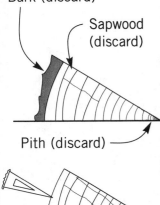

Bark (discard)

Sapwood (discard)

Pith (discard)

Rule of Thumb

So how dry should the rungs be? Around 5% moisture content. How can you tell? When rungs are dry enough to use, they will ping when tapped against a wooden work bench. Wet rungs give a thunk sound.

3. Remove and discard the bark and sapwood.

4. Use the froe to split out the billets of about the right size for the chair parts.

Green wood – A freshly cut tree may have 200% water content, where the bound water and the free water weigh twice as much as the wood. This wood is unsuitable for chair joinery. Like most water-saturated materials, green wood shrinks as it dries so joints made from wet wood will fall apart as soon as the wood dries. Chair assembly is done after the wood has been dried to the appropriate moisture content for the various parts.

That said, green wood of about 30% moisture content is a joy to work, it can be shaved and fashioned with great ease.

Shaping the Pieces

There were shaving horses for all of us and we fashioned all the parts to oversize squares with a drawknife. We shaved off the corners of the square billets to give an octagon shape near final dimension, ready for drying. This was very enjoyable and the resulting rough-hewn appearance of the handwork was satisfying.

Drying the Pieces

The posts and spindle blanks were made to near-finish dimensions while the wood was green then dried to about 15% moisture content and set aside.

The rungs were further dried in a home-made kiln made from 2-inch solid insulation. Ours was about 36-inches long x 24 wide and 24 high — enough space for all of our chair rungs. There were metal racks inside to lay the spindles on and a 60-watt light bulb for heat. Experience had shown that the 15% moisture content could be brought down to 5% by keeping the small diameter, octagonal rungs in the box for 24 hours. We never tested them for moisture and didn't know the actual MC. We used the sound method — wet rungs gave a thunk when struck against the wooden work bench; a rung pinged when it was dry enough to use. This sound method only worked when we dried our own wood.

Story Pole

Make a story pole to record all the dimensions for your chair — it's a lot faster and actually more accurate than using a tape measure. Use a smooth lath about ¼ inch thick x 1½ inch wide and the same length as the back leg. On the front of the pole record information for the front and rear legs — where the holes are drilled, the mortises cut and the tapers begin. On the other side of the pole record the lengths of the rungs. See **Figure 58**.

Moisture Content

All parts of the chair were shaped to approximate size at green-wood moisture content of 25% to 30% then air-dried to about 15% moisture content. At this point the posts were cut to exact length, smoothed and shaped with a spokeshave then the mortises were drilled. These pieces were stored in plastic bags until we were ready to use them to maintain their moisture content.

The octagonal rungs, also at 15% moisture content, were cut to length and placed in a home-made kiln to dry further.

Preparing the Rungs

The octagon rungs were taken out of the kiln for final shaping. We had put nearly-round pieces into the kiln; they came out elliptical. The dimension in the ray plane was greater than the dimension parallel to the growth rings. Some rungs also were curved — these were discarded. The rungs were rounded with a spoke shave, ready for use. **Figure 59** shows how the rungs looked.

The steps to shape the rungs:

1. **Cut the rungs** to exact length.

2. **Use a draw-knife** to round the elliptical-shaped piece to approximate diameter.

3. **Use a spoke shave** to do the final dimensioning and to

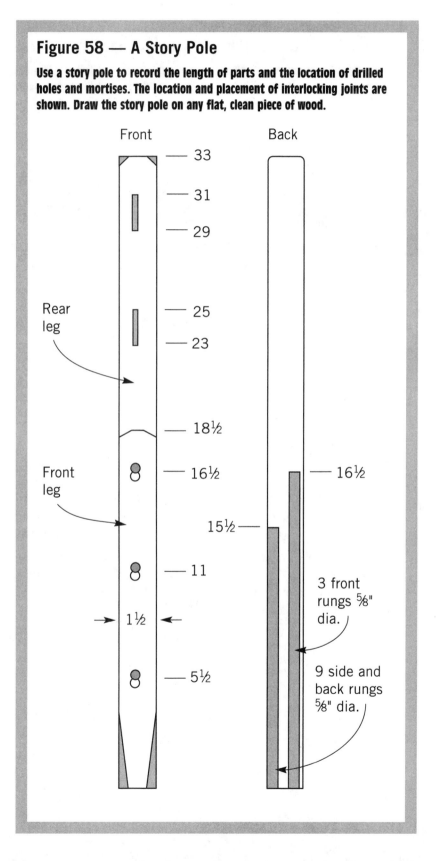

Figure 58 — A Story Pole

Use a story pole to record the length of parts and the location of drilled holes and mortises. The location and placement of interlocking joints are shown. Draw the story pole on any flat, clean piece of wood.

Figure 59 — How the Rungs Change Shape

The octagonal but nearly round spindles at 15% MC (a) were put into the kiln to dry. The dried rung (5% MC) was elliptical, having less shrinkage in the ray plane (b). The rungs were again rounded (c) and used in the chair where they absorbed moisture and swelled along the ray plane to form a tight joint (d).

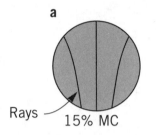  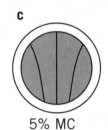 

a — 15% MC
b — 5% MC
c — 5% MC
d — 8% MC

Rays

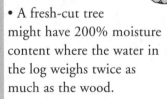

Rule of Thumb

• A fresh-cut tree might have 200% moisture content where the water in the log weighs twice as much as the wood.

• When all the free water is gone, the green wood is at 30% MC.

• Air dried wood is 15-20% MC.

• Kiln-dried wood is about 3% to 5% MC.

• Wood for furniture should be 6-8% MC.

smooth the rungs.

4. Form the tenons. If you use a spoke shave there will be no shoulders.

5. Put the final spindles back in the kiln until you are ready to use them in the chair.

Boring the Mortises

Our chairs needed twenty-four holes drilled for twelve spindles. This procedure was complicated because the front legs are further apart than the rear legs, see the two references at the end of this chapter for details.

Joinery Orientation

Tangential wood movement (movement tangent to the growth rings) is twice that of radial movement (movement parallel to the growth rings). In a post-and-rung chair the rungs should be oriented with the rays in line with the length of the posts. This way the biggest movement of the rung is parallel

to the post length. In tanoak the rays are more pronounced than the growth rings so it was easy to confuse the two and pop the spindles into the mortises the wrong way. I saw quite a few posts with splits due to the wrong orientation but I never saw a post split when the rungs were orientated with the rays in line with the length of the post. See **Figure 60**.

Interlocking Joints

After the two side panels of the chair were constructed, we drilled the mortises for the joining rungs. These were drilled so about 1/16 inch to 1/8 inch of the second tenon locked into the first tenon. See **Figure 61**.

Banging the Chair Together

First we made the two side panels and then we drilled mortises in them. The interior of the mortises were daubed with water-based glue (carpenter's white or yellow polyvinyl acetate) and the bone-dry rungs were inserted — usually with a wooden maul.

Casks and Wooden Tubs

White oak, redwood and cedar are used to make casks and wooden tubs because they are decay resistant and swell when the moisture content increases. In the construction, the staves are mitered so that the joints are mated. A metal band is then used to pull the staves together and to hold them tight. These wood slat containers always leak when they are first filled with a liquid — usually water. They then tighten up as the wet wood swells and they will stay water-tight as long as the water level is maintained. In this application, again wood movement is used to advantage.

References:

Make a Chair from a Tree by John Alexander, Astragal Press, 1994.

The Chairmaker's Workshop by Drew Langsner, Lark Books, 1997.

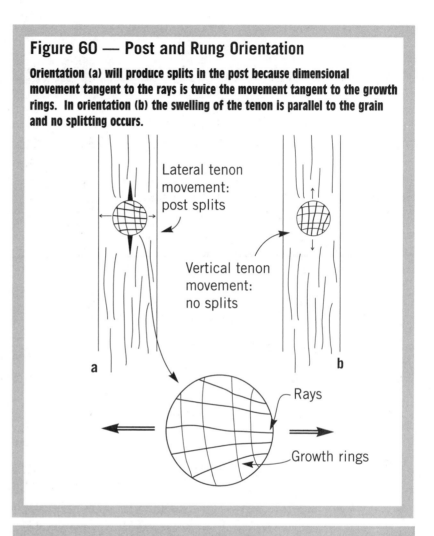

Figure 60 — Post and Rung Orientation

Orientation (a) will produce splits in the post because dimensional movement tangent to the rays is twice the movement tangent to the growth rings. In orientation (b) the swelling of the tenon is parallel to the grain and no splitting occurs.

Lateral tenon movement: post splits

Vertical tenon movement: no splits

a

b

Rays

Growth rings

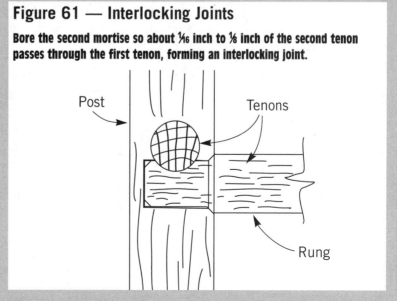

Figure 61 — Interlocking Joints

Bore the second mortise so about ¹⁄₁₆ inch to ⅛ inch of the second tenon passes through the first tenon, forming an interlocking joint.

Post

Tenons

Rung

CHAPTER 8

Column Strength and Entasis

A column is a rigid, relatively slender upright made in exacting proportions with minute detailing. It has both structural integrity and architectural beauty with a cylindrical shaft sitting on a base and topped with a capital. While a post or a pole is usually smooth with the same diameter from top to bottom, a column is tapered, with beautiful, intricate accompaniments top and bottom. It was early discovered that a column appeared more graceful if it diminished in diameter from base to capital. However, a row of tapered shafts with straight sides gives the disturbing optical illusion of curving inwards, therefore the woodworker must give the shafts a slight outward swelling, called entasis, to counteract this illusion and to enhance the impression of secure weight-bearing. This slight curvature must be done correctly without being exaggerated, or the column will appear to bulge unnaturally in the middle. Entasis does not apply at furniture scale, such as a chest with columns or a mantel. The optical illusion only occurs when tall columns are viewed from a distance.

Woodworkers should know how to design and build an architecturally refined column that is strong, attractive, and with proportions that are in comfortable relation to its surroundings. To do this he must understand the complex relationships between height, taper, diameter, and the swelling in the middle (entasis).

The Classical Columns

The first temples were rude wooden shelters in the forest where the columns were tree trunks supporting a thatch-type roof. As the temples grew larger and were made of mud bricks, three or more tree

Figure 62 — Two Classical Columns

The Doric and Ionic columns are the oldest of the five classical types. The Doric (a) is characterized by a capital (the top or crown) made of a circle topped by a square. The shaft is plain or has 20 facets. There is no base in the Doric order. In the Ionic (b) order the capital consists of a scroll above the shaft. The shaft is fluted and the base resembles a set of stacked rings. The Ionic column has a ratio of base diameter to shaft length of 7:1 that makes it look slender. The Doric shaft is set at a ratio of 6:1 and appears more substantial.

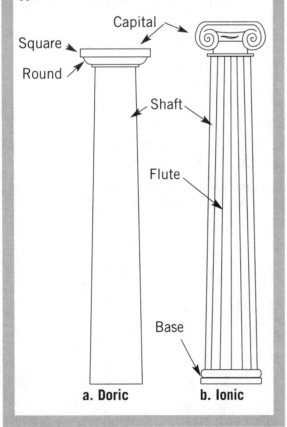

a. Doric   b. Ionic

trunks were lashed together for a stronger support. Later, when the temples were made of stone, so also were the columns made of stone — now fashioned in imitation of a tree trunk. The original meaning of the word 'column' is something that is high or rises in height. The Greeks considered the column an essential part of the architecture of their temples — in fact primitive Greek temples were little else than roofed columns.

A column is tapered from bottom to top and can be smooth, multifaceted, or fluted. The flutes can come to sharp points or to flats. To give the column an elegant appearance, the height must be made at a certain ratio to the bottom diameter, and this ratio varies according to the architectural style of column. The taper from bottom to top is mathematically set so the shaft seems to soar into the air.

The Doric order of architecture (c. 600 B.C.) had columns shaped like a tree with the ratio of 6:1; that is, a height six times the width at the base. The Doric column had a plain, cylindrical shaft and a head, called a capital, but no base — the shaft sat directly on the floor.

The Ionic order (c. 500 B.C.) had a column much like the

Doric, but with a base. The Ionic shaft had a 7:1 ratio and was more ornate — either circular or polygonal in cross-section, with flutes running vertically from bottom to top (**Figure 62**).

The other classical orders are the **Corinthian** (c. 200 B.C.), **Tuscan** (c. 1500 A.D.), and **Composite** (c. 1600 A.D.), the last a combination of the Corinthian and Tuscan orders. These columns have a height-to-base ratio of 8, 9, and 10 respectively. All columns have a top-to-bottom diameter ratio of 0.85. This means a column with bottom diameter of 12 inches will have a top diameter of 12 times 0.85 or 10¼ inches.

While the ratio of height to base initially was based on the dimension of a man, the columns actually symbolize the female figure — the grooves in the shaft represent the pleats of her skirt, the capital the woman's head and the entasis, the swelling that all columns have, symbolizes the woman's hips or her pregnancy. This swelling gives an effect of lightness to a structure and corrects the illusion of concavity that would be created by a straight taper from bottom to top. In the Doric style, there is no base because the women in the Dorian society wore long skirts and the shoes could not be seen.

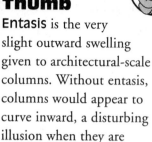

Rule of Thumb
Entasis is the very slight outward swelling given to architectural-scale columns. Without entasis, columns would appear to curve inward, a disturbing illusion when they are supporting a massive overhead portico.

Rule of Thumb
Classical columns originally **symbolized the female figure**: the grooves in the shaft represented the pleats of her skirt, the capital represented her head, and the swelling of the entasis represented her hips.

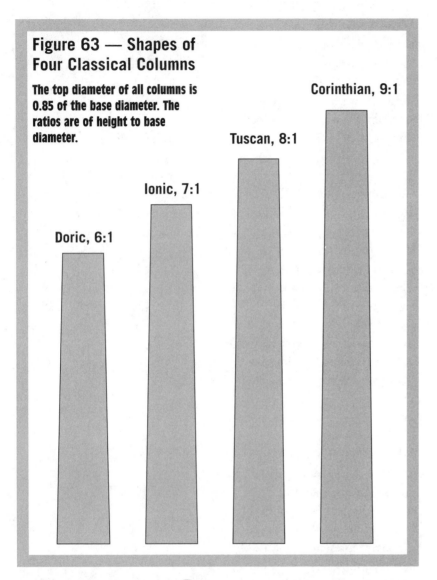

Figure 63 — Shapes of Four Classical Columns

The top diameter of all columns is 0.85 of the base diameter. The ratios are of height to base diameter.

Corinthian, 9:1

Tuscan, 8:1

Ionic, 7:1

Doric, 6:1

Rule of Thumb

In the **five classical orders** of architecture, columns have height-to-base diameter ratios ranging from 6-to-1 to 10-to-1. All columns have a smaller top diameter than their base diameter, by about 1 part in 6.

At the Erechtheon in Athens, the columns are not symbolic, they actually have the shape and features (legs, arms, and head) of women. The Parthenon nearby is known as the maidens' apartment and the Greek word parthenos means a young woman who is of marriageable age but unmarried.

Column Design

The manner of constructing the columns of all the orders rests on similar principles. Columns are divided into three primary parts or divisions — the base, the shaft, and the capital (see **Figure 62**) — except the Doric which has no base. The base diameter is the universal standard from which all measurements are taken. The shafts of the classical orders differ in height as do their capitals. Columns are either plain or fluted, and the flutes are different in the Ionic and Corinthian orders. Columns of all the orders taper gradually toward the top at a 0.85 ratio (**Figure 63**).

Mathematics

Mathematics and proportion determine size and shape of the columns. According to Vitruvius (Vitruvius, *Books on Architecture*, c.100 B.C., translated 1914 Harvard Univ., Dover Publ. 1960), a Roman engineer for both Julius and Augustus Caesar, "The masculine type Doric columns diameter-to-height ratio is based on the relationship between foot length and height in a man; whereas the slenderer Ionic column length-to-height ratio in a woman. As they wished to erect a temple with columns and had not a knowledge of the proper proportions of them, nor knew the way in which they ought to be constructed, so as at the same time to be both fit to carry the superincumbent weight, and to produce a beautiful effect, they measured a man's foot and finding its length the sixth part of his height, they gave the column a similar proportion, that is, they made its height six times the thickness of the shaft, measured at the base." Thus the Doric order draws its proportion, its strength, and its beauty, from the human figure.

Entasis

The Greeks developed the augmentation technique known as entasis (en'-Tay-sis) to avoid an optical illusion caused by the shafts and especially by the fluting (parallel vertical lines). In a tall structure like the Parthenon, such lines in a column would appear concave. To compensate, the Greek architects made the columns slightly convex. The swelling has little physical function — it makes the column only slightly stronger, but it does make it look more substantial, as though the stone is swelling like a muscle under its load.

The Greeks applied this curved profile to the whole length of the column, from the base to the capital. With the early Romans it became customary for the bottom third of the column to remain undiminished, in other words a cylindrical section, and for the upper two thirds to diminish in diameter and to be convex in profile. Later in this

chapter there are three methods for laying out a column. Method 1 follows the Roman design and Methods 2 and 3 follow the Greek design. Most columns commercially available today follow the Greek design and curve their whole length.

Shaft Design

The shaft of a column is laid out as follows:

1. Determine the length
(height) of the shaft needed.

2. Use drafting paper and
determine the taper that looks best. See **Figure 63** for height to diameter ratios of 6:1, 7:1, 8:1, or 9:1.

3. Use the tables in **Figures 67-70** to find the diameters for the base and top.

Problem 1: We want a 12-foot column and have decided a 9:1 ratio will look best. What are the top and bottom diameters?

Solution 1: Figure 70 shows data for a 9:1 ratio. Find 12 feet in the first column and read across to find a base diameter of 16 inches and a top diameter of 13⅝ inches. The rest of the data in **Figure 70** relates to entasis.

Entasis Calculation

The shaft of a column is tapered, but the line is not straight from

> ## Rule of Thumb
> Once you understand entasis, you can amaze your friends and perhaps win big on Jeopardy by eyeballing the difference between a classical Greek column and a Roman one. The Greeks applied the curve of entasis to the whole column, while the Romans left the bottom third of the shaft straight, applying entasis only to the top two-thirds.

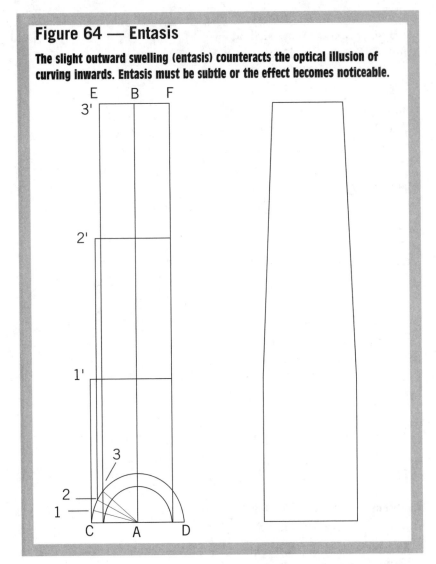

Figure 64 — Entasis

The slight outward swelling (entasis) counteracts the optical illusion of curving inwards. Entasis must be subtle or the effect becomes noticeable.

size pattern for the final column. It is the most rudimentary of the methods, yielding only two points between the top and bottom, but it does give satisfactory results. This method produces a pattern where the entasis begins at a point one-third of the way up the column according to the Roman design.

1. Draw the height of the column AB.

2. Draw the bottom diameter CD and the top diameter EF from **Figures 67-70**.

3. Draw a semicircle with center A and radius AC at the bottom of the column.

4. Also draw a semicircle with center A and radius BE at the bottom of the column.

5. Divide the column length into three equal parts 1', 2' and 3'.

6. Erect a perpendicular from the smaller semicircle to point 3' at the top of the column. Label the point where the large arc is cut as 3.

7. Divide arc C3 into thirds and label these points 1 and 2

8. Erect a perpendicular from point C on the larger semicircle to point 1' on the column.

9. Erect a perpendicular from point 2 to 2'.

10. Connect points C, 1', 2' and E for a half pattern.

bottom to top. The taper follows a convex curve to overcome the perception of concavity. Various methods have been used to find the curve. In using any of these methods, remember the curve must be subtle or the effect will be noticeable.

Method 1: Figure 64 shows one of the simplest ways to find the curve. It does not yield measurements but gives a full-

Method 2: This method (see **Figure 65**) is faster than Method

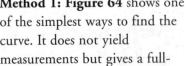

Rule of Thumb

Make entasis **subtle** or it will be noticeable.

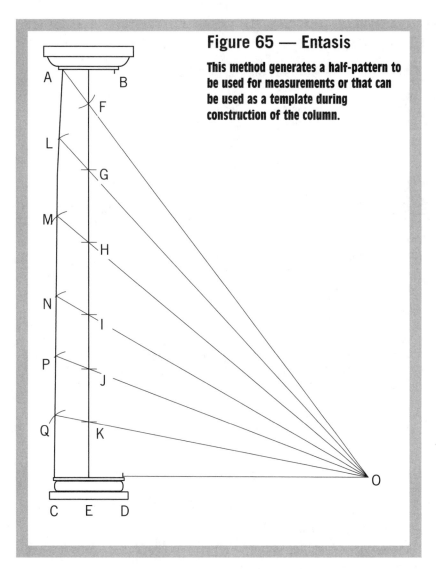

Figure 65 — Entasis

This method generates a half-pattern to be used for measurements or that can be used as a template during construction of the column.

Figure 66 — Divide the Shaft into Six Sections

Divide the column into six equal parts and use Method 3 (Figures 67-70) for the entasis calculations.

1 and gives multiple points along the shaft starting at a point one-sixth of the way up the column. Like Method 1, it also gives a full-size pattern and, thus, requires a large work area. Instead of giving only two points between top and bottom (as in Method 1) this method gives six points between the base and the capital according to the Greek design.

1. Draw the center line of the column.

2. Draw AB and CD which define the top and bottom diameters.

3. Set E as the midpoint of CD.

4. From A, with a radius equal to CE, draw an arc cutting the center line at F.

5. Project AF until it meets CD projected at O.

6. Divide the center line into as many parts as required e.g. F, G,

Figure 67 — Entasis Calculations (Ratio 6:1)

Use the figures in this table to find the diameters of the base, the top, and the five inner sections.

Column Height (Feet)	Column Height (Inches)	Base Diameter (Inches) (1)	Inches Section One (2)	Section Two (3)	Section Three (4)	Section Four (5)	Section Five (6)	Section Top (7)
6	72	12	12	11 6/8	11 4/8	11 1/8	10 6/8	10 2/8
7	84	14	14	13 6/8	13 4/8	13	12 4/8	11 7/8
8	96	16	15 7/8	15 6/8	15 3/8	14 7/8	14 3/8	13 5/8
9	108	18	17 7/8	17 6/8	17 3/8	16 6/8	16 1/8	15 2/8
10	120	20	19 7/8	19 5/8	19 2/8	18 5/8	17 7/8	17
11	132	22	21 7/8	21 5/8	21 1/8	20 4/8	19 6/8	18 6/8
12	144	24	23 7/8	23 5/8	23 1/8	22 3/8	21 4/8	20 3/8
13	156	26	25 7/8	25 4/8	25	24 2/8	23 2/8	22 1/8
14	168	28	27 7/8	27 4/8	26 7/8	26 1/8	25	23 6/8
15	180	30	29 7/8	29 4/8	28 7/8	28	26 7/8	25 4/8
16	192	32	31 7/8	31 4/8	30 6/8	29 7/8	28 5/8	27 2/8
17	204	34	33 7/8	33 3/8	32 6/8	31 6/8	30 3/8	28 7/8
18	216	36	35 7/8	35 3/8	34 5/8	33 4/8	32 2/8	30 5/8
19	228	38	37 7/8	37 3/8	36 4/8	35 3/8	34	32 2/8
20	240	40	39 7/8	39 3/8	38 4/8	37 2/8	35 6/8	34
21	252	42	41 7/8	41 2/8	40 3/8	39 1/8	37 5/8	35 6/8
22	264	44	43 7/8	43 2/8	42 3/8	41	39 3/8	37 3/8

(1) Base Diameter = Column Height / 6
(3) Section 2 = Base x 0.983
(5) Section 4 = Base x 0.932
(7) Top Section = Base x 0.85

(2) Section 1 = Base X 0.996
(4) Section 3 = Base x 0.962
(6) Section 5 = Base x 0.895

H, I, J, and K.

7. Through the points G, H, I, J, and K, project lines from O.

8. Draw arcs of radius CE from points G, H, I, J, and K which intersect the respective projection line at L, M, N, P, and Q.

9. The entasis is drawn through points C, Q, P, N, M, L, and A.

10. From this half-pattern, you can measure the six diameters.

11. Construct a full-size plywood model or take full-size measurements for use during construction of the column.

Rule of Thumb

A column will seldom **fail due to stress**. A 6 x 6 square, poplar column can withstand 134,000 pounds or 67 tons of weight before it is in danger of failing due to stress, that is fiber compression failure.

Method 3: This is the easiest way to find the correct measurements for a tapered column. Once you've determined the height of the column and the height-to-base ratio, you just divide the shaft into six equal sections (**Figure 66**) and read the dimensions from one of the charts (**Figures 67, 68, 69 or 70**). The charts are based on a mathematical method of finding the diameters of a column, including entasis. The steps are as follows:

1. Determine the height of the shaft — for example 12 feet.

Figure 68 — Entasis Calculations (Ratio 7:1)

Use the figures in this table to find the diameters of the base, the top, and the five inner sections.

Column Height (Feet)	Column Height (Inches)	Base Diameter (Inches) (1)	Inches Section One (2)	Section Two (3)	Section Three (4)	Section Four (5)	Section Five (6)	Section Top (7)
6	72	10 2/8	10 2/8	10 1/8	9 7/8	9 5/8	9 2/8	8 6/8
7	84	12	12	11 6/8	11 4/8	11 1/8	10 6/8	10 2/8
8	96	13 6/8	13 5/8	13 4/8	13 2/8	12 6/8	12 2/8	11 5/8
9	108	15 3/8	15 3/8	15 1/8	14 7/8	14 3/8	13 6/8	13 1/8
10	120	17 1/8	17 1/8	16 7/8	16 4/8	16	15 3/8	14 5/8
11	132	18 7/8	18 6/8	18 4/8	18 1/8	17 5/8	16 7/8	16
12	144	20 5/8	20 4/8	20 2/8	19 6/8	19 1/8	18 3/8	17 4/8
13	156	22 2/8	22 2/8	21 7/8	21 4/8	20 6/8	20	19
14	168	24	23 7/8	23 5/8	23 1/8	22 3/8	21 4/8	20 3/8
15	180	25 6/8	25 5/8	25 2/8	24 6/8	24	23	21 7/8
16	192	27 3/8	27 3/8	27	26 3/8	25 5/8	24 4/8	23 3/8
17	204	29 1/8	29	28 5/8	28	27 1/8	26 1/8	24 6/8
18	216	30 7/8	30 6/8	30 3/8	29 5/8	28 6/8	27 5/8	26 2/8
19	228	32 5/8	32 4/8	32	31 3/8	30 3/8	29 1/8	27 5/8
20	240	34 2/8	34 1/8	33 6/8	33	32	30 5/8	29 1/8
21	252	36	35 7/8	35 3/8	34 5/8	33 4/8	32 2/8	30 5/8
22	264	37 6/8	37 5/8	37 1/8	36 2/8	35 1/8	33 6/8	32

(1) Base Diameter = Column Height / 7
(2) Section 1 = Base X 0.996
(3) Section 2 = Base x 0.983
(4) Section 3 = Base x 0.962
(5) Section 4 = Base x 0.932
(6) Section 5 = Base x 0.895
(7) Top Section = Base x 0.85

2. Decide on the ratio of height to bottom shaft diameter — for example 6:1. Therefore the bottom diameter for a 12-foot shaft (144 inches) will be:

12' ÷ 6 = 2' or

144" ÷ 6 = 24"

3. Find the diameter of the top of the shaft. The ratio of top diameter to bottom diameter is 0.85 to one. Therefore the top diameter will be:

Top Diameter = Bottom Diameter x 0.85

24 x 0.85 = 20.4 ≈ 20⅜"

The 12-foot high shaft should have a 24 inch diameter at the bottom and a 20⅜ inch diameter at the top. These dimensions are independent of the base, the capital, and any mouldings.

4. To figure entasis, divide the length into six equal parts and use the charts (**Figures 67, 68, 69 or 70**) depending on whether the ratio is 6:1, 7:1, 8:1, or 9:1 to find the size at each section.

Problem 2: What will be the dimensions for a 12-foot column if we want the height-to-diameter ratio to be 6:1 (Doric)?

Figure 69 — Entasis Calculations (Ratio 8:1)

Use the figures in this table to find the diameters of the base, the top, and the five inner sections.

Column Height (Feet)	Column Height (Inches)	Base Diameter (Inches) (1)	Inches Section One (2)	Section Two (3)	Section Three (4)	Section Four (5)	Section Five (6)	Section Top (7)
6	72	9	9	8 7/8	8 5/8	8 3/8	8	7 5/8
7	84	10.5	10 4/8	10 3/8	10 1/8	9 6/8	9 3/8	8 7/8
8	96	12	12	11 6/8	11 4/8	11 1/8	10 6/8	10 2/8
9	108	13.5	13 4/8	13 2/8	13	12 5/8	12 1/8	11 4/8
10	120	15	15	14 6/8	14 3/8	14	13 3/8	12 6/8
11	132	16.5	16 3/8	16 2/8	15 7/8	15 3/8	14 6/8	14
12	144	18	17 7/8	17 6/8	17 3/8	16 6/8	16 1/8	15 2/8
13	156	19.5	19 3/8	19 1/8	18 6/8	18 1/8	17 4/8	16 5/8
14	168	21	20 7/8	20 5/8	20 2/8	19 5/8	18 6/8	17 7/8
15	180	22.5	22 3/8	22 1/8	21 5/8	21	20 1/8	19 1/8
16	192	24	23 7/8	23 5/8	23 1/8	22 3/8	21 4/8	20 3/8
17	204	25.5	25 3/8	25 1/8	24 4/8	23 6/8	22 7/8	21 5/8
18	216	27	26 7/8	26 4/8	26	25 1/8	24 1/8	23
19	228	28.5	28 3/8	28	27 3/8	26 4/8	25 4/8	24 2/8
20	240	30	29 7/8	29 4/8	28 7/8	28	26 7/8	25 4/8
21	252	31.5	31 3/8	31	30 2/8	29 3/8	28 2/8	26 6/8
22	264	33	32 7/8	32 4/8	31 6/8	30 6/8	29 4/8	28

(1) Base Diameter = Column Height / 8
(2) Section 1 = Base X 0.996
(3) Section 2 = Base x 0.983
(4) Section 3 = Base x 0.962
(5) Section 4 = Base x 0.932
(6) Section 5 = Base x 0.895
(7) Top Section = Base x 0.85

Solution 2: In **Figure 67** we see the dimensions will be:

Bottom: 24 inches

Section 1: 23⅞ inches

Section 2: 23⅝ inches

Section 3: 23⅛ inches

Section 4: 22⅜ inches

Section 5: 21½ inches

Top: 20⅜ inches

How Columns Fail

A wooden column can fail in one of two ways. First, it will fail if the compressive strength of the wood is exceeded, and second, it can fail by buckling.

Compression

A compression failure occurs when the wood in the column is simply crushed by the applied load. For compressive stress limits of various woods, see Chapter 5, **Wood Strength**. In general, the compressive limits range from red oak (2910 psi) to yellow birch (6130 psi). Compression, which engineers call stress, is measured by dividing the applied load (P) by the cross-sectional area (A) of the column. If this value exceeds the allowable, then failure occurs. In equation form this is:

Figure 70 — Entasis Calculations (Ratio 9:1)

Use the figures in this table to find the diameters of the base, the top, and the five inner sections.

Column Height (Feet)	Column Height (Inches)	Base Diameter (Inches) (1)	Inches Section One (2)	Section Two (3)	Section Three (4)	Section Four (5)	Section Five (6)	Section Top (7)
6	72	8	8	7 7/8	7 6/8	7 4/8	7 1/8	6 6/8
7	84	9 3/8	9 2/8	9 1/8	9	8 6/8	8 3/8	7 7/8
8	96	10 5/8	10 5/8	10 4/8	10 2/8	10	9 4/8	9 1/8
9	108	12	12	11 6/8	11 4/8	11 1/8	10 6/8	10 2/8
10	120	13 3/8	13 2/8	13 1/8	12 7/8	12 3/8	11 7/8	11 3/8
11	132	14 5/8	14 5/8	14 3/8	14 1/8	13 5/8	13 1/8	12 4/8
12	144	16	15 7/8	15 6/8	15 3/8	14 7/8	14 3/8	13 5/8
13	156	17 3/8	17 2/8	17	16 5/8	16 1/8	15 4/8	14 6/8
14	168	18 5/8	18 5/8	18 3/8	18	17 3/8	16 6/8	15 7/8
15	180	20	19 7/8	19 5/8	19 2/8	18 5/8	17 7/8	17
16	192	21 3/8	21 2/8	21	20 4/8	19 7/8	19 1/8	18 1/8
17	204	22 5/8	22 5/8	22 2/8	21 6/8	21 1/8	20 2/8	19 2/8
18	216	24	23 7/8	23 5/8	23 1/8	22 3/8	21 4/8	20 3/8
19	228	25 3/8	25 2/8	24 7/8	24 3/8	23 5/8	22 5/8	21 4/8
20	240	26 5/8	26 4/8	26 2/8	25 5/8	24 7/8	23 7/8	22 5/8
21	252	28	27 7/8	27 4/8	26 7/8	26 1/8	25	23 6/8
22	264	29 3/8	29 2/8	28 7/8	28 2/8	27 3/8	26 2/8	24 7/8

(1) Base Diameter = Column Height / 9
(2) Section 1 = Base X 0.996
(3) Section 2 = Base x 0.983
(4) Section 3 = Base x 0.962
(5) Section 4 = Base x 0.932
(6) Section 5 = Base x 0.895
(7) Top Section = Base x 0.85

Stress = Load (pounds) ÷ Cross-sectional Area (inches^2)

$$S = L \div A$$

Problem 3: We want to use a 6 inch x 6 inch poplar beam to hold up a 2,000 pound weight. Is this column in any danger of failure due to fiber crushing?

Solution 3: A total force of 2,000 pounds acts on 36 square inches, and develops a stress of:

$$S = L \div A$$

$$S = 2,000 \div 36 = 55 \text{ lb/in}^2$$

Poplar can withstand a compressive stress (load) of 3730 psi and still spring back.

Therefore the 55 psi in our problem is less than 2% of the fiber stress limit. Note that the height (or length) of the column was not a factor in the calculation. The height is relevant only when examining stiffness and the risk of buckling.

A column can be solid or hollow and still have enormous compressive strength. **Figure 72** shows solid square, solid round, hollow square, and hollow round columns, and the weakest can withstand 184 tons of weight.

Figure 71 — Compressive Strength of Wood

The Fiber Stress at Proportional Limit is the amount of load (weight) the material can withstand per square inch and still spring back.

Wood Type	FSPL(1)
Alder	4530
Ash	5790
Beech	4880
Birch, Paper	3610
Birch, Yellow	6130
Cherry	5960
Douglas Fir	5850
Elm	4030
Hickory	5900
Maple	5025
Oak, Red	2910
Oak, White	4760
Pine, Eastern White	3670
Pine, Western White	4480
Poplar	3730
Walnut	5780
Average	**4815**

(1) Fiber Stress at Proportional Limit (parallel to the grain)

Figure 72 — Comparing Compressive Strengths of Solid and Hollow Columns

Whether a wood column is solid or hollow, it seldom fails from compressive stress. The weakest column in the table will hold 184 tons without failure.

Column Type	Size	Cross Sectional Area (Sq In)	Doug Fir Strength (psi)	Column Strength (pounds)	Column Strength (tons)
Solid Square Column	12" x 12"	144	5850	842,400	421
Solid Round Column	12" Diam.	113	5850	661,050	331
Hollow Square 2" Walls	12" x 12"	80	5850	468,000	234
Hollow Round 2" Walls	12" Diam.	63	5850	368,550	184

Rule of Thumb

Of the common hardwoods, **yellow birch is the strongest** in compression parallel to the grain. Red oak us the weakest but can still withstand 2900 psi.

Column Load-Bearing Capacity

It helps to know how to calculate column loads — how much weight a column can carry without collapsing and what role height, load, cross-sectional area, and material stiffness play in column strength. The critical load formulas for columns are remarkable in that they do not include strength properties of the material, yet the formulas determine the carrying capacity of a column. The only material property involved is the E-value which represents stiffness.

Column Stiffness

The load applied to the top of a column is expressed in pounds. As weight is added, the column is susceptible to deflection and finally to buckling. In all discussions and formulas that follow, it is assumed that the load is applied directly upon the top of the column and that the column is straight and free of defects. This is hardly ever the case. To calculate the load that leads to buckling of a column, we need to examine four factors:

1. The property of the wood to resist deformation expressed as the modulus of elasticity (MOE). The E-value depends on the species of wood used.

2. The size of the ends of the column expressed as the moment of inertia (I). The I-value depends on the cross-sectional area.

3. The height of the column.

4. The end conditions of the column: whether the ends are fixed or free to rotate.

1. The property of wood to resist deformation is the modulus of elasticity (MOE). The E-value for different woods can be found in *Wood Strength*, Chapter 5 and is recapped in **Figure 71**, and varies from 1.2 to 2 million psi. It usually is abbreviated, for example 1,500,000 psi is written as E1.5. The higher the E-value of the wood, the more resistant it is to deformation. White oak and red oak average about E1.65, while the E-value of pine is 1.40. This means that, in general, oak is 15% stiffer than pine.

1.65 – 1.40 = 0.25 ÷ 1.65
= 0.15

2. The cross section of the column. The moment of inertia (I) of a column depends on the shape and area of the cross section. The dimensions are measured in inches.

For a Rectangle:
$I = (D_L \times D_S^3) / 12$

Where D_L = the large dimension and D_S = the small dimension.

For a square: $I = (D^4) / 12$
For a circle: $I = (\pi \times r^4) / 4$

Where r = radius.

Figure 73 shows the formulas for other geometrical figures.

3. The height or length of the column. As a column increases in height without a corresponding gain in cross-sectional area, it is increasingly subject to failure due to

Figure 73 — Moments of Inertia of Common Geometric Areas

Use these formulas to find the critical moment of inertia (Ic).

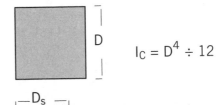

$$I_C = D^4 \div 12$$

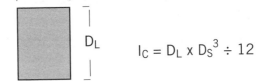

$$I_C = D_L \times D_S^3 \div 12$$

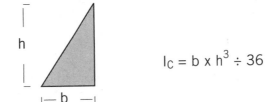

$$I_C = b \times h^3 \div 36$$

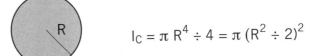

$$I_C = \pi R^4 \div 4 = \pi (R^2 \div 2)^2$$

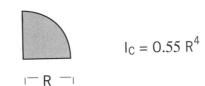

$$I_C = 0.55 R^4$$

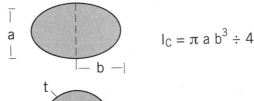

$$I_C = \pi a b^3 \div 4$$

$$I_C = \pi R^3 t$$

Figure 74 — End Conditions of Structural Columns

Columns fixed at both ends (a), fixed at one end (b) and free to rotate at both ends (c). Column (a) can withstand four times more weight before buckling than can column (c).

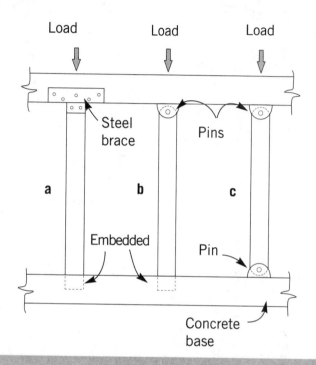

and bottom and are not fixed; the weakest condition. In construction, use square-ended columns and secure both ends — a column with top and bottom securely fixed is four times as stiff as an unfixed column.

Column Instability

To understand how instability occurs, consider a long, perfectly straight column, attached at both ends but not held tightly, as shown in **Figure 75**.

If a small force (P) is applied to the top of this test column, the column will compress fractionally but will remain straight. Then, with this force (P) still acting on the column, if a small lateral force (Q) is applied, then removed, the column will deform (flex) slightly but will return to its initial straight position. The same cycle may be repeated with the force (P) increasing in magnitude until a critical force (P_{CR}) is applied. When the weight reaches critical load, the column remains slightly deformed after the lateral force (Q) is removed. By applying force (Q) now in the opposite direction, the column will return to the straight position but will easily deform in some other direction. We now have a condition called neutral equilibrium — a most dangerous situation where even a small

buckling. Because the cross-sectional area of the column is expressed in inches, so must the height of the column be expressed in inches.

4. The end conditions of the column. There are three different ways to secure the two ends of a column: (1) top and bottom fixed, (2) one end fixed and one end pinned and (3) top and bottom pinned. See **Figure 74.** The pinned ends are able to rotate while the fixed ends are tightly attached. All calculations in this chapter assume the column ends are rounded top

Rule of Thumb

Use the 11-to-1 rule to estimate whether a column under load will **fail first from buckling** or from crushing — a column with length-to-diameter ratio greater than 11 will buckle at less than full compressive load.

additional lateral force or an extremely small increase in weight at the top will destroy the precarious equilibrium — causing instantaneous buckling.

Before the critical force (P_{CR}) point is reached, if the weight (P) on a column is doubled, tripled or quadrupled, there is no visible effect as it continues to stand upright. No gradual bending warns of a dangerous overload until sudden buckling occurs at or near (P_{CR}). For this reason, column failures due to buckling are unexpected, sudden, spectacular and incredibly dangerous.

Calculating the critical force (P_{CR}) is the most important quantity in column analysis, as, practically speaking, it represents the ultimate capacity of an ideal column. In real life, columns are never ideal. They are not perfectly straight, erected exactly vertical or loaded with the weight precisely centered at the top. Therefore, there is always a small amount of deflection (Q) from the start. Even so, finding the critical force (P_{CR}) of a column is the most significant measure of its stiffness. It is the starting point in calculating column strength.

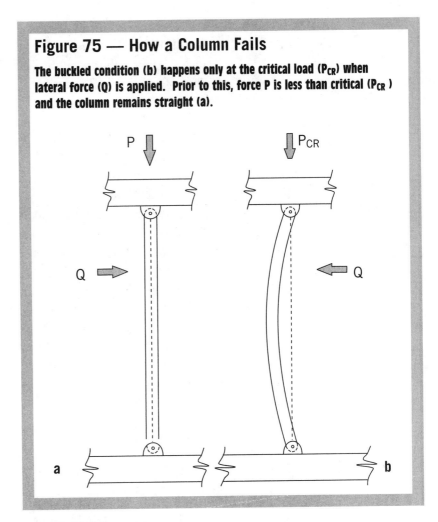

Figure 75 — How a Column Fails

The buckled condition (b) happens only at the critical load (P_{CR}) when lateral force (Q) is applied. Prior to this, force P is less than critical (P_{CR}) and the column remains straight (a).

Direction of Buckling

At the critical load (P_{CR}), an ideal, homogeneous column which is circular or tubular in its cross-sectional area may buckle sidewise in any direction. In the more usual case, a column does not flex equally in all directions. The moment of inertia (I) is a function of the cross-sectional area and the flexibility of the column depends on its minimum dimension. At the critical load a rectangular column buckles to one side or the other, in the direction of the smaller dimension. Thus a 6 inch x 8 inch column will buckle and collapse towards one of the 6 inch sides.

The Euler Formula for Pin-Ended Columns

In 1757 Leonhard Euler established the formula for calculating the force needed to buckle columns of this sort. To understand the basics, consider a column with its ends rounded and free to rotate around frictionless pins (**Figure 75a**). Such columns are called pin-ended columns. If we use this condition in our calculations a small safety factor will be built in because any amount of end-fixing during construction will only stiffen the columns.

The Euler formula states:

$$P_{CR} = (\pi^2 \times E \times I) / L^2$$

Where P_{CR} = critical load in pounds

π = 3.14

E = modulus of elasticity

I = least moment of inertia

L = length (height) in inches

And

$$I = (D_L \times D_S^3) / 12$$

Where D_L = Large Dimension and D_S = Small Dimension

Problem 4: How much weight can a 4 inch x 4 inch wooden column 25 feet long carry before

it is in danger of failure due to buckling? The column in question is not secured at the top or bottom. Assume the E-value of the wood is 1.5×10^6.

Solution 4:

Figure 73 shows the Inertia formula for square columns:

$$I = D^4 / 12$$

$$I = 4^4 / 12 = 256 \div 12 = 21.33 \text{ in.}^4$$

$$P_{CR} = (\pi^2 \times E \times I) / L^2$$

$$P_{CR} = (3.14^2 \times 1.5 \times 10^6 \times 21.33) / (25 \times 12)^2$$

$$P_{CR} = 9.86 \times 1.5 \times 10^6 \times 21.33 / 300^2$$

$$P_{CR} = 315.5 \times 10^6 / 0.09 \times 10^6$$

$$P_{CR} = 315.5 / 0.09 = 3505 \text{ pounds.}$$

This shows that the 25 foot long, 4 x 4 column can carry about 3500 pounds before it is in danger from buckling — however this assumes ideal conditions. Read *Safety Factors* at the end of this chapter for more on this.

Built-Up Columns

A composite area consists of two or more simple areas such as rectangles, squares and circles. Channels and I-beams are common examples. The moment of inertia of a composite area equals the sum of the moments of inertia of its components. if the axes of the composite areas are coincident. When an area such as a hole is removed from a

---

Rule of Thumb

If a post is in danger of buckling, make the post **half as high** and it will carry four times the weight.

larger area, its I-value is subtracted from the moment of inertia of the larger to obtain the net I-value.

Problem 5: What are the moments of inertia of the two built-up columns in **Figure 76**? Both are made of two ¾ inch x 6 inch boards and two ¾ inch x 4 inch boards.

Solution 5:

In this composite area, the moment of inertia of the outer rectangle is first determined, where D_L = the large dimension and D_S = the small dimension. Then the moment of the inner is determined and subtracted from the former.

Outer Rectangle (OR) for column in Figure 76a

$I_{OR} = (D_L \times D_S^3) \div 12$

$I_{OR} = (7.5 \times 4^3) \div 12$
$= 480 \div 12 = 40$ in.^{4}

Inner Rectangle (IR) for column (a)

$I_{IR} = (D_L \times D_S^3) \div 12$

$I_{IR} = (6 \times 2.5^3) \div 12$
$= 93.75 \div 12 = 7.8$ in.^{4}

Net Moment of Inertia for column (a)

I (net) = I (outer rectangle) minus I (inner rectangle)
$40 - 7.8 = 32.2$ in.^{4}

If the 4 boards are arranged as in **Figure 76b**:

Outer Rectangle (OR) for column (b)

$I_{OR} = (D_L \times D_S^3) \div 12$

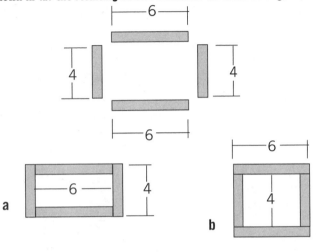

Figure 76 — Built-Up Columns

Columns (a) and (b) are both made from the four boards shown. To find the moment of inertia (I), the central 'hole' is subtracted from the 'whole'. The hollow column (a), 8 feet long, will carry nearly 50 times the weight (buckling strength) the 4 boards will carry. By arranging the boards as shown in (b) the resulting hollow column is 1.6 times stronger than (a).

$I_{OR} = (6 \times 5.5^3) \div 12$
$= 998 \div 12 = 83.2$ in.^{4}

Inner Rectangle (IR) for column (b)

$I_{IR} = (D_L \times D_S^3) \div 12$

$I_{IR} = (4.5 \times 4^3) \div 12$
$= 288 \div 12 = 24$ in.^{4}

Net Moment of Inertia for column (b)

I (net) = I (outer rectangle) minus I (inner rectangle)
$83.2 - 24 = 59.2$ in.^{4}

Problem 6: Which of the built-up columns in **Figure 76** will be stronger (relative to buckling)? Both are 12 feet long and are made of construction-grade pine (E=1.4).

Rule of Thumb

If a post is in danger of buckling, **fix the ends** and it will carry four times the weight.

Solution 6:

Critical Force where I = 32.2 for column (a)

$$P = (\pi^2 \times E \times I) / L^2$$

Where E = 1.40 x 10^6,
L = 12 feet and I = 32.2.

$$P = (3.14^2 \times 1.4 \times 10^6 \times 32.2) / (12 \times 12)^2$$

$$P = (9.86 \times 1.4 \times 10^6 \times 32.2) / 144^2$$

$$P = 444 \times 10^6 / 0.021 \times 10^6$$

$$P = 444 / 0.021$$
$$= 21{,}143 \text{ pounds.}$$

Critical Force where I = 59.2 for column (b)

$$P = \pi^2 \times E \times I / L^2$$

Where E = 1.40 x 10^6,
L = 12 feet and I = 59.2.

$$P = (3.14^2 \times 1.4 \times 10^6 \times 59.2) / (12 \times 12)^2$$

$$P = 9.86 \times 1.4 \times 10^6 \times 59.2 / 144^2$$

$$P = 817 \times 10^6 / 0.021 \times 10^6$$

$$P = 726 / 0.021$$
$$= 38{,}904 \text{ pounds.}$$

Thus the two composite columns 12 feet long constructed as in **Figure 76a** and **Figure 76b** theoretically can carry loads of 21,000 pounds and 39,000 pounds before they are in danger of buckling. Column (b) can carry nearly twice the weight of column (a) because the cross-sectional area is larger. Note that this is under perfect conditions with no safety factor.

Staved Hollow Columns

Most columns built for home construction are staved. Because wall thickness is extremely important in buckling strength, use the tube formula in **Figure 73** to calculate the I-value.

Problem 7: Compare the relative stiffness of two columns. Both are round, 6 inches in diameter and 25 feet long. One is solid wood and the other is made of ¾ inch staves. The E-value of both woods is 1.5 x 10^6. The staves will be glued and splined so they act as one solid ring.

Solution 7: Figure 73 gives the formulas for calculating the moment of inertia for circles and tubes.

$$I_{Circle} = \pi \times R^4 / 4$$

Where R = circle radius

$$I_{Circle} = 3.14 \times 3^4 / 4$$
$$= 3.14 \times 81 / 4 = 63.6 \text{ in.}^4$$

$$I_{Tube} = \pi \times R^3 \times t$$

Where R = inner circle radius and t = wall thickness

Let t = 0.75 and
R = 2.25 + ½t (0.375) = 2.625

$$I_{Tube} = 3.14 \times 2.625^3 \times 0.75$$
$$= 3.14 \times 18.1 \times 0.75 = 42.6$$

The same stiffness formula is used for both columns. The only difference between the tube and the solid pole is the different cross sectional areas and thus different moments of inertia.

Rule of Thumb

The effective length of a **braced column** is the total length minus two-thirds of the bracing length.

The general formula for both columns is:

$P_{CR} = \pi^2 \times E \times I / L^2$

$P_{CR\ Tube} = (9.86 \times 1.5 \times 10^6 \times 42.6) \div (25 \times 12)^2$

$= 630 \div 0.09 = 7,000$ lbs.

$P_{CR\ Circle} = (9.86 \times 1.5 \times 10^6 \times 63.6) \div (25 \times 12)^2$

$= 940 \div 0.09 = 10,452$ lbs.

$7,000 / 10,452 = 67\%$

Note also that the I-values differed by the same percent:

$42.6 \div 63.6 = 0.67$

This problem shows that the built-up stave column will carry 7,000 pounds of weight and the solid column will carry over 10,000 pounds before they are in danger of buckling. The two columns are the same length and outside diameter. The difference in strength is due to the cross-sectional area.

Tapered Columns

For tapered columns, either round or square, the representative dimension for the calculation of column strength is as follows:

$D_E = D_S + [(D_L - D_S) \times 1/3]$

Where D_E = effective dimension, D_S = small dimension and D_L = large dimension.

Problem 8: What is the effective diameter of a tapered column 15 feet high with base diameter 25¾ inches and top diameter 21⅞ inches?

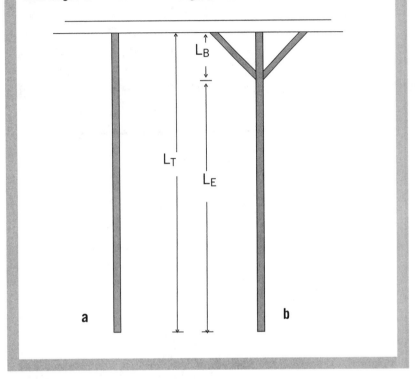

Figure 77 — Column Bracing

Every situation is different, but engineers will usually assign an Effective Length (LE) which is less than the bracing length. Column (a) is unbraced and LT = Total Length. In braced column (b), the effective length (LE) is total length (LT) minus 2/3 the length of the brace (LB).

a   b

Solution 8:

$D_E = D_S + [(D_L - D_S) \times 1/3]$

Where $D_S = 21.875$ and $D_L = 25.75$

$D_E = 21.875 + [(25.75 - 21.875) \times 1/3]$

$D_E = 21.875 + 1.29 = 23.165 \approx 23\frac{1}{8}$ inch

Bracing

What part does bracing play in column strength? Obviously, bracing plays no part in column compression as this depends only on the cross-sectional area of the column and the strength of the wood fibers. Bracing does, however, play a part in making the column stiffer, thus making it less likely to deflect and buckle. **Figure 77** shows a typical column braced at a 45° angle at the top of the column. The effective length of a column, after bracing, is the total column length minus two-thirds the bracing length.

$$L_E = L_T - (0.66 \times L_B)$$

Where L_E = effective length, L_T = total length and L_B = bracing length.

Both Ends Fixed

All the formulas we've used thus far have assumed the column ends were rounded and able to rotate freely. What if the ends are fixed?

When the ends are fixed, a column does not rotate when subjected to a lateral force. This makes a fixed column stiffer. The formula for critical force is:

$$P_{CR} = 4 \times (\pi^2 \times E \times I / L^2)$$

Note the fixed column is four times as stiff as the unfixed column.

One End Fixed

If the column is fixed at one end and pinned at the other, the formula is:

$$P_{CR} = 2.05 \times (\pi^2 \times E \times I / L^2)$$

Note the column fixed at one end is two times as stiff as the unfixed column.

Neither End Fixed

The formula for a column not fixed at either end is:

$$PCR = 1 \times (\pi^2 \times E \times I / L^2)$$

Safety Factors

Safety factors usually concern column buckling because a wooden column seldom fails due to compression stress. An engineer will assign fudge factors to his figures based on his experience. As a woodworker, if you use the 'worst case' formulas and then make the column as stiff as possible, you will automatically apply a safety factor. Secure ends, gussets, braces and shearing will all add stiffness and reduce the chance of buckling. One architect, who is also a woodworker, recommends that all weights be reduced by a factor of seven to insure stability. This means that if the theoretical maximum load is calculated to be 3500 pounds, then keep the load at $3500 \div 7 = 500$ pounds or less for safety.

Rule of Thumb
The fixed column is four times as stiff as the unfixed column. The column fixed at one end is two times as strong.

CHAPTER 9

Marquetry, Inlay and Intarsia

Creating a picture using wood is not new. Ancient Chinese and Indian artisans used thin wood to create beautiful scenes in the 3rd and 4th centuries BC, and King Tutankhamen's throne was decorated with inlay 3,000 years ago. Depending on how the wood pieces are shaped and how they are positioned — either on the surface or within — these wood paintings are called marquetry, intarsia, or inlay. Today woodworkers use these techniques to decorate trays, tables and chests as well as to produce pictures. The crafts can be practiced independently or as an integral part of other woodwork such as furniture making. This chapter will touch only briefly on inlay and intarsia, while delving deeply into marquetry, which is practiced by more woodworkers and also, is complicated and requires mathematical calculations to do properly.

What Are They?

There is confusion about the meaning of marquetry, intarsia, and inlay. Although they all take small pieces of material and blend them into a whole, the mechanics and the overall result are different. See **Figure 78**.

Intarsia – Marquetry and inlay were inspired by the ancient craft of intarsia — the making of decorative and pictorial mosaics by inlaying precious and exotic materials into or onto a background of solid wood. In the tomb of Pharaoh King Tutankhamen (c. 3000 BC), the throne and furniture are covered with inlay — precious stones, glazed tiles, and small pieces of wood, gold, and ivory.

With intarsia, one makes a mosaic by cutting and shaping relatively thick pieces of a pattern separately, then placing them together so they form a three-dimensional picture. Each piece is cut, carved, sanded, rounded over, or in some

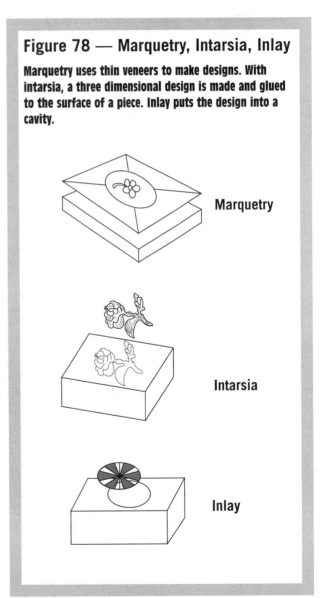

Figure 78 — Marquetry, Intarsia, Inlay

Marquetry uses thin veneers to make designs. With intarsia, a three dimensional design is made and glued to the surface of a piece. Inlay puts the design into a cavity.

Marquetry

Intarsia

Inlay

Figure 79 — Snowman, an Example of Intarsia

The snowman (Wood 75, Dec. 94, p.72) is made of pine, walnut, and mahogany. Each piece is cut independently, then shaped and glued to a background to produce a three-dimensional piece.

Front   Side

creating a design made of wood, shell, stone, metal, plastic, or bone — any material that can be cut thin or ground up. This material is then glued into a cavity that has been hollowed out or carved into the surface. Inlay began as early as 400 BC in India where artisans used knives to cut a cavity into furniture so a thin wood design could be placed into it.

Wood turners use the inlay technique to fill voids in turned bowls. Metal filings or ground-up turquoise, coral, abalone, malachite etc., are mixed with cyano-acrylate glue (super glue), and packed into the hole.

Marquetry – In marquetry, different types and colors of thin wood are carefully cut, and the pieces fit closely together, to create a design in a single sheet. Some marquetry artists also enhance their pictures with materials other than wood. This veneer picture is then glued onto a solid, stable surface. Marquetry covers a surface with assembled veneer instead of placing the design into a cavity like inlay. Table tops, chest lids, box covers, and pictures are favorite spots for marquetry. Artists use the colors and grain direction of different woods with dramatic effect. If the marquetry picture consists solely of geometrical designs, as in a checkerboard, it is called "parquetry."

way shaped, before being glued onto a backer board such as hardwood, plywood or MDF. While marquetry uses thin veneers, intarsia uses ¼ inch to 2 inch thick materials. Intarsia is used in wall plaques, on jewelry box lids and as decorations on the head and foot boards of baby cribs and beds. While different kinds of wood can be used in intarsia, such as walnut, mahogany and pine (see the snowman in **Figure 79**), beautiful three-dimension intarsia pictures may also be made using only one wood with the different pieces shaped, curved and sanded.

Inlay – Inlay is the art of

Marquetry requires very little wood — the veneers sold in the U.S. today are about ¹/₄₀ inch thick and, because veneers are sliced and not sawn, theoretically a 1 inch board could yield 40 pieces of veneer. The equipment required for marquetry is minimal — a method of cutting the wood (scroll saw, fret saw, coping saw, knife, chisel), a little tape, some glue, and a stable backer board.

Veneer allows the use of precious woods that, as dimensioned lumber, would otherwise be unavailable or too expensive, for example cocobolo, ebony, pink ivory, and the rosewoods. Some woods are too fragile structurally to be used in the solid form (such as burls, crotches, and short grain), and veneer is the only feasible way to use these woods. It is possible to buy hundreds of different kinds of veneer, each with their own characteristic hue and figure. Therefore the opportunity for color and pattern are practically endless and the end uses are equally diverse — a Ferrari dash board, a curved-front highboy, chests or a jewelry box.

The American Marquetry Association recently polled their members and found that 73% of them cut veneers with a scroll saw or fret saw, while 27% use a knife, scalpel, chisel, or blade of some kind. With a blade, the cut

is vertical and there is no kerf — thus there are no angles to figure. The focus of this chapter is on cutting veneers with a saw blade, where angles and math are very important.

Marquetry Tools and Materials
Veneers

At one time, veneers were sawn from logs, either by hand or at a saw-mill, to give sheets ¼ inch thick and, incidentally, wasting as much wood in saw dust as in usable veneer. Today veneers are cut by heavy slicing machinery. Logs are pre-treated by soaking in water or by steaming to soften the fibers, and then are sliced by rotating or swinging the log against a fixed blade. Cutting at various angles to the growth rings of the log produces different figures such as "crown cut," "rotary cut," "quartered," or "half-quartered."

Veneers use the wood very efficiently — a large tree will yield enough veneer to cover a football field, or more.

Transfer Paper

Marquetarians use transfer paper to copy a drawing onto the wood. The papers are available in colors including black (as in common carbon paper), white and yellow for marking on dark woods, and red or blue paper for light woods.

Rule of Thumb

Intarsia – This is a picture made of pieces of wood, each shaped, fit together and placed on top of a background.

Inlay – Inlay is a picture made of thin wood, rock, bone etc. placed in a recess in solid wood.

Marquetry – This is a picture made principally of veneer and overlaid onto a substrate.

Parquetry – This is marquetry where geometric shapes are used exclusively — an example is a checkerboard.

Rule of Thumb

MDF is dimensionally stable, comes in big sheets, is cheap, unattractive, and saves our forests because it's made of wood chips and glue. Veneers are thin, structurally unstable, rare, costly, and beautiful.

Unlike carbon paper, tracing paper does not leave an oily line that is difficult to remove.

Substrates

The substrate should be stable, flat and not too thick. Thick backing boards tend to spoil the overall balance of the picture. There are three good choices:

Solid timber. This is the least suitable material on which to mount pictures. Besides being wasteful — it will be covered with a veneer — it is prone to warping. The only case for solid wood is when the edge will be routed or otherwise machined, for example, as a game board.

Plywood. Plywood is a suitable baseboard material though care should be taken to select high-grade plywood with a well prepared surface and without voids. Position the plywood so the surface ply is at 90° to the predominant grain of the picture. If you choose a veneered plywood, only the front and the edges need to be covered.

Composite Materials. Man-made boards such as chip-board and medium-density and high-density fiber-boards are cheap, easy to work, and stable in use. MDF is available in various thicknesses. It is heavier than plywood, however, and may not be suitable for large pieces.

Saws and Knives

Scroll Saw – In the sixteenth century the thin jigsaw blade was first produced. Held in a frame, thin saw blades could cut the wood in tight turns with great intricacy. Stacks of veneers could be cut so multiple picture pieces could be made at once, and a sort of mass production was possible. In recent years, powered scroll saws have become available at prices anyone can afford. They are safe to operate — most woodworking accidents happen when someone tries to cut small pieces of wood on a machine. The scroll saw, however, is designed to cut small pieces very safely. Furthermore, there is no danger of kickback — a problem with many other woodworking machines. The constant-tension machines commercially available today allow swift changes in cutting directions without relief cuts, and permit sharp right-angle turns or complete 360° turn-arounds without blade breakage. The cut surface is so smooth it does not have to be sanded and the cut is square to the face without being angled or bellied.

The scroll saw has distinct advantages over hand sawing. First, a constant bevel can be maintained by tilting the table. Second, both hands are free to steer the wood through the saw blade. Third, the work has backup support from the narrow opening in the saw table so no waster board is needed with most veneers. Finally, the throat opening is large, allowing a large picture to be made.

Fret Saw – The fret saw is the ideal hand tool for cutting intricate shapes in thin veneers. It is light weight and the tension created by the tubular U-shaped steel frame keeps blades taut, both increasing cutting accuracy and reducing blade breakage (See **Figure 80**). The vise-like blade holders accept 5 inch or longer blades and the 12 inch throat is large enough for most veneer work. The unpinned blades are easy to thread through small drill holes, a necessity in most marquetry work.

Coping Saw – The coping saw is strong and rigid and the screw action of the handle keeps blades well tensioned. Replacement blades are available at most hardware stores. In complicated veneer work, the blade must be threaded through small holes and the pins make this difficult, if not impossible. Most experienced marquetry workers prefer unpinned blades.

Knife – About one-fourth of American marquetarians use a blade exclusively for veneer cutting. The percentage probably is higher in Europe. The blade may be a scalpel, X-acto® blade, chisel, or any sharp steel instrument capable of cutting thin wood.

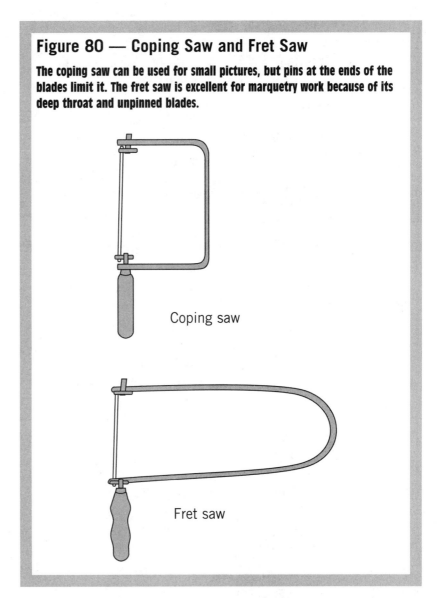

Figure 80 — Coping Saw and Fret Saw

The coping saw can be used for small pictures, but pins at the ends of the blades limit it. The fret saw is excellent for marquetry work because of its deep throat and unpinned blades.

Coping saw

Fret saw

Tape

Veneer tape is available from most woodworking supply houses and is preferable to masking tape which leaves a sticky residue. Clear Scotch Brand® type tape can be used but it is hard to remove because it is almost invisible. I've seen finished marquetry pieces (even one in a gallery) which, in just the right light, show traces of

Rule of Thumb

A coping saw uses blades with pinned ends that prevent them being fed through a tiny hole. A fret saw has a deeper throat and uses unpinned blades, which can be fed through very tiny holes.

Figure 81 — Saw Blades

Different manufacturers number their blades with various systems. It's always best to use calipers and check the width (across the teeth) of your blade.

Blade Number (1)	Blade Thickness (2)	Kerf Thickness (3)
8/0	0.006	0.008
7/0	0.007	0.009
6/0	0.007	0.009
5/0	0.008	0.010
4/0	0.009	0.011
3/0	0.009	0.011
2/0	0.010	0.013
02	0.028	0.035
03	0.032	0.040
04	0.035	0.044
05	0.039	0.049
06	0.041	0.051
07	0.045	0.056
08	0.050	0.063
09	0.053	0.066
0	0.011	0.014
1	0.012	0.015
2	0.013	0.016
3	0.014	0.018
4	0.015	0.019
5	0.016	0.020
6	0.017	0.021
7	0.018	0.023
8	0.019	0.024
9	0.021	0.026
10	0.022	0.028
11	0.024	0.030
12	0.024	0.030

(1) Blade manufacturers use different numbering systems.
(2) These numbers are close but not exact since each manufacturer produces blades of slightly different size.
(3) Use these numbers in the math formulas to determine miter angles.

clear tape that were never removed. Scotch Safe-Release Masking Tape® and the blue-colored, painters masking tape are both good for this kind of work – they are quite visible, easy to remove, and leave no residue. Avoid a tape that leaves a sticky residue or is so strong that it pulls slivers of wood off with it.

Saw Blades

Small fret saw blades are preferred for detailed veneer work where the cut direction is constantly changing. They are sold in thicknesses from 0.009 inch to 0.020 inch. Note that this is the width of the back of the blade and not the thickness of the blade across the teeth. When measuring, put the calipers across the teeth — it is the width of the kerf that is important not the width of the blade back. Usually for veneer work the best blades are the very thin (0.009 inch), very fine tooth (30 tpi) blades. They cut smoothly and leave nice edges. They are also small enough to be inserted through a hole made by a thumb tack or push pin through a pack of veneers. **Figure 81** shows the different sizes of blades.

Adhesives

Experienced marquetarians choose among four different glues — polyvinyl acetate (PVA), urea formaldehyde, contact cement, and epoxy. In a recent survey, most American marquetarians use PVA glues (63%) or contact cement (32%). The remaining 5% use either epoxy, plastic resin, cyano-acrylate, or urea formaldehyde.

Polyvinyl Acetate (PVA). This is the common, everyday white or yellow carpenter's glue. It is cheap, extremely strong, and can be found at any woodworking or hardware store. It requires clamping for at least one hour and because it is water-based, it can raise the grain on certain veneers. The yellow PVA glue can be reconstituted with heat for about ten days after initial set; the white PVA glue can be reactivated indefinitely. Woodworkers use this character-istic to good advantage, for example to add veneer to a curved surface like a tambour clock, or a marquetry band around the outside surface of a turned bowl. In use, both the veneer and the substrate are coated with glue and allowed to dry. The veneer is then placed in position, and using an iron as the heat source, the glue is reconstituted to attach the veneer. In this way, a curved surface can be veneered without clamping.

Contact Cement – Contact glue is often used in veneer work because it bonds instantly and holds well. Both the veneer piece and the substrate are coated with glue and allowed to dry for 30 minutes to 2 hours before assembly — follow the manufacturer's directions. A contact glue joint might fail, not because of the adhesive itself, but because of the finish that is ultimately applied over the veneer. If shellac dissolved in alcohol is used as a finish or sealer, the solvent can penetrate through the pores of the wood or between the pieces of marquetry and soften the adhesive below, causing delamination. If you plan to use a solvent-based finish, the water-based contact glues are very solvent resistant.

Urea formaldehyde – These glues are sold as powders which, when mixed with water, give a very strong adhesion. This is perhaps the best all-around glue for applying veneer to any flat surface — they don't bleed through, allow plenty of time for positioning, and don't allow veneers to creep. The dried glue is also impervious to paint thinner and alcohol — two solvents commonly used in marquetry finishes — varnishes and shellac.

Epoxy – The epoxies are expensive but bond almost anything to anything. They are sold as a two-part, cold liquid mixture (resin and hardener). The adhesion is rapid and

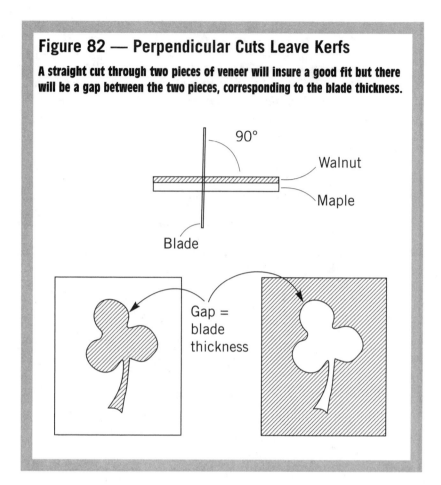

Figure 82 — Perpendicular Cuts Leave Kerfs

A straight cut through two pieces of veneer will insure a good fit but there will be a gap between the two pieces, corresponding to the blade thickness.

90°

Walnut

Maple

Blade

Gap = blade thickness

strong, waterproof, and because the reaction produces heat, will set in a cold shop.

Marquetry Cuts

In very broad terms, using a saw blade, there are only two methods of marquetry — the pieces can be prepared with a perpendicular cut or with a bevel cut. There are, however, many, many variations of each approach.

Perpendicular 90° Cuts

If we were to stack two pieces of veneer, one on top of the other, and cut out a design with a fret

Rule of Thumb

If you **stack two veneers** and saw with the blade square to the surface, the cut-out pieces from one layer will fit into the hole in the other, but with a gap. To eliminate the gap, tilt the saw blade just enough so one piece will fit tightly into the other.

Figure 83 — Perpendicular Cuts

Using the stack method, multiple coasters can be made. Four different species of veneer are held between two backer boards. The design is cut with the blade at 90° and the parts mixed-and-matched. When glued onto a substrate and cut into round disks, this technique will produce four drink coasters, all with the same scene, but each featuring different combinations of wood.

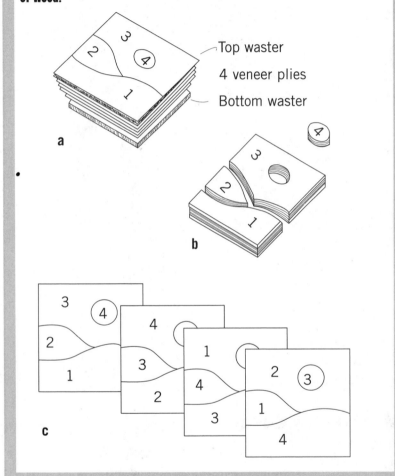

because of the kerf, that is, the gap created by the thickness of the saw teeth. Some marquetry is made this way with the kerf spaces filled with colored glue and sawdust. This is great for drink coasters and hot dish trivets where a dozen pieces can be made at one time.

Making Marquetry Drink Coasters

This procedure will make one set of four drink coasters using the pad or stacking method of marquetry. Each set will have the same scene but with a different mix of the same woods. See **Figure 83**.

1. **Cut four pieces** of ¼ inch cherry, oak, birch or maple plywood into 4⅛ inch squares. Use a wipe varnish (1:1 mixture of paint thinner and varnish) on the front (or good) side of the plywood — we'll glue the veneer to the back side. Applying a finish at this point protects the bottom of the coaster from dirt and glue during the procedures that follow.

2. **Gather four pieces** of veneer of near equal thickness. If you are using woods of similar grain and darkness, such as mahogany and walnut, turn these two pieces so the grains are not oriented in the same direction — one piece vertical and one horizontal.

saw held at 90° to the face, the design cut from the top piece would fit into the hole left in the bottom veneer; see **Figure 82**. At the same time, the design from the bottom piece would fit into the top background. By using this stack (or pad) method, we would have two pictures — but the inserts would not fit tightly

3. Cut two pieces of thin cardboard (cereal box material works fine) to the same size as the veneer pieces.

4. Place the cardboard pieces on top and bottom of the veneer pad and mark an arrow for "UP". A veneer with distinctive grain lines (such as oak) looks better as the sky when its grain runs crosswise.

5. Wrap tape tightly around the pad, two pieces of tape across and two pieces up-and-down. If one of the veneers appears to split easily, put that piece in the middle of the pile or put veneer tape across the back of it. The order of the wood pieces in the pad doesn't matter.

6. On the paper pattern, mark each section with numbers 1 to 4. If multiple pieces are the same feature, give them the same number; for example, when one part of a mountain range goes from left to right with a stream or tree dividing it. Glue the pattern to the top of the pad, making sure the top of the pattern is oriented with the "up" arrow.

7. Use the thinnest scroll saw blade you have and cut out each piece of the puzzle. Start outside the pad, cut across, and end at the opposite side. Set each sandwich section aside, being careful to not lose or break any

part. When all four pieces of the puzzle have been cut out, arrange them in order 1 through 4.

8. Separate and discard the top and bottom pieces of cardboard and distribute each piece of veneer in pack #1 along a board left to right.

9. Separate and discard the cardboard from puzzle pack #2 and distribute these pieces left to right also, except start at position 2. Continue in this manner until all pieces have been distributed and each of the four positions has a complete puzzle of different woods.

10. To assemble, put a piece of veneer tape under the bottom section of each puzzle. The tape I use is Scotch Safe-Release Masking Tape®. Position the next piece and press it onto the tape. Work from the bottom to top, adding tape as needed.

11. Hold the completed puzzle up to the light to see if the joints are closed. If there are poor joints, loosen the tape and readjust the pieces. Put the puzzle piece tape-side down and run a thin line of yellow PVA glue along each joint. Sprinkle on a little fine walnut saw dust and, with a spatula, rub and push the mixture into each joint. Let the piece dry for an hour. If the veneer piece starts to curl

Figure 84 — Six Coaster Patterns

These patterns can be used to make coasters. They all require six different veneers and when mixed-and-matched will make six different coasters.

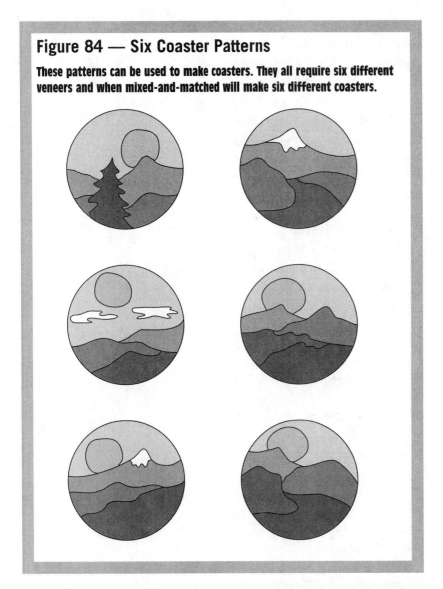

with waxed paper — and clamp. After an hour take the pieces out, carefully remove the tape, scrape off any extruded and still soft glue, and reclamp with a piece of paper towel between each layer.

13. After two hours, remove from the clamps and if necessary, fill voids with sawdust and glue. Sand the face of the marquetry piece with 120 grit sand paper. Wipe on a dilute coat of varnish (1:1, varnish to paint thinner).

14. Cut the pieces into circles on a band saw. I made mine 3⅝ inches in diameter. Sand the disk edges first on a power sander and finally with fine sandpaper by hand. Finish the top, bottom and edges with varnish. Finally, wax the top.

15. Do the above six times using six different scenes, then mix and match for six sets of coasters, each with six different scenes. **Figure 84** shows six different scenes for more coasters — each requires six pieces of veneer and will make six coasters.

Circle Cutting Jig

I had problems holding and cutting the disks on a band saw so I made a circle cutting jig with a peek-a-boo window. Because we are only cutting off ⁵⁄₁₆ inch on the four sides, it's easy to position the veneer

and warp, weight it down with a heavy, non-metallic tool. When the glue is dry, lightly sand the filled side.

12. Put PVA glue onto the substrate (unfinished, back side) and onto the marquetry piece (non-taped side) and join the two pieces. Do all four of the marquetry pieces and place them between two pieces of ¾ inch plywood — separate each layer squares a little off center and ruin the piece during the band saw procedure.

A circle-cutting jig for the band saw can be made as follows (**Figure 85**):

1. **Make a sliding table** out of ¾ inch plywood with a slat underneath to fit the band saw miter gauge slot.

2. **Drive a pin** into the sliding table 1¹³⁄₁₆ inch from the blade for the round plate to rotate on. The pin should be located one-half of the final disk diameter (3⅝ inch divided by 2) from the blade.

3. **Clamp** a wooden stop block on the back of the band saw table so the jig platform stops with the pin directly opposite the blade.

4. **Cut** a 3½ inch disk with a small hole in the center and put it on the pin. Note the rotating plate is slightly smaller than the finished marquetry piece.

5. **Prepare** a piece of cardboard about 6 inches by 8 inches and cut a 3⅝ inch hole in it. Three inches from the pin attach a ¾ inch by ¾ inch by 6 inch cleat to the board and attach the cardboard with thumb tacks (see **Figure 85**) so the round hole is centered directly over the 3½ inch plate.

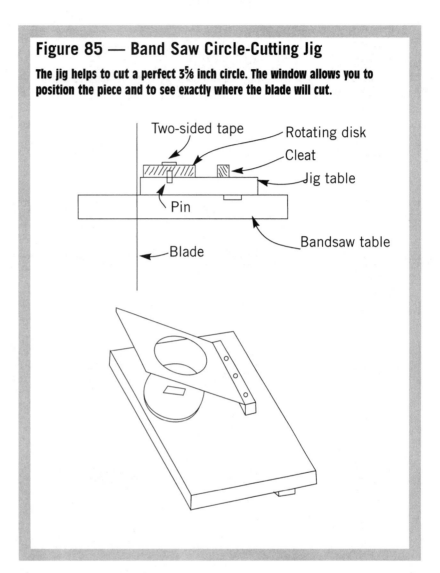

Figure 85 — Band Saw Circle-Cutting Jig

The jig helps to cut a perfect 3⅝ inch circle. The window allows you to position the piece and to see exactly where the blade will cut.

Two-sided tape — Rotating disk — Cleat — Jig table — Pin — Blade — Bandsaw table

6. **Using** the peek-a-boo hole in the cardboard, attach the 4⅛ inch marquetry squares to the rotating plate with double-sided tape. The cardboard arrangement allows you to see exactly where the blade will cut — there's only about ¼ inch of waste.

7. **Turn on the saw** and push the jig along the band saw table slot until it is against the stop. Rotate the marquetry piece and the plate to cut the circle.

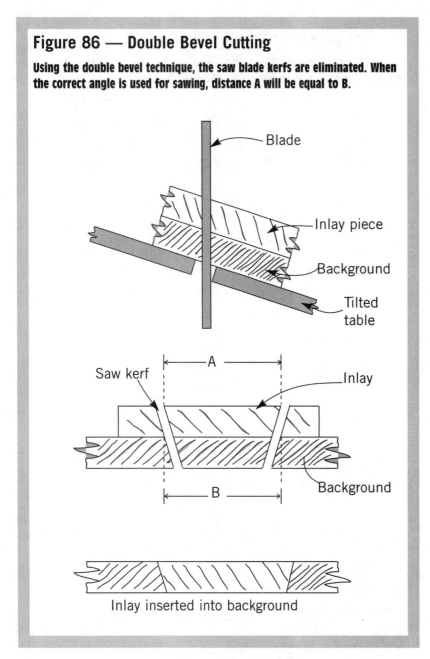

Figure 86 — Double Bevel Cutting

Using the double bevel technique, the saw blade kerfs are eliminated. When the correct angle is used for sawing, distance A will be equal to B.

Blade

Inlay piece

Background

Tilted table

A

Saw kerf

Inlay

B

Background

Inlay inserted into background

Double Bevel Marquetry

When you are composing a marquetry picture, the pieces should fit tightly against each other — and for this we need a better method than the 90º perpendicular cut.

In the 1700s the Germans started a technique of conical sawing of veneer pads where by angling the fret saw the blade kerf could be eliminated. By the 1900s the procedure was used extensively in furniture. The technique now is called double bevel cutting.

The most common technique used today is an additive process that starts with two sections of veneer, one on top of the other. The two pieces are cut simultaneously with the saw blade at an angle so that one piece will precisely fit into the opening of the other. The waste from each piece is set aside or discarded and the new piece is glued or taped into position in the picture. Then a third piece is cut and added and so on. This additive process continues until the whole picture is complete and ready for mounting. Because two pieces are cut together with the blade at the correct angle, they fit perfectly even if the blade didn't follow the pattern line exactly. See **Figure 86**. This technique is known as double bevel cutting.

A Complicated Procedure Explained.

The double-bevel method has the advantage of no visible kerf in the assembly, but there are two disadvantages. First, only one marquetry picture at a time is made. Secondly, there is wasted veneer. The technique can be confusing initially, but it is easily learned.

Calculate Blade Angle

The bevel-cut (double bevel, double-cut, conical-cut) method requires that the cut be made on a bevel. If you're using a hand-held fret saw, then construct a bird's mouth cutting table with the slope needed (**Figure 87**). If you're using a scroll saw, then tilt the table to the required angle.

In order to calculate the correct bevel angle, we need three important measurements:

   1. Thickness of background veneer;

   2. Thickness of insert veneer;

   3. Blade width (kerf).

Math

The working angle equals the arctangent of the blade width (BW) divided by the wood thickness (WT) (**Figure 88**).

   Angle = Arctan (BW ÷ WT)

   Where BW = blade width

   and WT = wood thickness

Problem 1: What angle should the table be set at if both the veneer and the background are ¹⁄₄₀ inch (0.025) thick and the blade kerf is 0.009 inch?

Solution 1:

   Angle = Arctan (BW ÷ WT)

   Where BW = 0.009
   and WT = 0.025

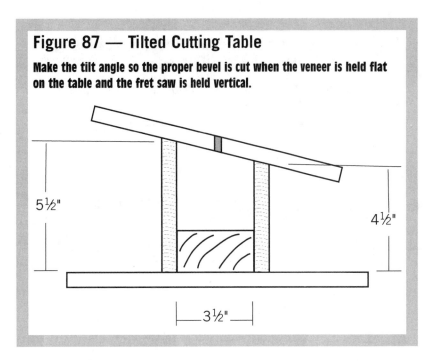

Figure 87 — Tilted Cutting Table

Make the tilt angle so the proper bevel is cut when the veneer is held flat on the table and the fret saw is held vertical.

5½"

4½"

3½"

   Angle = Atan (0.009 / 0.025)

   Angle = Atan 0.36

   Angle = 20°

This is a very big table tilt. What if the veneer were thicker, say ¹⁄₂₈ inch?

Problem 2: The blade is 0.009 and the veneer is ¹⁄₂₈ inch = 0.0357 inch. What is the tilt angle?

Solution 2:

   Angle = Arctan (BW ÷ WT)

   Where BW = 0.009 and WT = 0.0357

   Angle = Atan (0.009 ÷ 0.0357)

   Angle = Atan 0.2521

   Angle = 14°

Note that the angle difference is 6° (20° versus 14°) between

Figure 88 — Blade Width and Thickness of Insert Determine Blade Angle.

Angle = Tan (BW ÷ WT) where BW = blade width and WT= wood thickness.
Example: BW = 0.020, WT = 1/16" (0.0625).
Tan = (BW / WT) = 0.020 / 0.0625 = 0.32. Atan 0.32 ≈ 18°.

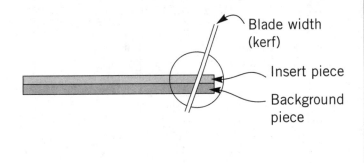

Blade width
(kerf)

Insert piece

Background
piece

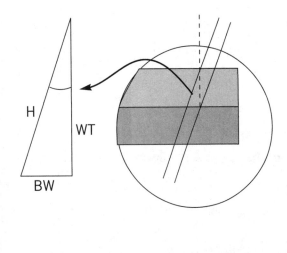

H

WT

BW

Where BW = 0.009 and WT = 0.125

Angle = Atan (0.009 / 0.125)

Angle = Atan 0.072

Angle = 4°

Problems 1, 2 and 3 show that as the wood gets thicker (or the blade thinner), the working angle is smaller. See **Figure 90** for the proper bevel angles.

Depth of Insertion

It's possible and sometimes necessary to use woods that differ in thickness, for example a ½ inch background with ¼ inch veneers. How do you figure the blade angle?

1. To set the insert even with the top of the background (marquetry) as in **Figure 89a.**

> Background = ⅜ inch (0.375 inch) thick
>
> Insert = ⅛ inch (0.125 inch) thick
>
> Blade = 0.045 inch wide
>
> Insertion Depth = ⅛ inch (0.125 inch)
>
> Tilt Angle = Atan (BW / ID)
>
> = Atan (0.045 / 0.125)
>
> = Atan 0.36 = 19.8° ≈ 20°

2. To set the insert in the middle of the background (**Figure 89b.**

> Insertion Depth = ¼ inch (0.250 inch)
>
> Tilt Angle = Atan (BW / ID)

cutting ¹⁄₄₀ inch and ¹⁄₂₈ inch veneers. Measure the veneer with calipers before starting.

Problem 3: To what angle should the table be tilted if the wood is ⅛ inch (0.125) thick and the blade is 0.009 inch wide?

Solution 3:

> Angle = Arctan (BW / WT)

= Atan (0.045 / 0.250)

= Atan 0.18 = 10.2° ≈ 10°

3. To set the insert at the bottom of the background as in **Figure 89c**.

Insertion Depth = ⅜ inch (0.375 inch)

Tilt Angle = Atan (BW / ID)

= Atan (0.045 / 0.375)

= Atan 0.12 = 6.8° ≈ 7°

4. To set the insert under the background as in **Figure 89d**.

Insertion Depth = ½ inch (0.500 inch)

Tilt Angle = Atan (BW / ID)

Where BW = 0.045 and ID = 0.5

= Atan (0.045 / 0.500)

= Atan 0.09 = 5.14° ≈ 5°

A Double Bevel Project

To demonstrate the double bevel method of marquetry, we can make a picture of a flower using six pieces of veneer (**Figure 91**). The same technique is used to make more complicated pictures; the first veneer piece is positioned on top of the background, the outline is drawn and it is bevel cut. The piece is dropped into the background.

The next piece is positioned on top and it is bevel cut along the lines and placed into the background. This process is repeated as each design element

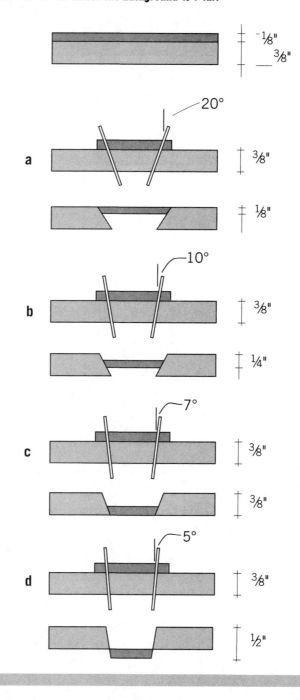

Figure 89 — Change the Bevel Angle to Put the Insert Even With the Top of the Background, in the Middle, at the Bottom, or Beneath it.

An insert ⅛ inch thick can be bevel cut at 20° so it will fit flush with the top of the ⅜ inch background (a), set in the middle (b) (10°), at the bottom (c) (7°) or under the background (5°) (d).

Figure 90 — Double-Bevel Angles

Find the wood thickness of the insert along the top of the chart and the kerf thickness along the left side. Read the angle of blade tilt in the center.

Double-Bevel Angles (In Degrees)

Kerf Thickness (Inches)	Wood Thickness (Inches)													
	1/50" 0.020	1/40" 0.025	1/32" 0.030	1/28" 0.035	0.040	0.050	1/16" 0.060	0.070	0.080	3/32" 0.090	0.100	1/8" 0.125	3/16" 0.188	1/4" 0.250
0.008	22	19	15	13	12	9	8	7	6	5	5	4	2.4	1.8
0.009	24	21	17	15	13	10	9	7	6.5	5.7	5	4	2.7	2
0.010	27	24	19	17	15	12	10	8	7	6	6	5	3	2
0.015	37	30	30	25	22	17	14	12	11	10	9	7	4.5	3
0.020				35	30	24	19	17	14	13	12	9	6	4.6
0.025					39	30	25	21	18	16	14	12	8	6
0.030						37	30	24	22	20	18	14	9	7
0.035							36	30	26	23	20	16	11	8
0.040								35	28	26	24	18	12	9
0.045									34	30	27	21	15	10
0.050									39	32	29	23	16	11.5
0.055										38	33	26	17	13
0.060											36	29	19	14
0.065												31	20	0.15
0.070												34	22	0.16
0.075												37	23	17
0.080													25	18
0.085													27	19
0.090													29	20
0.100													32	24
0.125														30
0.150														37

Note: 1/28" veneer = 0.036", 1/40" = .025", 1/50" = .02"
Note: Bandsaw blade = 0.045"

Example:
Angle = Atan(Blade Kerf / Wood Thickness)
Where Blade = 0.008", Wood = 0.036"
Angle = Atan(0.008 / 0.036) = Atan 0.222 = 12.5 deg.

is cut out individually, one part at a time and each successive cutout part becomes another inlay into the background. The advantage of this method is that the joints between pieces come out almost effortlessly perfect. The disadvantage is that only one picture can be made at a time.

Finishing

1. Glue the picture to a suitable substrate and clamp between ¾ inch plywood (with waxed paper) and let set for two hours. Remove the waxed paper and replace it with brown paper from a grocery bag and clamp for another two hours.

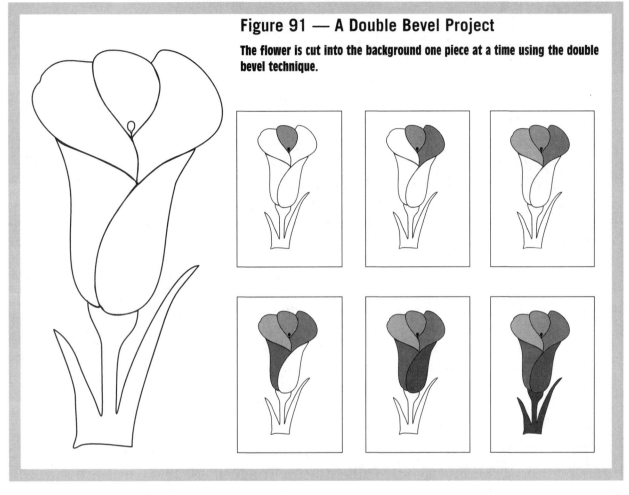

Figure 91 — A Double Bevel Project

The flower is cut into the background one piece at a time using the double bevel technique.

2. **Remove the tape** and scrape the veneer surface with a hand scraper.

3. **Glue veneer** to the back and the edges of the board. This helps stabilize the board and makes an attractive finish to your picture.

4. **Inspect** the front surface and fill any open joints with sawdust and white glue.

5. **Sand lightly** with 220-grit and 320-grit paper.

6. **Clean the surface** with a vacuum and seal each section of the picture with a wood sealer. Shellac and alcohol makes a good sealer if you're not using organic solvent-based contact cement.

7. **Apply the finish** (polyurethane, varnish, lacquer) as you would to any fine piece of woodwork.

Rule of Thumb

In double-bevel marquetry, as the saw blade gets thinner, the working angle becomes smaller. Therefore when you want a smaller angle, choose a thinner blade.

CHAPTER 10

Twists and Spirals

This is another one of those 'how'd you do that?' kind of projects. The twists common on Southwestern and Spanish-style furniture are often referred to as "spirals turned on a lathe." This statement is wrong — in two ways. First, 'spiral turnings' are not turned on a lathe; the lathe serves only to hold the work while the spiral portion is cut by hand. In this application the lathe is a fixture to hold the wood cylinder while the user moves the tool. Before cutting the spiral, however, a lathe is used to reduce the blank to a cylinder of the desired shape, by the usual methods.

Second, the twists around the cylinder are not spirals. The word 'spiral' comes from the word 'spire,' which means 'coil'. A spiral is a curve winding around a fixed point while continuously moving away from that point — all in the same plane — like a watch spring. A cross-section of a snail or nautilus shell is often used as an example of the spiral shape in nature. The spirals (we'll continue to use the word because it is so ingrained in our lexicon) we'll be talking about are evenly spaced and not moving away from a point. They wind around a cylinder, moving along its length, and are actually helices (plural of helix).

Figure 92 — A Helix and a Cylinder

If the helical coil is unwound from the cylinder, a right triangle is produced. The lead is the distance the spiral advances in one rotation. See Chapter 11, Mechanics, for more on "Screws and the Inclined Plane."

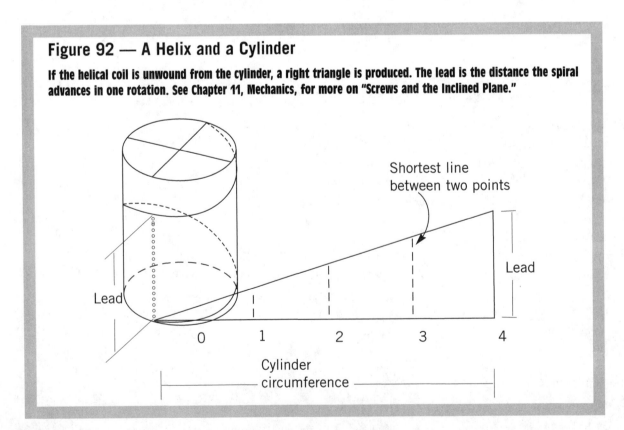

A helix is a straight line wrapped around a cylinder by the rotation of a point in a uniform manner. A screw thread is a good example of a helix. If the cylindrical surface upon which a helix has been generated is rolled out onto a plane, the helix becomes a straight line, as shown in **Figure 92**, and the portion below the helix becomes a right triangle. The triangle's altitude is equal to the lead of the helix and the length of the base is equal to the circumference of the cylinder. The lead (pronounced LEED) is the distance the spiral advances along the cylinder in one full rotation. A helix thus can be defined as the shortest line that can be drawn on the surface of a cylinder connecting two points not directly above each other. Later, when we lay out spirals, we will connect points and draw diagonal lines around a cylinder to find the lead we want.

Spirals come in both left- and right-handed forms. Standard screws, nuts and bolts are right-handed, as are both helices in a double-stranded molecule of DNA. Animal horns with helices usually appear as mirror images, having both a left-handed and a right-handed form.

Commercially there are two methods of cutting spirals: in the first, a router is driven along a slowly rotating workpiece. In the second, the workpiece is both

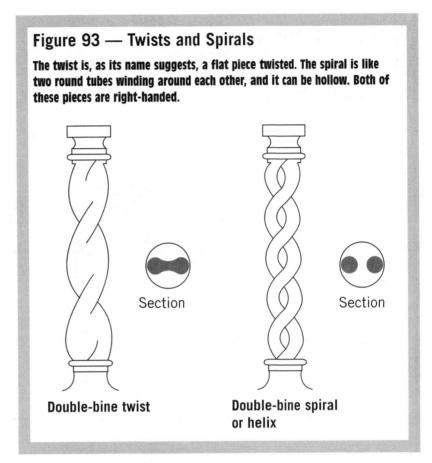

Figure 93 — Twists and Spirals

The twist is, as its name suggests, a flat piece twisted. The spiral is like two round tubes winding around each other, and it can be hollow. Both of these pieces are right-handed.

Section

Section

Double-bine twist

Double-bine spiral or helix

rotated and moved longitudinally past a stationary cutter. I'll explain how to make twists and spirals by hand — using a lathe, hand saw, drill, carving tools, chisels, rasps, and sandpaper. The lathe will be used to shape the starting blank to a cylinder, and then to hold the piece while you work on it by hand. Spiral cutting is actually pretty easy, though making multiple sets or mirror images takes a bit of preparation and care.

Twists and Spirals

You'll hear the terms 'single bine' and 'double bine' used in

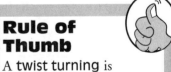

Rule of Thumb

A twist turning is not a spiral – which is flat – but a helix – which is three-dimensional. The thread on a machine screw is a helix. A steel tape wound inside its case makes a spiral.

Figure 94 — Walnut chair, mid-17th century

The square parts of the legs are 1⅝ inch. The chair was drawn from the original in the Victoria and Albert Museum, London, England. All spirals in this chair are right-handed.

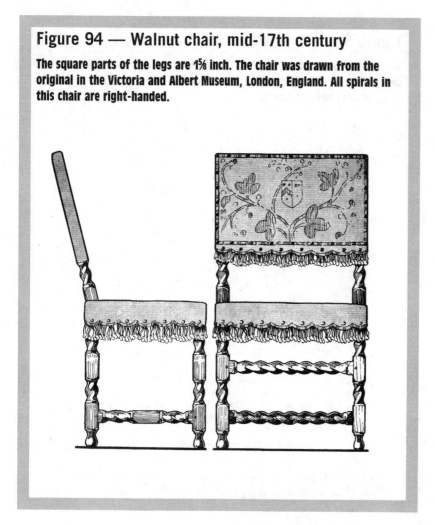

What is the difference between a twist and a spiral? **Figure 93** shows the face and end section view of both types. A twist can be thought of as a piece of flat material, for example a piece of ribbon, twisted but solid throughout. A single spiral can be thought of as a piece of thick rope twisted into a helix. A double spiral is like two ropes side by side also twisted into a helix. In a hollow spiral, each bine is separate and does not touch its neighbor as it twists. Today many people use the words 'twist' and 'spiral' as if they are the same thing.

History

Wooden threads for wine and olive presses were used as far back as 200 BC by both the Romans and the Greeks. It seems, however, that spiral turning for furniture originated in China in the 1600s. Examples of this form of decorative art were brought to Europe by Portuguese explorers and the spiral was incorporated into the prevailing furniture styles and became quite popular in the 1700s. **Figure 94** shows a chair dating back to the 1650s with spiral cuts on the stretchers, legs, and rails. Each spiral in the chair has a right-handed twist. Later, high-end chairs by the better craftsmen had spirals that were balanced by mirror-imaged spirals on opposite sides of the piece.

discussing spirals. The word 'bine' is defined as a twining stem and is an old English alteration of the word 'bind.' In fact the honeysuckle twining shrub was originally called a woodbine (or wood-bind) because of its penchant for winding and twisting around trees and trellises. In the U.S., the Virginia creeper, a tendril-climbing vine, is often called a woodbine. In woodworking, a bine refers to one of the twisting portions of a helix.

Left-Handed and Right-Handed Spirals

Spirals can be left-handed and right-handed. As viewed from any side, if the bines rotate clockwise, it is a right-handed spiral. Flipping a spiral piece upside-down does not change the direction of the twist. A right-hand spiral will always be right-handed, whether it's oriented top-up or top-down. If you have trouble deciding whether a spiral has a left- or right-hand twist, compare it to a screw. Virtually all screws are right handed. See **Figure 95**.

A look at contemporary mass-produced furniture shows that most of the spirals are left-handed. It is the mark of a careful craftsman to balance the spiral sections in a piece by placing mirror images in the upright sections. Pay attention to this small detail in furniture construction and it will stand out in the same way that hand-cut dovetails outshine machine-cut. Later when I describe cutting a spiral, we will carve from one end and then reverse the workpiece on the lathe and carve from the other end, so we always cut with the grain.

Types of Spirals

The main types of spiral twists are:

1. Single Twist – This spiral has a single bine worked from a single starting point to a single finishing point. This is sometimes known as a barley twist.

2. Double Twist — This is known as a double barley twist. It has two bines worked from two starting points.

3. Triple Twist – This spiral has three starting and finishing points. The three bines can be in a ribbon shape or a round shape.

4. Multi-Start Twist – This type of twist has four or five bines and four or five starting points.

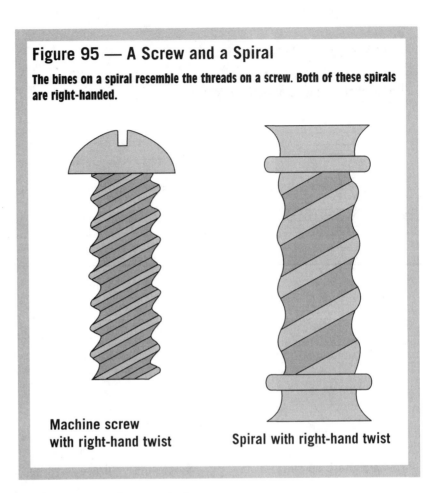

Figure 95 — A Screw and a Spiral

The bines on a spiral resemble the threads on a screw. Both of these spirals are right-handed.

Machine screw with right-hand twist

Spiral with right-hand twist

Rule of Thumb

The simplest way to **understand a helix** is to make a right-angled triangle of paper and to wrap it around a cylinder. The "lead" of the helix is the distance it advances along the cylinder in one complete wrap.

Figure 96 — Pitch and Lead

In a single-bine spiral (barley twist) the lead equals the pitch. In a double-bine spiral the pitch is one-half the lead.

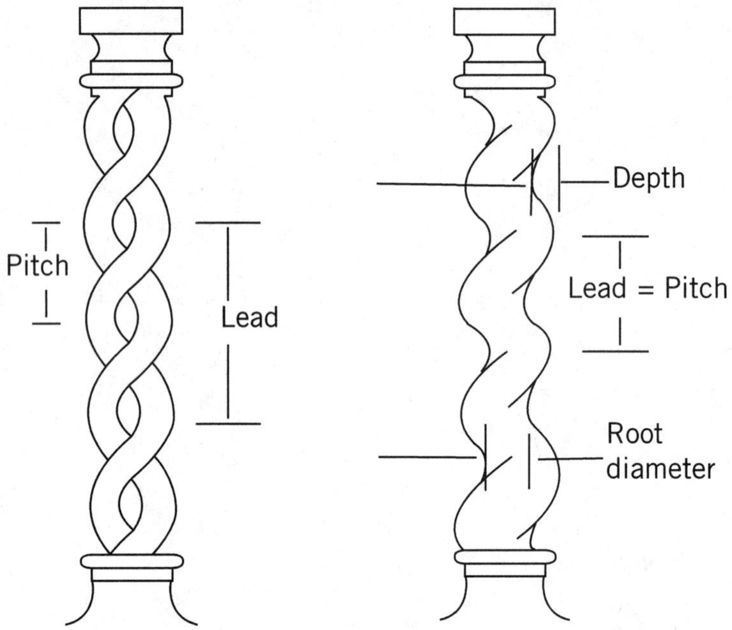

Pitch

Lead

Double-bine spiral

Depth

Lead = Pitch

Root diameter

Single-bine spiral

5. Rope Twist – This spiral has six bines and when done correctly, it resembles a rope.

6. Cable Twist – This type has nine bines and nine starting points. The bines are packed so closely together that the finished twist resembles a cable.

Wood

When you choose wood for a spiral, remember that most of the labor will be done with hand tools. Select straight-grained wood that carves well, such as walnut or mahogany — you'll be

carving and filing from all directions, so avoid a wood that splinters or breaks. Pick a wood with uniform colors throughout — the emphasis of the final piece will be on shape, so prominent wood grain will be a visual distraction. Omit very hard woods such maples, rosewood and teak — these are difficult to work with hand tools. Some kiln-dried woods, such as ash and oak, are prone to chip or tear-out when carved across the grain. You may want to practice on softer, less expensive wood such as pine, alder, or poplar. These woods are quite acceptable for mouldings and pieces that will be painted or stained.

Pitch and Lead

A spiral resembles a screw thread in that it has both 'pitch' and 'lead.' Pitch is the distance from center to center of consecutive ridges or bines. Lead is the distance one bine advances along the cylinder in one revolution. In a single-bine spiral, pitch and lead are the same. In a double-bine spiral, the lead is twice the pitch. See **Figure 96**.

A spiral with a short pitch and great depth will be weak because much of the long grain has been removed, leaving mostly cross grain. A longer pitch will be stronger but less pleasing to the eye. A delicate balance is needed.

Before starting on the spiral select a suitable pitch — the distance the twist will advance in one rotation. The most common pitch for a single bine roughly equals the diameter of the workpiece. So a workpiece 1½ inches in diameter commonly has a pitch of 1¼ inch to 1¾ inches. The exact pitch will be determined by the total length of the spiral because the length should be divided into a number of equal spaces each representing one complete rotation of the bine. The bine should begin and end on the same side of the cylinder.

Math

Problem 1: We are planning the layout of a single-bine spiral. If the diameter of the cylinder is 1½ inches and we want the spiral length to be about 18½ inches, what could the pitch be? (See **Figure 96**). Remember that the pitch should be approximately equal to the diameter and the bine should begin and end on the same side of the cylinder.

Solution 1a:

18.5" ÷ 1.5" = 12.33 turns

Using a pitch of 1½ inches will result in the bine starting on one plane at the top of the cylinder and ending one-third of the way around the cylinder at the bottom. Because we want a spiral bine to begin and end in the same plane, we have to adjust the pitch. Thus, we would

Figure 97 — Laying out a Single Spiral

A common,single spiral is laid out by dividing the cylinder into equal sectors each about the same length as the diameter of the cylinder (a). Each sector is then sub-divided into quarters (b). A paper tape (c) is used to measure the circumference and divide it into four quadrants. Four longitudinal lines are drawn (d) through the quadrant points — the left-handed spiral cut-line is drawn (e).

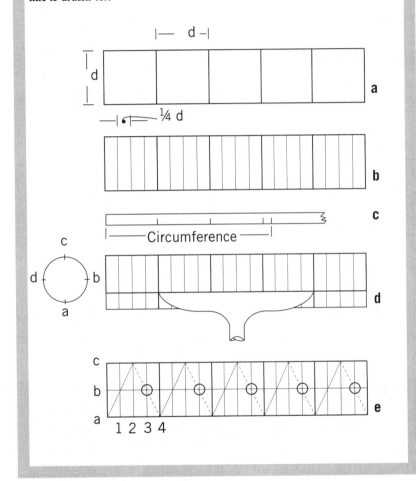

first try 12 equal-length sections.

12 x 1.5" = 18"

Therefore, we could shorten the length of the spiral from 18½ inches to 18 inches and use a 1½ inch pitch.

Solution 1b:

18.5" ÷ 1.5" = 12.33 turns

Rule of Thumb

1. **Design twists** to suit the furniture and not the other way around.

2. **Traditionally, furniture** should have left- and right-handed twists on the left and right sides.

3. **If the furniture piece** has an odd number of twists on it, the bines should all run in the same direction.

4. **A table** with four spiral legs should have alternating left and right twists.

Rule of Thumb

Normally the lathe is the only common woodworking machine that **moves the workpiece** against a stationary tool, all the other machines move the rotating tool into the stationary workpiece. However when you want to make a twist turning, or helix, you'd use the lathe as a jig to hold the workpiece while you carved it with other tools.

$$12.33 - 12.0 = 0.33$$
$$0.33 \div 12 = 0.0275$$
$$0.0275 \times 32 = 0.88 / 32$$
$$\approx \tfrac{1}{32}''$$

Make the pitch $\tfrac{1}{32}$ inches bigger:

$$1\tfrac{1}{2}'' + \tfrac{1}{32}'' = 1\tfrac{17}{32}''$$

This pitch ($1\tfrac{17}{32}$ inches) is close enough to $1\tfrac{1}{2}$ inches so the spiral will be pleasing to the eye.

Laying Out a Single Spiral

Figure 97 shows a method of laying out a barley twist on a turned piece, as follows:

Divide the Cylinder into Circular Sections

1. **Turn the part** to be carved as a plain cylinder. Keep the workpiece on the lathe.

2. **Measure** the diameter of the cylinder with calipers.

3. **Divide** the cylinder lengthwise into equal sections, each section being of a length approximately equal to the diameter. Make the spiral segment of the cylinder longer or shorter so the helix will end on an even sector or else adjust the size of the sectors. Rotate the cylinder by hand and mark these lines with a pencil, **Figure 97a**.

4. **Divide** each of the sections into four equal parts and mark these lines. See **Figure 97b**.

Divide the Cylinder into Four Longitudinal Sectors

5. **To divide** the circumference of the workpiece, wrap a piece of paper (or tape) around the cylinder and trim it so the ends meet. Put the paper on the workbench and divide it into four parts with a ruler or by folding it in half once and then in half again. The fold marks will quarter the cylinder (see **Figure 97c**). Use this paper ruler to mark the four quarters around the cylinder. You can also use the lathe index head to quarter the cylinder, or use the four corners of the original square piece.

6. **Use a long** lathe T-rest to draw four longitudinal lines at the points laid out by the paper strip dividing the circumference into fourths (a, b, c and d). See **Figure 97d**.

Draw the Spiral

7. **Start the spiral** line at the left end of the cylinder (for a left-handed thread) on one of the horizontal lines, for example 'a'. With a red pencil, join point 'a' to the intersection of the line 'b' and quadrant 1.

8. **Connect the points** to continue the spiral to line 'c' and quadrant 2, then to line 'd' and quadrant 3 and around the cylinder back to line 'a'. It isn't necessary to use a straight-edge to draw the red spiral line — just eyeball it.

9. One complete revolution of the spiral line has now been drawn. Continue drawing the spiral to the other end of the cylinder. See **Figure 97e**.

10. By starting the spiral line at 'a' and moving upward through 'b' to 'c', you will draw from left to right, creating a left-hand twist. To draw a right-hand twist, start from the right end of the cylinder and draw the diagonal upwards from right to left.

Cutting the Spiral

1. A handy depth marker can be made by clamping a straight piece of wood to one side of a backsaw, leaving enough blade exposed to cut the kerf as in **Figure 98**. If you don't use a depth gauge, count the saw strokes so you cut the kerf to the same depth throughout.

2. Saw along the heavy diagonal line as you slowly revolve the cylinder by hand. Use a hacksaw, a backsaw, or any handsaw that feels right. The usual depth is about one-quarter of the diameter of the cylinder. See **Figure 99a**. Any slight wandering made with the pencil will be straightened out by the saw.

3. Chop to the bottom of the kerf on one side with a ½ inch chisel.

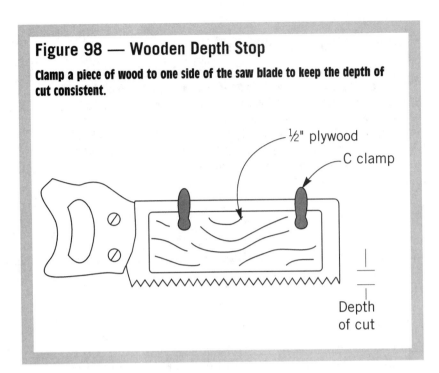

Figure 98 — Wooden Depth Stop

Clamp a piece of wood to one side of the saw blade to keep the depth of cut consistent.

½" plywood

C clamp

Depth of cut

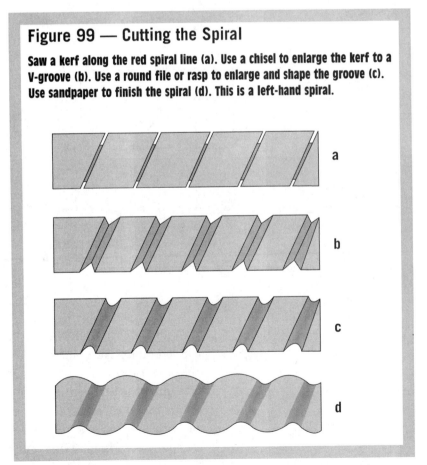

Figure 99 — Cutting the Spiral

Saw a kerf along the red spiral line (a). Use a chisel to enlarge the kerf to a V-groove (b). Use a round file or rasp to enlarge and shape the groove (c). Use sandpaper to finish the spiral (d). This is a left-hand spiral.

a

b

c

d

Figure 100 — Double Spiral

Divide the cylinder into equal sectors. The single-flute spiral (a) begins at point 1 and advances one diameter with each revolution. A double-bine spiral (b) starts at points 1 and 5 and each bine advances two diameters with each revolution. The three-flute spiral (c) begins at point 1 and at two other points one-third and two-thirds around the circle. The four-flute spirals begin at points 1, 3, 5, and 7. The three- and four-bine twists also advance two diameters with each revolution.

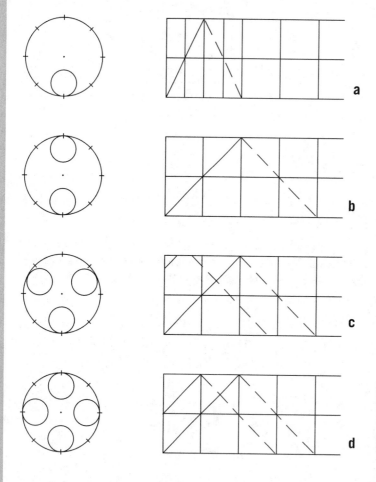

a

b

c

d

5. Round along the bottom of the V-groove with a round file or a Sur-form rasp. See **Figure 99c**.

6. Round over the edges with a half-round file, rasp, or small plane. These steps are shown in **Figure 99a** through **Figure 99d**.

7. Run the lathe at about 200 rpm and sand the entire surface, starting at 80-grit and moving through 120, 180, and 220-grit. Many light strokes will smooth out all the roughness. Because wood tends to heat-harden, work slowly though 80-120-220-320 grit sandpaper, removing the scratches from each grit before going to the next. It is difficult to remove 80-grit scratches using 320 paper after they have been heat-hardened.

8. If your lathe won't run as slow as 200 RPM, rig the spiral on your drill press. Power-sanding will save at least 30 minutes over hand-sanding time.

9. As a last resort, do the sanding by hand.

Laying Out a Double Spiral

1. A double spiral is laid out in much the same manner as the single-bine except that there are two starting points. One spiral starts at point 1 and another spiral begins at point 5. See **Figure 100b**.

4. Turn the workpiece end-for-end on the lathe and chisel the other side of the kerf making a V-groove. Reversing the piece allows you to cut with the grain on both sides of the kerf for less chipping. See **Figure 99b**.

2. One diagonal ridge line is drawn as before, but it will advance the distance of two pitch lines with each revolution of the workpiece.

3. An identical second ridge line is then drawn from Line 3, parallel to the first ridge line.

4. Three- or four-bine spirals can be made in a similar manner by starting the additional bines at the appropriate positions. See **Figure 100c and 100d**.

Cutting the Helix with a Table Saw

A table saw can be used to cut the initial kerf, as shown in **Figure 102**. A blank cylinder, held against an angled fence and rotated over the blade will feed itself along the fence in a regular manner. The pitch of the resulting helical kerf is governed by the angle of the fence. The bulk of the waste can be machined away on the table saw with a molding head on the saw arbor and a guide pin running in the kerf. Once the kerf is cut on the table saw you can also use a router mounted in a table with a guide pin to shape the groove. A band saw works also — tilt the table to the pitch angle and clamp a fence for depth. The process is as follows:

1. Turn a blank cylinder and drill center holes in each end. Attach square blocks to each end

Figure 101 — Cutting Spirals on the Table Saw

In all cases, the depth of cut is ¼ inch. Set the miter angle depending on the diameter of the inner cylinder; the outer diameter minus ½ inch. The pitch is equal to the diameter of the cylinder. Do not cut deeper than ¼ inch.

Cylinder Diameter (In. OD)	Kerf Depth (Inches)	Cylinder Diameter (In. ID)	Fence Angle (degrees)
1	0.25	0.5	32.5
1.25	0.25	0.75	28.0
1.5	0.25	1	25.5
1.75	0.25	1.25	24.0
2	0.25	1.5	23.0
2.25	0.25	1.75	22.3
2.5	0.25	2	21.7
2.75	0.25	2.25	21.3
3	0.25	2.5	20.9

Calculator: TanA = Pitch/Pi x Diameter at bottom of kerf
Excel Formula =ATAN(Cylinder OD/(3.14*Cylinder ID))*180/3.14

with wood screws so the cylinder is held securely but rotates freely. See **Figure 102**.

The blocks hold the cylinder securely, allow the cylinder to rotate freely and allow you to keep your fingers away from the blade.

2. Choose the pitch angle and set the miter gauge. When the fence slopes away from the operator from right to left as in **Figure 102**, the resulting helix will be like a left-hand thread. When the fence slopes away from left to right, the helix will be right-handed. The pitch angle (α) and the pitch (P) can be figured by the following formula, where (D) will equal the cylinder diameter minus two times the depth of the kerf.

Rule of Thumb

In a twist with a single strand, or bine, the pitch and the lead are the same, that is, the distance from one bine to the next is the same distance the twist advances in one revolution. In a twist with a double bine, the lead is twice the pitch. In single twists for furniture, the pitch and the lead should about equal the diameter of the workpiece.

Figure 102 — Cutting Spirals on the Table Saw

Position the fence so the cylinder is directly over the center of the blade. The end blocks allow the cylindrical stock to rotate freely. This setup will yield a left-hand twist with a pitch equal to the cylinder diameter.

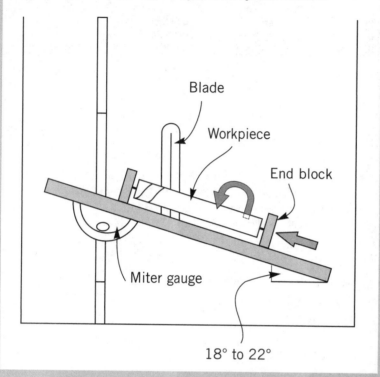

Blade

Workpiece

End block

Miter gauge

18° to 22°

Rule of Thumb

Sawing a spiral on the table saw can be dangerous. If the kerf is too deep — from the blade viewpoint it's an S-curve — the blade might jam and bind. Let the blade only cut ¼ inch deep.

See **Figure 101** for fence angle single-pitch settings for different cylinder diameters.

3. Raise the blade so it will cut a kerf ¼ inch deep in the cylinder. Note: a deeper kerf can cause the blade to bind.

4. Clamp a fence angled at 23° across the saw table just before the center of the saw blade such that the center of the cylinder will be directly over the center of the blade. The fence should be substantial, like a 2 x 4, and at least twice as long as the cylinder

blank plus the two end blocks.

5. Turn on the saw and lower the left end of the cylinder onto the blade with the end blocks tight against the fence. Rotate the cylinder as shown in **Figure 102** and allow the wood to feed along the fence from right to left as the blocks slide along the fence.

6. After cutting the helical kerf, remount the cylinder on the lathe for carving, or you can further shape it with a cutting head on the table saw arbor as follows:

7. Replace the saw blade with cove cutter heads or a dado blade and make a snugly fitting wooden insert for the table saw throat.

8. Drive a finishing nail into the face of the fence at mid-height of the cylinder and directly over the center of the blade. File the head of the nail smooth and let it protrude just enough to reach about 1/8 inch into the cylinder kerf. Test the cylinder to be sure that the workpiece rotates freely and that the nail rides in the kerf.

9. Now turn on the saw and rotate the workpiece slowly into the cutter, starting again at the left end. The pin will automatically feed the stock. This process must be done in one pass because the cut removes the guide kerf.

10. **Mount** the cylinder on the lathe and shape the twist with files and rasps.

Math

Tan α = P ÷ π D

Where α = the miter angle, P = pitch, π = 3.14 and D = diameter of the cylinder at the bottom of the kerf.

Problem 1: We have a cylinder 2 inches in diameter and we want to cut a helical kerf ¼ inch deep. The pitch of the helix is to be equal to the diameter of the cylinder.

Solution 1:

Tan α = P ÷ π D

Where P = 2 and D = 2 – (2 x ¼)

Tan α = 2 ÷ [3.14 x 2 - (2 x ¼)] = 2 ÷ 3.14 x 1.5 = 0.42

Arctan 0.42 = 23°

In a computer spreadsheet like Excel, use this formula:

=ARCTAN(2 ÷ (3.14x1.5)) * 180 ÷ 3.14

Tapers

To lay out a tapered spiral, the pitch diminishes as the diameter of the workpiece gets smaller. See **Figure 103**.

1. **Strike four lines** along the length of the taper to divide the

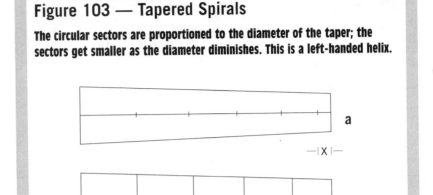

Figure 103 — Tapered Spirals

The circular sectors are proportioned to the diameter of the taper; the sectors get smaller as the diameter diminishes. This is a left-handed helix.

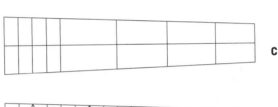

cylinder into four longitudinal sectors.

2. **Measure** the diameter of the taper's large end and mark this distance on one of the four longitudinal lines.

3. **At this mark** measure the diameter again, and mark this length along the same line.

4. **Repeat** this process until you reach the small end of the taper. Note in **Figure 103a** that the pitch lines do not reach the end of the taper. There is the extra length 'x'.

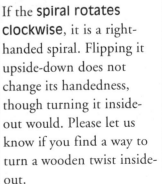

Rule of Thumb

If the **spiral rotates clockwise**, it is a right-handed spiral. Flipping it upside-down does not change its handedness, though turning it inside-out would. Please let us know if you find a way to turn a wooden twist inside-out.

Figure 104 — Flame Finial

The flame finial (b) looks very much like the morning-glory bud (c).

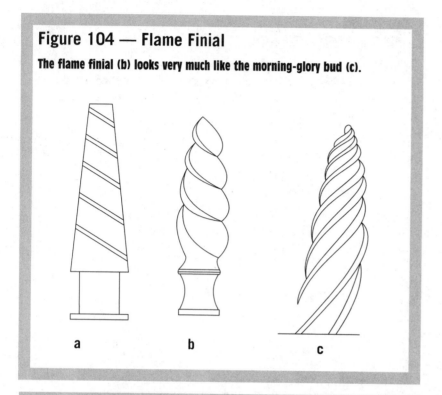

a   b   c

Figure 105 — A V-block Jig

Use this V-block jig to hold the cylinder while drilling for a hollow spiral. The workpiece needs to travel almost twice its length, so make the V-block plenty long.

into four parts, **Figure 103c.**

7. **Draw** in the helix ridge lines and proceed with the cuts, as in straight work. The line shown in **Figure 103d** will generate a left-handed spiral.

8. **To draw** a right-handed spiral, start at the right end, and rotate the cylinder towards you in the normal direction that a lathe rotates as you draw the diagonal line upward from right to left.

Flame Finial

To make a flame finial, follow steps 1 through 6 above for tapers, then:

7. **Draw** diagonal ridge lines starting from the large end of the taper. Use double lines about ⅛ inches apart. See **Figure 104**.

8. **Use gouges** and files to remove the waste in the hollows, avoiding the double lines.

Hollow Spirals

Another variation of the double or triple helix is the hollow twist where the bines are separated by an opening. Hollow or open twists generally lack sufficient strength for furniture legs but are quite effective as candlesticks or lamp bases.

Hollow Spiral – Method 1

The triple-bine hollow spiral is laid out as follows:

5. **Adjust** the four pitch lines so the distance 'x' is distributed equally among the five sections, as shown in **Figure 103b.**

6. **Divide** each of the sections

1. **Mark** the helix lines.

2. **Remove** the cylinder from the lathe and hold it in a V-block on the drill press. Drill holes in the cylinder, leaving the red ridge lines intact. Drill halfway through from each side to avoid splintering, **Figure 105**.

3. **Put the workpiece** back on the lathe and shape each bine with rasps, files, and finally with sand paper.

Hollow Spiral – Method 2

Short hollow spirals can be drilled out from the ends. The hole should be about 40% of the diameter. For example, if the cylinder is 1½ inches in diameter, then use a ⅝ inch drill.

1.5" x 0.40 = 0.60"
0.60" x 16 = 9.6/16"
≈ 10/16" = 5/8"

Drill a ⅝ inch hole down the center of the cylinder and proceed to cut the twist or spiral as before.

Laying Out a Spiral

Here is an easy way to mark a diagonal line around a cylinder:

1. **Wrap a string** around the workpiece the same number of times you want the bines to circle the cylinder — say, three times.

2. **Cut** the string.

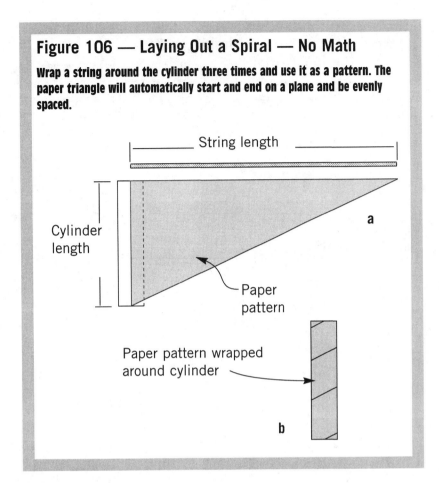

Figure 106 — Laying Out a Spiral — No Math

Wrap a string around the cylinder three times and use it as a pattern. The paper triangle will automatically start and end on a plane and be evenly spaced.

String length

Cylinder length

a

Paper pattern

Paper pattern wrapped around cylinder

b

3. **Cut** a piece of paper the same length as the string. At one corner of the paper, mark off the length of the cylinder.

4. **Starting** at this mark, cut a diagonal line to the other end of the paper (the hypotenuse), making a long triangle. See **Figure 106a.**

5. **Wrap** the triangle around the cylinder with its bottom edge aligned with the bottom of the wooden cylinder.

6. **Mark** along the edge of the triangle as you go. This

Rule of Thumb

When you want to make a **twist turning**, select straight-grained wood that will not splinter or break, and look for uniform color throughout. If you were to make a twist using highly figured wood like tiger maple, the shapes would be at war with the wood figure.

Figure 107 —
The Rope Twist

The rope twist has six tightly packed bines. This one is right-handed.

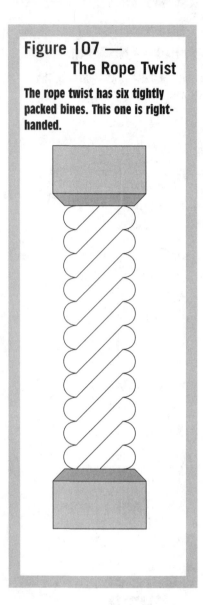

Figure 108 — The Rope Twist

The rope twist has six closely packed bines and looks like a rope. On the cylinder, draw six parallel lines along the length (one line for each bine) and then equally spaced circles around the cylinder. Each bine will make one complete rotation every six squares; the pitch will be six times the lead.

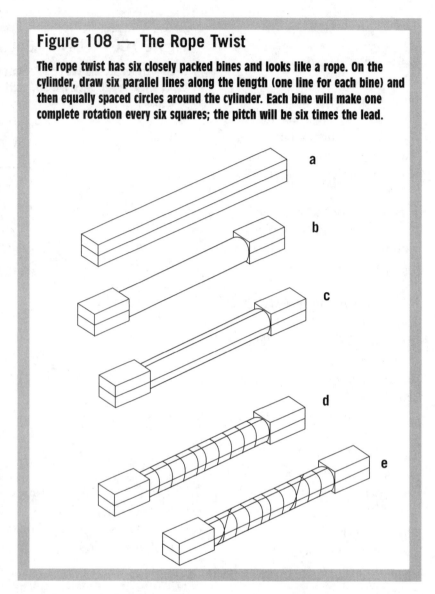

procedure works because a twist (screw) is merely an inclined plane (triangle) wrapped around a cylinder. See **Figure 106b**.

Making a Rope Twist

The Federal furniture period in the United States started about 1780 and lasted for nearly 50 years. Sheraton, Hepplewhite, and Chippendale designed and made furniture that was delicate and light in appearance. In addition to using twists as legs and stretchers for chairs and cabinets, they used carved spirals as decoration for mirrors, picture frames, and panels.

The design used most often for decoration was the rope twist, **Figure 107,** which has six bines perfectly parallel and tightly packed as they wind up the shank. After being carved, the piece was cut apart lengthwise and the back planed smooth. Usually, two twists were made and a left- and right-handed pair was used on the piece of furniture. This method left an identical set of twists for another piece of furniture. Instead of sawing the finished spiral apart, I suggest temporarily holding two pieces together and separating them later.

1. **Prepare the wood** piece by joining two pieces of straight-grained wood such as mahogany or walnut, see **Figure 108a**. If the decorative piece is to be stained or painted later, use poplar or another soft wood. Use double-sided tape in the middle and wrap the ends with fiberglass reinforced strapping tape. If the boards are overlong, the ends could be glued and later cut off to separate the pieces.

2. **Turn the cylinder** to the length and diameter required. See **Figure 108b**.

3. **Wrap a narrow** piece of paper around the cylinder and mark where the end laps the paper. Cut the strip at this point and divide the strip into six sections. Mark the points with a black pen.

4. **Wrap the paper** strip around the cylinder and mark off six

sections. See **Figure 108c**.

5. **Using** the long lathe tool rest, draw longitudinal lines with a soft pencil.

6. **Divide the cylinder** into equal sections (**Figure 108d**). If the last mark does not coincide with the end of the cylinder, then make marks on the cylinder starting from the opposite end. Divide these double marks and draw a line around the cylinder at each point.

7. **For a left-handed** twist, start at the left end and rotate the cylinder by hand toward you as you draw the diagonal line upwards.

8. **Draw all six** of the diagonals. See **Figure 108e**.

9. **Use a small backsaw** and cut on the diagonal lines to a depth of ⅛ inch to ¼ inch.

10. **Use chisels**, knives, rasps and files to cut the grooves. Sand smooth, and separate the two halves.

Reference: The chair in Figure 94 is from Charles Hayward's **_Period Furniture Designs,_** Sterling, 1956.

Rule of Thumb

Spirals and helices come in right-handed and left-handed forms. Standard screws and bolts are right-handed helices, as are the twisted strands of DNA. Twisted animal horns usually come in a right and a left, which may be why furniture decorated with twist turnings usually has one twisting one direction and the other twisting in the opposite direction.

Rule of Thumb

How to Lay out Left- and Right-hand Spirals

1. To lay out a right-handed spiral, start on the right end of the cylinder and draw the diagonal line up and to the left.

2. To lay out a left-handed spiral, start on the left end of the cylinder and draw the diagonal line up and to the right.

3. A right-handed spiral starts at the right end of the cylinder and a left-handed spiral starts at the left end of the cylinder.

CHAPTER 11

Mechanics — Simple and Complex

There are seven primary mechanical contrivances that are the basis for all our wood working machines and tools. These seven mechanical powers are based upon only two fundamental principles — the lever and the inclined plane. Understanding how these seven basic devices operate and the mechanical advantages derived from each will help you understand how your tools work.

Figure 109 — Seven Mechanical Powers

The lever (1), the wheel and axle (2), the cord and pulley (3), and the toothed wheel (4) all use the principle of the lever. The inclined plane (5), the wedge (6), and the screw (7) operate on the principle of the inclined plane.

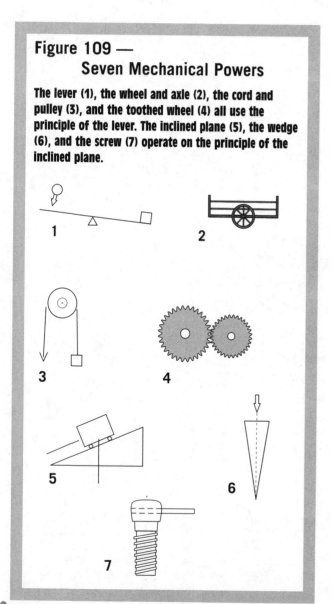

These mechanical powers (see **Figure 109**) are grouped according to which principle pertains: the lever (1), the wheel and axle (2), the cord and pulley (3), and the toothed wheel (4) — all operate on the principle of the lever. The inclined plane (5), the wedge (6), and the screw (7) follow the principle of the inclined plane.

These simple contrivances are commonly used for power transmission where some benefit is gained; for example the lever, where a small force applied over a long distance can move a heavy weight over a short distance.

The complex mechanisms discussed in the second part of this chapter are mostly devices to change the direction of a force, for example to change rotary motion to linear or linear motion to rotary. These inventions appear very complicated but a careful study of the principles employed by each will show they all still employ one or more of the seven basic mechanical powers.

Machines

A machine cannot generate work; it can only utilize or transmit the force that is applied to it. The mechanical advantage of any machine is the ratio of the resulting work to the applied force. Work is defined as the product of force times the distance through which the force acts. The efficiency of any machine is the ratio of the work done by the machine to the force applied. The efficiency is always less than 100 percent, because a certain amount of work is always expended in overcoming friction.

Definitions
The science of mechanics

deals with the effects of forces in causing or preventing motion. Different terms used in mechanics need clarification:

Statics deals with bodies in equilibrium and the forces acting upon them that cause them to remain at rest or to move with uniform velocity.

Dynamics deals with bodies not in equilibrium and the forces acting on them that cause them to move with non-uniform velocity.

Kinetics deals with both the forces acting on bodies and the motions they cause.

Kinematics deals only with the motions of bodies without reference to the forces that cause them.

Force is a push or a pull which may result from the force of contact between bodies, or from a force, such as magnetism or gravity, in which no direct contact takes place.

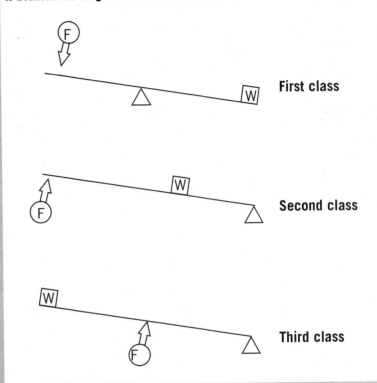

Figure 110 — The Three Classes of Lever

The three classes of lever differ as to whether the fulcrum (the support or pivot point) is between the force and the weight (First Class), the weight is between the fulcrum and the force (Second Class), or whether the force is between the weight and the fulcrum (Third Class).

First class

Second class

Third class

Matter is any substance that occupies space — gases, liquids, solids, electrons, molecules, atoms etc. These all fit the definition.

Inertia causes matter to resist change in its motion or state of rest.

Mass is a measure of the inertia of a body.

Work is the product of force multiplied by distance and is

Rule of Thumb

Work = Force x Distance

Figure 111 — First Class Lever

Force multiplied by the arm length (L) is equal to the weight multiplied by the length of the weight arm (l).

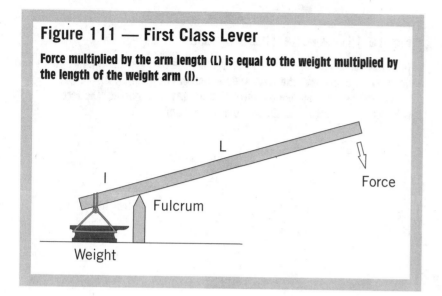

The Seven Simple Mechanical Powers
1. Levers

There are three classes of lever, differentiated by the relationship between fulcrum and weight (see **Figure 110**).

First Class Lever - The fulcrum is between the force and the load. This type of lever is illustrated by the teeter-totter, crowbar, prybar, and, when the levers are criss-crossed, pliers, shears, and scissors. The principle of the lever is that the force multiplied by the length of the power arm is equal to the weight multiplied by the weight arm (see **Figure 111**).

Math

Where F = Force, W = Weight, l = Weight arm length, L = Force arm length.

$$F = (W \times l) \div L$$
$$W = (F \times L) \div l$$
$$L = (W \times l) \div F$$
$$l = (F \times L) \div W$$

Problem 1: We have an anvil weighing 160 pounds (see **Figure 111**). We've hooked a harness around both ends and want to raise it up to slide a dolly underneath. We have a 6 foot iron bar and some wooden blocks. Will we be able to lift the anvil at least 6 inches off the ground?

expressed by a combination of units such as foot-pounds, inch-pounds, or meter-kilograms.

Power is the product of force times distance divided by time. It measures the performance of a given amount of work in a given time. Power is expressed in foot-pounds per minute, foot-pounds per second, or kilogram-meters per second.

Horsepower is the unit of power that has been adopted for engineering work. One horsepower is equal to 33,000 foot-pounds per minute or 550 foot-pounds per second. See Woodworkers' Essential Chapter 22, **Horsepower — Real & Imagined** for more on this.

Kilowatt, used in electrical work, equals 1.34 horsepower; 1 horsepower equals 0.746 kilowatt.

Solution 1: We can use the principle of the First Class Lever, where the force 'F' and distance 'L' are equal to the weight 'W' and distance 'l'.

Force F = (W x l) ÷ L

Weight W = 160, l = 1 foot, L = 5 feet. How much force will be required to lift the anvil?

F = (W x l) ÷ L

F = (160 x 1) ÷ 5

F = 160 ÷ 5 = 32 pounds

Note: in this problem, the height of the wooden block acting as the fulcrum is immaterial. If the anvil is raised and the dolly will not fit underneath, a higher block can be used and the same 32 pounds of force will raise the same weight higher.

Figure 112 shows the simplest weighing machine, another example of a First Class Lever, where the scale is balanced at its pivot point P. The smaller weight is hung seven divisions from the pivot; the larger weight is three divisions from P. Therefore, from the principle of the lever, seven times the smaller weight equals three times the weight of the larger. This means the larger weight is 7 ÷ 3 or 2⅓ times as great as the smaller.

Second Class Lever - The weight is between the force and the fulcrum. A good example of the second class lever is a long

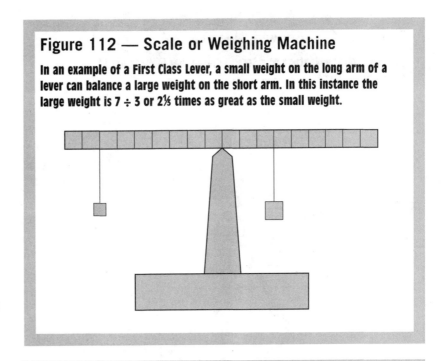

Figure 112 — Scale or Weighing Machine

In an example of a First Class Lever, a small weight on the long arm of a lever can balance a large weight on the short arm. In this instance the large weight is 7 ÷ 3 or 2⅓ times as great as the small weight.

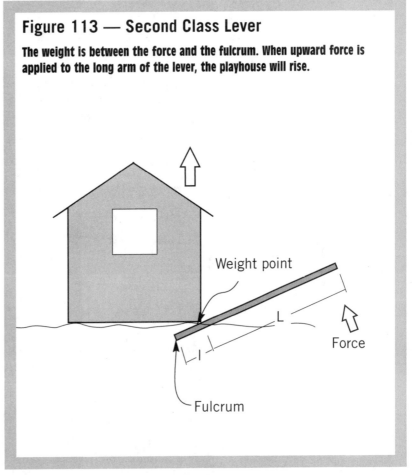

Figure 113 — Second Class Lever

The weight is between the force and the fulcrum. When upward force is applied to the long arm of the lever, the playhouse will rise.

Weight point

L

Force

l

Fulcrum

Figure 114 — Second Class Lever

The mechanical advantage of a Second Class Lever is illustrated by a shop mortising machine.

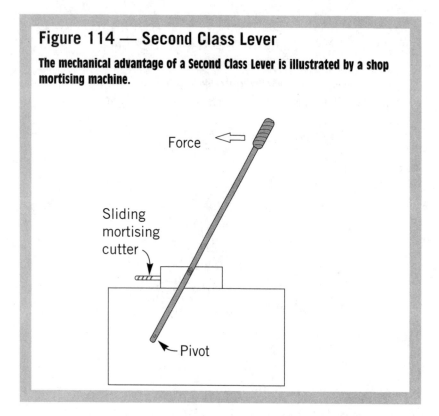

Force

Sliding
mortising
cutter

Pivot

pry-bar that is slid under a weight and the long end of the bar is lifted (see **Figure 113**). The wheel barrow is another example of a second class lever.

Math

$$F : W = l : L$$

$$F \times L = W \times l$$

$$\text{Force } F = (W \times l) \div L$$

$$\text{Weight } W = (F \times L) \div l$$

$$\text{Length } L = (W \times l) \div F$$

$$\text{Length } l = (F \times L) \div W$$

Problem 2: You want to raise the corner of the kid's playhouse to slide a concrete brick underneath. You figure the structure weighs about 1000 pounds so you may have to lift 500 pounds. You have a sturdy 8 foot long piece of 2x4 and can stick it under the house 12 inches. How much oomph is this going to require?

Solution 2: By putting 12 inches of the lever (l) under the house, you will have 7 feet for the force length (L).

$$\text{Force } F = (W \times l) \div L$$

$$F = (500 \times 1) \div 7$$

$$F = 500 \div 7 = 71 \text{ pounds}$$

Note that if you had dragged a concrete block over and used it as a fulcrum (First Class Lever) the math would have been the same. Lifting the house would still require 71 pounds of force but now you could use your body weight as part of the force.

Another example of a Second Class Lever is the shop mortiser, where the power of the arm is applied between the fulcrum and the force (see **Figure 114**). The longer the arm, the easier it is to push the cutter into the workpiece.

Third Class Lever – The force is between the fulcrum and the weight. In the Third Class Lever there is always a mechanical disadvantage where power is sacrificed for quick movement (see **Figure 115**). A good example of a double Third Class Lever is a set of salad tongs. The user squeezes the two handles and the jaws snap shut.

Math

$$F : L = W : l$$

$$F = W \times L \div l$$

The third class lever is also illustrated by the human forearm (see **Figure 116**) where the fulcrum is at the elbow joint, the weight is in the hand, and the force is applied through a tendon from the biceps muscle attached near the elbow. The fist, with the weight of a hardball, moves rapidly forward and throws the ball.

Complicated Lever Systems

The lever systems above were straightforward. In all cases the force times length was equal to the weight times length.

$$F \times L = W \times l$$

The lengths and the weights become harder to determine in the case shown in **Figure 117**, when three or more weights act on a single lever.

Math

$$F \times L = (W_1 \times l_1) + (W_2 \times l_2) + (W_3 \times l_3)$$

$$L = (W_1 \times l_1) + (W_2 \times l_2) + (W_3 + x l_3) \div F$$

$$F = (W_1 \times l_1) + (W_2 \times l_2) + (W_3 \times l_3) \div L$$

Problem 3: We are trying to remove a large tree stump and estimate the weight at 1000 pounds. I have a 12 foot long iron pipe for a lever and with my

Figure 115 — Third Class Lever

The force is between the fulcrum and the weight. The same math applies here as in the First and Second Class Levers. A salad tong is a double lever system.

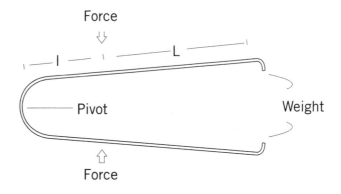

Figure 116 — Third Class Lever

In the human forearm, the force is between the fulcrum and the weight. The hand moves forward quickly and throws; force is sacrificed for rapid movement.

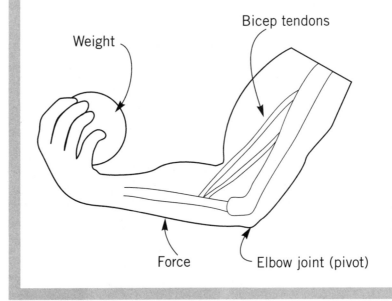

two buddies, Dan and Paul, can we pull this stump?

Solution 3: By pushing the lever 2 feet under the stump and using the edge of the hole as the pivot, we can use 10 feet of pipe

Figure 117 — A Complicated Lever System

Each weight and its corresponding arm length are added together to find the total weight and arm length. This value, placed in the formula, is used to solve the equation for Force F.

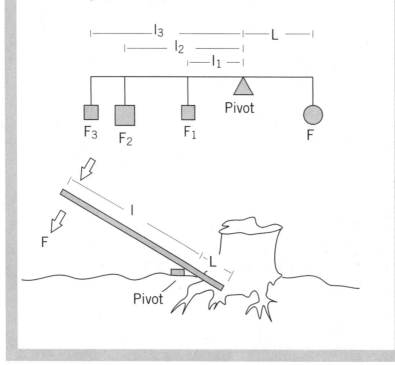

In this example, my two buddies and I should be able to pop that 1000 pound stump out easily. Editor's note: Ha.

2. Wheel and Axle

This contrivance consists of two cylinders of different sizes connected together and turning about a common axis. The two cylinders can be attached rigidly together or the wheel may rotate freely around the axle (see **Figure 118**). The wheel with the larger diameter will balance a larger force at the axle when a small force is applied at its circumference. If the axle is fixed to the body of a carriage and the wheel loosely mounted to revolve on it, the carriage can be drawn along with slight effort, requiring a push or pull representing only a small fraction of the weight of the carriage. The distance the carriage will travel for each revolution of the wheel depends on the diameter of the wheel.

$$\text{Distance traveled} = \pi d$$

Problem 4: With a 32 inch diameter wheel, what distance will a cart travel during one revolution of the wheel?

Solution 4:

$$\text{Distance traveled} = \pi d$$

$$\text{Distance} = 32 \times 3.14 = 100.5"$$

3. Cords and Pulleys

There is no mechanical advantage with a single fixed

as the force distance. We'll position ourselves at 10, 9 and 8 feet along the pipe.

Let $F_1 = 200$, $F_2 = 210$ and $F_3 = 185$ pounds.

Let $l_1 = 8$, $l_2 = 9$ and $l_3 = 10$ feet.

L = 2 feet and Force is unknown. We need to lift 1000 pounds.

$$F = (F_1 \times l_1) + (F_2 \times l_2) + (F_3 \times l_3) \div L$$

$$F = [(200 \times 8) + (210 \times 9) + (185 \times 10)] \div 2$$

$$F = (1600 + 1890 + 1850) \div 2$$

$$F = 5340 \div 2 = 2670 \text{ pounds.}$$

Rule of Thumb

The longer the lever, the less force needed.

pulley because the pulley wheel is considered to be a lever with the fulcrum at its center, thus the power arm and the weight arm of the lever each equal the radius of the wheel.

In **Figure 119**, the full force of the weight is carried by the cords around the weight pulley. The velocity with which weight W will be raised equals the velocity of the force at F.

Math

Force F = (W x l) ÷ L

Problem 5: If weight (W) is 100 pounds and the pulley is 10 inches in diameter, what force (F) is needed to lift the weight? See **Figure 119**.

Solution 5:

Force F = (W x l) ÷ L

F = (100 x 5) ÷ 5 = 500 ÷ 5 = 100 pounds

Windlass

In the windlass system, two different sized drums are mounted on the same shaft as in **Figure 120**. The weight is attached to the cord on the small drum and force is applied as a downward pull on the cord to the large drum. The force needed to lift the weight is directly proportional to the ratio of the diameters of the two drums.

F : W = r : R

F x R = W x r

F = (W x r) ÷ R

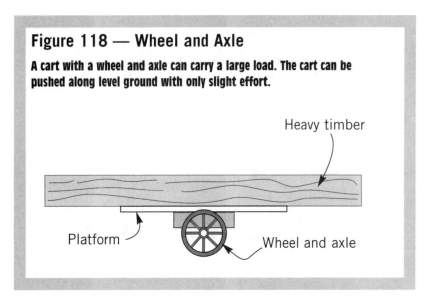

Figure 118 — Wheel and Axle

A cart with a wheel and axle can carry a large load. The cart can be pushed along level ground with only slight effort.

Heavy timber

Platform

Wheel and axle

W = (F x R) ÷ r

R = (W x r) ÷ F

r = (F x R) ÷ W

Problem 6: The radius (r) of the small drum on a windlass is 2 inches. What force (F) must be exerted to the large drum of 24 inches diameter, if one half ton (1000 pounds) is to be lifted? Here W = 1000, R = 12, r = 2.

Solution 6:

Force F = (W x r) ÷ R

F = (1000 x 2) ÷ 12

F = 2000 ÷ 12 = 167 pounds.

Note also that the rope on the large drum will travel six times farther than the rope on the small drum (12 ÷ 2 = 6).

Circumference C = πd = 3.14 x 24 = 75.4" (Drum #1)

C = πd = 3.14 x 4 = 12.6" (Drum #2)

75.4 ÷ 12.6 = 6

Figure 119 — Cord & Pulley

The velocity with which weight (W) will be raised is equal to the velocity of the force applied at F. There is no mechanical advantage (L = l) so, to balance, the force needed is equal to the weight.

L | l

Force

Weight

Figure 120 — Windlass

Force is applied as a downward pull on the cord to the large drum. The force needed to lift the weight is directly proportional to the ratio of the diameters of the two drums.

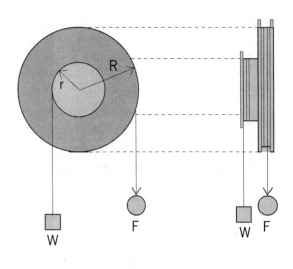

Figure 121 — Two Pulleys

One pulley is fixed and the second pulley carries the weight and moves freely. Because there are two cords attached to the weight-bearing pulley the mechanical advantage is two.

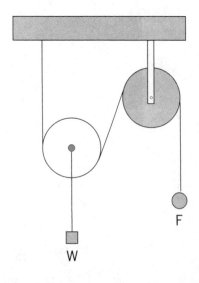

Two Pulleys

The two pulley system, as in **Figure 121**, features one fixed pulley and a second pulley that bears the weight and moves freely. The mechanical advantage in this system is two, thus a force of 50 pounds will lift 100 pounds of weight.

Four Pulleys

A hoist, as commonly used around the shop to lift heavy floor tools, is a combination of fixed and loose pulleys with one continuous rope connecting them as shown in **Figure 122**. In this diagram each block contains two movable wheels. The mechanical advantage of such an arrangement depends on the number of lines leading to the pulleys attached to the weight. Looking at **Figure 122** you see that the rope forms five vertical lines but that one of these leads from the upper pulley to the puller's hands; there are only four lines supporting the weight. Neglecting the loss due to friction and to the weight of the loose pulleys, a weight of four units can be balanced with a force of one unit. That is, a pull of 25 pounds will raise a weight of 100 pounds. But, in raising the 100 pounds one foot, each of the supporting lines must be shortened by the same amount so that the 25 pound applied force must move through four feet of rope.

Math

$$F = (1 \div n) \times W$$

Where F = Force, W = Weight and n = the number of ropes leading to the pulleys.

Problem 7: Referring to **Figure 122**, if weight (W) is equal to 450 pounds, what amount of force (F) will be required to lift this weight?

Solution 7:

Force $F = (1 \div n) \times W$

Where n = the number of pulleys and W = weight

Force $F = (1 \div n) \times W$

$F = (1 \div 4) \times 450 = 112.5$ pounds

If you had a combination of six pulleys in two blocks, there would be seven lines but only six would lead to a pulley bearing the weight, therefore n = 6.

Problem 8: If 200 pounds (W) is to be lifted, what force (F) will be required?

Solution 8:

Force $F = (1 \div n) \times W$

$F = (1 \div 6) \times 200$

≈ 33 pounds

Five Pulleys

While this setup (**Figure 123**) looks complicated, if you break it down you'll see it's a two-pulley system with five lines.

Math

$$F = (1 \div n) \times W$$

Where n = the number of lifting ropes

$F = 1 \div 5 \times 200 = 40$ pounds

The velocity with which W will be raised equals one fifth $(1 \div n)$ of the velocity of the force applied at F. Therefore if one pulls the line at 1 foot per second, the weight will lift at 1 foot every 5 seconds.

Problem 9: Referring to **Figure 123**, if weight (W) is 750 pounds, what force (F) is required to lift this weight?

Solution 9:

$F = (1 \div n) \times W$

$F = (1 \div 5) \times 750 = 150$ pounds

Elevator

The elevator (**Figure 124**) is a power-operated device for lifting and lowering passengers from one level to another and operates using the principle of a simple pulley. It consists of a car that runs between guide rails and is suspended from steel hoisting ropes. The weight of the car and its load is approximately balanced by the counter-weight. The weight to be hoisted or lowered by the drive motor is therefore never the total weight of the car and passengers, but only the relatively small difference between the counter-weight and the weight of the

Figure 122 — Four-Wheel Block and Tackle

In this hoist, the pulleys are put one above the other in a line. The mechanical advantage of this arrangement is 4.

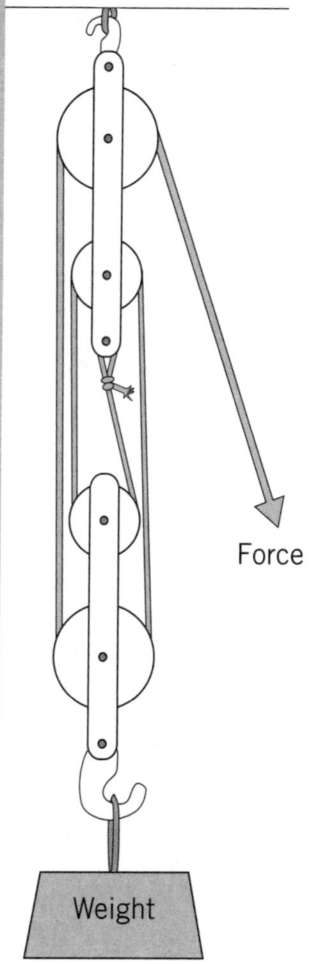

Force

Weight

Figure 123 — Block and Tackle

There are five parts of rope that touch a pulley at both ends, therefore n = 5 and the force (F) required to lift weight (W) is 1 ÷ 5.

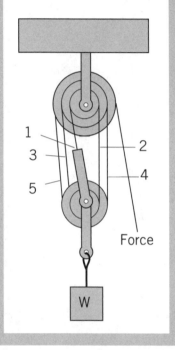

1
2
3
4
5

Force

W

Figure 124 — Elevator

The passenger car runs between guide rails and is suspended from steel hoisting ropes. The weight of the car and its load is approximately counter-balanced by the counter-weight.

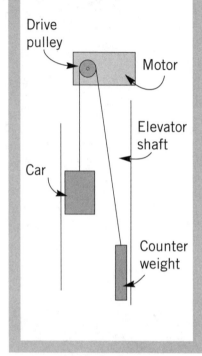

Drive pulley

Motor

Elevator shaft

Car

Counter weight

loaded car, which always varies to some extent.

Differential Pulley

In the differential pulley (**Figure 125**), a continuous chain engages sprockets so as to prevent the chain from slipping over the pulley faces. The chain shown in **Figure 125** is one continuous length passing around all three pulleys.

Math

Force F x R = 1 ÷ 2 x W x (R - r)

F = W x (R - r) ÷ 2 x R

W = (2 x F x R) ÷ (R - r)

Problem 10: Referring to Figure 125, where W = 800 pounds, r = 8 inches and R = 10 inches. What is the force (F) required to lift this weight?

Solution 10:

Force F = W x (R - r) ÷ 2 x R

F = 800 x (10 − 8) ÷ 2 x 10

F = 800 x 2 ÷ 20 = 1600 ÷ 20 = 80 pounds

4. Toothed Wheel

In these toothed, meshed wheels, the outer diameter of one wheel meets with the inner diameter of another wheel (**Figure 126**). In this way large weights can be lifted with small force.

Figure 125 — Differential Pulley

A chain (instead of a rope) is used here to prevent slippage. The chain is continuous, passing around all three pulleys.

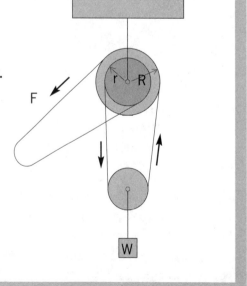

F

r   R

W

Math

$F = W \times r1 \times r2 \times r3 \div R1 \times R2 \times R3$

$W = F \times R1 \times R2 \times R3 \div r1 \times r2 \times r3$

Problem 11: Referring to **Figure 126,** what is the force (F) required to lift 1000 pounds (W) given the following: r1 = 17, r2 = 9, r3 = 7, R1 = 23, R2 = 16 and R3 = 20.

Solution 11:

$F = W \times (r1 \times r2 \times r3 \div R1 \times R2 \times R3)$

$F = 1000 \times [(17 \times 9 \times 7) \div (23 \times 16 \times 20)]$

$F = 1000 \times 0.1455 = 146$ pounds

Whatever weight is put on this toothed-wheel machine, it will require only about 15% (0.1455) force to lift it.

Gears

When one gear turns another gear, the number of teeth on the driving gear and the number of teeth on the following gear form a ratio (**Figure 127**). The gear ratio determines how the rotary force is transmitted from one gear to the next.

A high gear ratio is one in which the driver is larger than the follower. For example, in a gear ratio of 2 to 1, the driver has twice as many teeth as the follower, and twice the circumference. One revolution

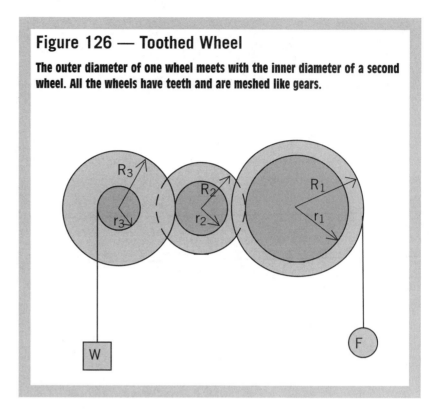

Figure 126 — Toothed Wheel

The outer diameter of one wheel meets with the inner diameter of a second wheel. All the wheels have teeth and are meshed like gears.

of the driver will produce two revolutions of the follower. Thus the applied force produces rapid rotation of the follower, at the expense of power.

A low gear ratio is one in which the driver is smaller than the follower. In a 1-to-2 ratio, the driver has half as many teeth as the follower, and must make two revolutions to produce one revolution in the follower. This arrangement magnifies the applied force, at the expense of speed or distance.

Number of Teeth Math

In general the following ratios hold:

The number of teeth on the

Figure 127 — Gears

When the driver has twice as many teeth as the follower, one revolution of the larger gear wheel will produce two revolutions of the smaller.

Driver   Follower

driver times the circumference of the follower equals the number of teeth on the follower times the driver circumference.

Driver Teeth = Number of teeth on driver

Follower Teeth = Number of teeth on the follower

Driver Cir. = Driver Circumference

Follower Cir. = Follower Circumference

Driver Teeth ÷ Follower Teeth = Driver Cir. ÷ Follower Cir.

Speed Math

The speed of the follower is directly proportional to the circumference of both the driver and the follower.

Follow Circ. ÷ Driver Circ. = Follow Speed ÷ Driver Speed

Problem 12: Referring to **Figure 127**, given the following: driver diameter = 16 inches and follower diameter = 10 inches. If the driver speed is 2400 rpm, what is the follower speed?

Solution 12:

FS = (DS x DC) ÷ FC

Where DS = 2400, DC = 16? and FC = 10?

FS = (2400 x 50.3) ÷ 31.4

FS = 3845 rpm

5. Inclined Plane

The principle of the inclined plane, sometimes called the ramp, applies when pushing a car up a ramp or pulling a sled up a snowy hill (see **Figure 128**). The use of an inclined plane does not lessen the total work of lifting the load, but it lengthens the distance traveled so that less power is used over a longer time. In the shop a jointer table is lifted by an inclined plane (see **Figure 128**).

The screw, an inclined plane wound helically around a cylinder, adds power at the expense of speed.

6. Wedge

The wedge is a double inclined plane and gives added power at the expense of speed. It is sometimes considered as a combination of two inclined planes placed base-to-base. The mechanical advantage increases as the angle of the wedge decreases. This relation, however, has little practical value since the resistance due to friction is very great. The principle of the wedge is applied to split logs, quarry stone, fasten tools to their handles, and lock tenon joints in chair legs (see **Figure 129**).

Math

The power required to drive a wedge is directly related to the size of the working angle ∂. In **Figure 129b** the working angle is double that of the working angle in **Figure 129a**. The force required to drive wedge (**Figure 129b**) is also doubled.

Force $F = (2Q \times b) \div l$

$F = 2Q \times \sin$ angle α

Where Q = Power quotient

If the working angle α in (a) is 10° then:

$F = 2Q \times \sin 10 = 2Q \times 0.1736 = Q0.3474$

When the working angle α is 20° as in (b) then:

$F = 2Q \times \sin 20 = 2Q \times 0.3420 = Q0.6840$

And $0.6840 \div 0.3420 \approx 2$

This shows that when the working angle is doubled the force required to drive a wedge is also doubled. The force applied in the form of a heavy blow from a sledge and the resulting strain is equal to the force of the blow multiplied by the length of the wedge divided by its width.

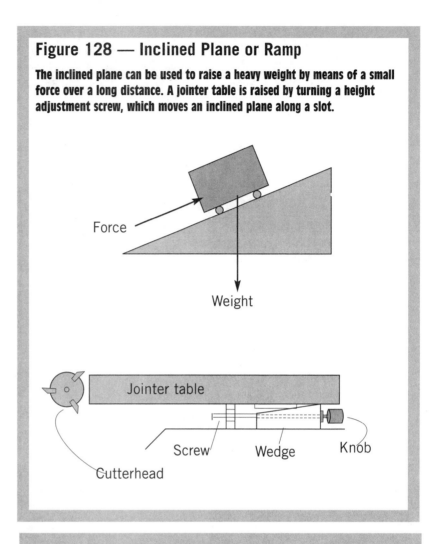

Figure 128 — Inclined Plane or Ramp

The inclined plane can be used to raise a heavy weight by means of a small force over a long distance. A jointer table is raised by turning a height adjustment screw, which moves an inclined plane along a slot.

Force

Weight

Jointer table

Screw   Wedge   Knob

Cutterhead

Figure 129 — Wedge

The wedge is a double inclined plane and sacrifices speed for power.

F

F

b

b

α

α

l

l

a

b

Figure 130 — Screw

The screw is an inclined plane wrapped around a cylinder.

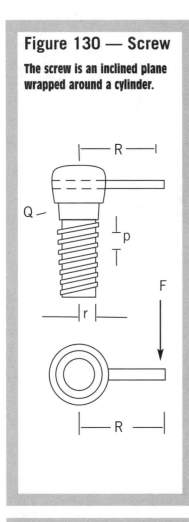

7. Screw

The screw is essentially an inclined plane wound helically around a cylinder (**Figure 130**). The principle of the screw is applied in the screw propeller for ships, in the lifting jack, in fine instruments for focusing and fine adjustments, and in common bolts and wood-screws.

Math

F = force at the end of the handle of a wrench, R = length of lever-arm, r = pitch radius of screw, p = lead of thread, Q = load. Then neglecting friction:

$$\text{Force } F = Q \times (p \div 6.28\,R)$$

Hydraulic Machines

Many machines involve more than the simple elements, the lever and the inclined plane. Some, such as the water wheel, hydraulic press, and hydraulic elevator make use of liquids (**Figure 131**). These are called hydraulic machines and depend upon the principle announced by Pascal (1623-1662) that a liquid in a closed vessel transmits pressure equally in all directions. The most valuable application of this principle is the hydraulic press, which Pascal described thus: "If a vessel full of water, closed in all parts, has two openings of which the one is a hundred times the other, placing in each a piston which fits it, the man pushing the small piston will equal the force of a hundred men who push that which is a hundred times as large."

The hydraulic press (**Figure 131**) offers a convenient means of exerting enormous forces, such as required for punching holes in metal plates, pressing oil from seeds, and stamping parts from sheet steel. Note, however, that if the large piston has 100 times as much surface as the small one, it moves only 1/100 of the distance that the small piston travels.

Math

Neglecting friction, the product of the great force on one piston times the small distance through which it moves equals the product of the small force on the other piston times the large distance through which it travels. The input equals the output.

Figure 131 — Hydraulic Press

A small force over a long distance applied on piston P₁ is capable of exerting a large force over a short distance on piston P₂.

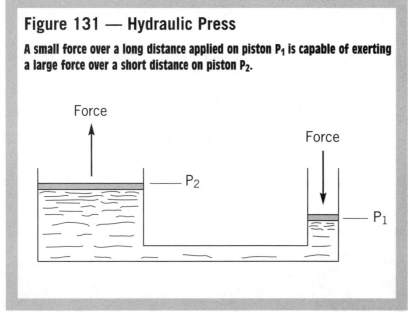

Area Large Piston P_2 x distance traveled = area small Piston P_1 x distance traveled

Area P_2 x d_2 = Area P_1 x d_1

For a hydraulic system where one piston has a diameter of 6 inches and the other piston has a diameter of 1 inch, the following relationship holds:

P_2 = 6-in. dia. Area = πr^2 = 3.14 x 3^2 = 28.26 sq. in.

P_1 = 1 in. dia. Area = πr^2 = 3.14 x 1^2 = 3.14 sq. in.

Ratio $P_2 : P_1$ = 28.26 ÷ 3.14 = 9

This means that when the small piston is depressed 9 units, the large piston will move 1 unit. Conversely, when 1 pound of pressure is put onto P_1, 9 pounds of pressure will be transmitted to P_2.

The input equals the output, just as when using the lever, wedge, or other simple device to obtain mechanical advantage. A machine can never produce more power than is put into it — and when real-world frictional losses are considered, the machine must always deliver less power than is put in.

Hydraulic elevators for lifting enormous weights are constructed on the same principle. When speed is demanded, as in elevators for high office buildings, the motion of the hydraulic piston or plunger is transmitted by a cable working over a series of pulleys that increase the speed of the elevator cage to four or more times that of the plunger.

Problem 13: What is the relationship in a hydraulic system between piston P_1 with diameter of 2 inches (r=1) and piston P_2 with diameter of 8 inches (r=4)?

Solution 13:

Area of P_1 = πr^2 = 3.14 x 1^2 = 3.14 sq. in.

Area of P_2 = πr^2 = 3.14 x 4^2 = 3.14 x 16 = 50.24 sq. in.

Ratio $P_1 ÷ P_2$ = 50.24 ÷ 3.14 = 16

Distance Traveled

Area P_1 x D_1 = Area P_2 x d_2

Problem 14: P_1 is 2 inches in diameter. P_2 is 8 inches in diameter. If Piston P_1 travels 12 inches how far will Piston P_2 travel? See **Figure 131**.

Solution 14:

d_2 = (P_1 x D_1) ÷ P_2 = (3.14 x 1^2) ÷ 50.24 = 0.75 inches

We also know the ratio between P_1 and P_2 is 16 therefore:

D_2 = d_1 ÷ 16 = 12 ÷ 16 = 0.75 inches

Force Transmitted

Force transmitted is in the ratio of the relative areas of the pistons — just as is distance traveled.

$$P_1 \times F_1 = P_2 \times f_2$$

Where P_1 = Area of P_1 piston, F_1 = Force at P_2, P_2 = area of P_2 piston and f_2 = force at P_2.

Problem 15: When a force of 25 pounds is applied at P_1, how much force is transmitted to P_2?

Solution 15: The ratio is still 16 therefore:

25 lbs. x 16 = 400 pounds

This is the principle that metal-stamping machines work on and is similar to the hydraulic braking system in a car. When the brake pedal (P_1) is depressed 4 inches, the wheel brake pad (P_2) is moved ¼ inch against the brake drum. If the automobile driver exerts 10 pounds pressure with his foot onto the pedal (P_1), then 160 pounds of pressure is transferred to the brake pad.

Complex Mechanical Movements

A complex mechanical movement is some contrivance that uses two or more of the simple machine elements described above to achieve some advantage. This advantage can be to change power or distance or to alter motion direction. We drive automobiles with rack and pinion steering; use hand drills with worm gears; have bench clamps with a screw and lever. The clutch of an automobile engine and the escapement of a watch are complex mechanical movements. The seven fundamental contrivances can produce some 750 combinations, which include practically all of the devices used in modern machines.

1. Rack and Pinion

The rack and pinion gear (see **Figure 132a**) is a combination of two geared devises and is used to convert rotary motion into linear motion or the reverse according to whether the rack or the pinion gear is the driver. Most autos use this mechanism for steering. The double rack with single pinion gear (**Figure 132b**) allows the piston stroke to double the distance. When the lower rack is fixed and the pinion rolls one foot, the upper rack will move two feet. In this way the stroke length of a piston can be doubled.

2. Gear-Wheel and Worm

The gear wheel and worm is a combination of the toothed wheel and a screw (see **Figure 132c**). It is used to change a rapid rotary motion into a very slow rotary motion. One rotation of the worm turns the gear wheel the distance of one tooth. Hand power saws and drills use this mechanism. The gear in the figure has 13 teeth

Figure 132 — Complex Machines

The rack and pinion (a) is used to steer automobiles. The single pinion with two racks (b) allows the stroke of a piston to be doubled in length. The gear-wheel and worm gear device(c) is used to change rapid rotary motion to very slow rotary motion. The screw clamp (d) uses a lever and screw as a bench hold-down. A sail boat uses the steering mechanism (e) in which a wheel is used to move the rudder. Metal shears (f) combine a lever with a rotary cam to create great shearing force. The foot treadle lever (g) used with a cam creates continuous rotary motion used in the past for wood lathes.

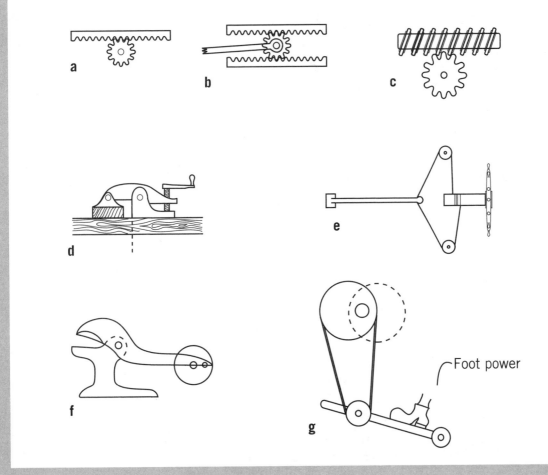

thus the gear speed will be $\frac{1}{13}$ of the transmitted speed.

3. Screw Clamp

The screw clamp is made of a screw and a First Class Lever (see **Figure 132d**). On turning the handle the screw pushes upward against the end of the lever. The holder, operating as a lever, clamps the piece of wood or other material placed under it on the other side of the fulcrum.

4. Steering Apparatus

Using a wheel and axle, two pulleys and a First Class Lever, this apparatus is used to steer sail boats (see **Figure 132e**). On the shaft of the hand wheel there is a barrel on which is wound a rope which passes around the guide pulleys and has its opposite end attached to the tiller which, in turn, is attached to the rudder. By turning the wheel, one end of the tope is wound onto the barrel and the other end is let off. The tiller is moved in one direction or the other, thus guiding the direction of the boat.

5. Shears

The shears (**Figure 132f**) use a First Class Lever and a wheel with offset axle. This cam arrangement is used to cut iron plate and other metals. The jaws of the cutter are opened by the weight of the long upper arm; the blade then closes as the cam rotates. The long leverage of the upper arm gives great shearing power.

6. Foot Treadle

This arrangement converts foot power to rotary power and was long used to power wood lathes when chair bodgers were deep in the woods (see **Figure 132g**). An endless band runs from a roller on the treadle to an eccentric on the upper shaft. In operation, the wheel is rotated in the proper direction by hand. Thus started, speed and direction can be maintained with the foot pedal. This arrangement is an improvement over older lathe

setups that relied on a spring-pole to return the treadle to its original position, resulting in a forward-reverse motion of the workpiece.

CHAPTER 12

Rust – Cause and Prevention

Rust is the bane of the woodworker and the curse of the tool collector. I remember the bench plane I inherited in 1960. It had the initials 'J.H.' (for John Horner) stamped on the rosewood handle so I knew it came from my grandfather and I felt a special affinity for this old tool. Gramps had made his living as a carpenter, starting in 1919 with the Santa Fe Railroad in Colorado. I spent hours truing the sole and then carefully sharpened the blade so it would shave hairs off my arm. After I made a few paper-thin curls of pine, I carefully laid the plane on its side in the back of a drawer and forgot about it. At the time I was living in eastern Pennsylvania and my shop was in the basement — the walls leaked and my shop became damp once the snow melted and the summer rains began.

A few months later I removed the plane from the dark reaches of the drawer. The beautiful tool my grandfather bought in 1890 and my father had used since 1935 was a mess. Through plain stupidity, I had managed, in a few months to turn a plane that had been in constant use in my family for 70 years into a wet, sticky, rust-covered lump.

I spent hours with sandpaper, steel wool, oil, rust remover and elbow grease. In the end the plane looked better but it was never quite the same. I have been wary of rust ever since and certainly agree with the fellow who said, "Rust is a four letter word."

Figure 133 — The Chemical Activity of Metallic Elements

The metals are arranged in decreasing order of their tendency to pass into ionic form by losing electrons. Metals at the top of the Electromotive Force (EMF) series are more active than those at the bottom of the list, and the higher metal will corrode (oxidize) when in contact with a metal lower on the list.

Metal	Symbol	Electrode Potential
Lithium	Li	2.96
Potassium	K	2.92
Barium	Ba	2.90
Calcium	Ca	2.87
Sodium	Na	2.72
Magnesium	Mg	2.40
Aluminum	Al	1.70
Manganese	Mn	1.10
Zinc	Zn	0.76
Chromium	Cr	0.56
Iron (Ferrous)	Fe++	0.44
Cadmium	Cd	0.40
Cobalt	Co	0.28
Nickel	Ni	0.23
Tin	Sn	0.14
Lead	Pb	0.12
Iron (Ferric)	Fe+++	0.05
Hydrogen	H	0.00
Bismuth	Bi	-0.23
Copper (Cupric)	Cu++	-0.34
Copper (Cuprous)	Cu+	-0.47
Silver	Ag	-0.80
Mercury	Hg	-0.81
Platinum	Pt	-0.86
Gold	Au	-1.36

More active

Less active

Because of chemical activity, some metals should never be in contact with each other. A storage battery and the electrical activity between metals explains corrosion. Iron has many great attributes but its one immense disadvantage is that it rusts. It's necessary to know what rust is, how it forms, and how to prevent it. Once you do have rust, learn how to remove it.

The Chemical Activity of Metals

To understand rust we first have to know a little about the chemistry of metals. Chemists have arranged the metallic elements in a list according to the ease with which they enter into a chemical reaction. This list is called The Electromotive Force Series (EMF), see **Figure 133**. We are particularly interested in how reactive a metal is in the presence of water and oxygen.

The first five metals on the list (lithium, potassium, barium, calcium, and sodium) oxidize very rapidly in the air and with considerable evolution of heat. All the metals down to copper also rust (oxidize) with comparable ease while the metals below copper (silver, mercury, platinum, and gold) do not rust. According to the electrolytic theory of rusting, these facts are just what we would predict.

Natural waters usually are dilute solutions of carbonic, nitric or humic acids. Carbonic acid is made in nature from carbon dioxide, nitric acid from nitrogen, and humic acid from the breakdown of carbohydrates (oil) and cellulose (trees and plant life). These naturally occurring acids contain displaceable hydrogen and react easily with metals above bismuth in the EMF series. These metals, therefore, almost never occur in the free state in nature, but instead are found in the combined state as sulfides, carbonates, etc. Metals below hydrogen usually are found in the free state — thus gold is found as nuggets of metallic gold. The metals below hydrogen are also found in combined states, e.g., mercury as cinnabar or as mercuric sulfide.

This difference in the activity of metals explains many reactions in everyday chemistry. For example, it explains the plating of one metal on another without outside current. When any metal is placed in a solution of a salt of a metal that stands below it, the first metal is dissolved and the second is thrown out of solution in metallic form. Aluminum pots and pans in the kitchen are often darkened by this swapping of metals. If you cook oatmeal, spinach, or other iron-containing food in an aluminum pot, some of the aluminum

Rule of Thumb

To **prevent iron tools from rusting**, keep the metal dry, since moisture starts the rusting process, and keep the shop warm, since cold metal attracts moisture. The worst situation is an unheated workshop during times of rapidly changing weather. When the air (and therefore the metal) is cold, then warmer and moister air moves in, the moisture will condense on the cold tools and rusting will begin.

changes place with some of the iron, the latter being deposited as a dark coating inside the pot. Although you can scour away this deposit, it's easier to remove it chemically by cooking some acidic food such as tomatoes, rhubarb, or sauerkraut in the pot. The iron thus regained is not only harmless but also a valuable food mineral.

A more specific way to describe the activity of metals is to say that they vary in their ability to ionize or give up electrons. All metals give up electrons differently and those at the top of the list (see **Figure 133**) give up electrons more easily than those at the bottom. This difference is what makes electric batteries possible, and it explains rust and electrolytic action between touching metals.

Storage Batteries

Count Alessandro Volta (1745-1827) demonstrated in 1800 that zinc and copper in a saline solution generated an electric current — the volt was named after him.

Thomas Edison (1847-1913) built a storage battery in 1886 using iron and nickel oxide in a strong alkali solution. **Figure 134** shows other storage cells using different metals.

A Simple Experiment

Electron transfer between metals

Figure 134 — Storage Cells

Dissimilar metals in an electrolyte solution generate a voltage. The metal higher on the EMF series gives up electrons and is the negative electrode. The metal lower in the series becomes the positive electrode and takes on electrons. The further apart the two metals are in the series, the larger the voltage.

Battery Name	Negative Pole	Electrolyte	Positive Pole	Voltage
Volta	Zinc	Salt (NaCl) Solution	Copper	1.00
Edison	Iron	20% Potassium Hydroxide Solution	Nickel Oxide	1.10
Regnier-1	Copper	Dilute Sulfuric Acid	Lead Oxide	1.30
Clark Standard	Zinc	Zinc Sulfate + Dilute Sodium Hydroxide	Carbon	1.50
Dry Cell	Zinc	Ammonium Cloride + Zinc Cloride	Carbon	1.60
Poggendorf	Zinc	Potassium Clorate + Dilute Sulfuric Acid	Carbon	2.00
Lead Accumulator	Lead	Sulfuric Acid Density = 1.25	Lead Oxide	2.20
Regnier-2	Zinc	Zinc Sulfate Solution	Lead Oxide	2.36
Main	Zinc	Sulfuric Acid Den. = 1.10	Lead Oxide	2.50

can be demonstrated with a simple experiment. If two metals of different activity are immersed in a salt (NaCl) solution and then connected by a wire, electrons will flow through the wire from the more active metal (top of the EMF list) to the less active (bottom of the list). The further apart the metals in the series, the greater will be the voltage. (See **Figure 135**).

Figure 135 — A Simple Single Fluid Cell

Two dissimilar metals in an electrolyte solution will pass a current from the negative electrode (Aluminum) to the positive electrode (Copper).

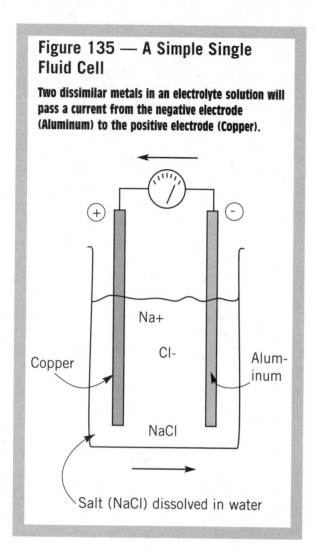

Copper

Na+

Cl-

Alum-
inum

NaCl

Salt (NaCl) dissolved in water

Figure 136 — The Potato Battery

When electrodes made of copper and zinc are placed in a potato, the more active metal (zinc) will corrode and transfer electrons to the less active metal(copper). The current produced is small, but an LCD watch can be powered this way.

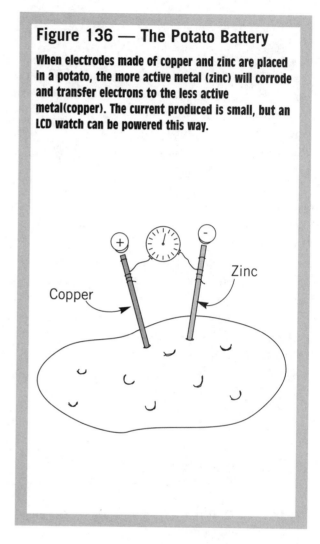

Zinc

Copper

In the experiment we would place an aluminum strip and a copper strip in a salt (NaCl) solution, attach a wire to each strip and join the wires to an ammeter. A small current can be detected.

Another Experiment

Another experiment that proves electrons flow from one metal to a dissimilar metal is one you might have tried in junior high school — the potato battery, **Figure 136**. In this experiment we insert two dissimilar metals into a potato. We can use copper and zinc; they are quite common and are far enough apart on the EMF series so that a current will flow. The potato's juices act as the electrolyte. The terminal voltage is more than 1 volt but the potato battery will only deliver a small current — just enough to run an LCD (liquid crystal diode) clock which demands only a few micro-amps.

Even if the metals are the same,

Figure 137 — Wet Cell and Dry Cell Batteries

The more reactive metal, that is, the one higher on the EMF series, gives up electrons and becomes the negative electrode. The further apart the two metals in the table in Figure 1, the larger the voltage generated.

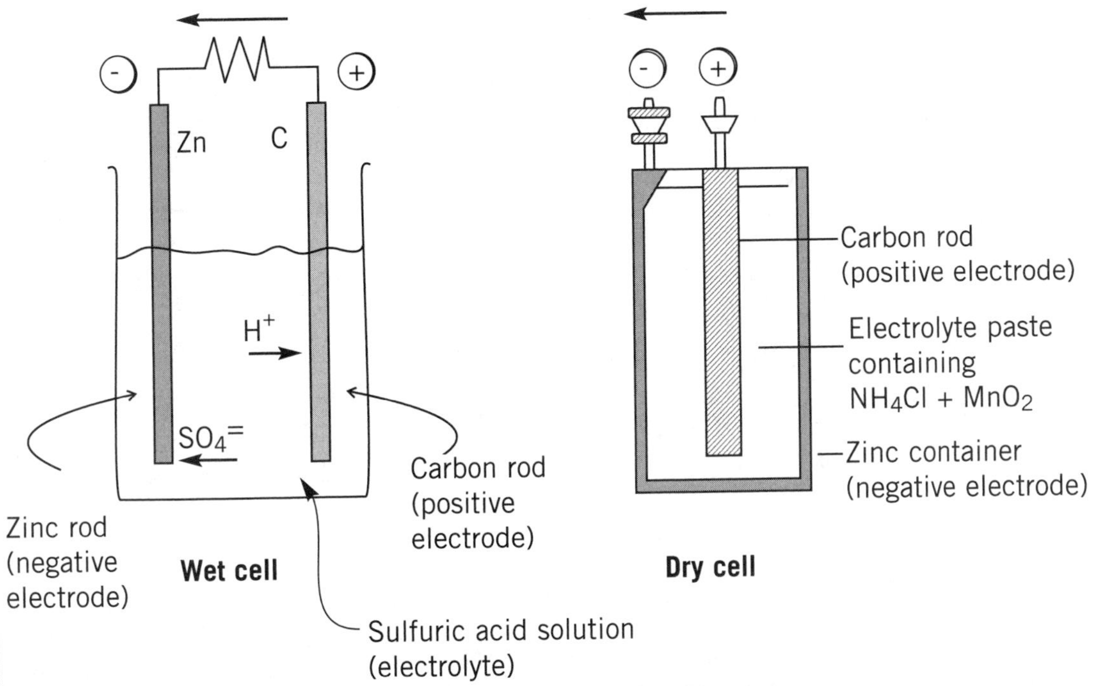

Zinc rod
(negative electrode)   **Wet cell**

Carbon rod
(positive electrode)

Sulfuric acid solution
(electrolyte)

Dry cell

Carbon rod
(positive electrode)

Electrolyte paste containing $NH_4Cl + MnO_2$

Zinc container
(negative electrode)

for example wrought iron and pig iron, there will be a flow of electrons. If the two metals are different, such as copper and iron, the metal higher in the EMF table will be anodic to (that is corroded by) the metal lower later in the table. Thus aluminum, which is very active, will be corroded by contact with copper, which is lower in the table.

A Simple Battery

We can construct a simple battery consisting of two different solid conductors as electrodes immersed in a solution of an electrolyte. Consider a cell with a dilute solution of sulfuric acid, a zinc electrode and a carbon electrode as in **Figure 137**.

When the zinc electrode is put into the solution, some of the positive zinc ions (Zn++) go into solution. The zinc becomes negatively charged while the solution becomes positively charged.

Connecting a wire across the terminals of the primary cell sets an electric charge in motion throughout the circuit. The direction of the current flowing through the wires outside the cell is from the positive terminal to the negative terminal; inside the cell the current flows from the negative terminal to the positive terminal.

This theory is put into practical use by the dry cell battery, **Figure 137**. The outer shell of the dry cell is made of zinc and is the negative electrode. The central post is made of carbon and is the positive electrode. In between the electrodes is the electrolyte, a paste containing ammonium chloride and manganese dioxide.

Electrical Activity Explains Corrosion

An electrical effect similar to a battery accounts for the accelerated corrosion that often takes place when two metals contact one another in the presence of moisture. In the early 1900s tin was used to plate and protect iron cans from rust (oxidation). In theory, when the tin coating oxidized, the resulting tin oxide would form a tight and impervious layer that would protect the iron underneath. It was found, however, that when the tin plating was scratched or broken,

the iron underneath corroded (rusted) faster than if it were not plated at all. The reason: tin and iron, in the presence of water, set up a current that accelerates the rusting process.

Today this type of tin coating is no longer used. Instead, zinc is used as a protective coating over iron — galvanization. The iron remains protected when the zinc coating is damaged because the zinc 'dissolves' (oxidizes to zinc oxide), and in doing so, 'flows' and forms a new protective coating. The iron under the scratch is protected.

Iron and Rust

Now back to iron and why tools rust. Iron ore is abundant and easy to mine. Iron itself is cheap, strong, and can be produced at low cost. By varying the carbon content from 0.30% to 1.02% and adding different chemicals (manganese, nickel, chromium, molybdenum, vanadium, silicon, boron, lead, sulfur, copper) alloy steels can be selectively produced from iron with nearly any property desired. Steels are made that have great, good or moderate hardness for use as springs, hand tools or ball bearings. The alloys can be malleable or hard enough to hold a sharp edge, hardened by flame or unaffected by heat. In 1860, the first steel rails lasted six years in a place where iron rails had to be replaced every three months. With all its positive attributes, iron has one immense disadvantage — its great tendency to rust.

When rust appears on a tool it should not be regarded as just the end effect of corrosion. I've heard rust referred to as 'graceful aging.' Rust is not just an effect nor is it an end product — and it certainly isn't graceful. Rust is an active contributing factor to the continued, on-going deterioration of iron.

What is Rust?

When we talk of iron we also mean cast iron, wrought iron, iron alloys, and steel. Steel and iron react in much the same way to oxidation because steel is just an alloy of iron with less amounts of carbon. The brownish-red deposit we call rust is ferric oxide, the same material we mine from the ground to make iron metal in the first place. Metallic iron is less stable than its ore therefore the rusting process (oxidization) is just an attempt by the metal to revert back to its natural form — hematite.

In 2004, the United States' Mars rover 'Opportunity', using infrared light radiated from rocks and soil, discovered hematite on the surface of the red planet. Scientists know that hematite forms only in the presence of water, therefore this proved that water is now, or at some time was, present on Mars.

Rust is about 20% water and permits the passage of water, gases, and electric currents through it to the metal underneath. By keeping these agents of corrosion always in contact with the surface of the metal, rust itself aids and abets the corrosion process. This characteristic, to absorb and to persistently retain moisture, is what makes possible the progressive corrosion that goes on beneath rust. Rust also tends to grow and spread outward from a spot where water has been deposited. Water spots appear on the surface of steel or iron whenever the metal temperature is lower than that of the surrounding atmosphere and there is sufficient moisture in the air to condense.

Rust (or ferric oxide, the name derived from ferrum, the Latin name for iron) does not adhere firmly to iron to form a tight protective coating, such as copper oxide over copper (green patina) or the oxides of aluminum, bronze, and magnesium. Instead, ferric oxide flakes away from the metal, continually exposing a new iron surface, which then rusts in turn. In this way an iron object will eventually rust completely away, returning to its natural state of ferric oxide.

Rule of Thumb

Newly cleaned tools often begin to rust immediately. Therefore, when you clean an iron tool, immediately protect it with oil, wax, or paint.

Steel, fresh from the smelter, has a tough coat of loose scale that is a natural consequence of the forge process. This mill scale (also called sub-oxide and black oxide) protects against rust formation so long as it remains intact. However, soon after leaving the factory, on exposure to air and with a few changes in temperature, the metal flexes and the scale begins to fall off. This makes the metal susceptible to rusting.

How Rust Forms

Electrolysis is the process where an electric current passes through a solution with the simultaneous chemical changes either in the electrodes or in the solutions in contact with the electrodes, or both.

It is believed that rust forms on iron and steel through electrolytic action on the metal surface when water separates into hydrogen ions and oxygen ions. The hydrogen ions then attack the iron and, in the presence of water, iron hydrate is produced. Chemically it looks like this.

Water plus electricity yields hydrogen ions and oxygen ions:

$$H_2O + e^- \rightarrow H^+ + O^{-2}$$

Iron plus hydrogen ions plus water yields iron hydrate:

$$Fe + H^+ + H_2O = Fe \cdot H_2O$$

The iron hydrate then combines with an oxygen ion to form ferric oxide (rust).

Iron hydrate plus oxygen ion yields ferric oxide plus water

$$Fe \cdot H_2O + O^{-2} \rightarrow Fe_2O_3 + H_2O$$

These equations show that both water and oxygen must be present for the formation of rust and that electricity speeds the reaction along as does the water produced by the chemical reaction. Note that water enters the reaction and then is later produced by the reaction.

Source of Electric Current

An electric current is necessary for rust to form. It can be set up by:

1. Impurities in the metal.

Trace amounts of a dissimilar metal within the iron can cause internal electrical currents. Because all iron and steel contain trace amounts of other metals (either naturally or added during the smelting process), iron will always contain small electrical currents. When a molten metal such as iron is cast, the hot but cooling metal is not homogenous — crystals form with dissimilar amounts of iron-plus-alloy and iron-plus-impurities. The cooled metal will be composed of crystals with different percents of impurities. Small electrical currents continually pass back and forth between the crystals in the metal, thus iron generates its own electric currents — enough to catalyze the rusting process.

2. Different metals in contact.

When two different metals are in contact with each other, an electrolytic current is produced and the less noble metal (the most reactive) will corrode. Plumbers never connect a copper pipe to an iron pipe without a bronze or plastic fitting between — both non-conductors. If these two dissimilar metals were to remain in contact, the iron pipe would oxidize and, with time, spring a leak. If steel nails were used to attach copper flashing to a building, the nails would corrode where the two different metals touched each other. Note that iron is higher in the EMF Series (see **Figure 133**) than copper, so to avoid corrosion use either copper or galvanized nails.

3. Stray electric currents.

An electric current, whether caused by different metals in contact, or from an external source using the metal as a conductor, will catalyze and accelerate the oxidation (rusting) process if water and oxygen are present. Floor tools in the workshop often have small current leakages that can't be detected, but in humid conditions these tools will rust faster than a tool right along side that doesn't have this small current flow.

What Causes Rust?

1. Exposure of the metal to moisture. Water is necessary to contribute hydrogen ions and active oxygen to the rusting process. Rusting proceeds rapidly in damp weather.

2. Electrical Current. A small current will cause iron to rust quickly. The current can come from within the metal, by two metals in contact, or from an external source.

3. Mechanical injury to the treated metallic surface. A scratch in the protective coating of electroplated or hot-dipped galvanized steel exposes bare metal — both metals can be scratched and while both will 'heal' somewhat, eventually rust will develop underneath. In highly corrosive environments, stainless steel or brass is preferred.

4. A chemical reaction. Certain chemicals can contribute to the rusting process. Steel will corrode quickly in the presence of swimming pool acid (muriatic, hydrochloric) or even in the presence of vinegar (weak acetic acid). Likewise, the tannic acid in redwood will speed up corrosion of an unplated nail and cause streaking in the wood.

Rule of Thumb

If rust does begin to form on a tool or machine bed, remove it immediately. Rust creates conditions that encourage more rust.

Cleaning Iron

Clean the surface before you apply any rust protection. The steel should have its surface in the best condition so the coating will adhere tightly. A coating of waterproofing material cannot stick closely and uniformly to a surface that is damp, rusty or greasy; neither does it serve any useful purpose when applied to loose or detachable scale. In new work, all rust, scale, grease and dirt should be removed from the surface of the metal before applying the first protective coat. A protective coating applied over rust allows the destructive electrolytic action to continue beneath the preservative film, with no outward sign of what is going on below.

1. Chemical Cleaners — In the

home shop, the common method of cleaning steel in preparation for applying a protective coating is to remove oil and grease with an organic cleaner such as paint thinner or alcohol, then to use acid jellies or other commercial rust removers. Most of the chemical jellies use phosphoric acid and they work in two ways: The acidic medium removes some rust by hydrogen ion exchange, common to any acid. The second manner is phosphoric acid reacts with rust to form iron phosphates which can be rinsed away. The iron phosphates do not form a protective coating.

2. Commercial Rust Removers — A study by a

woodworking magazine (<u>Wood</u>, Mar. 2004) found there is no commercially available rust remover that works on heavy rust without abrasion by steel wool or sandpaper. In fact abrasion plus mineral spirits was as effective as abrasion plus most of the rust removers.

3. Abrasion — The resident rust

and dirt is removed by scraping or with sandpaper, wire brushes, or grinders. Because the surface of the piece is left scratched, abrasion is a poor choice for antique tools or fine instruments but is often the best method for restoring shop floor tools. Use progressively finer grits of sandpaper to get a smooth surface.

4. Sandblasting — Sandblast-

ing is quite efficient because, in addition to leaving the surface clean, it leaves the surface dry — an important and essential condition when a coating is to follow. To some extent, pits and hollows are also cleaned.

5. Pickling — Pickling is an

industrial method of cleaning metal by immersing the piece in a dilute sulfuric acid bath (25% acid, 75% water). After the bath, the remaining scale and acid are removed with jets of water discharged at high pressure. Sulfuric acid is not available for home use.

Rule of Thumb

If you want to **store a tool** so no rust can form, you have to exclude either water, or oxygen, or both. The simplest way to do that is to put the tool in a sealable plastic freezer bag along with a little pouch of silica gel.

In home shops, muriatic acid (hydrochloric acid) is sometimes used to remove rust. This acid is stronger than sulfuric acid and is effective in removing rust from deeply pitted cast iron and some steels. After the acid treatment the piece should be washed thoroughly with water, neutralized with a solution of ammonia and water, then dried and immediately given a protective coating because pickled surfaces are particularly susceptible to rusting. Use 1 part acid poured slowly into 3 parts water.

Safety Note: When mixing, always add acid to water not the other way around. If you add water to acid an exothermic reaction ensues, sometimes violent, and the hot acid mixture can splatter and burn you.

Muriatic acid is available at home centers or where swimming pool supplies are sold, but should be used only in the most severe cases. Using a strong acid at home is always tricky and possibly dangerous. Before you decide to use this method also consider the disposal problem. Cities usually have drop-off centers where acids, poisons and other hazardous materials can be disposed of.

6. Electrolysis — This is a method of removing rust by immersing the rusted metal piece in an electrolyte solution and passing an electric current through it. This is the reversal of the rusting process so that instead of losing electrons, we add electrons to the rusted piece. This is especially useful for small tools and those too fragile or expensive for aggressive abrasion. See Chapter 13, *Electrolysis and Rust Removal* for a full explanation of this method.

Preventing Rust

Steel neither rusts in dry air (where there is no water to participate in or catalyze a reaction) nor does steel rust when submerged in water (where there is no dissolved air or carbon dioxide). Therefore, the best protection against rust is a coating that excludes both oxygen and water.

Protection from Rust

There are six general methods of protecting iron and steel from rust: (1) plating, (2) coating, (3) painting, (4) linseed oil, (5) waxes and oil, and (6) commercial rust protectants.

1. Plating with Other Metals.

Covering the surface with a non-oxidizing or less reactive metal protects iron from oxidation. Zinc is higher than iron on the EMF Series and therefore will corrode before iron, that's why zinc washers are used to protect iron boat propeller shafts. This sacrificial action of zinc is used quite often to protect iron from corrosion and galvanized washers are a good preventative in steel mechanisms and structures.

Iron can also be covered by a thin layer of zinc (galvanized). When used in this way, the zinc layer oxidizes to zinc oxide, which protects the iron. When the galvanized surface is scratched, zinc oxide heals itself somewhat and continues to stop oxygen and water from reaching the iron surface. However, with enough scratches or a deep gouge, air will finally get through to the iron and rust will begin, and because of the electric current between the two dissimilar metals, rust will proceed quickly.

Aluminum is also a good plating material because, being higher on the list, it will corrode (oxidize) before iron and protect it. Aluminum has other advantages: its oxide is tough, adheres tightly, and will self-heal when subjected to small scratches.

Early 20th century tools made of iron were often plated with nickel or tin to prevent oxidation. Nickel is still used in industry but generally is not available to the home wood-worker, and tin cans haven't been made for over 100 years now.

Chromium is another metal used to protect iron, for example, automobile bumpers. Because chromium doesn't adhere strongly to iron, the usual procedure is first to plate the iron with successive layers of copper, then nickel, and finally with chromium. The final chromium plate is strong and protective for years, although over time the metallic bonds weaken and the chromium flakes off.

2. Applications of independent coatings. Asphalt and waterproof cements can be used to protect metallic surfaces. Old hand planes made of cast iron were japanned using an asphalt-based coating that adheres tenaciously and resists abrasion. This black material is still available from woodworking stores and catalogs.

3. Painting. Oil-based paint especially designed to protect and to improve the appearance of surfaces are universally used in industry for coating steel tools. Experience shows that these paints are excellent coatings for preservation and protection. Special paints to prevent rust are sold as sprays or for brush application in most hardware stores.

The essentials of a preservative and protective paint for steel are as follows:

Rule of Thumb

It's a good idea to **unplug stationary power tools** when you will be away from the workshop for more than a few days. That's because any current leakage in the tool's electrical circuitry will encourage rusting.

Mechanical Properties — The paint must be workable, that is, go on easily with brush or sprayer and flow over the surface evenly.

Chemical Properties — The protective paint must not only dry quickly but also dry simultaneously throughout, that is not harden on the surface or skin over while remaining soft underneath. The paint (or primer) should not dry and leave pinholes that are a starting point for rust.

Physical Properties — The paint must be able to accept more coats of paint without softening under them (hardness), it must wear well (durability), and it must exclude moisture (imperviosity).

4. Linseed Oil — When linseed oil dries (or to be more precise, when it polymerizes) it changes from a liquid to a solid, rubber-like substance that not only holds itself together but also clings to any dry surface. Dried linseed oil is only slightly soluble in dilute acids, weak alkaline solutions, paint thinner, turpentine, alcohol, acetone, water, and itself. Whether used as an ingredient in paint or applied directly to metal, it is a durable and effective protective coating. It is a key ingredient in many primers and paints for metal.

5. Oil and Wax — A light coating of oil will protect the metal from moisture and oxygen but it is not permanent. Wax rubbed on the surface will give protection for a short time. Wood workers commonly protect steel tools and machines with oil and wax but should regard this as only a temporary fix.

6. Commercial Rust Protectants — Recently a woodworking magazine (***Wood*** Mar. 2004) tested nine commercial rust preventatives. They built a wet box to produce rust quickly and tested the effectiveness of rust protectants. Using a piece of cast-iron, they sanded, cleaned, and sectioned off sections with tape. The products were applied according to the manufacturer's instructions and then the cast iron test piece was placed into the wet box. Moisture was pumped in continuously, and the time was noted when rust first began to form and when each test area was completely rusted over. This test accelerated rust formation beyond what might be expected in even the most rust-prone areas of the country. The results:

Ineffective — Ordinary paste wax, carnuba wax, and a spray-on surface lubricant were ineffective. In some cases rusting started within 15 minutes after application.

Fair — A wax with a rust block, a spray used to seal metal surfaces, and a topcoat used mainly to make metal surfaces slick were all only fair in the tests.

Good — Two products deemed to be somewhat effective in preventing rust were Bullfrog® tool wipes and Empire Topsaver®.

Excellent — The one product that stood out head-and-shoulders above all the rest was Boeshield T-9®. All the areas protected by the other eight preventatives were completely rusted over after 24 hours while the T-9 product was effective in the "rust machine" for over two weeks.

T-9 is a paraffin wax in a solvent vehicle. Once the solvent evaporates, the remaining film of dry paraffin wax protects the metal surface. Developed by Boeing Aircraft, it has been around for years. Two weeks of protection in the "rust machine" would probably translate to at least a year's protection in the normal shop.

CHAPTER 13

Electrolysis and Rust Removal

To remove rust on shop tools, we usually chip, sand, and scrape the surface then paint or rub on wax or oil to protect the clean metal. This is labor intensive, dirty, and often removes more metal than is necessary. Pits and small crevices are difficult, if not impossible, to clean this way. Expensive instruments and small items are too fragile for this brute force treatment. In fact, cleaning badly rusted metal does not have to be hard work. Removing rust with electrolysis requires a lot less effort because an electric current does the work.

When iron corrodes and red rust (ferric oxide) forms, we say the iron has rusted. Chemically, metallic iron has oxidized, that is, it has been stripped of two electrons. Using electrolysis, we can reverse the oxidation (rusting) process by restoring those two electrons.

Hematite iron ore plus coke yields cast iron

Ferric oxide plus carbon yields carbon dioxide plus iron

$$Fe_2O_3 + C \rightarrow CO_2 + Fe$$

Iron and Steel

Iron is the second most common metal in the earth's crust (aluminum is first) and it is our most common metal because so many everyday objects are made of it. The chief iron ores are the oxides, Fe_2O_3 or hematite and Fe_2O_4 or magnetite. These ores can be converted to metallic iron by heating them strongly with burning carbon in the form of coke, which is coal or wood that has been burned in the absence of air to drive off volatile non-carbons. The fairly pure carbon (coke) combines with the iron ore and strips off the oxygen, leaving metallic iron behind. A chemist would write it like this:

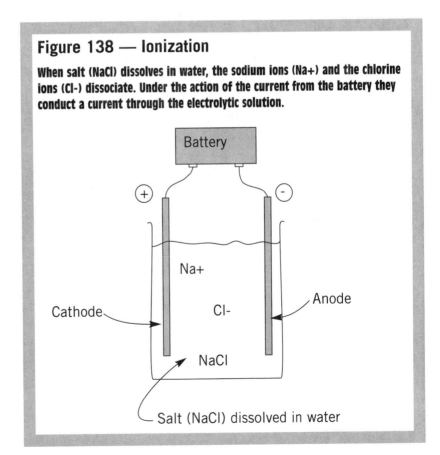

Figure 138 — Ionization

When salt (NaCl) dissolves in water, the sodium ions (Na+) and the chlorine ions (Cl-) dissociate. Under the action of the current from the battery they conduct a current through the electrolytic solution.

Battery

(+)   (-)

Na+

Cathode   Cl-   Anode

NaCl

Salt (NaCl) dissolved in water

Rule of Thumb

Instead of scraping and sanding, you can **use an electric current** to clean rust off metal, using the process called electrolysis. This is the most non-invasive way to remove rust, much easier on tools than scraping and sanding.

Cast iron (sometimes called pig iron) contains about 4% carbon as an impurity, plus traces of sulfur and phosphorous along with small amounts of other metals. Cast iron is hard but brittle. The top of your table saw, drill press table, jointer bed and plane bodies are all made of cast iron. The graphite particles in the iron concentrate stress and promote crack propagation. This is why cast iron cracks easier than wrought iron and steel.

Wrought iron is made by heating cast iron in the presence of oxygen to remove some impurities and to reduce its carbon content to about 2%. Wrought iron is not as hard as cast iron, but it is tougher and more malleable, thus it does not crack as easily. Iron fences, decorative railings, and outdoor furniture are made of wrought iron.

Steel is iron that has a still lower content of carbon, with fewer impurities. Steel-making is really nothing but the removal, by combustion, of some carbon and some impurities contained in the iron. This is done by bringing the molten metal into contact with air so the impurities are burned, that is, transformed into their oxides by the oxygen in the air. These oxides are lighter than the molten metal so they float on it as liquid slag, which is drained off before the steel itself is poured. The structure and composition of steel makes it more resilient, more flexible and — what is more important — easier to cut. The alloy has great strength and considerable ductility, that is, it can be drawn or hammered into new forms. High-speed steels can get hot without losing their hardness, or temper, and are alloys of iron and tungsten, chromium, cobalt, and/or vanadium.

Rust

Rust, or ferric oxide, is formed by the gradual oxidation of iron or steel when exposed to air and moisture. The rusting proceeds faster if an electrical current is present. The chemistry looks like this:

1. Water plus electricity yields hydrogen ions and oxygen ions

$$H_2O + e^- \rightarrow H^+ + O^{-2}$$

2. Iron plus hydrogen ion plus water yields iron hydrate

$$Fe + H^+ + H_2O \rightarrow Fe \cdot H_2O$$

3. Iron hydrate plus oxygen ion yields ferric oxide plus water

$$Fe \cdot H_2O + O^{-2} \rightarrow Fe_2O_3 + H_2O$$

In the three equations above, note that water is introduced in equation 1, then water combines with iron in equation 2, and then water is a product in equation 3. Water is a common, active ingredient in all three equations yet it is never consumed. This means that when water gets on iron, it produces rust and once the rusting process starts, additional water isn't necessary for the rusting process to continue. In the widely accepted hydrolytic theory of corrosion of metals, this moisture-holding property of rust becomes of the greatest importance, for except in the presence of moisture, electrolytic action is impossible. For more on the rusting process see Chapter 12, *Rust — Cause and Prevention*.

Ionization Theory

The ionization theory, first proposed in 1887 by Swedish scientist Svante August Arrhenius, states that whenever an electrolyte is placed in a dissociating medium, such as water, part or all of the electrolyte molecules separate into ions. Some of the ions carry a positive electrical charge and others are charged negative. In all cases the oppositely charged ions are present in exactly equivalent quantities.

When salt (NaCl) dissolves in water, the sodium ion carries a single positive charge (the symbol for the singly charged sodium ion is Na^+), while the chlorine ion carries a single negative charge (it is written as Cl^-). The current between the electrodes sets these ions in motion: the positive sodium ions move toward the cathode and the negative chlorine ions move toward the anode. The motion of these ions, both positive and negative, constitutes the current in the solution. See **Figure 138**.

Electrolysis Theory

The theory behind electrolysis is as follows: In chemistry we know that oxidation (rusting) is the loss of electrons. When iron oxidizes and loses electrons it is converted into iron oxide or red rust. If we could reverse this process, that is, add electrons to iron oxide we could convert iron oxide to metallic iron. Actually, during electrolysis only a small amount of rust is converted back to metallic iron. The main product of electrolysis is ferrous oxide, or black rust.

Electrolysis is the most non-invasive way to remove rust and is certainly easier on the rusty tool than other methods of rust removal. Whether you sand, grind, sandblast, use wire wheels or chemical rust removers, these all remove good metal along with the rust and the tool usually ends up scratched. Electrolysis removes only the rust and leaves the tool surface smooth and unscratched — provided that is the way the tool was before it rusted.

Rule of Thumb

The chemistry of rusting requires the presence of water, but it does not consume the water. That's why, once water gets on iron and starts the rusting process, additional water isn't needed for the rusting to continue.

The process involves passing an electrical current through the rusted piece to convert the red rust (ferric oxide), which often clings tenaciously to iron, into black rust (ferrous oxide), which easily sloughs off. To do this conversion we have to reverse the rusting process, so instead of removing electrons (rusting) we have to add electrons. By adding electrons via an automobile battery charger, we can convert red rust to a mixture of metallic iron and black rust, and by changing one rust state (red) to a different rust state (black), we make it easier to remove the iron oxide (rust) from the metal. Some of the black rust actually is further reduced to yield some metallic iron, but it is a thin film not firmly attached and is easy to rub off. There is no appreciable metal build-up.

Chemically, electrolytic removal of rust looks like this:

Red rust plus electricity yields black rust

Ferric oxide plus electrons yields ferrous oxide

$$Fe_2O_3 + e- \rightarrow FeO$$

A little of the black rust is converted (reduced) to iron metal.

Black rust plus electricity yields metallic iron

Ferrous oxide plus electrons yields iron

$$2FeO + e^- \rightarrow 2Fe + O_2\uparrow$$

Electrolysis in The Shop

The basic concept is to use a 12-volt car battery charger to pass a small electrical current through a rusty tool that's submerged in an electrolyte solution. An exchange of ions takes place, resulting in removal of the rust.

Two things are reduced (they gain electrons) at the cathode — water and rusty iron. The reduction of the water produces hydrogen gas, which you see as bubbles.

Water plus electricity yields oxygen and hydrogen

$$2H_2O + e^- \rightarrow O_2 + 2H_2\uparrow$$

These tiny oxygen and hydrogen bubbles form at the surface of the metal and help to loosen the rust. Red rust (ferric oxide) is reduced to ferrous oxide (black rust) and in the process the rusty clump is loosened from the tool. Some of this black sludge falls to the bottom of the bucket, although on heavily rusted items some is held tightly and must be cleaned from the surface with an abrasive pad. Because hydrogen is combustible and lighter than air (remember the Hindenburg?) conduct the electrolysis with a good draft and away from open flames.

The electrolyte can be as simple as baking soda (sodium bicarbonate) which is dissolved in water. In solution the bicarb salt becomes a sodium ion (Na^+) and a bicarbonate ion (HCO_3^-). These positive and negative ions carry the current in the solution — the negative ions move to the positive electrode (anode) and the positive ions migrate towards the negative electrode (cathode). Like electrons moving in a wire, the result is a current. The ions thus provide a pathway for the electrical current from the battery charger to travel from one electrode to the other.

Once the rust has been converted from red to black, it loosens its hold on the steel and the solution helps to convey it to the bottom of the bucket, baring more rust to work on.

Equipment Required for Electrolysis

There are four components in the process: a battery charger (current source), ionic solution (electrolyte), sacrificial iron connected to the positive battery charger terminal (anode), and the rusted part connected to the negative charger terminal (cathode).

1. A Battery Charger — A 12-volt car battery charger capable

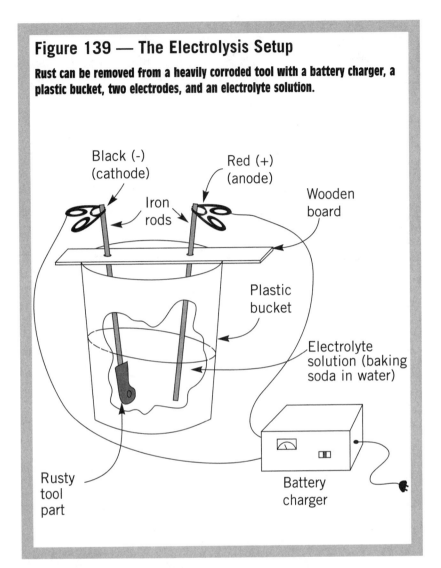

Figure 139 — The Electrolysis Setup
Rust can be removed from a heavily corroded tool with a battery charger, a plastic bucket, two electrodes, and an electrolyte solution.

Black (-)
(cathode)

Red (+)
(anode)

Iron rods

Wooden board

Plastic bucket

Electrolyte solution (baking soda in water)

Rusty tool part

Battery charger

of generating 4 amps is ideal. A 6-volt charger will work but the process will be slower. Try to use a charger with a built-in ammeter; that way you can tell if the process is working. I use a 6/12 volt charger with a 2 amp slow charge and a 6 amp fast charge, equipped with an ammeter and resettable circuit breaker.

2. The Anode (red) — This positive electrode will be a piece

Rule of Thumb

Cast iron, such as your hand plane body and saw table, is liable to crack because it contains graphite particles that concentrate the stress.

Rule of Thumb

Safety —

Before getting started there are a few safety points:

1. Don't put your hands in the electrolysis solution and don't touch either electrode when the charger is turned on.

2. A by-product of the process is hydrogen so keep the process outdoors and away from open flames.

3. Keep children and pets away from the electrolysis.

4. Don't let the anode and the cathode touch outside of the bath or inside when the charger is on.

of concrete reinforcement bar (rebar), a spoon, a pot lid, or any piece of iron that conducts electricity. It should be free of rust or scale and not galvanized. Its function is to provide electrical contact between the positive lead of the battery charger and the solution. The copper connector from the charger should make good contact with the metal bar, but should not be immersed in the solution. If it does touch, some copper will be ionized and disappear into the solution, possibly to be deposited on the iron tool.

3. The Cathode (black) — The rusty tool is attached to the negative terminal; another piece of rebar will do the trick. The rod is connected to the negative terminal of the charger and delivers electrons to the reaction.

4. The Ionic Solution — An electrolyte is any substance that, when in solution, forms a liquid that will conduct an electric current. Any substance that dissolves in water will conduct electricity to some degree and therefore can serve as the electrolyte. Acids, bases, and salts are common electrolytes. The electrolyte literature mentions sodium chloride (common table salt), sodium carbonate (washing soda), sodium bicarbonate (baking soda), hard water (has minerals

dissolved), sea water (salt dissolved in water), lye (sodium or potassium hydroxide), vinegar (dilute acetic acid), and laundry detergent (washing soda plus bleach and detergent). For the purposes of this discussion we'll use sodium bicarbonate, a common household product that dissociates easily, is cheap, readily available and non-toxic. If it is spilled, it is non-corrosive and it is easy on the environment when disposed of.

Electrolysis, Step-by-Step

1. Dissolve 2 tablespoons of sodium bicarbonate (Arm and Hammer Baking Soda®) per gallon of warm water. The solution has two purposes: (1) to conduct the electrical current from one electrode to the other and (2) to help loosen the black rust. Use a plastic bucket or any non-conducting container large enough to submerge the rusty tool. A 5-gallon plastic bucket works nicely. See **Figure 139**.

2. Drill two ¾ inch holes in a board and lay it across the top of the bucket. Put two iron rods through the holes to rest on the bottom of the bucket. If you use concrete-reinforcing rods, file off the ridges on the side where the tool will be attached — you want a good connection.

3. Prepare the rusty tool by removing any non-iron parts and any wood pieces. Clean the tool with paint thinner to get rid of any grease and oil. It's important that the current have a good path to travel from the battery charger down one rod, into and through the rusty tool, through the solution to the other rod and back to the charger.

4. Attach the rusty tool to one of the metal rods with iron wire making sure there is good electrical contact, which can be difficult with heavily rusted objects. Use string or rubber bands but not copper wire.

5. Attach the leads from the charger to the iron rods — the black (negative) lead to the rusty tool rod, the red (positive) lead to the other sacrificial rod.

6. Set the charger to 'trickle' or 'charge' (not 'start') and plug it into a 120-v circuit. Make sure the two rods (or the tool and the other rod) are not touching.

7. Turn on the charger. When the process is working, the ammeter on the charger will record 1 to 2 amps and bubbles will soon appear on the surface of the rusty tool and on the positive (red) rod. If everything is set up correctly and you still don't see bubbles, toss in some more baking soda or move the rods closer together.

8. Experiment to learn how

long to leave the charger going. Thirty minutes will be sufficient for tools with just a little rust. Leaving the tool in the solution for a longer time is not injurious to the metal because, when the red rust has been converted to black rust, nothing else happens, the reaction is over. As long as the iron is underwater and away from oxygen, it won't rust and the slightly alkaline solution won't do it any harm either — although Japanning, a common coating for protecting steel, and paint may begin to lift after a prolonged period. The only problem with leaving the tool in the solution overly long would be if the ionic solution itself attacked the tool. This would only happen if the solution were a strong alkali or acid.

9. The electrolysis will work first on the rusted surface that directly faces the anode. Every 30 minutes, rotate the tool so a new surface faces the anode. Turn off the charger before you touch either electrode.

10. Unplug the charger and remove the tool from the solution. It won't look bright and shiny at this point. Rub it under running water with a plastic pot scrubber and, depending on the amount of original rust, you may have to repeat the process. Sound plating and japanning will not be affected but plating under which

Rule of Thumb

1. Remove non-ferrous metallic parts and wood before you begin.

2. Clean the metal with paint thinner to remove oil and grease.

3. Set the process up outside.

4. Hook the rusty tool or part up to the black battery lead.

Figure 140 — For Large Objects

Use two battery chargers for big items in a large bath. Put the negative (black) leads of both chargers on the rusted piece and the positive (red) leads on pieces of metal suspended in the electrolyte bath.

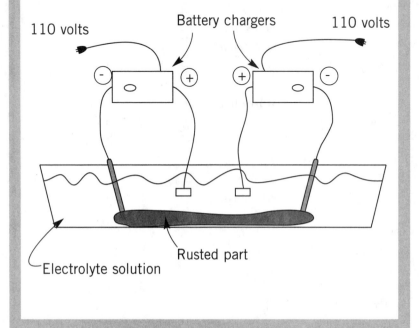

110 volts   Battery chargers   110 volts

Rusted part

Electrolyte solution

the thin, grey metal deposit — actually newly minted iron — rub lightly with 1000-grit paper or fine steel wool.

13. The cleaned metal will rust again very quickly so coat it with wax, paint, oil or grease.

Variations

The item to be de-rusted can be the inside of the electrolyte container itself. Hook the black (negative) electrode to the container, fill the cavity with electrolyte, and suspend the red (positive) electrode so it is in the solution but not touching metal.

If the rusty item is very large, use a children's plastic swimming pool or a non-metal garbage can as the electrolyte container. A long item can be treated by immersing half of it in the solution, then turning it around to treat the other half. There'll be no lap marks. Use two battery chargers if the electrolyte bath is large. See **Figure 140.**

To clean rusty spots on large objects or items that can't be submerged, soak a sponge in the electrolyte and apply it to the rust. Stick the negative (black) electrode into the sponge and apply the red (positive) electrode to the metal.

Rule of Thumb

You can use electrolysis to clean the rust off **a large item** like the table for a woodworking machine by submerging it in a plastic wading pool or a large plastic garbage can. To speed the process along, use two battery chargers in stead of one.

rust has formed will usually be lifted, and the solution will soften some paints.

11. Once all the rust is gone, dry it immediately with a soft towel. It's a good idea to put it in an oven set on 'warm' for a half-hour to make sure all the moisture is gone — this will dry all the little nooks and crannies.

12. The surface of the rusted area will be black and the rusted pits will still be pitted, but free of rust. Shiny, non-rusted metal remains unchanged. To remove

CHAPTER 14

Coopering

Coopering is the barrel maker's art, the technique of making wooden containers by edge-joining vertical staves into a cylinder. The word "cooper" derives from the French word "cupe" which means cask, and historically a cooper was one who "made or repaired wooden casks." From about 1640 until the early 1900s, there was a cooper in nearly every town in the United States. Wooden casks, barrels, buckets, kegs, and vats were needed to hold, store, and transport hundreds of dry and liquid materials. And every Saturday night a large, wooden washtub was pulled into the kitchen, filled with water heated on a coal stove, and thousands of Americans scrubbed themselves clean — whether they needed it or not.

In the early 1900s, cardboard was introduced in the United States. These wood pulp-based boxes and liquid-tight containers were cheaper, lighter than wooden containers, and could be turned out by the thousands. They soon became the choice for shipping and storing foods and goods. By 1925 the barrel had gone the way of the buggy whip and the cooper was standing in the unemployment line alongside the buggy maker.

The few coopers still doing commercial work today use machines to make a relatively small number of barrels mostly for low-volume, specialty wineries. Hand cooperage is practiced by only a few artisans who make casks for museums, historical restorations, and amateur wine and beer makers. A woodworker today may knock out six- and eight-sided flower buckets and other decorative containers but this work can hardly be called cooperage. Perhaps of more interest to cabinetmakers and the serious woodworker is the use of the coopering

Figure 141 — Cooperage

The cooper's technique is used to construct staved containers — buckets, tubs, and casks. It also is used to make curved-front drawers, cabinet doors, chest lids, and chair seats.

technique to fashion more complicated items such as a curved drawer front for a chest of drawers, a rounded door for a cabinet, arched lids for chests, and curved seats for chairs. In each of these cases, the end product is a piece of furniture shaped like the segment of a circle — that is, a partial arc. Whether the construction is a complete cylinder or a partial segment, the curve (arc) is strong, predictable, reproducible, stable, and visually interesting. **Figure 1** shows some of the projects made by coopering.

History

The cooper is depicted in paintings and murals dating back thousands of years. For at least 2000 years, the construction methods remained essentially the same. The shape of the barrel also has not changed because it has proved rugged enough to be rolled down the gangplank of a ship or to be banged around in the back of a wagon. It can withstand great force from the weight of flour, apples, and fish, or the pressure from fermenting beer. Tight casks for molasses, fish, wine, and whiskey were known as wet cooperage, while slack cooperage was for dry goods such as flour, nails, and apples. Nail kegs and other light-duty containers had nearly straight sides, while the barrels for wine and ale had wide staves with a

mid-section larger than the ends

A "barrel" refers to a capacity or a measurement similar to a bushel or a peck. In the United States, a hogshead, or double-barrel, is 63 gallons and a barrel is 31.5 gallons. Dry goods like flour and grain, and wet goods like whiskey and molasses, could be purchased and delivered in wooden casks, by the barrel, hogshead, half-barrel, or firkin. A half-barrel measures 15½ gallons (about 100 pounds dry measure) and a firkin is a quarter barrel, or about 8 gallons. These amounts are approximate because the dry and wet measures are different — a barrel of flour is 26¼ gallons, while a barrel of whiskey is 31.5 gallons. Also, England and the colonies didn't agree on the basic quantity of a barrel — a barrel of apples in London was 36 gallons, while a barrel of apples in Boston was 26 gallons. The savvy buyer knew whether he was buying wet or dry goods, and whether the product was coming from the United States or England.

Over the years the word barrel has come to refer to the container rather than the amount. **Figure 142** shows the parts of a round, wooden cask that bows outward in the middle and is held together with metal hoops — the container we now call a barrel.

Barrels

The cooper determined the number of staves needed for each barrel by estimating the size and then figuring one stave for each inch of diameter at the barrel head. This is mathematically sound when each stave is just a smidgen over 3 inches wide, because the diameter times pi (π) equals the circumference.

Circumference
= Diameter x π (3.14)

The wooden cask of barrel size was about 34 to 36 inches high and 16 to 18 inches in diameter at the head, although these dimensions varied from cooper to cooper. Straight-grained white oak was the wood of choice for watertight barrels, while slack barrels were made of red oak, ash, and chestnut. The logs were cut to length then split and quartered with ¾ inch by 4 inch wedges and a sledge. A froe was used to split out wide slabs that, were air-dried for about a year. The boards were shaped with a side axe to 3¾ inches wide in the middle, tapering to 3 inches at each end, then beveled along the two long edges using a cooper's jointer — a 6 foot long board with a plane mounted upside down in its middle. Working on a shave-horse, the cooper used a draw knife to round over the outside of each stave so it matched the outer radius of the barrel. The inside of the stave was slightly hollowed out to make it easier to bend.

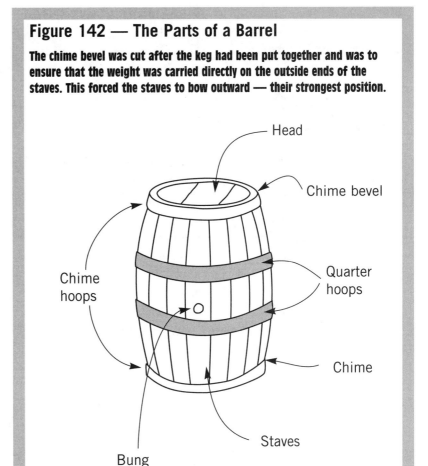

Figure 142 — The Parts of a Barrel

The chime bevel was cut after the keg had been put together and was to ensure that the weight was carried directly on the outside ends of the staves. This forced the staves to bow outward — their strongest position.

The staves were stood upright in a circle in an iron hoop. A fire was placed inside in a metal basket and the staves were heated for 15 to 30 minutes, until they were hot to the touch along their entire length. Another hoop was then driven over the outside of the staves to shape the barrel. The remaining hoops were added and the cask fitted with heads. The barrel was filled with water and tested for leaks, which were plugged with sharpened pegs. The barrel was ready for delivery.

Rule of Thumb

The traditional cooper fitted staves together to make barrels and casks, but you can use the same technique to make curved panels for furniture — the coopered construction does not have to be a full circle.

Figure 143 — Finding the Length of Sides

The inner circle (a) radius is measured from the center to one side of the polygon. An outer circle (b) radius is the distance to a point of the polygon.

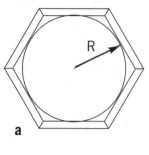

a

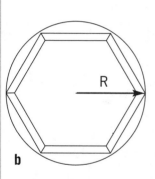

b

Regular Polygons

A regular polygon is a multisided figure having all sides and all angles equal. If we know the width of the polygon from side to side (inner circle), or the width from point to point (outer circle) (**Figure 143**), we can determine the length of a side by using an appropriate constant (**Figure 144**).

Problem 1: We need to construct a wooden tub with six sides to hold a round flower pot 12½ inches in diameter. What should be the length of each side?

Solution 1: Note that the hexagon must be constructed so a 12½ inch circle will fit inside as in **Figure 143a**, so we must use the inner circle radius constant in **Figure 144**. To ensure ample room, we will make the wooden tub 13 inches side to side.

Math

The length of a side of a polygon equals the radius divided by the circle constant.

Side length (L) = Radius (R) ÷ Constant (K)

Where R = 13 ÷ 2 = 6.5" and hexagon, inner circle K = 0.866

L = 6.5" ÷ 0.866 = 7.51"

Therefore each of the six sides of the hexagon should be 7½ inches wide (inner board measurement) so that when they are joined, a 12½ inch circular pot can be placed within.

Problem 2: We want to make some eight-sided cedar buckets to fit into a garden flower cart. The cart has 8½ inch diameter holes in the surface. What width should the sides of the octagon be? See **Figure 143b**.

Solution 2: Use **Figure 144** to find the outer circle radius constant. Find octagon and read the constant (1.307).

The length of a side of a polygon equals the radius divided by the circle constant.

Side length (L) = Radius (R) ÷ Constant (K)

Where R = 8.5" ÷ 2 = 4.25" and K = 1.307

L = 4.25 ÷ 1.307 = 3.25"

Therefore each of the eight sides of the octagon should be 3¼ inches long (outer board measurement) so that when they are joined, the cask will set in an 8½ inch hole.

Problem 3: Let's make a little 16-sided bucket to set on the stove to hold wooden spoons and cooking utensils. It will be 6 inches high and 4¾ inches wide (side to side).

Solution 3: A check of **Figure 144** shows a 16-sided polygon is not listed. The general equation for a polygon constant is:

Math

Side Length Constant = 1 ÷ (Sin 360/n ÷ Cos 180/n)

Where n = number of sides

For the sixteen-sided polygon:

Side Length Constant = 1 ÷ (Sin 360/16 ÷ Cos 180/16)

Side Length Constant = 1 ÷ (Sin 22.5 ÷ Cos 11.25)

Side Length Constant = 1 ÷ (0.3827 ÷ 0.9808)

Side Length Constant = 1 ÷ 0.3902 = 2.56

Now, find the length of the side:

Side Length = Circle Radius ÷ Side Length Constant K

Where K = 2.56

Side Length = (4.75 ÷ 2) ÷ 2.56

Side Length = 2.38 ÷ 2.56 = 0.93" ≈ $^{15}\!/_{16}$"

So, we make the little sixteen-sided spoon holder with slats $^{15}\!/_{16}$ inches wide. The rip bevel angle will be:

180° ÷ 16 = 11.25°

For more on polygons and side lengths, see Woodworkers' Essential Chapter 8, p. 80, ***Size and Measurement***.

Construction of Regular Polygons

Now, how do we actually construct one of these multi-sided casks?

Problem 4: Make a ten-sided bucket 14 inches high and 10 inches across (side to side).

Solution 4:

1. Check **Figure 144** to find the width of the ten slats.

Figure 144 — Constants for Side Lengths of Regular Polygons [1]

Name	Number of Sides	Inner Circle Radius Constant [2]	Outer Circle Radius Constant [3]
Triangle	3	0.289	0.577
Square	4	0.500	0.707
Pentagon	5	0.688	0.851
Hexagon	6	0.866	1.000
Heptagon	7	1.038	1.152
Octagon	8	1.207	1.307
Nonagon	9	1.373	1.462
Decagon	10	1.539	1.618
Undecagon	11	1.703	1.775
Dodecagon	12	1.866	1.932

(1) Side Length = Circle Radius ÷ Constant
(2) Use this constant to construct a polygon when the circle goes inside.
(3) Use this constant to construct a polygon when the circle goes outside.

Decagon, Inner Circle, K = 1.539

2. Slat width = Radius ÷ Constant

Slat Width = (10 ÷ 2) ÷ 1.539

Slat Width = 3.25" = 3¼"

3. Cut ten slats 14 inches long and about 4 inches wide.

4. Figure the bevel angle.

Angle = 180° ÷ number of sides = 180° ÷ 10 = 18°

5. Set the table saw blade to 18° and bevel-cut one edge of each slat.

6. Set the fence to 3¼ inches and bevel-rip the other side of each stave.

7. Glue the staves together and make a bottom.

Rule of Thumb

When making a barrel with staves that are about 3 inches wide, you'll need one stave for each inch of diameter.

Figure 145 — Calculate the Bevel Angle

1. Draw the full-size curve.
2. Divide the arc into individual staves (S).
3. Find the radius of the arc.
4. Measure the total angle (A) with a protractor.
5. Calculate the bevel angle (B) using the equation:
B = A ÷ 2 x S
6. Example if A = 60° and S = 6, then
          B = 60 ÷ 2 x 6 = 60 ÷ 12 = 5°

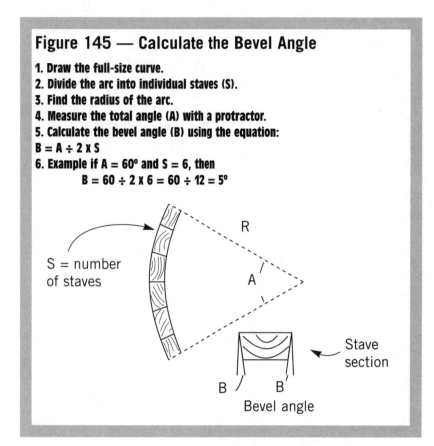

S = number of staves

R

A

Stave section

B   B'

Bevel angle

Arcs of Partial Polygons

The tubs, pots, and casks we made before were complete circles. The next projects — doors, chest tops, etc., are only partial circles, that is, arcs. To illustrate, we will construct an arc 20 inches wide with a height of 2 inches. We will use six staves.

The angle to cut the staves can be determined in two ways:

> **Without Math:** Draw the pattern full-size and measure the stave thickness, width, and bevel from it.

> **With Math:** Determine the circle radius and calculate the angle, **Figure 145**.

a. Without Math

There is a fairly easy way to figure out the width of the staves and angles:

With Center Divider

1. **Cut a piece** of plywood with the same width (20 inches) and height (2 inches) of the arc **(Figure 146a)**.

2. **Draw the arc** full size with trammel points **(Figure 146b)**.

3. **Cut away** the waste with a bandsaw and smooth the edges, and use dividers to step off the six staves **(Figure 146c)**.

4. **Use a combination** try-square with a center head to make angle lines **(Figure 146d)**.

5. **Use a sliding** T-bevel to record the angle lines **(Figure 146e)**.

6. **Transfer** the angle lines to the saw blade **(Figure 146f)**.

7. **Bevel-rip** each stave and compare its width and angle with the full-size pattern.

8. **Adjust** the blade and re-cut each stave until the angle is correct.

9. **Adjust** each stave width by comparing it to the pattern.

b. With Math

Refer to **Figure 147**.

1. **Determine** the length of the arc chord (AC). This is the width of the door.

2. **Find** the height (h).

3. **Determine** the Radius (R) using the equations:

AB x BC = h y

Where, in our case, h=2", AC = 10", AB = 5" and BC = 5".

5 x 5 = 2 y

y = 25 ÷ 2 = 12.5"

To find the diameter (DE) of the circle:

Diameter = y + h

Where y = 12.5" and y = 2"

Diameter = 2 + 12.5 = 14.5"

To find the Radius (R) of the circle:

Radius = Diameter ÷ 2

Radius = 14.5 ÷ 2 = 7.25"

4. **Find the total angle.**

Arc Angle
$= 2 \times \sin^{-1} (AC \div 2R)$

Where AC = 10"
and R = 7.25"

Arc Angle
$= 2 \sin^{-1} [10 \div (2 \times 7.25)]$

Arc Angle
$= 2 \sin^{-1} (10 \div 14.5)$

Arc Angle $= 2 \sin^{-1} 0.6897$

Arc Angle $= 2 \times 43.6 = 87.2°$

5. **Choose** the number of slats (6) and step them off.

6. Find the bevel for each slat. Bevel angle equals the total angle divided by twice the number of slats.

Bevel Angle
= Arc Angle ÷ 2 x Slats

Bevel Angle = 87.2° ÷ (2 x 6)
= 87.2 ÷ 12 = 7.26° ≈ 7¼°.

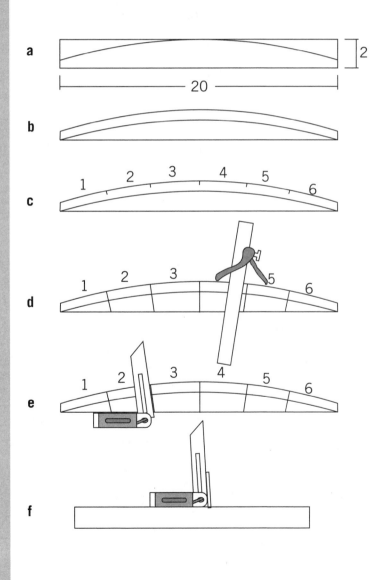

Figure 146 — Making the Staves without Math

(a) Cut a piece of plywood to the same width and height as the arc and draw the top of the arc.
(b) Cut away the waste and draw the rest of the arc.
(c) Divide the arc into six sections and mark the position of each stave.
(d) Use a combination try-square with a center head to draw each stave angle.
(e) Use a sliding T-bevel to find the angle.
(f) Transfer the angle from the pattern to the saw blade.

Figure 147 — The Arc

Finding the angles with Math

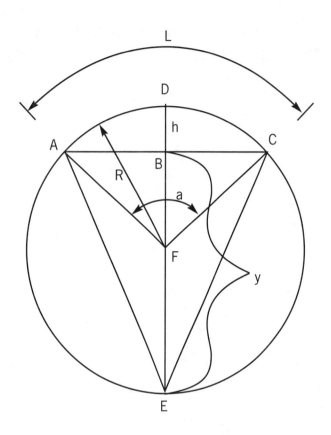

AC = Arc Chord
h = Arc Height
R = Circle/Arc Radius
a = arc angle
DE = Circle Diameter
L = Arc Length
y = circle diameter minus h
F = Circle Center

Arc Radius $R = [(\frac{1}{2}AC)^2 + h^2] \div 2h$
Arc Length $L = \pi R a \div 180$
Arc Height $h = R - \frac{1}{2}\sqrt{4R^2 - (AC)^2}$
Arc Angle (in degrees) $a = 2\sin^{-1}(AC \div 2R)$

7. Find the length of the arc:

Arc Length (L)
$= (\pi R a) \div 180$

Arc Length (L)
$= (3.14 \times 7.25 \times 87.2) \div 180$
$= 1985 \div 180 = 11"$

8. Find the slat sidth:

Slat Width = Arc Length ÷ Number of Slats

Slat Width $= 11" \div 6 = 1.83"$
$\approx 1^{13}\!/_{16}"$

Now rip each slat at a $7\frac{1}{4}°$ bevel and to a width of $1^{13}\!/_{16}$ inches.

Projects

The following four projects use the same coopering techniques as the barrel maker but instead of a whole circle, we need only a partial circle, that is, an arc.

1. Chest Lid

Making a chest lid is, in some ways, different from making a stand-alone curved surface because the shape of the arc is defined by the ribs of the chest. The beveled staves will be attached to the ribs and the ends of the chest instead of being glued together in a stand-alone manner. Each stave can be cut, adjusted, then attached. The next stave is then cut and attached until the top is complete. See **Figure 148**.

Problem 5: We want to make a toy chest. The box will be 34 inches long by 21 inches wide and 21 inches high. The rounded lid will rise 6½ inches.

We want the staves to be 1 inch to 1½ inches wide. How many staves will we need and what is their width and bevel angle?

Solution 5: Before we can determine the number of staves, the width and the bevel angle, we need to find the arc radius, the angle of the arc and the length of the arc (**Figure 147**).

Math

Find the Arc Radius:

Where AC = 21 and h = 6.5

Radius (R)
= $[(\frac{1}{2}\,AC)^2 + h^2] \div 2h$

Radius (R)
= $[(\frac{1}{2} \times 21)^2 + 6.5^2] \div 2 \times 6.5$

Radius (R)
= (110.25 + 42.25) ÷ 13

Radius (R) = 152.5 ÷ 13
= 11.73" ≈ 11¾"

Find the Angle of the Arc:

Arc Angle (a)
= 2 Arcsine (AC ÷ 2R)

Arc Angle (a)
= 2 Arcsine [21 ÷ (2 x 11.73)]

Arc Angle (a)
= 2 Arcsine 0.8951

Arc Angle (a)
= 2 x 63.5 = 127°

Find the Length of the Arc:

Arc Length (L) = π R a ÷ 180

Arc Length (L)
= (3.14 x 11.73 x 127) ÷ 180

Arc Length (L) = 4679 ÷ 180
= 25.99 ≈ 26"

Find the Number of Slats:

Divide the arc length (L) by

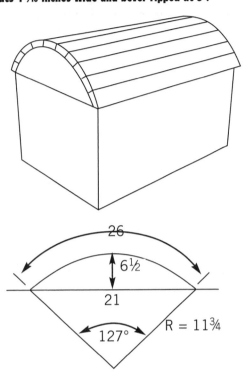

Figure 148 — Chest Lid

Use ten slats 1¹⁵⁄₁₆ inches wide and bevel-ripped at 5°.

the slat width wanted (1.25").

Number of Slats
= Arc length (L) ÷ 1.25"

Slats = 26 ÷ 1.25 = 20.8

Therefore we will use 21 slats.

Find the Slat Width:

Slat Width = Arc Length (L) ÷ Number of Slats (21)

Slat Width = 26 ÷ 21 = 1.24 ≈ 1¼"

Find the Corner Angle:

Corner Angle = Arc Angle ÷ Number of Slats

Corner Angle = 127 ÷ 21 = 6.05° or 6°

Find the Bevel Angle:

Figure 149 — A Curved Door for a Small Cabinet

Because it is so difficult to predict the exact width and curve of a coopered door, make the door first and then construct the cabinet to fit.

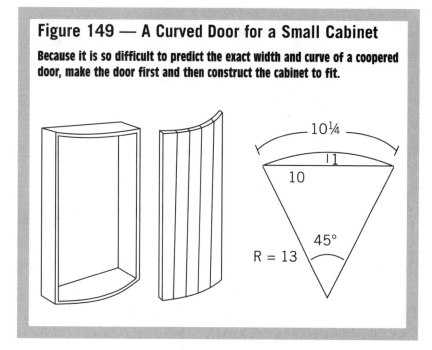

Problem 6: We want to construct a curved door for a small cabinet as in **Figure 149**. The door will be 15 inches high by 10 inches wide. There will be five staves and the arc height (h) is 1 inch. What will be the width of each stave and at what bevel angle should the saw blade be set?

Solution 6:

Find the Radius:

$R = [(\frac{1}{2} \times AC)^2 + h^2] \div 2h$

$R = [(\frac{1}{2} \times 10)^2 + 1^2] \div 2 \times 1$

$R = [(5)^2 + 1] \div 2 = 26 \div 2$
$= 13"$

Find the Arc Angle:

Arc Angle
$= 2$ Arcsine $(AC \div 2 R)$

Arc Angle
$= 2$ Arcsine $[10 \div (2 \times 13)]$

Arc Angle $= 2$ Arcsine $(10 \div 26)$

Arc Angle $= 2$ Arcsine 0.3846
$= 2 \times 22.6° \approx 45°$

Find the Arc Length (L):

Arc Length (L) $= \pi R a \div 180$

Arc Length (L)
$= (3.14 \times 13 \times 45°) \div 180$

Arc Length (l) $= 1837 \div 180$
$= 10.2" \approx 10\frac{1}{4}"$

Find the Slat Width:

Slat Width = Arc Length (L)
$\div$ Number of Slats

Slat Width $= 10.2 \div 5 = 2.04$
$\approx 2"$

Find the Bevel Angle:

Bevel Angle
$=$ Arc Angle $\div 2 \times$ Slats

Bevel Angle $= 45° \div (2 \times 5)$
$= 45° \div 10 = 4.5°$

Bevel Angle= Corner Angle ÷ 2

Bevel Angle = 6.0 ÷ 2 = 3°

So we will cut twenty-one slats to 1¼ inch width at a bevel-rip angle of 3°. When the twenty-one slats are attached to the ribs of the chest lid, they will span 21 inches, form an arc 26 inches long and the height of the arc will be 6½ inches. If the slats do not lay flat and rock on the ribs, use the cove cutting technique described in **Chapter 21**, *Coves on the Table Saw.*

2. Cabinet Door

It is difficult to set the blade of a table saw to precisely 5° (or 4.5° or 5.5°). Because the bevel angle cut on the staves determines the length and curve of the door, most cabinetmakers make the door first. They then take direct measurements from the door and make the cabinet to fit.

Set the saw blade at 4.5° and make one bevel-rip cut. Set the fence to 2 inches and cut the other side of each slat.

3. Curved Drawer

To make a curved-front drawer, cooper the ends. See **Figure 150**.

The curved drawer is an example of coopering to make a piece that is incorporated into furniture. The curved drawer could be made by band-sawing a large block of solid stock, or by bent lamination. Coopering the curves is a nice touch because a circle can be made and one-quarter or 90° used for each end of the drawer face. If you make two drawers, a full circle can be made and then cut into quarters.

Construction — If you're making more than one drawer, glue up a cylinder and turn it round on a lathe. Cut the cylinder in quarters and use two per drawer.

Math

Radius = 5", Slats = 6, Arc Angle = ¼ circle = 90°

Find the Arc Length:

Arc Length = π R a ÷ 180

Arc Length
= 3.14 x 5 x 90 ÷ 180

Arc Length
= 1413 ÷ 180 = 7.85"

Find the Slat Width:

Slat Width = Arc Length ÷ Number of Slats

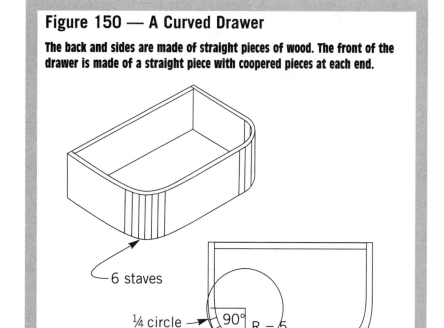

Figure 150 — A Curved Drawer

The back and sides are made of straight pieces of wood. The front of the drawer is made of a straight piece with coopered pieces at each end.

6 staves

¼ circle → 90° R = 5

6 staves

Slat Width
= 7.85" ÷ 6 = 1.3" ≈ 1⁵⁄₁₆"

Find the Corner Angle:

Corner Angle = Arc Angle ÷ Number of Slats

Corner Angle = 90 ÷ 6 = 15°

Find the Bevel Angle:

Bevel Angle =
Corner Angle ÷ 2

Bevel Angle = 15 ÷ 2 = 7.5°

4. Chair Seat

A chair seat can be made from a thick plank by hogging out the seat to create a hollow top and a flat bottom. This is the usual method for Windsor chairs. Coopering produces a seat that is curved across both the top and bottom surfaces and is not heavy

Figure 151 — Chair Seat

(a) Draw a full-size box one half of the seat width. Sketch the half-seat section inside the rectangle.
(b) Cut pieces of poster board to the size of the seat slats and lay them on the pattern. The shaded areas show overlaps.
(c) Mark the overlaps (dotted lines).
(d) Cut the pieces of cardboard so they fit together.
(e) Use these patterns to set the saw blade and bevel-rip the seat pieces.

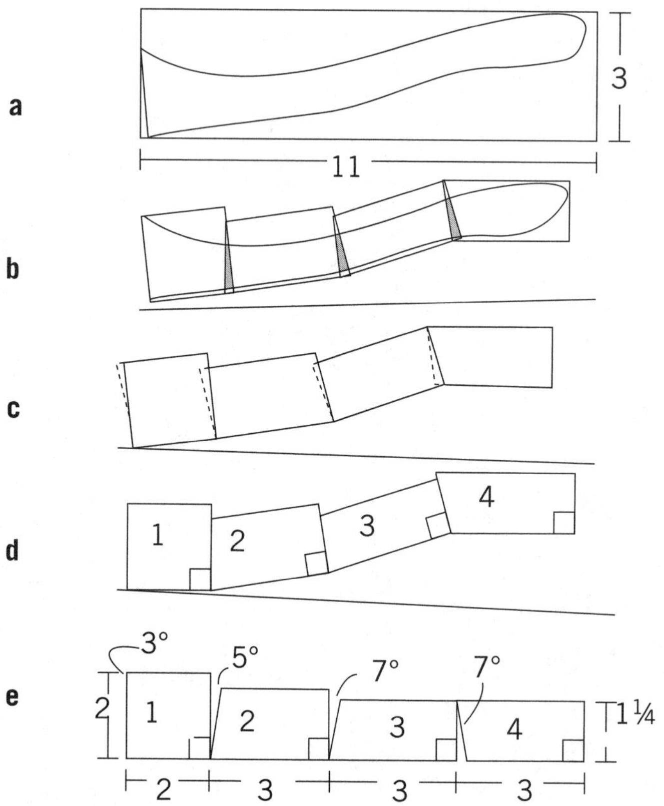

looking. See **Figure 151**.

1. Draw a full-size rectangle with the outer dimensions of the half-seat, 3 inches x 11 inches.

2. Draw the outline of the half-seat inside the rectangle.

3. Divide the width into four sections to represent the wooden staves.

4. Make pieces of poster-board to the same dimension as the seat slats, for example, 2 inches x 2 inches, 1½ inches x 3 inches, and two pieces 1¼ inch x 3 inches.

5. Lay these cardboard pieces on the pattern.

6. Mark the overlap angles and use scissors to cut the pieces so they fit together. Keep one edge of each stave at 90° and bevel the other edge. This way each stave only has to be beveled once.

7. Use these patterns to size the staves (height and width) and as a gauge to set the saw blade angle. It is not necessary to measure the angles.

8. Rip the seat pieces and compare with the pattern. Adjust. Note the center piece (#1) will be 2 inches high x 4 inches wide.

9. Use a band saw to cut away waste from each stave.

10. Glue the eight pieces together and finish shaping with scorp, chisel, and sanders.

Each of the staves that form each section can be sculpted before gluing together to save time later. With planning the front pommel, the concavities to each side, and the high flat outside rim for spindles, can all be done on the band saw before glue-up.

5. Drawer in Sideboard

The drawer in a 1785 sideboard with serpentine front is a good example of stave construction by coopering. The original plans make no mention of how to figure the miters.

Using the same procedure as in the previous project 4, Chair Seat, the drawer front **Figure 152** can be constructed. Follow the same steps 1-10 as for the chair seat to make this piece. Keep one edge of each stave at 90° and bevel-rip the other edge.

Use Equal Bevels?

When putting together a cask with eight slats it would be easier to bevel only one edge of each slat. The bevel angle would be twice that of a double bevel and therefore easier to set on the table saw. Also, only eight bevel cuts would be needed instead of sixteen. However, the beveled edge will be longer than the non-beveled, 90° edge (**Figure 153**). So how much is this difference and how will it affect the surface of the cylinder?

Problem 7: We want to construct an eight-sided cylinder (cask, tub, barrel, whatever) and would like to bevel only one edge of each slat, leaving the other edge square. What will be the difference in length of the mating edges? We plan to use ¾ inch boards.

Solution 7: The width of the slats is immaterial; the thickness of the wood stock and the number of sides in the polygon

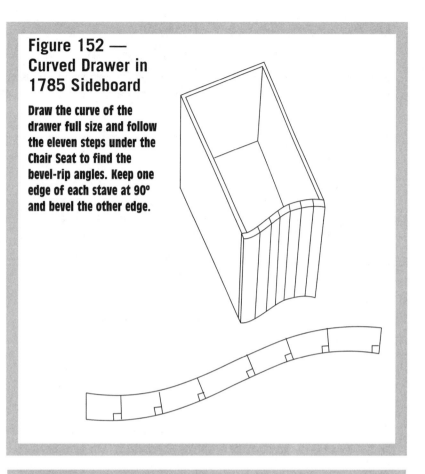

Figure 152 — Curved Drawer in 1785 Sideboard

Draw the curve of the drawer full size and follow the eleven steps under the Chair Seat to find the bevel-rip angles. Keep one edge of each stave at 90° and bevel the other edge.

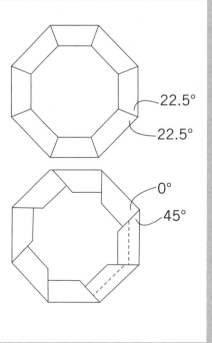

Figure 153 — An Eight-sided Cylinder with Double Bevels or Single Bevels.

An eight-sided cylinder can be constructed with both edges of each stave beveled at 22.5° (a) or only one edge of each slat beveled at 45° and the other left at 90° (b). The variation in length of each mating edge depends on the thickness of the wood and the number of sides in the polygon. The dotted lines show that the difference in length of the mating sides lessens as the thickness of the staves diminishes.

22.5°
22.5°

0°
45°

Figure 154 — Difference in Lengths of Mating Edges [1]

When an 8-sided polygon is made of 1-inch stock, the difference between the 90° edge and the 45° edge is over ⅜ inch (1 versus 1.41). If a 16-sided polygon is made of 1-inch stock, the difference is only ¹⁄₁₆ inch (1 versus 1.09).

Polygon Sides	Wood Thickness (in inches)									Corner Angle	Angle Cosine
	0.50	0.75	1	1.25	1.50	1.75	2.00	2.50	3.00		
6	1.00	1.50	2.00	2.50	3.00	3.50	4.00	5.00	6.00	60.00	0.5000
8	0.71	1.06	1.41	1.77	2.12	2.47	2.83	3.54	4.24	45.00	0.7071
10	0.62	0.93	1.24	1.55	1.85	2.16	2.47	3.09	3.71	36.00	0.809
12	0.58	0.87	1.15	1.44	1.73	2.02	2.31	2.89	3.46	30.00	0.866
14	0.56	0.83	1.11	1.39	1.67	1.94	2.22	2.78	3.33	25.72	0.9009
16	0.54	0.81	1.09	1.36	1.63	1.90	2.17	2.72	3.26	22.50	0.9205
18	0.53	0.80	1.06	1.33	1.60	1.86	2.13	2.66	3.19	20.00	0.9397
20	0.53	0.79	1.05	1.31	1.58	1.84	2.10	2.63	3.15	18.00	0.9511
22	0.52	0.78	1.04	1.30	1.56	1.82	2.08	2.61	3.13	16.36	0.9595
24	0.52	0.78	1.04	1.29	1.55	1.81	2.07	2.59	3.11	15.00	0.9659

(1) One joining side is 90 degrees, the other joining side is the Corner Angle.

Rule of Thumb

To find the correct bevel angle to set the table saw blade:

1. Find the radius of the arc

2. Find the arc angle

3. Find the arc length

4. Find the slat width

5. Find the bevel angle

are all that matters. In an octagon the side angles are:

Corner Angle=360° ÷ 8 = 45°

To find the length of the beveled edge:

Length = Wood Thickness ÷ cosine Corner Angle

L = 0.75 ÷ Cos 45

L= 0.75 ÷ 0.7071

= 1.06" ≈ 1"

The length of the two sides will be 0.75 inch versus 1.06 inch, or more than ¼ inch difference, probably too much.

Problem 8: What if we wanted to construct the door in **Figure 149** out of ⅝ inch cherry and instead of beveling both edges of the six slats, bevel only one? What would be the difference in length of the mating edges?

Solution 8: Again the width of the slats is immaterial. **Figure**

149 shows the bevel angle is 5°.

Side Angle = Bevel Angle x 2

Side Angle = 5° x 2 = 10°

To find the width of the beveled edge:

Length = Wood Thickness ÷ Cosine Corner Angle

L = 0.625" ÷ Cos 10°

L = 0.625 ÷ 0.9848

= 0.635" ≈ ⅝"

There will be no appreciable difference in the length of the two edges, one is 0.625 inch and the other is 0.635 inch, and the 10° setting on the table saw probably will be more forgiving than a 5° setting.

The chart in **Figure 154** shows the difference in length of the mating edges for different-sized polygons and different thicknesses of wood.

CHAPTER 15

Torsion Boxes

A torsion box is an excellent way to make strong and lightweight table tops, shelves, bench tops, and modular furniture. A torsion box is a structural assembly of core pieces, skins, and glue that can be used as a horizontal or vertical panel where strength and stability are needed. The engineering principles follow the deflection and torque principles of aerodynamics – like an aircraft wing. A torsion box can be made any width, length, or thickness and can be square, rectangular, or round. The design can be flat or curved and the skin can be covered before or after construction. The core materials are cheap, and the exterior can be finished with paint, stain, varnish, plastic laminate, tile, cloth, or leather. Further, it can stand alone like a shelf or be attached to other boxes to form cabinets and furniture. A T-box is extremely strong and very light in weight.

With all these attributes, industry has embraced the torsion box wholeheartedly — the design is used for hollow-core doors, desk tops, benches, table tops, work surfaces, room dividers, and large cabinetry — any situation where a strong, flat, stable, lightweight piece is needed.

But the concept is seldom used by the average woodworker, mostly because they do not understand how a torsion box works or how to build one. I'll try to demystify the job and show you where the strength and stability come from.

Introduction

When we first design a project, we consider the basics: dimensions, proportions and overall size. Then we settle on the type of wood and the joinery, along with types of glue and clamping procedures. Next we decide on the hardware we'll need and finally the sanding and the finish. If we have doubts about any step, we cast about for substitutes and coming up empty, we

redesign the project or abandon it altogether. This happened with a recent project of mine.

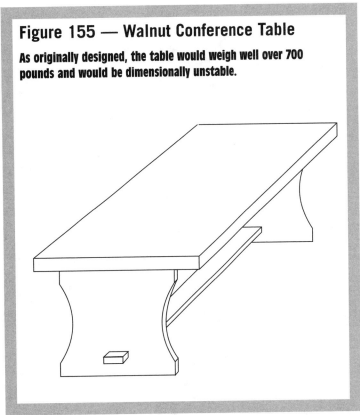

Figure 155 — Walnut Conference Table

As originally designed, the table would weigh well over 700 pounds and would be dimensionally unstable.

Rule of Thumb

A torsion box gets most of its stiffness from the top and bottom skins, provided they are firmly attached to the core pieces. The role of the core is to transfer the forces from one skin to the other, where any deflection is converted into sideways movement. In effect, load added to the torsion box causes the bottom skin to stretch or to move sideways on the core pieces.

I agreed to help a friend design and build a large conference table — 12 feet long and 4 feet wide. The client specified that it be made of walnut and that the top should be 3 inches thick. The configuration of the meeting area required that the table occasionally be moved off to one side of the room. We came up with a design that included a glued-up slab for the table top and two near full-width pedestals (**Figure 155**). Our design called for 3 inch solid walnut throughout.

We had a few misgivings. First, we knew that any wide, glued-up slab would have dimensional problems no matter how many props and underpinnings we added. Wood expands and contracts because of changes in internal moisture content in response to external humidity. Also, large glued-up pieces have a tendency to warp, twist, cup, and bow. Strike one.

We then checked on the availability of walnut and found no local source for the 12 foot long by 3 inch thick stock we needed. Ordering more than 200 board feet from a mill in Pennsylvania, at $20 per board foot, would have cost more than $4000 plus shipping. Strike two.

The third problem was size. How were we going to handle these large pieces of wood?

Wrestling 12 foot lengths of walnut onto a table saw or putting them through a planer would be a big job. I shuddered at trying to joint and glue these pieces. Strike three.

The fourth problem was the weight of the finished piece. A few calculations showed that the table with pedestal and stretcher would top 700 pounds. See **Figure 164** Page 220.

Top: 4' x 12' x 3/12'
= 12 cu. ft.

Pedestals: 2 (3' x 3' x 3/12')
= 4.5 cu. ft.

Stretcher: 2" x 6" x 12' =
2/12'x 6/12' x 12' = 1 cu. ft.

Total weight: 17.5 cu. ft. x 42
lbs. per cu. ft = 735 lbs.

The client was an accounting firm and not a health club full of bodybuilders — so, unless we put this huge piece of furniture on rollers, a 735 pound table was out of the question. Strike four.

Because of the problems with stability, availability, size, and weight, the original design was not feasible and an alternative was needed. The new design needed to be lighter while still maintaining strength and flatness. The construction needed to be dimensionally stable. We also hoped to be able to use local materials without having to order walnut, sight unseen, from across the country. We finally decided that a better choice for both the table top and the two pedestals might be three torsion boxes.

Torsion Boxes

The word torsion comes from the Latin torsus meaning to twist. In engineering, torsion is defined as the twisting of a body by the exertion of forces tending to turn one end about a longitudinal axis while the other end is held fast or turned in the opposite direction. In wood-working we encounter this twisting motion with shelves, table tops, doors, partitions, and other large, relatively thin structures. The job of a torsion box is to resist both deflection and twisting.

Torsion boxes offer design possibilities that solid wood cannot — including freedom from problems of wood movement, reduced weight, less material, cheaper costs, structural rigidity, and the ability to casually manipulate thickness and width without regard to the availability of solid stock. These features should make the torsion box a concept that woodworkers would be eager to embrace.

However, the torsion box is a well-kept secret in woodworking and the rudiments of construction are relatively unknown. A search of one index of 1010

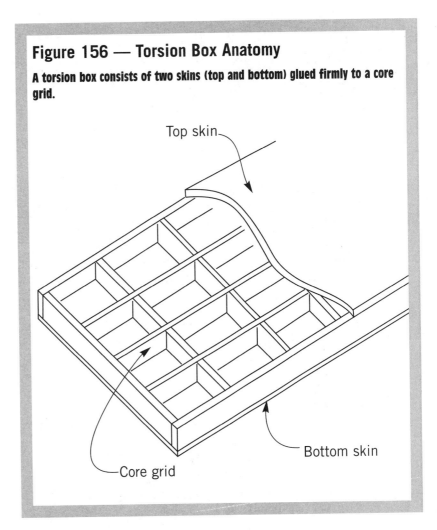

Figure 156 — Torsion Box Anatomy

A torsion box consists of two skins (top and bottom) glued firmly to a core grid.

Top skin

Core grid

Bottom skin

issues of nineteen different wood-working magazines showed only three articles on torsion boxes out of more than 22,000 listings. It's no wonder woodworkers don't use it more. Also none of the articles gave mathematical data on the strength and stiffness of a torsion box — woodworkers don't know how to calculate its strength.

When we want to substitute this shop-made beam for a solid piece of wood, several questions arise:

Rule of Thumb

To make a torsion box stiffer and thus capable of supporting a heavier load, increase the thickness of the skins, and/or the width (depth) of the core parts. These two factors are much more important than changing from one wood species to another, changing the thickness of the core parts, or changing their spacing.

1. How do you construct a torsion box?

2. How big should the core pieces be?

3. How close should the core pieces be spaced?

4. How thick should the skins be?

5. Where does the strength of a torsion box come from?

6. Does the skin or the core contribute more to the stiffness?

7. Is a torsion box as strong as solid wood?

8. How do the weights of solid wood and a torsion box compare?

These questions will be answered in the following pages.

How a Torsion Box Works

A torsion box consists of two skins of plywood, or similar thin material, firmly attached to an inner grid of wood strips (see **Figure 156**). When constructed correctly, the force from one surface is transferred through the core to the other surface (see **Figure 157**). In woodworking, the construction usually consists of ½ to ¾ inch wide core materials and ⅛ inch, ¼ inch or ⅜ inch plywood for the skin surfaces. The resulting structure has strength not present in either the core or the grid alone and gets its strength in the same way an airplane wing does.

Beam Strength Math

We can think of a torsion box as a special type of beam. Beam strength (stiffness) is calculated using this formula:

$$Y = (0.021 \times W \times L^3) / (E \times I)$$

In this formula the beam ends are fixed but not pinned and the load is centered. See Woodworkers' Essential Chapter 16, **Shelf Loads** for more on this.

Y = Maximum deflection or sag at mid-span in inches.

0.021 = A constant.

W = Weight of the load in pounds.

L = Length of the board or beam in inches.

E = Modulus of Elasticity (MOE) in pounds per square inch.

I = Moment of Inertia.

We can see by examining the beam stiffness formula above that resistance to bending depends on four factors:

1. The type of wood. The property of the wood to resist deformation is its modulus of elasticity (MOE). All woods have values between 1.23×10^6 (fir and chestnut) and 2.00×10^6 (locust). In calculating beam stiffness, the wood type is less important than the length or thickness of the beam. See **Figure 161** for a list of woods and their MOE.

2. The cross section. The moment of inertia (I) of a beam depends on its cross section (width times thickness). Because the cross-section of most woodworking projects (shelves, table tops, doors, etc.) is rectangular, the I-value is the horizontal dimension (width) times the vertical thickness (height) cubed and divided by 12. Width and thickness are measured in inches. Huge gains in 'I' are achieved when we increase the thickness (vertical) number. This is why a 2 x 6 floor joist is so much stiffer on edge than when laid flat.

A 2 x 6 beam laid on edge.

$$I = W \times T^3 / 12$$

$$I = 2 \times 6^3 / 12$$

$$I = 2 \times 216 / 12 = 36 \text{ (on edge)}$$

A 2 x 6 beam laid flat.

$$I = W \times T^3 / 12$$

$$I = 6 \times 2^3 / 12$$

$$I = 6 \times 8 / 12 = 4 \text{ (flat)}$$

These calculations show the 2 x 6 beam on edge is nine times (36/4) as stiff as when the same beam is laid flat.

3. The length. The length of the beam is important because this value is cubed in the deflection equation. By doubling the length, the deflection increases eight times. For example, if a 4 foot shelf sags ½ inch, an 8 foot shelf would sag 8 x ½ = 4 inches.

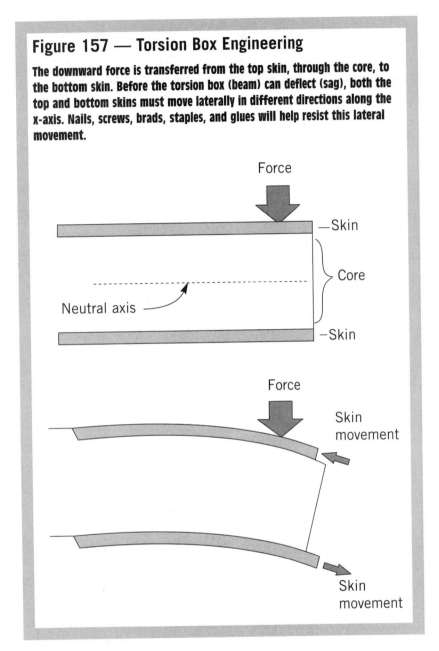

Figure 157 — Torsion Box Engineering

The downward force is transferred from the top skin, through the core, to the bottom skin. Before the torsion box (beam) can deflect (sag), both the top and bottom skins must move laterally in different directions along the x-axis. Nails, screws, brads, staples, and glues will help resist this lateral movement.

4. The load. The load or the weight a beam will carry may be distributed evenly or centered. In our calculations the load is considered to be centered. If the load is evenly distributed, the deflection will be less.

Figure 158 — Contribution of Core and Skin to Stiffness.

A ⅛-inch skin contributes more than one-half (53%, 60% and 69%) of the strength in torsion boxes made of ¾ inch core members. The ¼ inch skin contributes 72%, 77% and 83% of the strength.

Core Material Size	Number Of Long 2-inch Struts	Comb. Inertia 'I' Value of Struts(1)	1/8-in. Skin 'I' Value = 2.26 (2)		1/4-in. Skin ' I' Value = 5.06 (2)		3/8-in. Skin 'I' Value = 8.46 (2)	
			Grid Contrib. (3)	Skin Contrib. (4)	Grid Contrib.	Skin Contrib.	Grid Contrib.	Skin Contrib.
⅜ x 2	2	0.5	18%	82%	9%	91%	6%	94%
	3	0.75	25%	75%	13%	87%	8%	92%
	4	1	31%	69%	17%	83%	11%	89%
¾ x 2	2	1	31%	69%	17%	83%	11%	89%
	3	1.5	40%	60%	23%	77%	15%	85%
	4	2	47%	53%	28%	72%	19%	81%

1. Core Inertia Value = $W \times D^3 \div 12$ where W = Width, D = Depth
Inertia Value Combined is the single I-value times the number of long struts
2. Skin Inertia Value = $A \times D^2$ where A = Area, D = Distance from neutral axis of the section to the center of the skin.
3. The grid contribution to the stiffness of the T-box is the skin's I-value divided by the total I-value.
4. The core contribution to the stiffness of the T-box is the core's I-value divided by the total I-value.
5. The total T-box depth will be the core depth (2 inches) plus twice the skin thickness.

Torsion Box Strength

A torsion box gets its strength from the outer skins plus the inner grid — but perhaps not in the proportions you would suspect. The strength (stiffness) of a wooden beam is easy to calculate because it depends almost entirely upon the cross section (I value) and the length (L). The type of wood plays only a small part in the formula.

A torsion box is mostly hollow and the main role of the core is to transfer the force from one surface (for example, the top) to the other surface (for example, the bottom). See **Figure 157** and **Figure 158**.

Math

In a solid beam, the strength comes from the ability of the wood fibers to resist tension under load. A torsion box gets its stiffness (strength) and resistance to deflection (sag) from force transference. While the stiffness of a beam depends on width and thickness (I= W x T³ ÷ 12) the stiffness of a torsion box depends on the cross sectional area of the skin and the distance from the skin to the center of the box (I = A x D³). See **Figure 160**, Page 214.

$$I = A \times D^3$$

Where I = Inertia, A = Area and D = Distance from the neutral axis of the section to the center of the skin.

Before the torsion box can deflect, the top and bottom skins must slide in opposite directions along the x-axis. Glues are very strong in resisting shear movement (see **Figure 157**). Here are a couple of examples to review the basics:

Problem 1: We've constructed the core for a torsion box from pieces of ¾ inch x 2 inch stock. The core is 8 inches wide and 48 inches long. We've put four long boards and then cross pieces at equal spaces of 1⅛ inches (see **Figure 159**). If we cover this box with ⅛, ¼, and ⅜ inch skins, what will be the comparative strength of the core and the skin?

Solution 1:

Core: In all cases we kept the core the same size, therefore whether the skin is ⅛, ¼, or ⅜ inch, the core contributes the same I value.

$$I = W \times T^3 \div 12$$

Where W = Width of each board (¾ inch) and T = Thickness of each board (2 inches).

$$I = 0.75 \times 2^3 \div 12$$

$$I = 0.5$$

And because there are four long

boards in each core:

The total I value for the core = 4 x 0.5 = 2

The cross pieces of the grid do not enter into the calculations.

Skin: The skin contributes a different I value for each skin thickness:

$$I = A \times D^2$$

Where A = Area (cross section) of the skin, D = Distance from the center of the core to the center of the skin. See **Figure 160**, page 214.

⅛ inch skin (0.125 inch) with 2 inch core:

$$I = A \times D^2$$

Where D = 1 + (0.125 ÷ 2) = 1.0625

And A = Width x Thickness = 8 x 0.125 = 1

$$I = 1 \times (1.0625)^2$$

$$I = 1 \times 1.13 = 1.13$$

Because there is a top skin and a bottom skin this I value is doubled:

Total I value = 2 x 1.13 = 2.26 for ⅛ inch skin with 2 inch core.

¼ inch skin (0.25) with 2 inch core:

$$I = A \times D^2$$

$$I = (0.25 \times 8) \times (1.125)^2$$

$$I = 2 \times 1.27 = 2.54 \text{ for one skin}$$

Total I-value = 2 x 2.54 = 5.06 for two ¼ inch skins

Rule of Thumb

Wood girders used as floor joists often have the cross-sectional shape of an I-beam, with most of the material collected in large flanges at the top and bottom and with the joining plywood web rather thin. Why is this?

If you take a solid wooden beam and support both ends, then place a weight (force) along the length, the top layers of the beam will be compressed to a slightly shorter length while the bottom layers will be lengthened slightly by the tension force. In between the top and bottom surfaces there is a neutral wood layer that will remain the same length and is useful solely in connecting the top and the bottom together while maintaining the distance between them. This connecting piece need not be massive and in fact in an I-beam, is fairly thin.

One downside: in a fire, these I-beams burn much faster than a solid beam would.

Figure 159 — Full-size Core

If this ¾ inch core with 1⅝ inch spaces were covered with ⅛ inch plywood skin top and bottom, the core would only contribute 47% to the strength of the box. With ⅜ inch skin, the core contributes only 19%. Most of the strength comes from the skins and their attachment to the core.

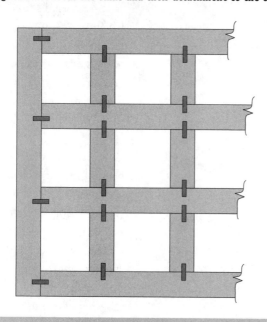

Figure 160 — Torsion Box Math

The Moment of Inertia (I) equals the area (cross section) of the skin (A) times the square of the Distance (D) from the center of the skin to the neutral axis of the section.

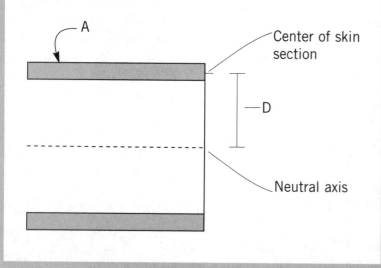

with 2 inch core.

⅜ inch skin (0.375) with 2 inch core:

$$I = A \times D^2$$

$$I = (0.375 \times 8) \times (1.1875)^2$$

$$I = 3 \times 1.41 = 4.23 \text{ for one skin}$$

Total I-Value = 2 x 4.23 = 8.46 for two ⅜ inch skins with a 2 inch core.

Comparative Contribution of Skin and Core

The comparative contribution of the skin and the core to the total stiffness (strength) of the torsion box depends on the I-Values of each:

⅛ inch skin:

I (skin) = 2.26

I (core) = 2.0

Total I value = 2.26 + 2.0 = 4.26

Skin contribution = 2.26 / 4.26 = 53%

¼ inch skin:

I (skin) = 5.06

I (core) = 2.0

Total I value = 5.06 + 2.0 = 7.06

Skin contribution = 5.06 / 7.06 = 72%

⅜ inch skin:

I (skin) = 8.46

I (core) = 2.0

Total I value = 8.46 + 2.0 = 10.46

Skin contribution
= 8.46 / 10.46 = 81%

These calculations show that the skin contributes most of the strength of the torsion box. To be effective, however, it must be firmly attached to the grid so the force acting on one surface is fully transmitted to the other surface. Glue and small brads serve that purpose well for woodworkers.

Comparing Solid Wood to a Torsion Box

So how strong is a torsion box compared to a solid beam? We'll design one shelf of solid wood and another using a torsion box. We'll put an unusually large weight of 1000 pounds (centered) on both the solid shelf and on the torsion box shelf, and calculate the deflection of both.

Problem 2: The shelf will be 8 inches wide, 2½ inches thick and 48 inches long. We plan to store our cannonball collection here and at present it weighs 1000 pounds. The weight will be centered and we'll assume the MOE value of both woods (the core and the skin) is 1.6×10^6, a typical wood value (**Figure 161**). For more on shelf deflection and MOE values of wood, see Woodworkers' Essential, Chapter 16, *Shelf Loads*.

Solid Wood Shelf: The solid wood shelf is assumed to be

Figure 161 — E-Value Table

Stress factors of some common hardwoods and softwoods. The Modulus of Elasticity (E-Value) can be used to calculate stiffness and deflection of a beam.

Hardwoods	E-Value*	Softwoods	E-Value*
Alder	1.38	Balsam Fir	1.23
Ash	1.77	Cedar	1.19
Beech	1.60	Douglas Fir	1.95
Cherry	1.50	Pine	1.40
Chestnut	1.23	Redwood - old growth	1.34
Elm	1.40	Spruce	1.40
Locust	2.00		
Maple	1.70	**Average**	**1.42**
Oak	1.65		
Poplar	1.58		
Walnut	1.68		
Average	**1.61**		

* x 1,000,000 PSI

fixed but not pinned at the ends and the load is centered. The formula for beam deflection (Y) is:

$$Y = (0.021 \times W \times L^3) \div (MOE \times I)$$

Where W = 1000 pounds,
L = 48 inches and
MOE = 1.6×10^6.

The formula for Inertia (I) is:

$$I = Width \times (Thickness)^3 \div 12$$

Where Width = 8 inches and
Thickness = 2½ inches.

$$I = 8 \times 2.5^3 \div 12$$

$$I = 8 \times 15.6 \div 12 = 10.4$$

$$Y = (0.021 \times W \times L^3) \div (MOE \times I)$$

$$Y = (0.021 \times 1000 \times 48^3) \div (1.6 \times 10^6 \times 10.4)$$

$$Y = 2.3 \times 10^6 \div 16.6 \times 10^6$$

Rule of Thumb

If a torsion box beam or shelf is held firmly at both ends, the deflection is 60 percent that of a similar beam that merely rests on end supports.

For example we have a six foot shelf that is fixed but not pinned. This shelf deflects 0.5 inch under a load. By firmly attaching the ends of the shelf, the deflection can be reduced by 60 percent.

$$0.50" \times 0.60 = 0.30"$$

$$Y = 2.3 \div 16.6$$
$$Y = 0.14" \text{ deflection}$$
$$0.14" \approx \tfrac{4}{32}" = \tfrac{1}{8}"$$

This tells us that a solid board 8-inches wide x 2½ inches thick x 48 inches long will deflect 0.14 inch under a centered weight of 1000 pounds. The eye can perceive a sag of ¹⁄₃₂ inch per running foot or ⅛ inch for the four-foot length. This sag might not be noticeable.

Torsion Box Shelf: Now let's construct a torsion box shelf. Again it will be 8 inches wide x 2½ inches thick x 48 inches long. We'll put four ¾ inch x 2-inch boards in the core with ¼ inch plywood skins on the top and bottom. The I-value will be that calculated before for the core (2.0) and for the skin (5.06), total = 7.06. The deflection formula assumes the shelf ends will be fixed but not pinned and the load will be centered. The deflection (Y) at center span will be:

$$Y = (0.021 \times W \times L^3) \div (MOE \times I)$$

Where I (Moment of Inertia) = Core Value + Skin Value

$$I = 2 + 5.06 = 7.06$$

$$Y = (0.021 \times 1000 \times 48^3) / (1.6 \times 10^6 \times 7.06)$$

$$Y = 2.32 \times 10^6 / 11.3 \times 10^6$$

$$Y = 2.32 / 11.3$$
$$= 0.21" \text{ deflection}$$
$$0.21" \approx \tfrac{3}{16}"$$

This tells us that a torsion box with four ¾ inch core members and with ¼ inch skins will deflect about 0.21-inch under a load of 1000 pounds.

The torsion box, so constructed, is almost as strong as solid wood — 0.14 inch deflection versus 0.21 inch. If we had used ⅜ inch plywood for the skin, the deflection would have been 0.15 inch, nearly identical to that of solid wood (0.14 inch).

Note that these calculations did not use the size or spacing of the cross pieces at all. The cross pieces are useful only to keep the long pieces upright and evenly spaced during construction. Later we'll find that the solid shelf weighs four times as much as the torsion box — 6.9 pounds versus 1.7 pounds.

Constructing a Torsion Box

So, how do we actually build a torsion box? Here are the steps:

1. Draw a detailed plan with all the pockets, extra side pieces, and solid sections.
2. Build the frame.
3. Add the long pieces.
4. Add the spacers.
5. Build the solid areas.
6. Add the joint strengtheners.
7. Fasten the skin.
8. Add any edge pieces.

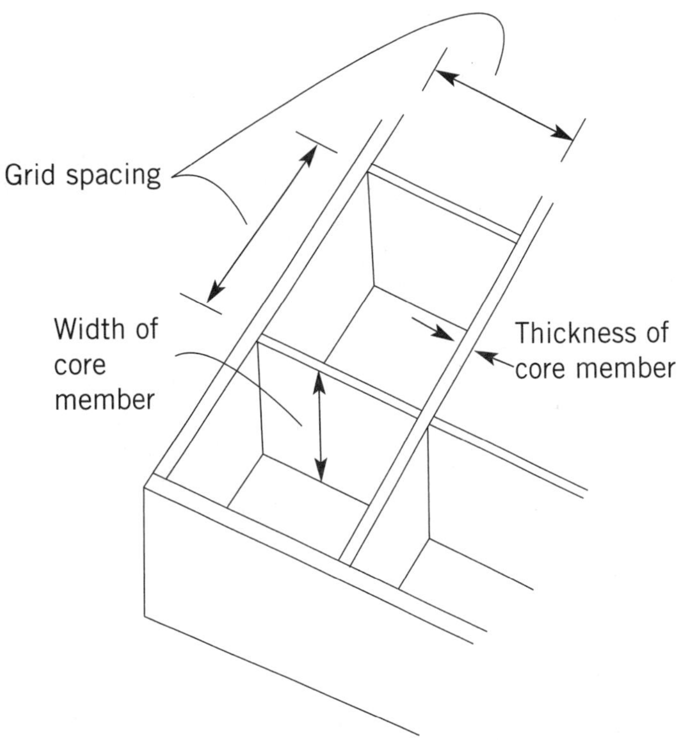

Building the Core

Before you start to build the core, carefully plot it out. Your drawing should show where legs will be attached and where this box will be joined to others or attached to a wall. Also note the location where tools such as a small drill press, metal vise, or such will be attached. A torsion box isn't like working in solid wood where a little can be added or taken off later. The plan is everything.

The basic core of a torsion box consists of an outer frame, the long inner pieces, and the short spacer boards. The outer frame is often made of a good wood such as walnut. This makes an edge treatment unnecessary. There also may be extra back-up boards for ledger pockets or edge treatments, and additional built-up blocking for hardware. Ledger pockets are necessary to join the boxes together or to another piece of cabinetry, and solid blocking is needed when legs or hardware are to be attached later.

The core can be made of a soft wood like pine or poplar, low-density fiberboard, MDF, or plywood so long as the material is strong, stable, and will make a firm glue joint with the skin. The core spacing depends mostly on the thickness of the skin. If the spacing is too far apart the box may sound like a drum and

Figure 162 — Torsion Box Specifics

The width of the core materials is important for stiffness. The thickness and grid spacing are less important. The glue bond between the core and skins is most important.

Grid spacing

Width of core member

Thickness of core member

the thin skin will sag into the voids. With a thin skin the core pieces may telegraph through.

To start, rip all the core material to width; remember the width becomes the height of the core. The wood for the core can be from ¼ inch to ¾ inch thick and the pieces can come directly from the table saw. If you use solid wood, be sure it is well dried to avoid any movement later. Once the core pieces are built into the box, movement

Rule of Thumb

In a torsion box, space the long pieces about 3 inches apart for ⅛ inch skin, 4 inches for ¼ inch skin, 5 inches for ⅜ inch skin, and 6 inches for ½ inch and thicker skins.

Rule of Thumb

The Torsion Box

1. A strong bond between the skins and the core members is most important.

2. If possible, in addition to glue, also staple or nail the skins to the core members.

3. The thickness of the core members (⅜ inch, ½ inch or ¾ inch) and spacing (5 inches, 6 inches, or 8 inches apart) of the grid (see **Figure 162**) makes little difference in the strength of the box.

4. The skin contributes most of the strength to a torsion box — the thicker the skin, the stronger the box.

5. The width of the core members (2 inches, 3 inches, or 4 inches) is very important in the strength of the box. The larger the cross section, the stiffer the box. All other things being the same, if the box depth is doubled, the stiffness will increase by eight.

due to changes in temperature and humidity isn't really an issue because the internal pieces are not especially wide (the direction of most wood movement) and they are isolated from the atmosphere.

After cutting the boards to length, build the outside frame. This can be put together with nails, screws, or just stapled together, with or without glue. In the case of a table or shelf, this outer frame can be made of a good hardwood.

Add the internal solid core pieces and run them in the direction of the greatest force — usually the longest dimension. Use the cross pieces as spacer blocks to keep the long pieces vertical while they are stapled in place.

Also add any long back-up pieces at this time. Be sure to include whatever ledger pockets are needed to join the box to the wall or to other cabinet elements. Next add the short spacers and glue solid pieces of wood into the core in places where legs, hardware, or other attachments will be fastened.

All the core pieces should fit together tightly but it isn't necessary to use half-lap joints or even glue. Staples will hold the pieces together until the skin is attached. Before adding the skin,

hammer all staples slightly below the surface. The strength of a torsion box relies on strong attachment of the skin to the core pieces so make sure there is no interference from protruding staples.

Attaching the Skin

The thickness of the skin depends on the weight the beam must hold and the attachments that will be added later. A thicker skin will make a stiffer box. You wouldn't want to attach folding leg hardware to a ⅛ inch skin. You also wouldn't need a ½ inch skin for a narrow bookshelf that will hold paperbacks. Use good plywood or other man-made materials because if the skin delaminates the torsion box will be weakened. If the skin is to be covered with plastic laminate or veneer after the box is completed, you can use nails and staples in addition to glue in attaching the skin because they will be hidden later.

If you want veneer on the final box, it usually is easier to attach the veneer before you glue the skin to the inner core — especially if you use glue that needs a vacuum press. Gluing a thin skin with heavy force onto a finished torsion box may deform the veneer so that the grid pockets are visible in the final product. Veneer can be added after the box is complete by using contact cement or yellow carpenter's PVA glue with moderate pressure from weights or clamps. Old-timers used bags of sand to hold the veneer in place until the hide glue could set. Veneer added to the completed box will also cover up screws and nails used in the core construction.

Figure 163 shows the difference in stiffness between solid wood shelves and torsion box shelves. In each case the shelf ends are assumed to be fixed but not pinned and the 500 pound weight is centered and not evenly distributed. The 2 inch x 8 inch x 48 inch solid wood shelf deflects 0.15 inch while the torsion box counterpart deflects 0.20 inch. In most cases the torsion box shelves are sufficiently stiff, even with 500 pounds of weight.

Because the strength of the torsion box comes from the transfer of shear force from the top surface to the bottom surface (see **Figure 157**, Page 211), the skin must be attached firmly to the grid. Almost any glue can be used here because most glues have great strength in resisting movement from shear force. Polyvinyl acetate (white, yellow, and high-performance PVA carpenter's glue), hide, resorcinol, urea formaldehyde, epoxy, and polyurethane glues can all be used. The only glues not recommended are hot melt,

Figure 163 — Comparing Stiffness of Solid Wood Shelves versus Torsion Box Shelves with ⅜" Skins

A torsion box is nearly as strong as a solid beam of the same size. A 2 inch x 12 inch solid wood shelf 48 inches long will deflect 0.05 inches under a 500 pound load. The same size torsion box shelf, with the same 500 pound load, will sag about 0.09 inches. If you double the thickness of either the solid or the torsion box shelf, it will be eight times stiffer.

	Shelf Size	Solid Wood Shelf Length in Inches 36	42	48	52	60	66	72
		Deflection in Inches with 500 Pound Weight (Centered)						
Solid Wood	2 x 8	0.05	0.10	0.15	0.20	0.25	0.35	0.45
Solid Wood	2 x 10	0.05	0.07	0.10	0.14	0.22	0.29	0.37
Solid Wood	2 x 12	0.02	0.04	0.05	0.07	0.10	0.13	0.17

	T-Box Size	Torsion Box Shelf Length in Inches 36	42	48	52	60	66	72
		Deflection in Inches with 500 Pound Weight (Centered)						
T-Box	2 x 8	0.07	0.14	0.20	0.27	0.34	0.48	0.61
T-Box	2 x 10	0.07	0.11	0.16	0.20	0.31	0.41	0.53
T-Box	2 x 12	0.04	0.06	0.09	0.11	0.17	0.23	0.30

cyano–acrylate, and contact adhesives — which all have short open times. For more on the seven different types of adhesives, see Woodworkers' Essential, Chapter 28 ***All About Glues.***

Figure 164 — Weight of Wood

The weight of different woods can be figured by using the specific gravity. Specific Gravity x 62.1 = pounds per cubic foot.

Wood (1)	Specific Gravity (2)	Pounds Per Cubic In. (3)	Pounds Per Cubic Ft. (4)
Apple	0.75	0.027	47
Ash	0.76	0.027	47
Balsa	0.12	0.004	7
Basswood	0.34	0.012	21
Beech	0.81	0.029	50
Birch	0.59	0.021	37
Black Locust	0.78	0.028	48
Blue Gum	1.01	0.036	63
Box	1.05	0.038	65
Butternut	0.38	0.014	24
Cedar	0.32	0.012	20
Cherry	0.51	0.018	32
Chestnut	0.41	0.015	25
Cottonwood	0.33	0.012	20
Cypress	0.53	0.019	33
Douglas Fir	0.48	0.017	30
Ebony	0.91	0.033	57
Elm	0.48	0.017	30
Hemlock	0.45	0.016	28
Hickory	0.75	0.027	47
Lignum Vitae	1.25	0.045	78
Mahogany, Honduras	0.66	0.024	41
Mahogany, Spanish	0.85	0.031	53
Maple, Soft	0.62	0.022	39
Maple, Hard	0.75	0.027	47
Oak	0.64	0.023	40
Padauk	1.01	0.036	63
Pine, White	0.35	0.013	22
Pine, Yellow	0.55	0.020	34
Poplar	0.35	0.013	22
Redwood	0.35	0.013	22
Rosewood	1.01	0.036	63
Satinwood	0.95	0.034	59
Spruce	0.41	0.015	25
Teak, Indian	0.76	0.027	47
Teak, African	0.98	0.035	61
Walnut	0.67	0.024	42
Willow	0.51	0.018	32

(1) Average Value at 12% Moisture Content
(2) The ratio of wood density to water density.
(3) Equals Pounds per Cu. Ft. / 1728
(4) Equals Spec. Grav. Times 62.1
Note: Water weighs 62.1 lbs. per Cu. Ft.

Relative Weight

The relative weights of different woods can be found by comparing their specific gravity (or density), **Figure 164**, which is the ratio of the weight of a substance to that of an equal volume of water at the same temperature.

Specific Gravity walnut= 0.67

Specific Gravity pine= 0.35

0.35 ÷ 0.67 = 0.52

This means pine is 52% as heavy as walnut, or that pine weighs 48% less than walnut. Wood density varies within the same variety because of moisture content, when the wood was cut, how long it was stored, and the ratio of heartwood to sapwood among other things. See Chapter 5, *Wood Strength* for more on wood density.

Walnut weighs 42 pounds per cubic foot and 0.024 pounds per cubic inch (see **Figure 164**). Therefore, a solid piece of walnut 12 inches x 12 inches x 2 inches weighs about 7 pounds (see **Figure 165a**).

12" x 12" x 2" = 288 cu. in.

288 x 0.024 lbs. per cu. in. = 6.9 lbs.

In **Figure 165b** a torsion box, also 12 inches x 12 inches x 2 inches, with the core made of ¾ inch pine with four cells and covered top and bottom with ¼ inch plywood, weighs only 1.7 pounds (the box is 54% air). This is 5.2 pounds lighter or only one-quarter as heavy. The box in **Figure 165c** weighs only 2.0 pounds, and again about one-half of the shelf is air. Note that building the torsion box out of pine (0.013 lbs. /cu. in.) instead of walnut (0.024 lbs. /cu. in.) also saved weight.

Joinery

Torsion boxes can be used alone as in shelves, benches and table tops, or can be joined with other torsion boxes in units. The best way to join two torsion boxes edge-to-edge (see **Figure 166a**) is to butt them together and glue them. Double up the core stock at the join points and use splines or biscuits for better alignment and a stronger joint. Torsion boxes can be joined at right angles (**Figure 166b**) with the skin of one box overhanging its core so it can conceal the joint. Use a floating spline to align the joint. The mating edges of the boxes can be mitered and glued as in **Figure 166c**, although again the core stock must be doubled or tripled up to provide for the miter cut. Boxes can also be joined edge-to-edge or at right angles by gluing an intermediate piece of solid wood at the corner as in **Figure 166d**.

To attach one torsion box to another, for example as a shelf to a cabinet or a pedestal to a table top, use a slightly different strategy. Attach a ledger board to the side of the cabinet or under

the table top and build a pocket into the end of the torsion box. Slip the pocket onto the ledger strip and attach it with glue and brads or screws (**Figure 166e**).

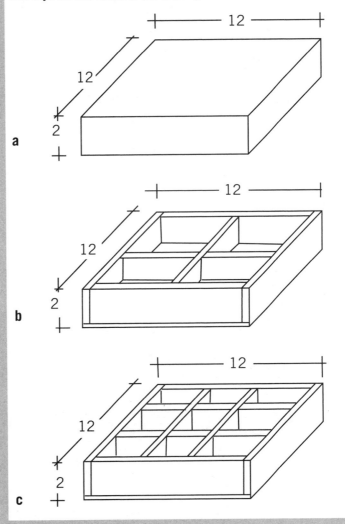

Figure 165 — Relative Weights of a Torsion Box versus a Solid Beam

A solid piece of wood (a) 2 inches x 12 inches x 12 inches weighs 6.9 pounds. The Torsion Box with four cells (b) weighs one-fourth that of solid wood (less than 2 pounds). The nine-cell box (c) weighs about 2 pounds. The weights of both (b) and (c) include ¼ inch plywood tops and bottoms (the tops are not shown in the drawing).

Figure 166 — Joining Torsion Boxes

For edge-to-edge joinery, double up in the core and use splines to keep the surfaces even (a). Let one skin run long before joining two boxes (b) or cut at 45° (c). Two boxes can be glued to a solid piece of wood (d). To join a torsion box at right angles to another torsion box or a panel, use a ledger board and a pocket with brads and glue (e).

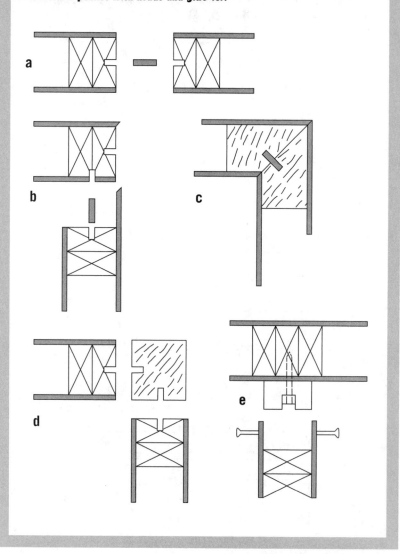

then build a pocket into the torsion box (**Figure 167a**). The pocket then slips onto the ledger strip and is attached with glue and screws or nails. The lipping on the box hides the ledger.

The ledger board should be a piece of clean, knot-free hardwood that can withstand considerable tension without breaking or tearing away from the wall. If the box skin is at least ⅜ inch plywood then the screws can be seated and the holes filled. If the skin is ⅛ inch or ¼ inch material, make a double or triple thickness inside the pocket (**Figure 167b**) to minimize the risk of the screws tearing out under load. The extra thickness will also permit countersinking the finish nails.

When the torsion box goes into a corner, ledgers should be attached to both walls. The method of attachment must be considered when building the torsion box. Once it is built, it's too late to add a pocket or double up on a core side.

Curved Panels

A torsion box can be made as a curved panel for a chair back or a table pedestal. The curved end boards and the curved core pieces are cut as continuous strips and attached to straight outside pieces (**Figure 168a**). The short spacer pieces are then added (**Figure 168b**). The

Wall Mounting

A torsion box can be mounted to a wall and will hold considerable weight with no visible means of support. Locate the wall studs and screw a ledger strip to the surface of the wall, spacers are straight and serve to keep the arcs evenly spaced and upright.

It's important that the curved pieces do not twist and that the surfaces are flat to take glue and make a tight bond with the skin. The skin should be attached to the convex side first. If the skin surface has a finished veneer already, use curved battens, clamps, and glue to attach it to the core. If paint, leather or another finish is to be added later, use brads or staples plus glue to attach the skin.

Edge Treatments

The outer frame pieces of the core are visible edges of the final box and can be finished by adding a flat cap (**Figure 169a**), half round (**Figure 169b**), molded (**Figure 169c**), a leather wrapping (**Figure 169d**), a drop lip with reveal (**Figure 169e**), or other typical edge treatments.

A Project — The Conference Table

Now that we know that a torsion box is extremely stable, that it gets most of its strength from the skin, that it weighs about one-fourth as much as a solid beam, and we also know the basics of T-box construction, let's make the 4-foot x 12-foot conference table. It's nice that if the client decided at the last minute that the top would look better 3½ inches thick instead of

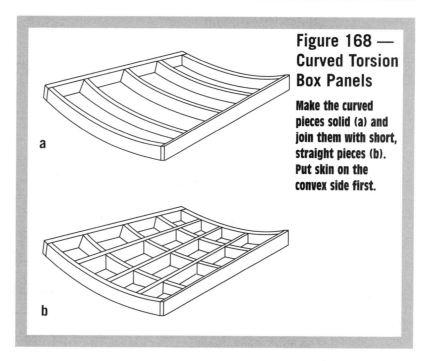

Figure 167 — Wall Mounting

Attach a ledger board to the wall and slip the T-Box pocket over it (a). If the skin is thin, double up so you can use a screw or nail without tear out (b).

a

b

Figure 168 — Curved Torsion Box Panels

Make the curved pieces solid (a) and join them with short, straight pieces (b). Put skin on the convex side first.

a

b

3 inches, it's easy to do. Just nudge the rip fence over a little and cut the core material a little wider. This is certainly not something you can do with solid stock.

The Core

We drew up a design for the torsion box top using ¾ inch

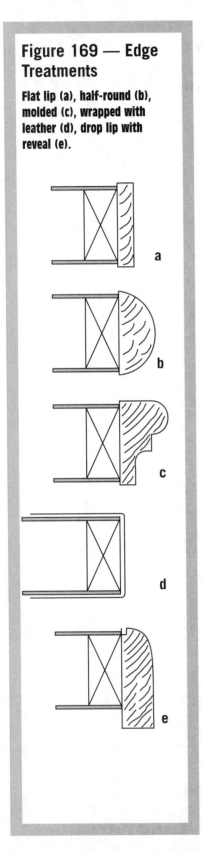

Figure 169 — Edge Treatments

Flat lip (a), half-round (b), molded (c), wrapped with leather (d), drop lip with reveal (e).

thick x 2¼ inch wide core members to be covered top and bottom with ⅜ inch plywood. This combination will yield a 3-inch thick shelf. We planned on spacing the grid members about 8 inches apart both for strength and so the top wouldn't resonate when someone drummed on it with a pencil. **Figure 170** shows the design.

We selected some ¾ inch walnut to make the table top edges and ripped the boards to 3 inch width (see **Figure 171**). We cut two long pieces to 144 inches long and two short pieces to 46½ inches long.

We found some ¾ inch, kiln-dried poplar (about 6% moisture content) in various lengths between four feet and fourteen feet long. We set the rip fence at 2¼ inches and cut eight pieces for the long members of the core. We checked that they were all 142½ inches long. We ripped some of the shorter lengths of poplar for the cross-bracing also at 2¼ inches. We figured we needed 110 of them so we started chopping away, setting a stop at 7 inches.

When all the long and short pieces had been cut, we started putting the core together — first by fastening the two long walnut pieces to the two 46½ inch walnut end-pieces with staples to make a 48 inch x 144 inch frame. We then built the inner

core out of the poplar boards. We put two long pieces lengthwise in the center of the core because two pieces of plywood skin meet here. We used a piece of core cross-bracing as a spacer and put in the other four long pieces with staples at each end.

We stapled the cross braces every 7 inches then carefully turned the core over and stapled all the bottom joints. We added extra bracing exactly 96 inches from each end to accommodate the plywood joints where the 8-foot and 4 foot panels meet. We decided we didn't need any special bracing inside the core to fasten the pedestals; I'll explain why later. The core was done.

The Skin

For the skins, we used ⅜ inch Baltic birch, solid-core plywood that came in 4 foot x 8 foot sheets. Because we needed 12 foot lengths, we bought five sheets (three for the table top and two for the pedestals). We ripped the three sheets for the top into 24 inch panels. The strongest pattern for the torsion box would be two 8 foot pieces and two 4 foot pieces joined like brickwork (see **Figure 170**).

We made sure the shop floor was flat because a level working surface is essential so the final panel doesn't end up twisted. We placed the core on the floor and squared it up by measuring diagonals. We rolled polyvinyl acetate glue (carpenter's yellow, PVA) on the top side of the core and quickly laid a 23¼ inch x 8 foot piece of plywood down on it, good side up. We used a staple gun hooked to an air compressor to fasten the plywood to the core at one end. After squaring up the frame again, we stapled the piece at the 8-foot mark, and then worked along the side of the frame and also along the middle with a staple about every 7 inches both lengthwise and crosswise. We put on the short 46½ inch piece of plywood and fastened it securely with glue and staples. The other half of the top went quickly. We made sure to stagger the plywood so a joint didn't extend across the box and within 15 minutes the two of us had the top covered on one side.

We flipped the partial T-box over and repeated the gluing and stapling on the other side. We made sure the skin joints on the under side did not correspond with the joints on the top side. The next day we tapped all the fasteners to make sure they were not setting proud, filled the small dents made by the staples, and sanded the surface smooth.

We found a source for ¹⁄₄₂ inch phenolic-backed walnut veneer in large sheets. The plastic backing makes the veneer moisture-resistant. We ordered two 50-inch x 12-foot pieces for

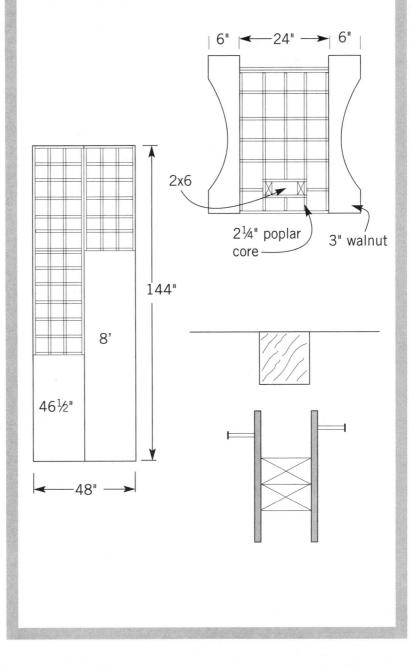

Figure 170 — Torsion Box Table

The table will be strong, stable, and weigh less than 200 pounds. The outer frame of the table top core is made of solid walnut pieces. The rest of the core is ¾ inch x 2¼ inch poplar and the skin is ⅜ inch plywood. Both the top and bottom surfaces of the top will be covered with walnut veneer after the plywood skin has been attached. Each pedestal is made of two pieces of solid walnut cut on the band saw to the arc shape with inner core members made of poplar. The pedestal is mostly hollow-core. The stretcher beam is a solid piece of 2 inch x 6 inch walnut.

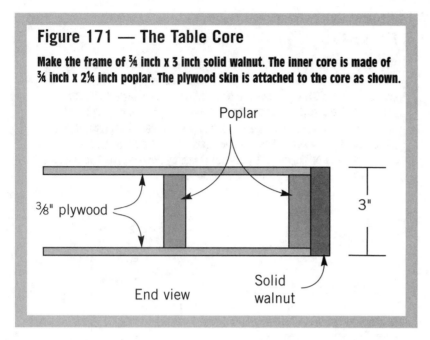

Figure 171 — The Table Core

Make the frame of ¾ inch x 3 inch solid walnut. The inner core is made of ¾ inch x 2¼ inch poplar. The plywood skin is attached to the core as shown.

Poplar

⅜" plywood

3"

End view

Solid walnut

$4/sq. ft. When the roll arrived we spritzed it with water and laid it flat for a day, then attached it with contact glue. After a light sanding we applied a finish.

Pedestals

The cores for the pedestals were made a little differently from the top cores. The curved end-blocks of the pedestals were made of 3 inch thick, solid walnut. Between these walnut end curves we put 2¼ inch core pieces (see **Figure 170**). Because we needed to penetrate the middle of the pedestal (through both the skin and the core area), we installed a hollow box structure in the core so we could cut a hole later and pass a 2 inch x 6 inch stretcher through. We attached the plywood skin as shown in **Figure 170** to make a pocket at the top so we could attach the pedestal

to the underside of the table top. We added the pressure-sensitive walnut veneer and cut out the mortise areas for the solid stretcher.

Putting them all Together

Two 2¼ inch ledger boards 24 inches long were attached with screws and glue to the underside of the table top exactly 18 inches from each end to serve as attachment pieces for the pedestals. The seven long, 2¼ inch grid pieces inside the top core, plus the ⅜ inch plywood skin, provided enough grab for screws so the ledger was quite solid. The pedestals were attached with PVA glue (carpenter's yellow glue) and finishing nails. We slid the solid 2 inch x 6 inch stretchers through the mortises in the pedestals and toe-nailed it in place. The table was now complete except for a finish.

Recap

The initial design using solid wood had four problems: stability, size, weight, and availability of the wood. Here's how the torsion box table stacked up.

Stability — A torsion box is incredibly stable because it is made of many little pieces of wood held together with staples and glue. It does not warp, twist, or move, and it remains flat and stable. We used kiln-dried wood for the core and the pieces are insulated inside the box so humidity and temperature changes do not affect them. The plywood skin is also stable.

Size — Size of the core members was no problem. The biggest pieces were the 12-foot long pieces of ¾ inch x 2¼ inch poplar and walnut. The ⅜ inch plywood sheets for the skin were easily handled by two people. The walnut pedestal pieces were band sawn from 3 inch stock.

Weight — If you remember, the original table design would have weighed over 700 pounds. The torsion box table weighs about 200 pounds.

Strength — Will the table be able to withstand the rigors of CPA conference-room life?

The deflection formula is:

$$Y = (0.021 \times W \times L^3) \div (E \times I)$$

In this formula:

Y = Maximum deflection or sag at mid-span in inches.

W = Weight of the load centered (in pounds).

L = Length of the board or beam in inches.

0.021 = A constant.

E = Modulus of Elasticity (MOE) of the wood in pounds per square inch.

I = Moment of Inertia.

Where: W = 500 pounds — let's assume two hefty accounting chaps are both going to sit on the center of the table at the same time.

L = 108" — remember the pedestals are inset 18 inches from each end.

144" − 36" = 108"

$E = 1.6 \times 10^6$ — a normal wood value.

Skin Inertia

$$I = 2 (A \times D^3)$$

Where:

I = inertia.

A = area of skin.

D = distance from the neutral axis of the section to the center of the skin. (See **Figure 160**).

$I = 2 (A \times D^3)$
$A = 0.375 \times 48 = 18$
$D = 0.1875 + 1.125 = 1.3125$
$I = 2 (18 \times 1.3125^2) = 47$
$I = 2 (18 \times 1.72)$
$I = 2 (31) = 62$

Core Inertia

$I = W \times T^3 \div 12$ (for each long core member)
$I = 8 \times (0.75 \times 2.25^3) \div 12$
$I = 8 \times (0.75 \times 11.4) \div 12$
$I = 8 \times 8.5 / 12 = 68 \div 12 = 5.7$

Deflection

$Y = (0.021 \times W \times L^3) \div (E \times I)$
$Y = 0.021 \times 500 \times 108^3 \div 1.6 \times 10^6 \times (62 + 5.7)$
$Y = 13.23 \times 10^6 \div 108.3 \times 10^6$

Step-by-Step

1. Lay the skin, good side down, on a flat surface and fasten four positioning blocks at the corners with hot-melt glue.

2. Spread PVA glue on one surface of the core. A 2 or 3 inch roller is perfect.

3. Lay the core on the skin and square it up with the alignment blocks.

4. Add weights until the glue has grabbed — thirty minutes to one hour.

5. Turn the box over and spread glue on the other grid surface.

6. Lay the other skin (with alignment blocks) on the grid, square it up and clamp or use weights. If a plastic laminate or veneer is to be added later, use a staple gun or nails to attach both skins to the grid — of course, use glue too.

7. After the glue has set, trim the skins.

Figure 172 — Comparing Torsion Box Skin Thickness

A torsion box is incredibly stiff — a shelf 2 inches thick by 10 inches wide and 72 inches long with only a ⅛ inch skin will deflect less than ¼ inch under a load of 250 pounds. A shelf made of solid wood will deflect about ⅛ inch but will weigh four times as much as a torsion box.

All shelves are 2" thick x 10" wide x 72" long.

T-Box Skin	Inertia Value	Deflection 1000-lb. Load (inches)	Deflection 500-lb. Load (inches)	Deflection 250-lb. Load (inches)	Deflection 125-lb. Load (inches)
		Decimals			
1/8"	3.54	0.91	0.46	0.23	0.11
1/4"	4.67	0.69	0.35	0.17	0.09
3/8"	5.44	0.60	0.30	0.15	0.08
1/2"	5.88	0.55	0.28	0.14	0.07
Solid Plank	6.67	0.49	0.25	0.12	0.06
		Fractions			
1/8"	3.54	15/16	7/16	1/4	1/8
1/4"	4.67	11/16	3/8	3/16	1/16
3/8"	5.44	5/8	5/16	3/16	1/16
1/2"	5.88	9/16	1/4	1/8	1/16
Solid Plank	6.67	8/16	4/16	2/16	1/16

$$Y = 13.23 \div 108.3 = 0.12" \approx \tfrac{1}{8}"$$

Thus, under an unusually heavy weight (500 pounds, in the center of the table), the torsion box will deflect about ⅛ inch.

Conclusion

This should demonstrate that the torsion box design is a viable alternative to solid-wood construction. We made a table out of local, inexpensive poplar and plywood. It was flat and extremely stable and its weight was one fourth of a solid-wood table. Under a load of 500 pounds, the table deflected only ⅛ inch. The construction was easy and the finished table will not move, warp, or twist in the years to come.

So, in practice, what is the best torsion box? Should the skin be ⅛ inch, ¼ inch, or what? **Figure 172** gives some interesting data.

We want to store 80 large books (⅞ inch spine) each weighing 1.6 pounds on a 72-inch long shelf. If the shelf is completely filled, the total weight will be 128 pounds evenly distributed. **Figure 172** shows that the torsion box shelf made with ⅛ inch skin top and bottom over a core of ¾ inch material 1¾ inches wide (the core will be 1¾ inches high) will sag only ⅛ inch under this weight. A shelf made of solid wood will deflect ¹⁄₁₆ inch under a weight of 125 pounds.

Figure 172 shows that an increase in skin thickness with a corresponding decrease in core thickness (the overall dimension of the shelf remains the same), increases the shelf stiffness. When you're designing a shelf, first determine the deflection using ⅛ inch material. If the deflection is more than you can tolerate, try ¼ inch material or ⅜ inch until the sag is tolerable. Use the data in **Figure 172** to help in your design.

CHAPTER 16
Off-Center Turning

When we turn something on a lathe we expect it to be round. The piece spins about its central axis in a circular motion and we hold a metal tool against it to cut beads and coves and fashion a round, turned object. Off-center turning, however, is a little different. The lathe still turns in a circular motion but the work piece is attached so that it now spins about a new, secondary axis and by making a shallow cut, we are able to produce a partial arc, rather than a round shape. By using two off-center points we can turn an oval. If the work piece is attached at both ends in this off-center way, its entire length will all be oval-shaped. However, if only one end of the piece is attached off-center, only that end of the piece will be shaped like an oval while the other end will remain round like a normal lathe turning. Somewhere in between the top and the bottom, the oval shape and the round shape will merge.

You can see that this gives rise to a lot of possibilities. Hammer handles are not round. They are shaped like an ellipse at the bottom to fit the human hand, but round at the top to fit into the metal head. Using this off-center tuning technique you can fashion handles to fit both the tool and your own hand. Club-foot legs have been made to adorn fine American furniture since the 1700s and they, too, can be turned on the lathe. The foot design decidedly is not round but the top of the leg is. Oval-shaped candle-stick holders and triangular or deltoid bud vases

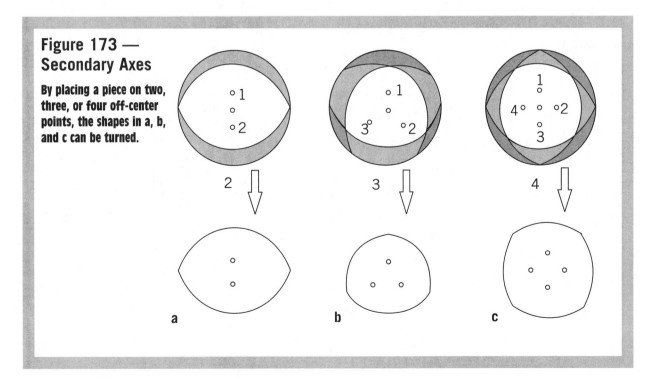

Figure 173 — Secondary Axes

By placing a piece on two, three, or four off-center points, the shapes in a, b, and c can be turned.

229

Caution and Safety

We've all had close calls — usually on the table saw and the shaper. The wood lathe is not especially dangerous but off-center turning is the exception. Because of the eccentric movement, there are special safety measures to heed.

Safety Measures

1. Check that the piece can rotate. The wood is mounted off center at one end, or at both ends, so that it swings in an arc. Always rotate the lathe a few turns by hand before turning it on to make sure the workpiece clears the bed and the tool rest. Failure to do this pre-check could result in two things — the piece comes around and crushes your hand against the tool rest, or the piece is knocked off the lathe and hits you. If it were to strike you in the head the damage could be quite severe, even fatal.

2. Start turning at low speed. The piece is swinging out-of-round and will vibrate. If it is heavy enough, it might even try to walk your lathe across the floor. If the low speed seems manageable, go ahead and turn carefully. If it's not manageable, cut away some of the out-of-round wood with a band saw or hand tools. As you cut, the piece will begin to balance and you can increase the speed. Usually, you should work on the lathe at the fastest speed that is safe.

3. Hold the tool firmly and take little bites. I like to tuck the handle of my gouge under my arm and against my waist. Watch the top of the rotating piece and cut away the shadow, see **Figure 174**. When the shadow is gone, you are no longer cutting the out-of-round portion of the workpiece. It's time to stop.

4. Stop the lathe and check the work frequently. Make sure the wood hasn't loosened. You should work from a pattern or follow marks on the piece to show where the starting and ending points are, and how deep to cut.

5. Be careful when you are sanding an off-center piece. It is often better to sand while it is not turning. Some turners prefer the looks of a piece with the lathe marks intact rather than the blurred look of a sanded piece. If a piece is hand made, there is nothing wrong with it looking hand-crafted.

also can be made this way.

Of course, we are not confined to just one secondary axis. Two, three, or more axes can be used, each one giving a different effect. To visualize the possibilities of multiple off-center axes, refer to **Figure 173**.

Theory and Calculations

The turning axis on a lathe is the straight line that runs between the driver (spur) at the headstock to the driven center at the tailstock. When a stick is turned on the lathe in a normal manner the turning axis coincides with the middle line of the piece. A turner will shape the piece using skews and gouges and the end product will be circular beads and coves centered on the turning axis.

With off-center turning the stick is attached so its mid-line does not coincide with the turning axis of the lathe. This means one section of the workpiece passes closer to the tool rest than the other parts of the piece. This off-center section is selectively removed (cut off) to produce a non-circular shape because only that portion of the workpiece that is out-of-axis is removed. If the piece is turned too far, a cylinder will result.

It's more complicated when a workpiece is mounted with one end off-center and the other end at true center. The lathe tools will cut a circular profile at the end mounted on the True Center (TC) and a partial arc at the end mounted Off Center (OC). The two profiles merge somewhere in between.

Oval Tool Handles

This project will introduce the simplest type of off-center turning, where only one end of the piece is off-center. Oval tool handles allow a worker to grasp the tool with maximum strength and better hand control when driving screws, hammering nails, or cutting wood. Some woodworking chisels and knives are made with oval handles so that the cutting edge will be in the most useful plane when the tool is picked up. Other tools are sold with oval handles so they will not roll off the workbench and fall to the floor.

Almost any hardwood is suitable for making a turned tool handle. We'll make a handle for a wood rasp by laminating three pieces of wood and then turning one section by the off- center procedure. **See Figure 175.**

1. Cut two pieces of hardwood ¾ inch x 1¾ inches x 6 inches and one piece of a contrasting wood ¼ inch x 1¾ inches x 6 inches long.

2. Cut a slot for the rasp tang in the narrow piece, and then

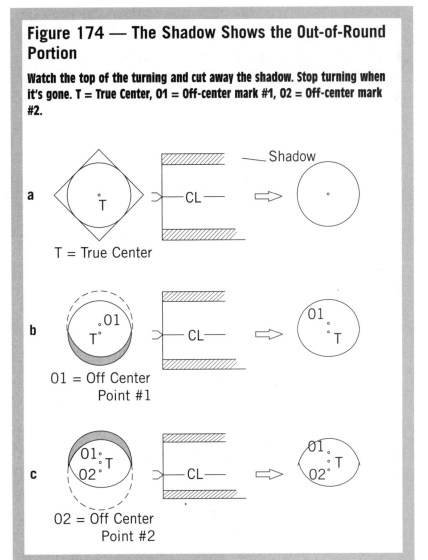

Figure 174 — The Shadow Shows the Out-of-Round Portion

Watch the top of the turning and cut away the shadow. Stop turning when it's gone. T = True Center, O1 = Off-center mark #1, O2 = Off-center mark #2.

a — T = True Center

b — O1 = Off Center Point #1

c — O2 = Off Center Point #2

glue the three pieces together as shown in **Figure 175.** Normal carpenter's yellow glue is fine for this job (see ***Woodworkers' Essential,*** All About Glues, Chapter 28). If the tang is round or if you decide to make the handle from solid wood, drill a hole in the end before turning, instead of sawing a slot. We'll use the tang hole (whether drilled or cut beforehand) to

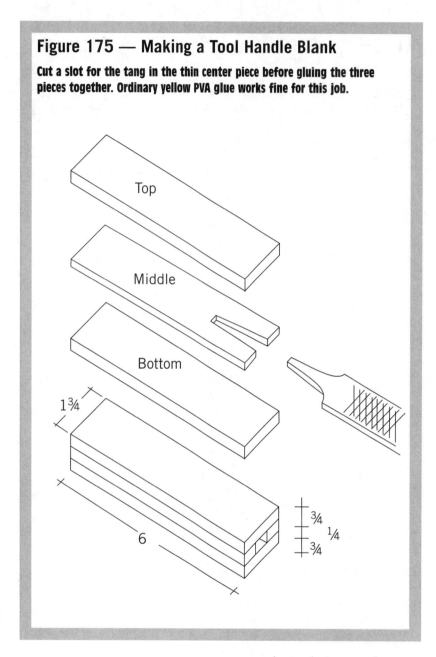

Figure 175 — Making a Tool Handle Blank

Cut a slot for the tang in the thin center piece before gluing the three pieces together. Ordinary yellow PVA glue works fine for this job.

Top

Middle

Bottom

1¾

6

¾

¼

¾

center lamination. This hole placement will produce an oval shape with its major axis in line with (parallel to) the flat edge of the file — the most comfortable hand position.

4. Mount the handle blank on the lathe at the true centers both head and tail, and turn to a cylinder using a skew or gouge. Turn the tailstock end to a diameter that will fit a ferrule. I make my own ferrules from pieces of copper tubing. Tap the ferrule on to the end and turn the handle to the shape shown in **Figure 176**.

5. Now mount the handle in one of the off-center holes at the tail end, with the ferrule end still mounted at true center. Rotate the piece a few times by hand to make sure it clears the bed and the tool rest. Start the lathe at slow speed and observe the shadow — the part of the wood we want to remove (see **Figure 174**). Start turning near the center and move the tool right to left — this way you'll be moving from true center to off-center. Take small bites and cut until the shadow is gone, then stop. Learn to watch the top of the wood while you're working.

center the workpiece on the lathe.

3. Draw diagonals on one end of the laminated piece and drill a small hole at the center. Also drill two holes ⅛ inch off center. **Figure 176** shows the off center marks on either side of the

6. Move the tail to the other off-center hole, leaving the ferrule end at true center and, again, remove wood until the shadow is gone. Stop the lathe and sand the piece by hand or if you were skillful in your turning, don't sand at all. Apply a finish and you're through. You've just made your first off-center turned piece.

Letter Opener

This wooden letter opener is a great gift item but to make it strong enough to open a big envelope and to remain sharp, it must be made of a hardwood carefully selected so that the grain runs straight from end-to-end and the growth rings are parallel with the wide part of the turning. Caution — woods that are soft or have wild grain or wide growth rings need not apply.

1. **Start** with a stick of hard wood 1½ x 1½ x 12 inches long.

2. **Draw diagonal** lines at each end to locate the true centers.

3. **Mark the grain** direction and draw a line through the center point perpendicular to the grain, see **Figure 177**.

4. **Mark offset** center points on this perpendicular line ⅜ inch on either side of true center at both ends. The narrow blade should be positioned here along the strongest section of the wood. Drill small holes at the true center and at the off-center points.

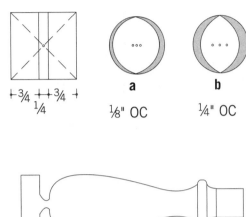

Figure 176 — Turning the Off-Center Tool Handle

Find the center of the blank and drill one hole to mark the true center and two other holes to mark the off-center points. If the marks are ⅛ inch off center oval shape (a) is produced. Marks ¼ inch off center will produce shape (b).

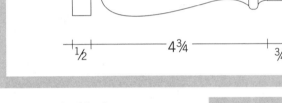

5. **Mount** the blank on true center at each end and turn a 1 inch diameter cylinder 9¼ inches long, leaving the ends of the stock square, **Figure 179**.

6. **Make a** full-sized template from **Figure 178**, and mark the beads and coves on the cylinder. Use a parting tool and calipers to cut each section to the correct diameter.

7. **While the piece** is on true center at both ends, turn the handle to its finished shape. Then turn the blade to form a taper. Stop the taper ¼ inch from the true end for support.

Figure 177 — Grain Alignment for Letter Opener

Find the center of the blank then determine the direction of the growth rings (G). For the greatest longitudinal strength, draw a line perpendicular to the growth ring direction and locate the off-center marks on this line.

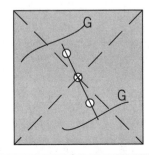

Figure 178 — Letter Opener Template

Use this template to shape the letter opener.

Figure 179 — Turning the Letter Opener

The cylinder is turned with both ends on center (a). The handle and blade cylinder are also turned with both ends on center (b). Move the blade off center to shape one side (c) then move the wood to the other off center position and turn the remainder of the blade (d).

8. Remount the blank at corresponding off-centers at each end, and turn one face of the blade. Don't touch the handle.

9. Remount the blank at the other off-centers and turn the other side of the blade.

10. Remount the stock at true center to finish-sand the handle. Turn off the waste at the handle end, working this diameter down to ⅛ inch. Remove the blank from the lathe and saw off the ends.

11. File the edges of the blade until they are sharp then sand the handle and the blade. Put on a finish, and then wax.

Club Foot Leg

The club foot is the simplest leg for an out-of-round turning. This project can be done entirely on the lathe but is made significantly more difficult because all four legs must be the same — maybe not identical but certainly similar enough so a casual observer doesn't notice a difference. In baluster turning if the heights of the turned elements match, people do not notice differences in the profile or in the diameter. In club foot turning, if the heights of the coves and the size of the feet are uniform in appearance, the diameter or precise shape of the curves won't be noticed.

The club foot is often confused with a cabriole leg. **Figure 180** shows the difference between the two types of furniture leg.

A club foot, as in **Figure 180a,** can be turned using two parallel turning axes, however we're going to make a leg with the top always on true center and only the foot off-center as in **Figure 181**. The procedure is:

1. **Cut a piece** of wood about ¾ inch longer than the length of the finished leg. If you're going to build a table or a chair, cut four pieces. In our example I used walnut 1½ inches x 1½ inches x 16¼ inches long.

2. **Make a template** with the important dimensions marked on it. In this example I made marks at 2, 14, 14½, 15 and 15¼ inches, and a notch to mark the top of the leg. Then take a sharp knife and make notches at these points. See **Figure 181c.**

3. **Cut mortises** for the aprons on two adjacent sides at the top end of the blank. Strike diagonals across the ends of the

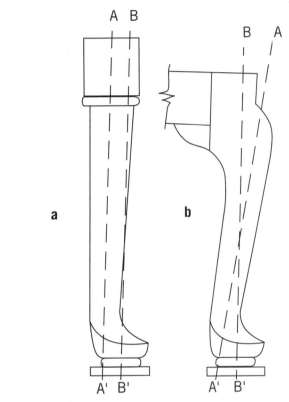

Figure 180 — Club Foot and Cabriole Legs

The club foot leg (a) can be turned entirely on the lathe —first at true centers A-A' and then at offset B-B' and the two turn lines are parallel. The cabriole leg (b) is characterized by a knee at the top which is fashioned with a handsaw and by hand carving. Only the bottom half is turned — first on true centers B-B' and then at the off-center points A-A'. The tilt of the leg is achieved because the two turn lines are not parallel.

blank at both top and bottom to locate the true center point as in **Figure 182.**

4. **Mount the leg** blank on the lathe between true centers and use a skew to cut the angled shoulder, or pommel, just under the top squares. This will prevent splintering during turning. Turn the piece so you have a cylinder between the mortised area and the end.

Figure 181 — Club Foot Leg

The first profile (a) is turned with the top on True Center (TC) and with the foot off center (OC). The second profile (b) is turned with both ends on true center (TC). Use the pattern (c) to mark positions on the leg blank.

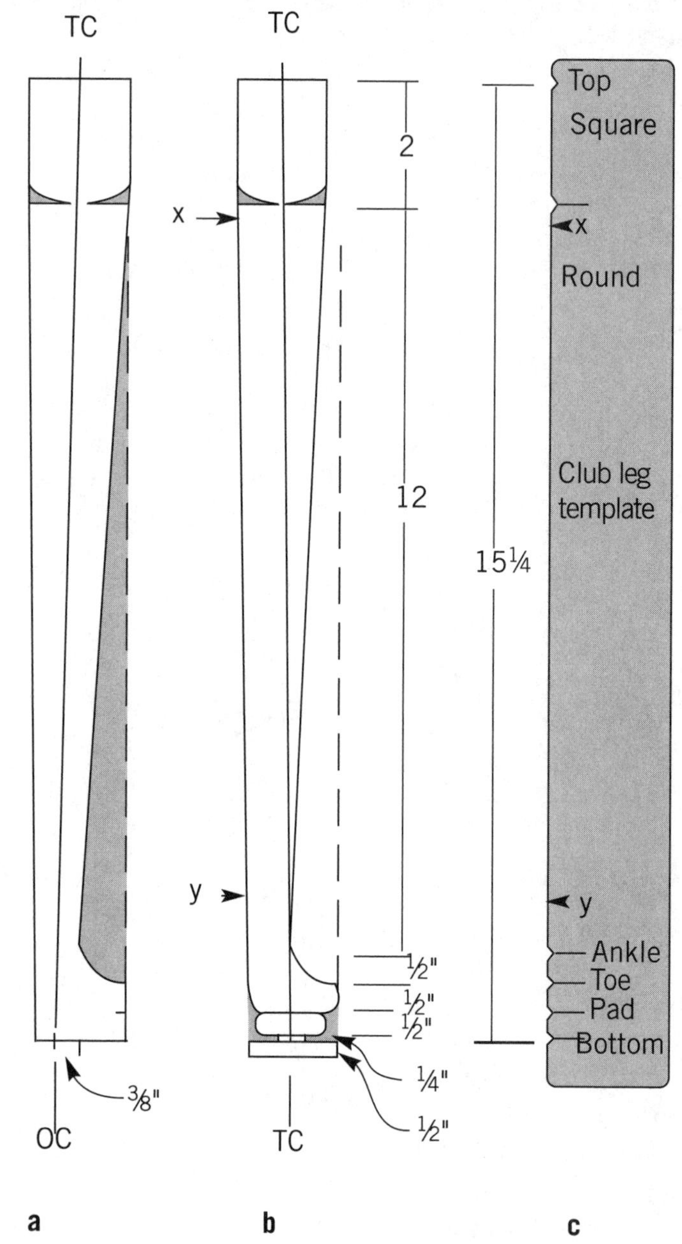

TC   TC   Top
Square

x →

2

←x

Round

12

15¼

Club leg
template

y →   ← y

Ankle
½"   Toe
½"   Pad
½"   Bottom

¼"

⅜"   ½"

OC   TC

a   b   c

5. Make a ¼ inch cut with a parting tool to mark the bottom of the leg at 15¼ inch.

6. Remove the blank and measure the diameter of the cylinder immediately below the square section. Divide this figure by two. This will be the diameter of the leg at the ankle. Divide this figure in half. This will be the offset value for the bottom of the leg.

Math

Leg Diameter at x = 1.5 inches

Leg Diameter at y = x ÷ 2 = 1.5 ÷ 2 = 0.75 inches

Foot Offset = y ÷ 2 = 0.75 ÷ 2 = 0.375 inches

7. In our example the diameter at the top of the leg is 1½ inches, the ankle will be ¾ inch, and the offset will be ⅜ inch. At the foot end, measure ⅜ inch out from the original center along the diagonal line that separates the two mortises, as shown in **Figure 182**. It is important that this be done correctly or the foot will point under the table or out to the side instead of pointing out diagonally from the table.

8. Remount the leg blank on the off-set point at the foot and at true center at the top. Taper the leg from the square area down to the ankle at the top of the foot. The piece will vibrate at first because the blank is off center. The shadow is visible and this is the area to be removed.

9. **Blend the ankle** into the foot carefully but don't cut the circumference of the foot yet. This can't be done until the leg is remounted on the true centers. Follow **Figure 181** carefully.

10. **Remount** the leg on the true centers and turn the bottom of the foot and the pad under the foot. Reduce the diameter of the material under the pad with a parting tool and finally remove the club foot from the lathe and saw off the remainder of the tab.

You probably noticed that the foot is formed because of the off-center placement of the bottom portion of the leg. When the off-center point is on a diagonal, the foot points towards a corner of the leg. This is the conventional position for chairs, tables and case work. When the off-center point is not on a diagonal, that is towards a side, the foot will point towards the side of the leg. This orientation is seen on foot stools, coffee tables, and hassocks, because these items set in the middle of a room and are viewed from all four sides. Some Chinese tables and chairs have the toes pointed inwards. By proper placement of the off-center points, you can point the toes in any direction you choose.

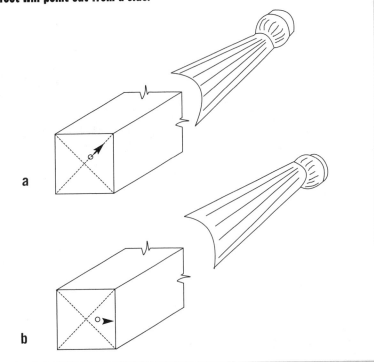

Figure 182 — Locations of Off-Center Points for Club Foot Leg

When the off-center point is located on the diagonal as in (a), the foot will point diagonally out from a corner. When the off-center hole (b) is used, the foot will point out from a side.

a

b

Cabriole Leg

The cabriole leg is the more elegant cousin of the club foot — having a bend at the knee and a tilt in its profile. It represents a stylized animal leg and sometimes ends with a hoof or a claw-and-ball. The cabriole probably evolved from a 16th century Chinese leg form which ended with a dragon's claw or a lion's paw clutching a large pearl. During the mid- to late 1700s, first in England then in the American Colonies, cabriole legs were integrated into all forms of furniture — chairs, tables,

Figure 183 — Turning the Cabriole Leg

Three separate operations are necessary to turn a cabriole leg.
(a) The pad and foot outline are turned on true centers (TC).
(b) The middle or ankle portion is turned off center (OC).
(c) The knee is shaped with saws and rasps.

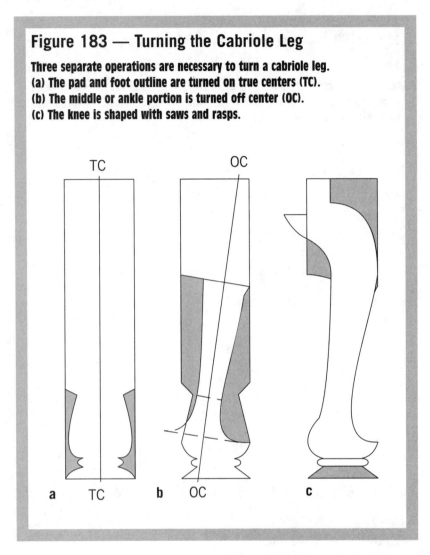

turning technique you can create elegant legs with a pleasing shape that have the advantage of uniformity not easily obtained by hand shaping. There's still a lot of hand work because only the bottom half of the leg can be turned. After the knee bracket has been glued on, the upper half is shaped with a table saw, band saw, rasp and chisels. Here's the procedure:

1. Make a full size pattern of the side view as in **Figure 183c** and draw the true center (TC) line as in **Figure 183a**.

2. Find center points at the ankle and mid-leg and draw the off-center (OC) line, extending it top to bottom as in **Figure 183b**.

3. From the pattern, make a marking guide with the important points — bottom of the leg, pad, toe, ankle, and knee.

4. Begin by squaring the pieces for the legs. Because the legs will have a square-to-round transition, the blanks must be milled exactly the same. Draw diagonals on each end to mark the true centers (TC). Using the pattern, mark the locations of the off-center (OC) points. Note that the off-center points are derived by drawing a line through the pattern and not by calculations or measuring.

casework, and even beds. The cabriole is a main feature of Queen Anne (1702-1714) furniture and today not only defines the American Colonial period but also distinguishes this furniture from all other styles.

The traditional method of making a cabriole leg is with the band saw and rasps. Old timers still believe the best cabrioles are entirely shaped by hand — however by using the offset

5. Cut any mortises at this time, while the blank is square.

6. Mount the blank on the lathe on true centers (TC), top and bottom. Use the marking guide (**Figure 183a**) and cut the lower profile to remove the shaded area.

7. Remount the blank at the off-center points (OC) and cut the shaded area as shown in **Figure 183b**. Do not cut the toe or the pad. Remove from the lathe and begin the hand work.

8. Glue on the knee bracket and using a band saw, table saw, rasps, spoke-shave, drawknife, sanding block, files, teeth etc., shape the top of the leg.

9. Put the piece back on the lathe but don't turn it on. Rotate the piece by hand and smooth the transition points at the bottom of the leg.

10. Saw off the waste under the pad and you're through.

Dogleg Spindles

The back legs of chairs pose a special problem when they are angled and turned, see **Figure 184**. A spindle can be turned for a chair back but then it can't be steam bent with predictable success. Also any beads or coves will cause the wood to break during the bending process. The point where the lathe cuts were

made is weak because layers of grain have been severed.

That same spindle can be steam bent first but then can't be easily turned however, by using an off-center technique we can solve this problem. We'll form the dogleg first, and then make a special jig to hold the crooked spindle. With a little care and a lot of attention, the bent leg can be turned. This is a special case of off-center turning and this Rube Goldberg-like contraption actually works.

1. To make a balancing jig, start by tracing the leg profile on a piece of cardboard or paper. See **Figure 185**.

2. Measure distance (x) from the center line A-A' to the top of the crooked leg.

3. Glue up pieces of plywood to the same thickness as the leg and make the jig using distance (x)

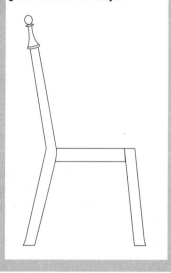

Figure 184 — Dogleg Spindles

Turning the angled back legs of chairs poses a special problem. Special jigs compensate for the off-center contours. First prepare the crooked legs by bending, lamination, or band saw. If the legs are steam bent or laminated, make sure they are dry so they won't spring back after turning. If band sawn, avoid short grain at the bend — select wood whose grain follows the shape.

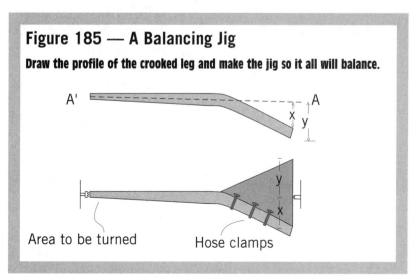

Figure 185 — A Balancing Jig

Draw the profile of the crooked leg and make the jig so it all will balance.

Area to be turned

Hose clamps

Figure 186 — Desk Caddy Holds Five Cups

This is an example of an off-center turning using the face plate.

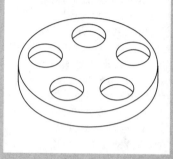

Figure 187 — Placement Jig

Use a ¾ inch dowel (or the same ID as the threaded bore in your face plate). Tap a nail point into the center of one end of the dowel and use this jig to position the face plate.

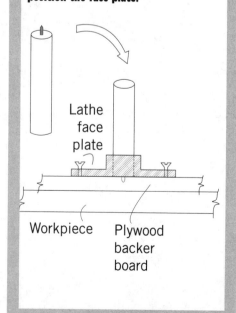

Lathe face plate

Workpiece   Plywood backer board

and distance (y). Make sure the jig extends from the end of the spindle to the bend.

4. If the leg portion is round, cut a V-groove along the edge of the jig to cradle it.

5. Cut slots along one edge of the jig to accommodate hose clamps, then attach the spindle to the jig and mount it on the lathe.

6. Remember that even though the turning is balanced along the 'x' and 'y' axes, it is out of balance along the 'z' axis. Run the lathe at its lowest speed and watch out for the eccentric. It swings around about 600 times a minute — don't stick your fingers or your turning tools into this spinning propeller. By being careful, you can turn this portion of the leg.

Carousel Caddy

This type of off-center lathe work uses a face plate instead of turning between centers. Like the other off-center work, the piece swings in an eccentric manner and you have to be careful. This piece, as designed (**Figure 186**), requires a lathe with a 6 inch swing. Measure the distance between your drive spur and the lathe

bed, this is the maximum radius you can turn. If your lathe doesn't have enough clearance, adjust the size of the caddy.

1. Start by preparing the wood. I used a ¾ inch piece of maple 8 inch x 8 inch square. Attach the hard wood to an equal sized piece of plywood (the backer board) with double-sided tape.

2. Make a placement jig as in **Figure 187**. Use a dowel the same diameter as the threaded center bore of your lathe face plate and drill a ⅛ inch hole ½ inch deep in the center of one end. Clip the head off a small nail and tap the blunt end into the hole so ¼ inch of the sharp point protrudes.

3. Draw diagonals and mark the center point of the backer board. Drill a small hole at the center point, tap the point of the centering jig into this hole, and drop the face plate over it. Drive the attaching screws home.

4. Put this wood sandwich on the lathe and turn to a 7½ inch disk.

5. Remove the face plate and mark the backer board for the off-center turning. Using the center hole as the center, draw a 4 inch circle (2 inch radius). Drill a ⅛ inch hole anywhere on this circle.

Math

Problem 1: Find the length of the side of a five-sided figure where the inside diameter is four inches. Refer to **Figure 188**.

Solution 1: The equation to find the length of a side of a pentagon where all sides are of equal length is:

Side Length = Diameter x constant

Where diameter = 4 inches and the constant = 0.588

Side Length = 4 x 0.588 = 2.352 inches

For more on circle division see Woodworkers' Essential **Circles,** Chapter 9.

Converting the decimal 0.352 to inches:

$0.352 \times 16 = 5.6/16 \approx \text{^{6}/16}$

$0.352 \times 32 = 11.3/32 \approx \text{^{11}/32}$

Therefore $2.352 = 2^{11}/_{32}{}''$

For more on number conversion see **Woodworkers' Essential,** Converting Numbers, Chapter 6.

Perhaps we should use the metric system.

1 inch = 2.54 cm

2.352 x 2.54 = 5.97 cm

≈ 6.0 cm

Starting at the first hole on the circle, measure $2^{11}/_{32}$ inch (or 6 cm) and mark the second point on the drawn circle. Continue along the circle and mark all five points. Drill ⅛ inch holes at each mark.

6. **Position** the centering jig in one of the marks and attach the face plate. Put the workpiece on the lathe and turn by hand to make sure it clears the ways and tool rest.

7. **Start the lathe** at a slow speed. Set calipers to 1 inch and hold them to the turning disk. Find the center point with one leg and mark a 2 inch circle with the other leg.

8. **Turn the first** recess and sand.

9. **Repeat** the operation for each of the required five recesses, making each the same diameter and depth.

10. **Reattach** the turning to the face plate at the original center and use a parting tool to cut part way through the softwood. Round the edges of the hardwood, sand it smooth, and pry the disk off the softwood.

Figure 188 — Desk Caddy

Draw a 4 inch diameter circle on the plywood and then step around it from any point and mark the five sectors. The length of a sector is $2^{11}/_{32}$ inch (6.0 cm).

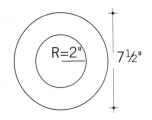

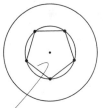

2¹¹⁄₃₂" typ.

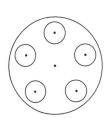

CHAPTER 17

Reverse Lathe Turning

As soon as folks see a reverse turning their first comment is, "How did you hollow out the inside?" I tell them that the inside was actually turned on the outside first, then put on the inside so the outside could be turned to match the inside — and I still have a bit of explaining to do — in fact I've almost confused myself.

Figure 189 — How an Inside-Out Turning Works

Four sticks are temporarily joined and the profile area is turned round (a). The inside silhouette is made by turning the outside pattern (b) on a lathe and then reversing the four sticks — the cove shape now becomes a quatrefoil (c) in the end view. An eye-pleasing outside shape (d) completes the ornament. The depth of cut 'x' is one-half the size of the window '2x'. The final view (d) is rotated 45°.

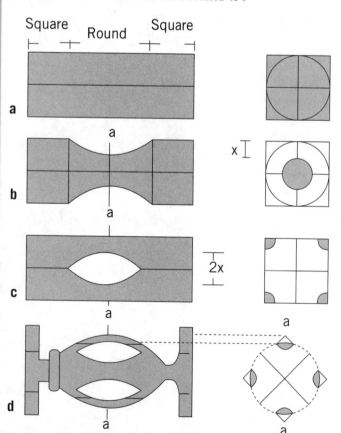

This inside-outside turning process isn't just complicated for casual observers; it's also hard for experienced wood turners to grasp. The lathe work itself is easy — most of us have turned more intricate doo-dads. Reverse turning or double turning is a process where you temporarily fasten four pieces together and turn a profile. This turning is then taken apart, each stick is rotated 180° and the pieces are then glued back together with the initial profile buried inside. Everything that was outside is now inside and the shapes are reversed — the cylinder that was on the outside becomes a four-lobed quatrefoil on the inside visible through the windows. The depth of every cut is doubled in width.

Shaping the new outside on the lathe now compliments the inside profile — this is why the process is called inside-out turning. Beautiful Christmas ornaments can be made from small pieces of ordinary woods and because they are hollow, they are quite light and delicate. In the following pages you will learn how to design and turn these tantalizing inside-outside ornaments.

The Basic Process

Our minds aren't used to flip-flopping images By studying the process you'll find ways to grasp this reversing process and to visualize the final profile.

1. **Four square** sections of wood are temporarily fastened together.

2. **The four-piece** assembly is chucked in a lathe and an outside profile is turned.

3. **The sections** are removed from the lathe, the pieces are separated, rotated 180º and permanently glued back together with the outside profiles now facing inwards.

4. **The glued**, permanent assembly is rechucked and turned again so the outside is a pleasing shape that complements the windows and the inside profile.

Profile and Shape

To visualize the final profile, imagine that you are cutting from the middle line outwards. Therefore when you cut a cove, the reverse will be a half circle and when mated with the second piece the two will make a circle. By cutting a slot, the final window will be rectangular and when you cut a "V", the reverse shape will be a diamond.

Theory

How does a reverse turning work? **Figure 189** shows the four sticks, the outside profile,

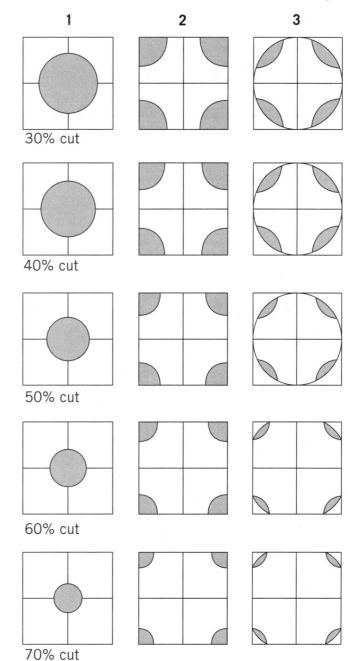

Figure 190 — First Cut Depth

The depth of the first cut (column one) is directly related to the size of the outer staves of the profile (column two). The walls (column three) of the final ornament becomes thinner as the depth of the first cut deepens. Make the first cut 50% and work from there. Any depth deeper than 70% will give a wall size on the final ornament too small to hold the ornament together.

1   2   3

30% cut

40% cut

50% cut

60% cut

70% cut

Figure 191 — Finding 30% and 50% Cut Depth.

Use dividers to set the depth of the first cut. When the dividers are set equal to the width of one stick (a) and used to measure the turned area, the depth will be 50%. When the distance is across the diagonal of one stick (b), the depth will be 30%. Most turnings should start at 50%.

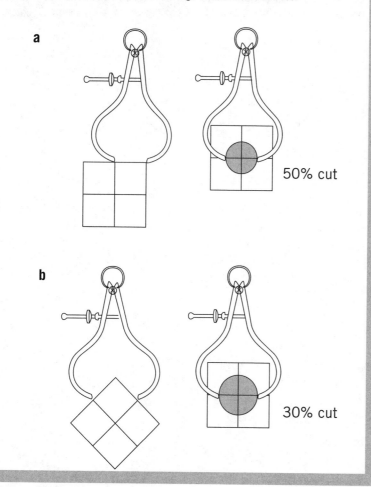

50% cut

30% cut

Rule of Thumb

Make the first cut about one half the width of a single stick as viewed from the side. This means if you're using 1½ inch square sticks, the first cut should be ¾ inch deep.

the window when the sticks are reversed and the final shape of the ornament after the second turning. If the first cut is too deep, the second turning will cut away the thin walls and the ornament will fall apart. If the first cut is too shallow, the window openings between segments will be too narrow. Because the depth of cut from

the flat face (or from the largest cylinder possible) is equal to one-half of the finished window, a one-half inch cut depth will produce a one-inch window width. So how deep should this first turning be?

The depth of the first cut depends on the size of the sticks, the size of the half-profile to be cut and on how thick you want the walls of the finished ornament to be. **Figure 190** shows first cuts of 30%, 40%, 50, 60% and 70% of the width of one stick. As the initial cut deepens, the walls of the final ornament become thinner and in the case of the 70% first cut, the walls are so thin the turning probably will collapse.

Make the first cut 50% of the thickness of one stick, reverse the sticks and check on progress. Tape the sticks together and cut some more if you want a deeper cut and thinner walls on the finished piece.

Finding Cut Depth

Try a depth of 50% for the first cut. **Figure 191** shows a neat way to gauge this distance.

When the dividers are set to the width of one stick, the first cut will be 50% depth. When the dividers are set to the diagonal of one stick, the initial cut will be 30% depth. **Figure 192** shows why this is so.

Preparing the Wood

Start with flat, kiln-dried boards and rip them on the table saw. Make sure the blade is set at 90° because the four sticks must be all the same size and with square corners. To conserve lumber and to give a nice, smooth glue joint I use a narrow kerf, fine-tooth blade — the pieces are smooth enough to glue-up without sanding or planing.

To Double-Saw or Not To Double-Saw

For accurate preparation on a table saw, I use the double-saw method — I rip all four pieces to ⅟₁₆ inch greater than the desired dimension then readjust the saw to the exact dimension and rip them again. Woodworkers, in general, agree that the double-cut method gives more accurate cuts for both crosscuts and rip cuts. They separate into two camps however, as to the reason.

1. The worst case scenario:
You have an under-powered motor, a thin blade which is dull, blade stabilizers are not used and the feed rate is too fast. This multitude of ripping sins will cause the motor to chug and the blade to distort resulting in an off-square cut. The problem here is mechanical. The double-cut method will produce better results because the small motor can run at full speed and the

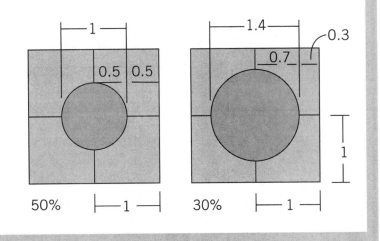

Figure 192 — The Math

Let the width of one stick equal 1 inch. When the cylinder diameter is 1 inch, the radius is ½ inch. This means the first cut is also ½ inch — or 50%. The hypotenuse of a 1 inch square is 1.414-inch. When the cylinder diameter is 1.4 inch, the radius is 0.7 inch. This means the first cut is 0.3 inch — or 30%.

blade will not be distorted when it is only cutting a sliver of wood.

2. The best scenario:
You have a powerful motor, a sharp blade with stabilizers and the feed rate is slow. The blade will cut through solid wood with no distortion — there is no mechanical problem here and any difference in cutting will be human error. The double-cut method will result in better sticks in this case only because the operator is better able to hold the smaller sticks tight against the fence and watch carefully as the blade slices a small sliver from the edge.

In both instances, the double-cut

Figure 193 — Cutting Four Pieces from a Large Chunk of Wood

To have consistent figure in the final assembly, use a large piece of wood and cut it as shown. Be sure to number the pieces and, as they are cut, hold them together with a rubber band.

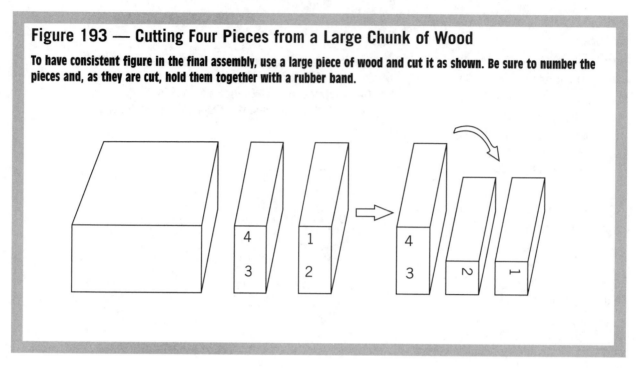

method will give superior reproducible cuts.

Woods for Turning

I've found that woods with consistent grain and regular colors are the best for these turnings, because in the final ornament, the emphasis should be on the shape of the window and the outer profile, not on the prominence of the wood figure. Wild figure patterns and obvious growth rings will show definite glue lines when the parts are reassembled. Walnut, mahogany, maple, and cherry turn nicely and, when glued together, give pieces that are homogenous in color and figure. By cutting all four pieces from the same board, you can arrange the final glue-up so that the figure is continuous,

and the turning will look like it was made from a solid piece of wood — especially with accurate sawing and good glue joints. See **Figure 193.**

If you start with a dimensioned board use the table saw to cut the length needed, say 6 inches. Set the fence to the size of a quarter-square and cut two pieces. Cut these two pieces in half. Number the ends to keep track of grain alignment and rubber band the pieces together when doing quantity batches.

Another method is to start with a large piece of lumber and put it through the planer first. Then use a band saw to cut pieces at least ½ inch over the final dimensions of the four assembled segments to allow for jointing and squaring up. Make the pieces as large as possible without including the pith or any sap wood. They can be cut smaller later. Square the pieces on the planer.

Design

Almost any profile can be turned inside out, but it's hard to visualize the final shape while turning, so a drawing and a gauge are useful. The wood that is removed actually forms the shape of the design — kind of like a photo negative. The steps to make a design, a pattern and a gauge are as follows:

1. Draw a rectangle the size of your assembled four-piece blank on a piece of ¼ inch cross hatched paper (**Figure 194**).

2. Hold a piece of stiff card stock next to the design and draw a half-pattern along one edge. Write in depth of cuts. This pattern shows the position and depth of cut for important points of the design. You also can fold the drawing in half, cut out the half silhouette, and paste it on card stock or a piece of plastic.

3. Transfer the position of each cut to the other edge of the card stock and make notches. During the turning, these notches will be used to indicate the top and bottom extremities of the pattern, and to mark important

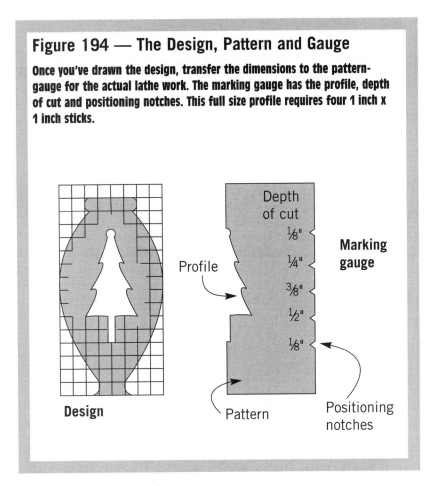

Figure 194 — The Design, Pattern and Gauge

Once you've drawn the design, transfer the dimensions to the pattern-gauge for the actual lathe work. The marking gauge has the profile, depth of cut and positioning notches. This full size profile requires four 1 inch x 1 inch sticks.

Design

Profile

Depth of cut

⅛"

¼"

⅜"

½"

⅛"

Marking gauge

Pattern

Positioning notches

points.

Draw up your own design or use one of the designs in **Figure 195** to turn a Christmas ornament. Remember to size the profile so the deepest cut is no deeper than 50% of the width of one stick.

Holding the Four Pieces

How you hold the pieces while turning them depends on the size of the turning and whether this is a one-time project or an assembly line piece. The assembled pieces can be held for turning by using chucks, glue,

Figure 195 — Designs

Transfer one of these designs to make your pattern. Make the deepest first cut only 50% of the width of one stick.

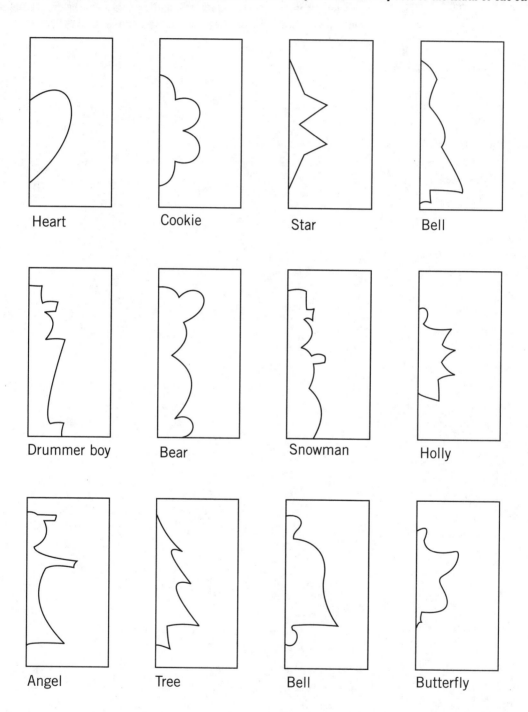

Heart   Cookie   Star   Bell

Drummer boy   Bear   Snowman   Holly

Angel   Tree   Bell   Butterfly

tape, rubber bands, screws, plastic pipe rings and clamps.

Metal Chuck

By far the easiest way to hold the pieces is with a four-jaw metal chuck. Wrap a few turns of masking tape around each end of the bundle and then put one end into the chuck. It helps if you remembered to make the four pieces a little long so you can cut off the ends in case they are marred by the jaws. You can hold the tail end with a cup chuck (**see Figure 196**) or even with a live cup. Either way, make sure the assembly won't budge during the lathe work.

The four-jaw metal chuck and tape are my preferred method of holding the four loose pieces because you can take the assembly apart and rotate the pieces to look at the final design. If it's OK then glue it up, but if it needs more work then reverse the pieces again, chuck them back up and cut some more.

Cup Chuck

If you plan to turn a lot of the same size pieces, a wooden cup chuck makes a lot of sense, see **Figure 196**. These shop-made jigs are recessed ¼ inch deep and shaped to hold the four-piece assembly. The driver chuck is 3 inches to 5 inches in diameter, and made to fit your metal faceplate. You can also turn a tenon on the rear of the cup

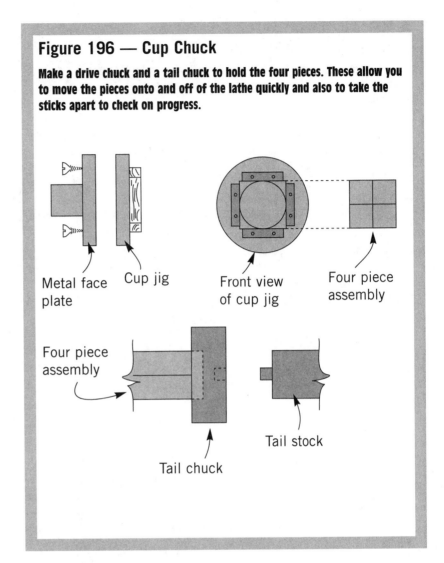

Figure 196 — Cup Chuck

Make a drive chuck and a tail chuck to hold the four pieces. These allow you to move the pieces onto and off of the lathe quickly and also to take the sticks apart to check on progress.

Metal face plate

Cup jig

Front view of cup jig

Four piece assembly

Four piece assembly

Tail chuck

Tail stock

chuck so it can be held by a regular four-jaw metal chuck.

To make the wooden cup chuck, band saw a piece of ¾ inch plywood to the diameter of the metal faceplate. On the lathe as the piece is rotating, use a pencil to draw a series of circles. Glue and tack four pieces of ½ inch x ½ inch slats to the plywood using the outside dimensions of the four-piece assembly. See **Figure 196**.

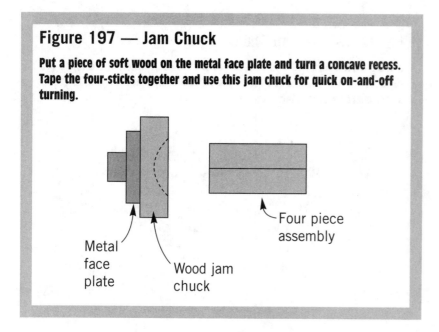

Figure 197 — Jam Chuck

Put a piece of soft wood on the metal face plate and turn a concave recess. Tape the four-sticks together and use this jam chuck for quick on-and-off turning.

Four piece assembly

Metal face plate

Wood jam chuck

into the glue lines between them.

Jam Chuck

Mount a piece of pine or poplar on the face plate and turn a cup cavity as in **Figure 197**. Tape the four sticks together and test the bundle until it fits tightly. It doesn't take a lot to hold four small sticks. This method is fast and lets you take the bundle out for inspection.

Hot Melt Glue

This is the best method if you're going to use glue. It is fast, the glue holds well, and it can be taken apart easily to check progress.

Don't spread the hot melt glue over the entire surface — just put a blob at each end on the joint face of one piece, put it on a flat surface and bring the adjacent piece to it. The hot melt will allow you 10 to 15 seconds to align the two pieces before it cools. Do the same with pieces 3 and 4. Finally glue the two two-piece subassemblies pieces into one assembly. Total time spent is probably less than a minute.

Using hot melt glue this way will leave a slight gap between the pieces. These gaps won't influence the final assembly and will actually help correct misalignment caused by imperfectly squared wood. Try to

The tail chuck is made in a similar way. Prepare the rear of this chuck by drilling a hole that just fits your tail stock. The four pieces need to fit into both cups snugly. If there is any play, build up the ends with wraps of masking tape. This method is simple and the pieces can be put in and taken out quickly. It is probably not worth making the chucks unless you intend to turn a number of same-size pieces — or unless, like many of us, you enjoy making jigs.

If you don't have a metal chuck or don't want to make cup chucks, the literature is full of other methods. Most of these methods allow you to drive the assembly with a regular four-prong spur in the headstock and a cup center in the tailstock. Make sure the driving spurs bite into each piece of wood, not get the outside of the assembly square even if the inside has gaps and isn't perfectly square. The inside corners will be turned towards the outside later, and will be cut away.

PVA Glues

If the wood is flat and square you can hold the assembly with a dab of glue on the ends of the pieces. Make a pencil mark around each piece ¼ inch from the end and band saw a slot ¹⁄₁₆ inch deep on both interior faces of each block. This slot acts as a glue barrier when gluing up the assembly.

Glue the pieces together applying polyvinyl acetate glue (PVA, Carpenter's, white, yellow or high performance) only to the ¼ inch area at the end of each piece. Glue two pieces together and then the other two, then join these two pairs together for the final piece. PVA glues require clamping for at least one hour. After the turning is complete, take the assembly apart by cutting ¼ inch off each end. Mark the freshly cut end with the same numbers and lines as they were initially.

This method is slow and the assembly can't easily be taken apart to check progress.

PVA Glue and Paper

Spread PVA glue on the two surfaces and put a piece of brown paper bag between. These pieces should be clamped together while the glue dries and the two pieces can't be shifted after the first 5 minutes. The paper joint is more secure than the hot melt joint and keeps the wood aligned properly, but it takes longer than other methods to set up and take apart. It also requires driving a chisel into the crack to split the paper, which might cause a divot. The small space created by the paper-glue line won't show up as a space in the final silhouette if you keep the joints tight.

Use this method if your assembly is big and you're worried about it coming apart during the turning. It is messy, slow, and requires clamping for at least an hour. You also have to remove the paper and glue from the wood — no problem on the central part which you'll be turning away. On the square end parts, wet the wood and scrape with a chisel. Other methods allow you to take the temporary assembly apart and check it out. This one doesn't.

Some complex designs can be helped by using black construction paper, pre-cut to the silhouette of the design. Turn close with gouge and skew then carefully scrape until you see a bit of black sawdust in the shavings — you've turned far enough.

Cyano-Acrylate Glue

Cyano-Acrylate glue or super glue can also be used. Put the glue on both ends of one piece, bring the other piece to it, and spray with accelerator. This glue sets quick and hard but can be broken apart easily with a wide chisel for disassembly — in fact the joint may be brittle enough to knock apart with a hammer. One reason you might want to use this method is if the woods are oily and you have a great supply of the expensive CA glue and accelerator.

Polyurethane Glue

Polyurethane glue is good for any type of wood and is especially useful with oily woods. Use only a drop or two on one piece. Wet the mating piece and clamp for an hour or so. This glue foams so be prepared to clean the assembly with a sharp chisel.

Nylon Reinforced Tape

Reinforced tape is the preferred method if you don't have a metal, four-jaw chuck. Hold the four pieces together tightly and bind each end with two wraps of the nylon filament tape. This method is strong, fast, and the assembly can be cut apart easily to check on progress.

Double-Sided Tape

Modern woodworker's double-sided tape is incredibly strong so don't tape along the whole length of a piece or you're liable to break the pieces to get them apart. A short piece of tape at each end will hold the assembly quite well. This method is strong and fast but you may pull slivers of wood from the face of your assembly, and fragile turnings may break while trying to separate the pieces.

Masking Tape

Masking tape is strong enough for small assemblies; when the sticks are one inch or less. Make sure the pieces are held squarely and that the lathe drive spurs are in solid wood and not in the assembly joints. If you've decide to use tape and don't have nylon filament tape, go ahead and try three or four wraps of masking tape.

Rubber Bands

Strong rubber bands will hold small pieces up to ¾ inch x ¾ inch and less than 5 inches long — I've used them for a lot of Christmas ornaments. Just make sure all four pieces are square. Use a cup center at the tail stock end instead of a cone center, and make sure the driving spurs are in wood and not in a joint.

Hose Clamps

Hose clamps can be used after first joining the four pieces

together tightly with masking tape at each end to keep the four sticks from shifting while the clamp is tightened. I don't recommend this method because it is dangerous. The clamp screw and the tail of the metal band make a large arc and can take a major chunk out of your hand very quickly. If you do decide to use this method, wrap the clamp with tape — this will make them hurt a little less if you get a finger or knuckle too close.

A Screwy Method

This method is used mostly for large furniture type turnings. Use a blank disk on the face plate as the chuck and drive a screw through the disk into the center of the ends of each of the four pieces. The same screw hole will work when you rotate the pieces. This method is extremely strong and can be used for large pieces, for example 6 inches square and 24 inches long.

Plastic Pipe

Cut a ¾ inch section from the end of a piece of three inch, white PVC drain pipe. The male end is a little over 3 inches inside diameter and will hold four 1¹⁄₁₆ inch pieces nicely. The female end of the same PVC drain pipe is 3⁵⁄₁₆ inches inside diameter. A narrow band cut from here will hold four 1⁵⁄₃₂ inch pieces for turning. **Figure 198** shows how the square pieces fit into the PVC pipe.

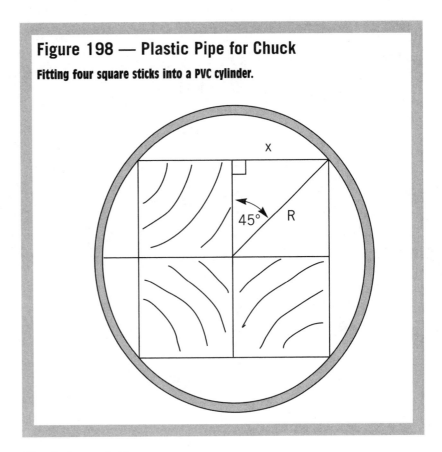

Figure 198 — Plastic Pipe for Chuck
Fitting four square sticks into a PVC cylinder.

Here's the math if you want to cut your own banding.

Stick Size=0.7071xPipe Radius

Problem 3: We have a piece of PVC pipe with inside diameter of 77 mm (3¹⁄₃₂ inches). What size stick shall we prepare so that four pieces will fit into the cylinder? Note, it's sometimes convenient to use the metric system for math problems.

Solution 3:

Stick Size=0.7071xPipe Radius

Where Radius= 77 ÷ 2 = 38.5

Stick Size = 0.7071 x 38.5 = 27.2 mm

1 inch = 25.4 mm

Rule of Thumb

To find the **approximate size** of four pieces of wood (all the same size) that will fit into a piece of round plastic pipe:

Divide the inside diameter of the pipe by three.

For example, the female end of a 3 inch PVC drain pipe is about 3¼ inches inside diameter.

3.25 ÷ 3 = 1.08 inches.

So cut four 1 inch sticks, tape the ends and nudge them inside.

27.2÷25.4=1.07 inches≈1¹⁄₁₆"

Therefore cut four sticks 1¹⁄₁₆ inch square to fit into the pipe band.

On The Lathe
Turn the Inside Profile

1. Nick the inside ends of each stick and mount the block in the lathe using a chuck, tape, glue or whatever. If you're using a drive spur, set the points in solid wood and not between the glue joints. Nick the inside ends of each stick before you do the glue-up. Put the drive spur center in the hole.

2. Bring up the tailstock but don't apply too much pressure to the narrow glue/tape joints.

3. Place the gauge on the block and mark the left and right (top and bottom) extremes of the pattern.

4. Score these points with the tip of a skew chisel to prevent tear out.

5. Turn the section between the marks down to a straight cylinder only where the silhouette will be — don't round the whole piece. Without flat sections on the ends, you will be trying to glue a curve to a curve; the four flat areas become the glue joints for the final piece.

6. Use the gauge and, with a pencil in the notches, make marks on the cylinder for position points.

7. Use a parting tool and calipers to make depth cuts according to the measurements on the pattern gauge.

8. Join the depth cuts to complete the first turning shape. Use skews, gouges and scrapers depending on the shapes you want and your skill with these tools. Smooth the turning with sandpaper, if necessary.

9. This outside surface will not be exposed in the final ornament but it will be visible, so now is the time to put on a finish. Don't finish the flat portions because these surfaces form the glue joints when you assemble the ornament. Dip a rag in some shellac and apply it lightly. In a few minutes follow with a coat of paste wax. Turn on the lathe and buff it. This will give it a nice finish and the wax allows most dust to be blown away in the years to come. You can also use acrylic paint on the inside — for example, use yellow if the ornament will be a lantern with a wooden candle inside or red for a Christmas ornament..

Reverse the Pieces and Turn the Outside

1. Remove the assembly and nick each end of the eight outside corners with a knife.

Shaving off a sliver will mark the exact center of the top and bottom for remounting and of the finished piece for mounting hooks or for drilling to add finials and icicles.

2. **Remove** the tape from each end of the assembly and rotate each piece 180°. The small nicks that we just cut should now be in the center of each end. This will help in remounting the bundle on the lathe.

3. **Instead** of gluing the pieces together, just hold the four pieces and look at the windows carefully. If they need any adjustment, rotate the pieces back to their original position, remount on the lathe and refine the silhouette. You may need to turn through the finish and then refinish later.

Assembling the Ornament

1. **If the ornament** looks okay, glue the sections together using PVA glue. It's best to use a thin application because the ornament will be under no stress and glue squeeze-out on the inside will be hard to remove.

2. **After the glue** has set, remount the assembly on the lathe and turn the entire piece to its maximum diameter so the walls are circular arcs.

3. **Mark the ends** of the final

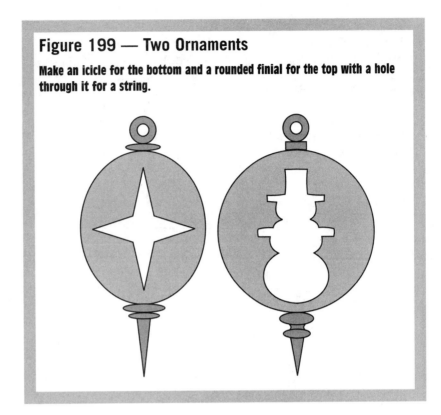

Figure 199 — Two Ornaments

Make an icicle for the bottom and a rounded finial for the top with a hole through it for a string.

ornament on the cylinder and turn the outer shape as in your original design. As you start turning the outside, you will see how deep to cut by watching the inside 'ghosts'. This view of the interior shape can guide you in cutting the outside contour. Follow the shadow outline in the spinning piece to shape the outside.

4. **Sand** and apply finish.

5. **Turn** separate pieces for the finial and the icicle. The centered holes top and bottom will help in drilling to attach these pieces. **Figure 199** shows two completed ornaments.

Glues

Figure 200 — Christmas Ornament

The first cut '1' will shape the inside profile of the finished ornament. After the four sticks are rotated, the second cut '2' shapes the outside profile.

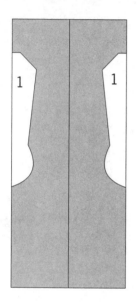

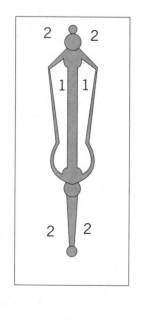

Almost any adhesive can be used for the final glue up. There are nine different types of adhesives and they differ mainly in strength, open time, closed time, whether they are waterproof and whether they work on oily woods. With the inside-outside turnings, open time and water resistance aren't important.

For the ordinary woods — cherry, mahogany, walnut, oak and maple — use ordinary yellow carpenter's glue. This is polyvinyl acetate (PVA) and is sold as white, yellow and high perform- ance. The white glue takes longer to set (30 minutes) than the yellow (15 minutes) or the high performance (5 minutes).

If you are using an oily wood such as teak, cocobolo or one of the rosewoods, you can still use PVA adhesives — just be sure that the joints have been freshly cut (within 24 hours) and then sanded lightly with 180-grit paper. Wiping the joints with paint thinner or acetone doesn't help as much as having a fresh surface and light sanding. Polyurethane glue is excellent with oily woods it but does expand and foam. Shave off the excess glue with a chisel.

A good adhesive should dry and set in a short time, the glue line should be invisible and strong, and it should be inexpensive and have a long shelf life. It should

also be easy to use, easy to clean up and be non-toxic. Most of the time, normal PVA glues fit this bill nicely.

A Christmas Ornament

Figure 200 shows a complex Christmas ornament.

1. The first cut '1' will shape the inside profile of the finished ornament.

2. Carefully sand the turned area.

3. Paint the turned portions yellow.

4. Rotate each stick 180° and glue them together with PVA glue.

5. Turn the outside as shown in the second cut '2'.

Asymmetrical Turnings

The previous projects involved symmetrical figures. For a non-symmetrical turning you need to turn two separate ornaments, disassemble each, then mix and match. See **Figure 201**.

Note that with an asymmetrical turning there is no waste, you'll be able to make two ornaments; they'll just be mirror images.

Flared Vase

Another example of a reverse turning is a flared vase as in **Figure 202**. Instead of a closed form, like the ornaments, the flared vase is open at one end.

Figure 202 shows how four pieces of wood can be turned on a lathe, then reversed and shaped to make the flared vase. Because there is no tailstock connection for the final shaping, a plug is made to support the "petals". The plug should fit snugly inside the blank so there is no movement.

The plug is made by turning a soft piece of wood between centers to the shape of the inside of the vase. The plug needs to be a good fit, so use calipers to gauge the depth and diameter.

1. **Mount** the four-piece assembly in a chuck and turn as in **Figure 202a.**

2. **Sand** and finish this portion.

3. **Remove** the four pieces and turn each 180° and glue the pieces together.

4. **Make a plug** to fit the inside contour.

5. **Turn the final** outside shape.

6. **Sand** and finish outside.

References

Figure 199, Susan Hardenbrook, West Bay Area Woodturners, 1997

Figure 200, Tom Howard, West Bay Area Woodturners, 2003

Figure 201, *American Woodturner*, Sept. 1991

Figure 202, *Woodturning*, 1996

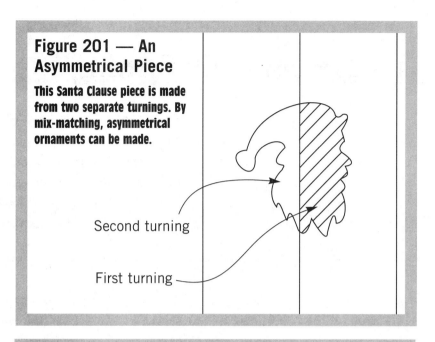

Figure 201 — An Asymmetrical Piece

This Santa Clause piece is made from two separate turnings. By mix-matching, asymmetrical ornaments can be made.

Second turning

First turning

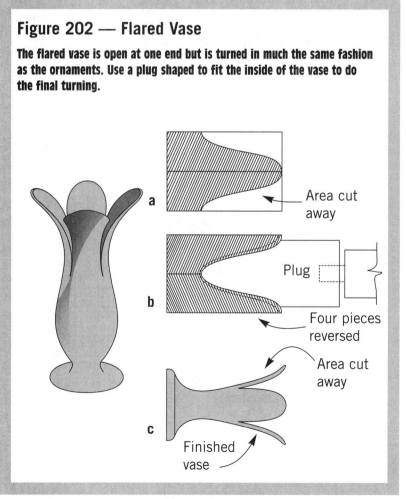

Figure 202 — Flared Vase

The flared vase is open at one end but is turned in much the same fashion as the ornaments. Use a plug shaped to fit the inside of the vase to do the final turning.

a — Area cut away

b — Plug — Four pieces reversed

c — Area cut away — Finished vase

CHAPTER 18

Segmentation Turning

Pueblo Indians of the American Southwest were making beautiful pottery before Columbus sailed to the New World. The method was similar at all the pueblos, most of which were in what is now New Mexico. Clay was dug from a nearby deposit, dried, pulverized and cleaned of stones and other impurities. Water was added and the clay was tempered by adding an inert material to keep the mixture from being too sticky and to reduce the risk of cracking during firing. The tempering materials were specific to each pueblo. This continued for centuries and accordingly affords a way to identify the place where a vessel was made then — and is made today. Tempering materials include fine sand, powdered volcanic ash, and crushed pottery fragments.

Figure 203 — Outlines of Pueblo Vessels

(a-d) San Ildefonso (New Mexico); (e) Hopi (Arizona); (f) Zuni (New Mexico); (g) Hopi (Arizona); (h) Zuni (New Mexico) and (i) Acoma (Arizona).

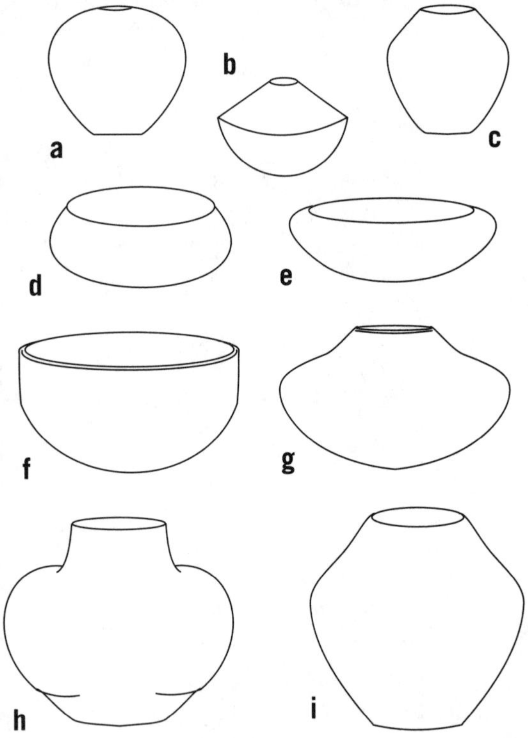

No potter's wheel was used to form those pots. The clay was rolled into short sections of rope, which were coiled to build up the walls. Thinning and shaping was done with a scraper made from a piece of gourd, then decorations were scratched or carved into the surface. The rough surface was painted with a slip — fine red or white clay in a water suspension. It was mopped on and then, while still damp, the surface was polished with a smooth stone. Colored decorations were added with a yucca brush and pigments obtained from the boiled juice of plants.

On a windless morning the vessels were laid out on a framework of rocks, and then covered with dried cow dung, bark, or sticks that were set afire. The fire was smothered with urine to yield jet black vessels, and let burn for longer times to give shades of tan, cream, yellow, orange and red. The temperature was no more than 950° F. and often even lower, which preserves luster. Today potters fire at temperatures in the range of 1200° to 1400° F.

The bowls and vases made by the Hopi, Zuni, and Acoma, were used to carry water, store grains and to cook food — just part of their daily chores. Today these vessels represent a part of our country's history and are collector's items that command premium figures at art galleries from Santa Fe to New York City. **Figure 203** shows shapes of some typical ancient pueblo Indian pottery.

When I visited the Indian Cultural Center in Albuquerque, NM, a few years ago, I was struck by the similarity of the old sculpted bowls on display there and the bowls still being made at the San Ildefonso Pueblo — the shapes and designs haven't changed that much. At an Indian trading post on the reservation just a few miles north of Santa Fe, I showed the owner a wooden, segmented bowl that I had made — trying to emulate a classic American Indian style. He commented favorably on the shape and design and noted that there were several lathes in use locally — the Indians today are making solid and segmented wooden bowls of indigenous woods like oak, maple, pinon, and cottonwood, using the same designs and shapes their ancestors used to make pots of clay.

Segmented Bowls

The Hopi artisan first rolled the wet clay into a snake and then coiled the material bottom to top to shape the vessel. Segmented turning techniques allow modern-day wood turners to construct bowls by stacking built-up rings in somewhat the same way. By varying the color and size of the wood pieces, one can make designs resembling those of the past.

Intricate designs can be built when 16, 18 or even more wedges are joined together in one ring. Extremely complicated designs may require 72 segments or more. Each ring is stacked upon another ring as the design and shape of the pot slowly builds up. A pot 10 inches high and 10 inches in diameter might have 15 rings with 18 segments in each ring, or 270 different wedges of wood. Each wedge can be of any wood of any color, and each wedge can itself be made of multiple pieces. The more intricate bowls might contain thousands of pieces of wood.

The most difficult part of segmented turning is cutting and gluing the small pieces into rings, then building up the design, layer by layer. The actual lathe turning is straightforward.

Corner Angles and Miter Angles

The math involved in segmented turning concerns finding the proper miter angle for each segment of the ring and the length of each these pieces. The

> ### Rule of Thumb
>
> **Segmentation turning** can produce beautiful and interesting shapes, but the key to it is perfect joints between segments, and one way to achieve them is with a stationary disk sander.

Figure 204 — Corner and Miter Angles

The central joint angles of a polygon always add up to 360°. The miter angle, that is the angle to set the table saw miter gauge, is one-half of the center angle.

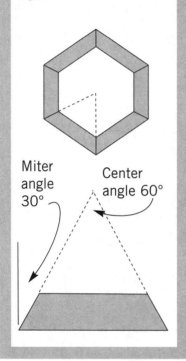

Miter angle 30°

Center angle 60°

miter angle depends on the number of segments in the circle. The segment length at the wide end of the wedge (**Figure 205**) depends on the diameter of the circle. The height of each ring is the thickness of the board. The width of the segment from outside to inside is determined by the shape you intend to build.

Math

A full circle has 360°, therefore to make a closed construction out of straight pieces, the center angles must add up to this same 360°. In a figure with six equal-length sides, the six 60° central angles add up to 360°. But you don't cut the corners of each piece at 60° — because two sides come together to make a corner and each side must be miter-cut to one half the corner angle, or 30°. To find the center angle for a figure with any number of equal-length sides, divide 360° by the number of sides. To find the miter angle, divide the corner angle by two, **Figure 204**.

> Center Angle = 360° ÷ Number of Segments
>
> Miter Angle=Center Angle ÷ 2

Problem 1: We are planning to make a segmented bowl and one ring will have 12 pieces. At what angle should the miter gauge on the table saw be set?

Solution 1:

> Corner Angle = 360° ÷
> Number of Segments
>
> Corner Angle = 360° ÷ 12
>
> Corner Angle = 30°
>
> Miter Angle=Corner Angle ÷ 2
>
> Miter Angle = 30° ÷ 2 = 15°

Therefore we should set the miter gauge at 15° and cut 12 pieces of equal length — plus one extra piece, just in case. Now that we know how to determine the angles of a polygon, we can find the length of the segments.

Side Length of Regular Polygon

Knowing the size of the polygon, as measured by the radius of the circle that lies inside and touches all the sides (the inner circle), we can determine the length of the sides. The inside circle is also called the inscribed circle. The outside circle, in which the polygon neatly fits touching all the points, is mathematically useful too, but of little relevance to segmented woodturning.

Math

The radius of a circle inscribed inside a regular polygon makes up one side of a right triangle as shown in **Figure 205**. Side X of the triangle is one-half the length of one side of the polygon (L). Geometry will help us solve for the length of side X of the triangle, and thus find the length of one side of the polygon. For a right triangle:

Let n = number of sides

Let X = the opposite side of the right triangle and ½ of the polygon side.

Tangent of the angle = opposite side / adjacent side

Tan angle = X / Radius

X = Radius x Tan angle

Angle = 180 / n

X = Radius x Tan (180/n)

Side = 2X

Side = r[(tan 180/n)2]

Application

Problem 2: We want to build a twelve-sided figure with diameter of 11.5 inches. What is the length of a segment?

Solution 2:

Side = r[(tan 180/n)2]

Where n = 12 and r = 5.75 inches

Side = 5.75[(tan 180 ÷ 12) 2]

Side = 5.75 [(tan 15) 2]

Side = 5.75 x 0.5359

Side = 3.08" ≈ 3⅛ inches

We would cut twelve pieces 3⅛ inches long (the long side) and at an angle of 15°, see **Figure 206**. When these segments are assembled we will have a twelve-sided polygon whose diameter is 11½ inches as measured by the inscribed circle.

The tangent of the center angle, 0.54 in the formula above, is constant for all regular 12-sided figures. Once you know the

radius of the inscribed circle, this constant can be used to find the length of the segment. This same number, 0.54, can be found in **Figure 206** along with the other inside-radius constant K values for other polygons.

Using a Constant

We can use the constant derived for each polygon to find the segment length (see **Figure 206**) instead of using the intimidating formula above. The procedure is as follows:

1. Choose the number of segments in the ring, for example, nine.

2. Determine the radius of the ring to be made, for example, 9½ inches diameter ÷ 2 = 4.75 inches.

3. Look up the inside radius constant K in **Figure 206** for the polygon, for example nine-sided K = 0.73.

4. Multiply the radius times the K value to find the segment length:

Length of Segment = Radius x Inner Radius Constant

LS = R x K

LS = 4.75-in. x 0.73
= 3.47 inches ≈ 3½ inches

This segment length (3½ inches) is correct for a nine-sided figure with a 9½ inch diameter ring.

Figure 206 gives number constants K which, when multiplied by the radius of the

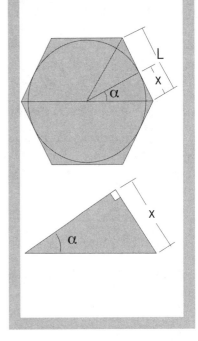

Figure 205 — A Regular Polygon Can Be Broken Down into Right Triangles

Use geometry to find the length of opposite side X which is one-half the length of one side of the polygon.

Figure 206 — Regular Polygons

Multiply the radius of any polygon by the given inner radius constant K to find the length of a segment. For example to find the length of a segment of a hexagon (n = 6) with diameter of 10 inches (r = 5) multiply 5 x 1.15 = 5.75 inches.

Name	Number Of Sides n	Constant for Radius of Inner Circle[1] K	Corner Angle	Miter Angle (degrees)
Triangle, Equilateral	3	3.46	120	60.0
Square	4	2.00	90	45.0
Pentagon	5	1.45	72	36.0
Hexagon	6	1.15	60	30.0
Heptagon	7	0.96	51	25.7
Octagon	8	0.83	45	22.5
Nonagon	9	0.73	40	20.0
Decagon	10	0.65	36	18.0
Undecagon	11	0.59	33	16.4
Dodecagon	12	0.54	30	15.0
Triskadecagon	13	0.49	28	13.8
Quadradecagon	14	0.46	26	12.9
Pentadecagon	15	0.43	24	12.0
Hexadecagon	16	0.40	23	11.3
Octadecagon	18	0.35	20	10.0
Twenty	20	0.32	18	9.0
Twenty two	22	0.29	16	8.2
Twenty four	24	0.26	15	7.5

(1) Constant K = (Tan 180/n) x 2
Example, let n = 6. Then K = (Tan 180/6) x 2 = Tan 30 x 2 = 0.5774 x 2 = 1.1547

inner circle, produce the length of each segment for rings of three to twenty-four segments. For more on regular polygons and radii of inner and outer circles see Woodworkers' Essential, Chapter 8, *Size and Measurement.*

Bowl Diameter

The largest circle that can be drawn touching the edges of the outside of each segment (not the points) will also be the maximum size ring that can be turned or sawn from the polygon. Using the constants in **Figure 206**, we can calculate the size of the bowl by knowing the length of each segment.

Problem 3: If we have a 12-sided ring and the long length of each segment is 3 inches, what bowl diameter can be turned?

Solution 3: Find the inner radius constant K in **Figure 206**.

Radius = Length of Side / Inner Radius Constant

Radius = 3 ÷ 0.54
= 5.55 inches

Diameter = 2 x radius

Diameter = 2 x 5.55
= 11.1 inches

This means when we glue up a 12-sided ring with each segment 3 inches long, we will be able to turn a circular ring with a diameter of 11⅛ inch.

Wood Length

The total length of wood needed for a ring is found by adding the length of one segment and the width of your saw's kerf (usually about ⅛ inch) and multiplying that number by the number of segments in the ring.

Problem 4: How much wood is needed to cut 24 pieces each 2¼ inches long?

Solution 4:

Wood Length = Segment Length + ⅛ inch x Number of Segments

Wood Length = (2.25 + 0.125) x 24 = 57 inches

You need a longer piece for extra segments plus a foot of wood for a hand-hold. If you can flip-flop the wood as you cut (see **Figure 209**) you'll use less wood.

Designing the Bowl

An accurate drawing of the proposed bowl is necessary to figure out the number of rings, the dimensions of each segment, and the position of each ring, **Figure 207**.

1. Draw the full-size profile (inside and outside contours) on ¼ inch graph paper. Include horizontal lines to show the thickness of the wood for each ring. Use colored pencils to show wood color and grain patterns.

2. Number each horizontal ring from the top down.

3. Make a worksheet as in **Figure 208**.

4. Start filling in the worksheet, listing the ring numbers in column A and the types of wood for each ring in column B.

5. Draw rectangles around each section of the profile (**Figure 207**) at each ring, allowing ¼ inch waste inside and outside. Use a 12 inch ruler and measure the width of each block to fill in column C. When you rip the boards, use **Figure 208**, column C for width. If one of the rings is solid, that is will not be made of segments, mark this fact in

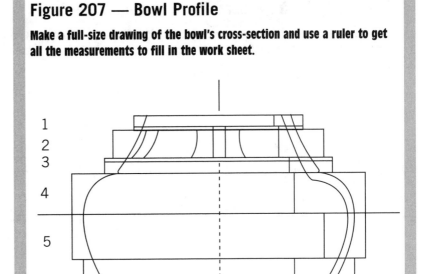

Figure 207 — Bowl Profile

Make a full-size drawing of the bowl's cross-section and use a ruler to get all the measurements to fill in the work sheet.

column G with the size of the disk in column F.

6. Column D is for the thickness of the wood for the segments — quite often this is regular ¾ inch stock. Add a veneer ring after the segments are glued into a ring and sanded flat.

7. Measure the outside diameter of each ring (Column F) plus ½ inch.

8. Determine how many segments there are to be in each ring and record it in column G along with the miter angle. The figures 10/18 means 10 segments are to be cut at an 18° miter.

Rule of Thumb

When you are **sawing blocks** to be glued up into segmented rings, calculations for the corner angles might involve tiny fractions of a degree — hard to hit with a table saw. So get as close as you can, then assemble two half-rings. Flatten their ends on the stationary disk sander to make the two half-rings fit perfectly together.

Figure 208 — Worksheet for a Segmented Bowl

Make a worksheet like this for each vessel you design. The rings are numbered 1 to 8 in the left column, then add the types of wood stock used (width, thickness and length), the ring diameter, and the outside length of each segment.

Ring Number (From Top Down)	Type (1)	Width (5)	Thickness	Length (2)	Ring Diameter	Segments & Degrees	Segment Length (4) (Fraction)	Segment Length (Decimal)
A	B	C	D	E	F	G	H	H
1	Holly + V1	3/4	1/4	10	2-7/8	10/18	15/16	0.93
2	Mixed	3/4	1/2	11-3/8	3-1/2	10/18	1-1/8	1.13
3	Holly + V1	3/4	1/4	12-1/2	3-7/8	10/18	1-1/4	1.25
4	Walnut	1-1/4	3/4	16-1/4	5	10/18	1-5/8	1.63
5	Walnut	3/4	3/4	16-1/4	5	10/18	1-5/8	1.63
6	Walnut	1	3/4	15-1/2	4-3/4	10/18	1-9/16	1.54
7	Walnut	1-3/8	3/4	12-1/4	3-3/4	10/18	1-1/4	1.22
8	Holly + V2	Disk	5/16	—	2-7/8	Disk	—	0

(1) V1 = Black Dyed Veneer, V2 = Yellow Dyed Veneer
(2) Wood Stock Length = Segment Length x 10
(4) Segment Length = Radius x K Value (0.65)
(5) Ring 8 is a solid disk.

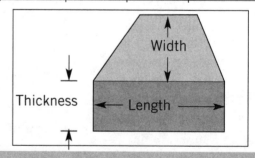

Rule of Thumb

To find the miter angle divide 180° by the number of sides. For example, to cut segments for a 12-sided polygon, 180 / 12 = 15° miter angle.

The different rings do not have to contain the same number of segments but make sure they line up nicely. An intricate design may require 16, 18, or more segments. The rest of the vessel can have rows of 8, 10, or 12 segments. It just so happens that every ring in this vessel has 10 segments.

9. Find the length of each segment from **Figure 211** and record it in column H.

10. Now calculate the length of stock you'll need for each row by multiplying the segment length (column H) times the number of segments (column G). Record this for each row in column E. Remember, this piece should be longer for safety in cutting the miters and for a few extra segments.

You now have all the information you need to plane and rip the boards and to miter-cut the various pieces for your turning.

Making the Bowl

1. Use the worksheet to mill the wood. You have the width (C), thickness (D) and length (E) for each ring, see **Figure 208**. Cut the segments to the lengths in column H with the miter gauge set at the angle listed in column G.

2. Dry-fit each segment into a ring and hold them with a hose clamp. Hold the ring up to the window and if you see light, adjust two segments on opposite sides. A disk sander works fine. When the joints are tight, apply carpenter's yellow glue to each edge and place the ring on a flat surface. Compress the ring with the hose clamp, tap the pieces flat, and let set for an hour. Use chalk or a piece of tape and number each ring as in **Figure 207**. If you want to glue up the ring later, put the pieces in a plastic sandwich bag and label it.

3. Do the same with each ring until all are glued up. Scrape the glue off the faces and flatten one face on a disk sander. Glue the bottom disk (ring 8, **Figure 207**) to a waste block on a metal faceplate and turn the ring flat using a scraper. Glue on a veneer ring.

4. Glue the next ring (# 7) in place and flatten the top. Glue each ring in place, adjusting each so the joints are attractively offset.

5. When the bowl blank is dry, bring up the tailstock and turn

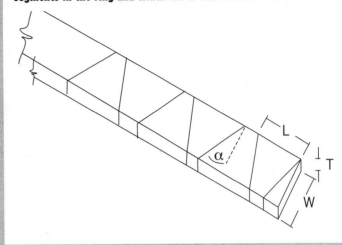

Figure 209 — The Various Pieces

The wood thickness (T) is the same as the ring height, segment length (L) determines the ring size, miter angle (α) depends on the number of segments in the ring and width (W) is the thickness of the bowl wall.

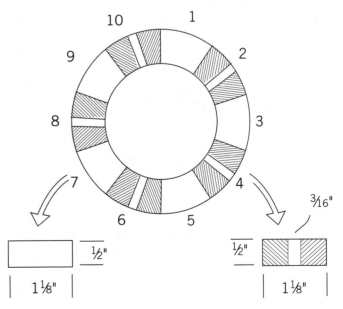

Figure 210 — A Complicated Ring

The complicated ten-segment ring #2 is made of five maple pieces ½ inch thick x ¾ inch wide x 1 ⅛ inch long cut at 18° at each end. Each of the five holly-bloodwood segments is made of two pieces of bloodwood and one piece of holly.

Odd numbered pieces   Even numbered pieces

Figure 211 — Segment Lengths

Find the diameter of the ring in the first column and the number of segments along the top. The segment length is to the nearest 1⁄16 inch. Example: Find the segment length of a 16-sided figure with diameter = 8 inches; read 1⅝ inches. To find the exact length, multiply the constant K (from Figure 206) times the radius.

Diameter	6 pcs	8pcs	10pcs	12 pcs	14 pcs	16 pcs	18 pcs	20 pcs	22 pcs	24 pcs
2.0	1-1/8	13/16	5/8	9/16	7/16	3/8	3/8	5/16	5/16	1/4
2.5	1-7/16	1 1/16	13/16	11/16	9/16	1/2	7/16	3/8	3/8	5/16
3.0	1-3/4	1-1/4	1	13/16	11/16	5/8	1/2	1/2	7/16	3/8
3.5	2	1-7/16	1-1/8	15/16	13/16	11/16	5/8	9/16	1/2	7/16
4.0	2-5/16	1-11/16	1-5/16	1-1/16	15/16	13/16	11/16	5/8	9/16	1/2
4.5	2-9/16	1-7/8	1-7/16	1-3/16	1-1/16	7/8	13/16	3/4	5/8	9/16
5.0	2-7/8	2 1/16	1-5/8	1-3/8	1-1/8	1	7/8	13/16	3/4	5/8
5.5	3-3/16	2-5/16	1-13/16	1-1/2	1-1/4	1-1/8	15/16	7/8	13/16	11/16
6.0	3-7/16	2-1/2	1-15/16	1-5/8	1-3/8	1-3/16	1-1/16	15/16	7/8	3/4
6.5	3-3/4	2-11/16	2-1/8	1-3/4	1-1/2	1-5/16	1-1/8	1-1/16	15/16	7/8
7.0	4	2-7/8	2-1/4	1-7/8	1-5/8	1-3/8	1-1/4	1-1/8	1	15/16
7.5	4-5/16	3-1/8	2-7/16	2	1-3/4	1-1/2	1-5/16	1-3/16	1 1/16	1
8.0	4-5/8	3-5/16	2-5/8	2-3/16	1-13/16	1-5/8	1-3/8	1-1/4	1-3/16	1-1/16
8.5	4-7/8	3-1/2	2-3/4	2-5/16	1-15/16	1-11/16	1-1/2	1-3/8	1-1/4	1-1/8
9.0	5-3/16	3-3/4	2-15/16	2-7/16	2-1/16	1-13/16	1-9/16	1-7/16	1-5/16	1-3/16
9.5	5-7/16	3-15/16	3-1/16	2-9/16	2-3/16	1-7/8	1-11/16	1-1/2	1-3/8	1-1/4
10.0	5-3/4	4-1/8	3-1/4	2-11/16	2-5/16	2	1-3/4	1-5/8	1-7/16	1-5/16
10.5	6-1/16	4-3/8	3-7/16	2-13/16	2-7/16	2-1/8	1-13/16	1-11/16	1-1/2	1-3/8
11.0	6-5/16	4-9/16	3-9/16	3	2-1/2	2-3/16	1-15/16	1-3/4	1-5/8	1-7/16
11.5	6-5/8	4-3/4	3-3/4	3-1/8	2-5/8	2-5/16	2	1-13/16	1-11/16	1-1/2
12.0	6-7/8	5	3-7/8	3-1/4	2-3/4	2-3/8	2-1/8	1-15/16	1-3/4	1-9/16
12.5	7-3/16	5-3/16	4 1/16	3-3/8	2-7/8	2-1/2	2-3/16	2	1-13/16	1-5/8
13.0	7-1/2	5-3/8	4-1/4	3-1/2	3	2-5/8	2-1/4	2-1/16	1-7/8	1-11/16
13.5	7-3/4	5-5/8	4-3/8	3-5/8	3-1/8	2-11/16	2-3/8	2-3/16	1-15/16	1-3/4
14.0	8 1/16	5-13/16	4-9/16	3-3/4	3-1/4	2-13/16	2-7/16	2-1/4	2	1-13/16
14.5	8-5/16	6	4-11/16	3-15/16	3-5/8	2-7/8	2-9/16	2-5/16	2-1/8	1-7/8
15.0	8-5/8	6-1/4	4-7/8	4-1/16	3-7/16	3	2-5/8	2-3/8	2-3/16	1-15/16
15.5	8-15/16	6-7/16	5-1/16	4-3/16	3-9/16	3-1/8	2-11/16	2-1/2	2-1/4	2
16.0	9-3/16	6-5/8	5-3/16	4-5/16	3-11/16	3-3/16	2-13/16	2-9/16	2-5/16	2-1/16
16.5	9-1/2	6-7/8	5-3/8	4-7/16	3-13/16	3-5/16	2-7/8	2-5/8	2-3/8	2-1/8
17.0	9-3/4	7-1/16	5-1/2	4-9/16	3-15/16	3-3/8	3	2-3/4	2-7/16	2-3/16

(1) The Side Lengths are figured to the nearest 1/16-inch. To find the exact length
  Multiply the Constant (K) from Figure 206
Example: 12-sided figure with dia. = 17. K=0.54, radius = 8.5. 0.54 x 8.5 = 4.59-in. The table lists 4-9/16-in.

the finished shape. You'll be surprised how nicely it turns — all the segments are oriented so you're always turning long grain.

6. **Use** the bowl profile (**Figure 207**) to make a pattern on cardboard and use it to shape the outside of the turning.

Making a Complicated Ring

Row #2 (**Figure 207**) is built up of five maple wedges and five mixed wedges of bloodwood and holly (see **Figure 210**). Here's how to proceed.

1. **Prepare** the maple stock ½ inch thick x ¾ inch wide and cut five pieces 1⅛ inch long at 18°. These are pieces 1, 3, 5, 7, and 9 in **Figure 210**.

2. **The mixed** wedges (segments 2, 4, 6, 8, and 10) are made this way: prepare the bloodwood stock ½ inch thick x ¾ inch wide and cut ten pieces ¹⁵⁄₃₂ inch long at 9° as in **Figure 210.**

3. **Prepare** the holly stock ¹⁄₁₂ inch thick x ¾ inch wide and cut five pieces ³⁄₁₆ inches long. These pieces are not miter cut.

4. **Put all together** as in **Figure 210**. This ring will contain 20 pieces of wood.

Rule of Thumb

Reproduce and hang the chart in **Figure 211** in your shop. It's all you need to find the length of a side of any ring.

CHAPTER 19

Bowls and Baskets from Boards

It has been estimated that 90% of the wood is wasted when a bowl is turned from a solid block. If you make bowls from boards, the only waste is the small amount of sawdust that comes from the band saw kerfs. There are four methods of making bowls from boards (**Figure 212**): rings sawn at 90° from multiple boards (a), beveled rings sawn from a single board (b), or beveled rings sawn from multiple boards (c), and spiral rings sawn so they overlap (d).

Figure 212— Four Ways to Make Bowls from Boards

The square ring method (a) uses more material but gives leeway in bowl shape and colors. The beveled ring method uses a single board (b) or two boards (c). The spiral ring method (d) can make collapsible baskets.

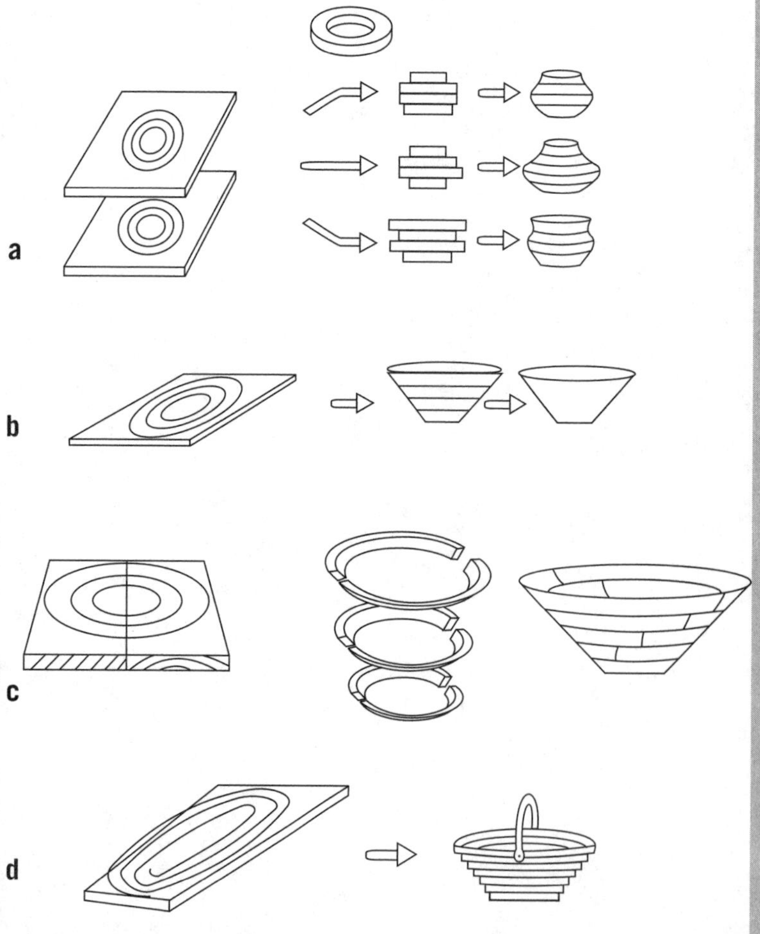

Making a large bowl from a solid piece of wood is hard work — from finding a large chunk of wood, mounting it on the lathe, and then cutting 90% of it away. The turner still has to worry about the bowl splitting and distorting as it dries. None of these problems occur with bowl blanks glued up from kiln-dried boards and the size of the final bowl is limited only by the size of the lathe.

Making a bowl from a board is easy, fast, and saves a lot of wood. The height, shape, and wall thickness are governed by the initial shapes cut out of boards you can find in your wood pile. Ring lamination bowls are stronger than bowls turned from solid blocks and lathe time and material costs are significantly lower.

Techniques

Making a bowl from a board is an interesting concept — flat, two-dimensional planks sawn into rings produce bowl blanks of remarkable complexity and beauty. The principal is simple — saw successively smaller rings from a board (or boards), glue these rings together one on top of another and then sand or turn the rough bowl blank into a pleasing shape.

1. Square Rings

— With this procedure different sized rings are cut from two or more boards with the blade set at 90º (hence the term 'square rings'). These rings are then assembled to make the bowl blank. The shape and composition of the final bowl depends only on the whim of the craftsman — any shape using any wood. By using a mixture of wood types, multi-colored bowls can be produced. This method is easy because there are no bevel cuts and any rings left over can be used on another bowl. See **Figure 212a.**

2. Beveled Rings from One Board

— This system involves bevel-cutting successive rings so each outer ring fits on top of an inner ring. The stacked and glued rings are shaped with abrasives or turned. The shape of the final bowl is usually conical with straight sides and, unless two boards are used, always homogeneous (see **Figure 212b**).

3. Bevel Cut from Two or More Boards

— This method also involves bevel cutting successive rings — but from two boards instead of one (see **Figure 212c**). No lathe is required to finish these bowls; they can be finished by sanding.

4. Spiral Rings from Continuous Cuts

— Using this method, a spiral is cut from a board and the outer edges are raised so each coil is higher than its neighbor but still in contact. This helical shape is then glued in place to produce a permanent bowl, or joined in a way to make it collapsible, see **Figure 212d.**

Square Rings Cut from Multiple Boards

With this method, the rings are cut at 90° from two or more boards and the different pieces, selected for color and diversity, are glued together to make the bowl blank. This technique is easier than the other methods because the band saw (saber saw, coping saw, fret saw, scroll saw) doesn't have to be tipped at a precise angle, see **Figure 212a.**

Experimenting with this concept can produce a wide range of shapes and, by using different woods, will produce multi-colored bowls not possible with solid blocks or with the beveled single board procedure.

Procedure

1. Draw the silhouette of the

bowl using ¼ inch, cross-hatch

Rule of Thumb

When you turn a bowl from a solid block of wood, **90% of the wood** becomes shavings, chips and dust. But when you construct a similar bowl using rings sawn from a flat board, you might lose only 10% of the wood to sawdust.

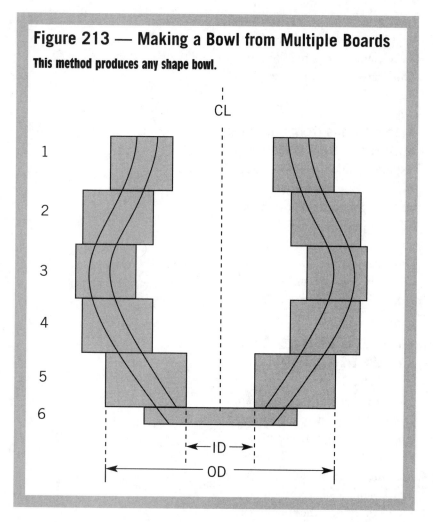

Figure 213 — Making a Bowl from Multiple Boards
This method produces any shape bowl.

4. Make a list of all the different rings you'll need for the bowl blank then draw the rings on multiple pieces of wood. In our example we used ¾ inch stock.

5. Cut the rings using whatever saw you've chosen. I use a band saw and enter the wood circle with the grain, not across. When this scarf joint is glued back together it will be nearly invisible. Walnut, oak, mahogany, cherry, and many other woods have such consistent grain pattern and color that it will be hard to see these joints. Save the unused rings for another bowl.

6. Stack the rings and glue them together. Be sure to stagger the scarf joints for strength and to make them less visible. To clamp the rings, use weights or place them in a press until the glue has set.

7. Mount the bowl blank on the lathe and turn to shape.

Beveled Rings Sawn from a Single Board

With this method, rings are sawn from a single board at an angle and width such that when the rings are reassembled they form a conical bowl blank, see **Figures 214 and 215**.

The outside surface pattern of the finished piece can be affected

paper. Also draw the inside wall (assume the walls are ¼ inch to ⅜ inch thick). See **Figure 213**.

2. Make horizontal lines to indicate the thickness of the wood and number each layer 1 to 6 starting at the top. Note that it isn't necessary that all layers be the same thickness.

3. Mark the inside diameter (ID) and the outside diameter (OD) of each ring on the paper. Leave at least ¼ inch extra on the inside and outside.

Rule of Thumb

Square-cut rings are the simplest way of building a bowl, since there are no bevel cuts and no calculations, and you can use any wood to make almost any shape.

by using contrasting rings at the rim or the foot of the bowl but in general it will be homogeneous.

Math

The working angle (band saw table tilt) equals the arctangent of the ring width divided by the wood thickness.

Angle = Arctan (RW ÷ WT)

Where RW = ring width and WT = wood thickness

Problem 1:

We have a 12 inch x 12 inch x ¾ inch thick piece of California claro walnut and want to bevel-cut it to make a 12 inch diameter laminated bowl blank. We want each ring to be ⅝ inch in width to allow some flexibility when shaping the final bowl on the lathe. At what angle should the band saw be set?

Solution 1:

Angle = Atan (RW ÷ WT)

Where ring width RW = ⅝ inch (0.625) and wood thickness WT = ¾ inch (0.75)

Angle = Atan (0.625 ÷ 0.75)

Angle = Atan 0.8333

Angle = 39.8056º ≈ 40º

Set the band saw table at 40º

Figure 216 shows the steps if you use a calculator.

You can also find the correct blade angle using the chart in **Figure 217.** In the previous example, find ¾ inch Stock

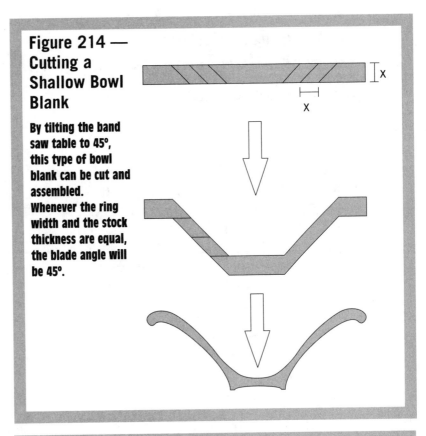

Figure 214 — Cutting a Shallow Bowl Blank

By tilting the band saw table to 45º, this type of bowl blank can be cut and assembled. Whenever the ring width and the stock thickness are equal, the blade angle will be 45º.

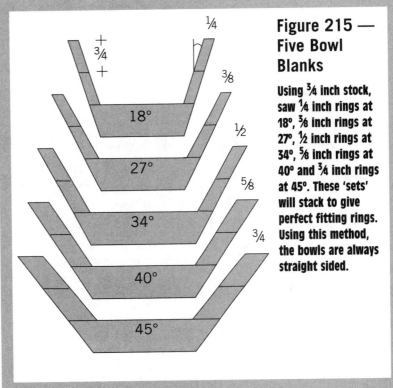

Figure 215 — Five Bowl Blanks

Using ¾ inch stock, saw ¼ inch rings at 18º, ⅜ inch rings at 27º, ½ inch rings at 34º, ⅝ inch rings at 40º and ¾ inch rings at 45º. These 'sets' will stack to give perfect fitting rings. Using this method, the bowls are always straight sided.

Figure 216 — Using a Calculator

Follow these steps to find the correct answer. Ring Width (0.625) ÷ Wood Thickness (0.75) = 0.833. Arctangent of 0.833 = angle 39.8056°. We should set the band saw table to cut each ring at 40°.

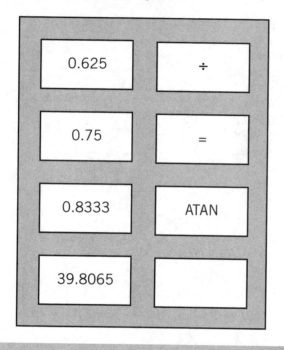

0.625	÷
0.75	=
0.8333	ATAN
39.8065	

Thickness in the left column, to the right and under ⅝ inch Ring Width read 40°.

Computer Math

To do these calculations on a computer spread sheet such as Excel, use the following formula:

Atan(Ring Width ÷ Stock Thickness)*180/3.14

To find the correct angle to cut 1-inch rings in 2-inch stock, enter the following:

"=Atan (1/2)*180/3.14". The answer, 26.5651, is rounded to 27°. See footnote at end of chapter.

Rule of Thumb

If the **Ring Width** and the **Wood Thickness** are equal, (for example ¾ inch rings cut from ¾ inch stock), then the blade angle is always 45°.

Procedure

1. **On ¼ inch** cross-hatch paper, choose a profile in **Figure 215**.

2. **Set the band saw** table to the correct angle. Note that the blade thickness is not important — the diameter of each ring will differ from its neighbor by the width of the blade.

3. **Draw concentric** rings on a paper pattern and tape it to the stock.

4. **Cut the rings** from one board using scarf cuts tangent to the rings.

5. **Assemble** and glue.

6. **Turn the bowl** on a lathe.

Beveled Rings Cut from Two Boards

With this method two boards are butted together and concentric circles are drawn (see **Figure 218**). For a 45° bowl, the rings' thickness should equal the board's thickness. There's no need to cut wider rings because the cutting angle remains constant and thicker rings will just make the glue-up and the turning more difficult.

The two boards can be the same type of wood or different — for example maple and walnut. The pieces should be equal in thickness and jointed along one edge. See **Figure 218**.

Figure 217 — Blade Angle for Bowls from a Single Board [1]

The correct blade angle depends on the width of the ring and the thickness of the board. The width of the saw blade is immaterial. Both the formula for your calculator and an Excel spread sheet formula are given.

Stock Thickness (Fraction)	Stock Thickness (Decimal)	. . . . Ring Width								
		¼ in. 0.25	⅜ in. 0.375	½ in. 0.5	⅝ in. 0.625	¾ in. 0.75	⅞ in. 0.875	1 in. 1	1⅛ in. 1.125	1¼ in. 1.25
		Blade Angle in Degrees [2]								
¼ in.	0.25	45								
⅜ in.	0.375	34	45							
½ in.	0.5	27	37	45						
⅝ in.	0.625	22	31	39	45					
¾ in.	0.75	18	27	34	40	45				
⅞ in.	0.875	16	23	30	36	41	45			
1.0 in.	1	14	21	27	32	37	41	45		
1⅛ in.	1.125	13	18	24	29	34	38	42	45	
1¼ in.	1.25	11	17	22	27	31	35	39	42	45

(1) Blade Angle: Atan (Ring Width / Stock Thickness)
Excel Formula: =Atan(C$7/$B9)*180/3.14
(2) No figures given for angles greater than 45 degrees.

Procedure

1. **Butt two** jointed boards together and draw concentric circles where the width of each ring is equal to the thickness of the wood stock.

2. **Separate** the two blanks and set the band saw table to 45°.

3. **Cut the semicircles**, first from one of the halves and then from the other.

4. **Glue the** half ring pieces together using staples, masking tape or large rubber bands to keep the rings together.

5. **Sand the top** and bottom surfaces of each ring smooth on a belt sander.

6. **Put the biggest** disk on a flat surface and stack the other rings on top. If they tend to slip, use staples to tack them in place.

7. **Place a weight** on the top or use clamps or a shop-made a bowl press and let the glued up blank dry overnight.

8. **Mount the blank** on a lathe faceplate and turn using a bowl gouge.

Figure 218 —Make Rings from Two Different Boards

Use a compass to draw concentric circles. The finished bowl can be homogeneous if the two boards are the same species, or it will have different colored rings if the boards are different.

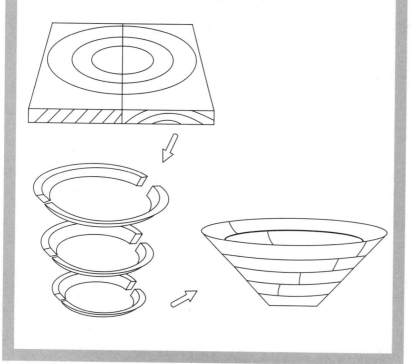

Rule of Thumb

When you build a bowl by stacking beveled rings sawn from a single board, you'll get a conical shape with straight sides — and almost no waste.

When you build a bowl by stacking beveled rings sawn from two or more boards, you can make almost any shape, but you will have some wood left over.

Bowls Cut at Multiple Angles

Rings sliced from a single board do not all have to be cut at the same angle like those in **Figure 214**. **Figure 219** shows bowl blanks made from a single board by cutting rings at different angles. By combining these rings, bowls with curved sides can be made.

Procedure

To make a bowl as in **Figure 219b**, do the following:

1. **Rip** an 8 inch x 8 inch board in half.

2. **Butt these** boards together

and hold with a few pieces of masking tape.

3. **Locate the center** and draw an outer circle with diameter 7¾ inch. This ring will be cut with the band saw table set at 90º.

4. **Measure inwards** (toward the center mark) from this outer ring and make marks at ¼ inch, ⅜ inch, ½ inch, ⅝ inch, and ¾ inch.

5. **Draw circles** at each of these marks.

6. **Separate** the boards and cut the semi-circles on the band saw. Cut the outer ring at 0º.

7. **Cut each** succeeding ring as shown in **Figure 219b**: at 18º, 27º, 34º, 40º, and 45º. Cut the other board the same way to make another set of half rings.

8. **Assemble** each ring by placing carpenters glue on the joints and holding the ends together until the glue is tacky. Use a paper stapler to join the rings and let set for at least 4 hours.

9. **Assemble** the rings and glue them together with yellow carpenters glue.

10. **Mount** on a faceplate and turn the profile as shown in **Figure 219b**.

Spiral Rings Sawn from a Single Board

To make an elliptical or round collapsible basket, bandsaw a continuous spiral into a flat board at an angle such that the spirals wedge against each other when the basket is opened. Use the pattern in **Figure 221**. These baskets can be used to hold fruit and flowers on the table and when collapsed make nice trivets for hot dishes.

Math

The working angle (Table Tilt) equals the arctan of the Blade Width divided by one-half the Wood Thickness. See **Figure 220**.

Angle = Arctan (BW / ½ WT)

Where BW = blade width and WT = wood thickness

Problem 2:

Calculate the correct angle to set the band saw table so that each succeeding spiral drops down one half the width of the stock when the band saw blade kerf is 0.045 inch, the wood thickness is 0.75 inch and one-half wood thickness is 0.375 inch.

Solution 2:

Angle = Arctan (BW / ½ WT)

Where BW = 0.045 and ½ WT = 0.375

Angle = Atan [0.045 ÷ 0.375)]

Angle = Atan 0.12

Angle = 6.8428° ≈ 7°

With the table tilted to 7°, each succeeding spiral will drop ⅜ inch or half-way down. Note that the size (width) of the spirals, whether they are ¼ inch,

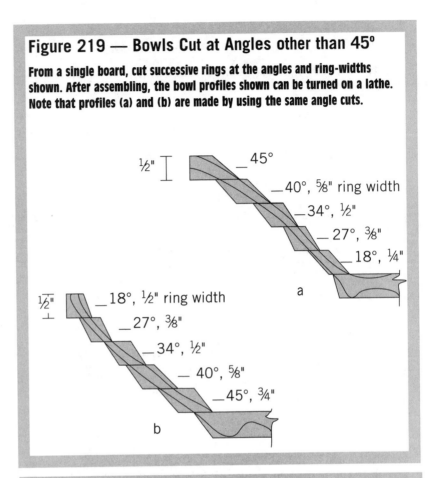

Figure 219 — Bowls Cut at Angles other than 45°

From a single board, cut successive rings at the angles and ring-widths shown. After assembling, the bowl profiles shown can be turned on a lathe. Note that profiles (a) and (b) are made by using the same angle cuts.

½"   45°
—40°, ⅝" ring width
—34°, ½"
—27°, ⅜"
—18°, ¼"
a

½"   18°, ½" ring width
—27°, ⅜"
—34°, ½"
—40°, ⅝"
—45°, ¾"
b

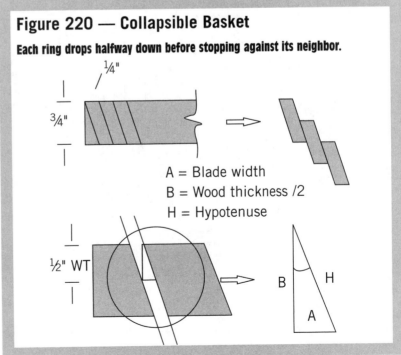

Figure 220 — Collapsible Basket

Each ring drops halfway down before stopping against its neighbor.

¼"
¾"

A = Blade width
B = Wood thickness /2
H = Hypotenuse

½" WT

B   H
A

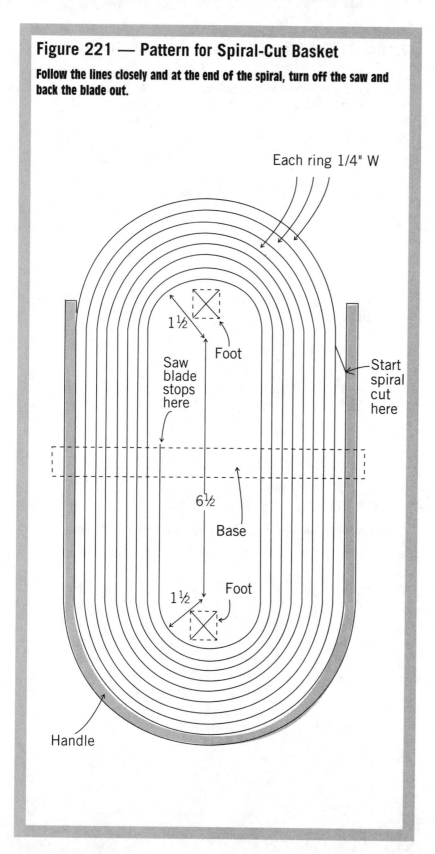

Figure 221 — Pattern for Spiral-Cut Basket

Follow the lines closely and at the end of the spiral, turn off the saw and back the blade out.

Each ring 1/4" W

1½

Foot

Saw blade stops here

Start spiral cut here

6½

Base

1½

Foot

Handle

⅜ inch or ½ inch makes no difference in the angle of the blade. All that matters is the thickness of the blade and the thickness of the wood.

Procedure

1. Choose a straight-grained, knot-free, ¾ inch hardwood like mahogany or walnut that measures about 6½ inches x 13 inches. Make sure the wood is reasonably flexible and not too brittle to bend. Sand both sides of the board until smooth.

2. Make a pattern or use the one in **Figure 221**. Attach the pattern to the work piece with a 'temporary bond' spray adhesive.

3. Mark the handle and cut it out with the band saw set at 90º (the table is flat). Discard the waste wood at one end. Sand the outside edges of the board.

4. Cut a small piece of wood with the band saw and measure the width of the kerf. Use the formula above under Math or use **Figure 222** and tilt the table to the correct angle. The usual setting will be 6º to 7º for ¾ inch stock.

5. Start the cut at the point noted and carefully follow the line to the end. Turn off the saw and back the blade out.

6. Glue the free end where the saw entered (the scarf) back in place and sand the edges of the spiral cut.

7. Prepare the long bottom cleat (¼ inch high x ¾ inch wide x 6¾ inches long) and attach it to the bottom.

8. Round over one corner of the handle as shown in **Figure 223** and attach it.

9. Make two balancing feet each ¾ inch x ¾ inch x ¼ inch high and glue them to the underside of the basket base as shown in **Figure 221**. **Figure 223** shows the collapsible basket.

Figure 222 — Spiral Baskets

Find the thickness of the wood stock in the left column and the band saw blade thickness (kerf) along the top. Set the band saw table to the angle indicated. For example, a ¾ inch board cut with a blade with 0.05 inch kerf should have a table angle of 7.6°.

Wood Fractional Size	Wood Decimal Size	----Band Saw Thickness (inches) ---			
		0.04	0.045	0.05	0.055
		---- Table Tilt Angle [1] ----			
3/8"	0.375	12.0	13.5	14.9	16.4
1/2"	0.5	9.1	10.2	11.3	12.4
5/8"	0.625	7.3	8.2	9.1	10.0
3/4"	0.75	6.1	6.8	7.6	8.3
7/8"	0.875	5.2	5.9	6.5	7.2
1.0"	1	4.6	5.1	5.7	6.3

(1) Table Tilt Angle = Atan (BT / 0.5 * WT)
Excel Formula: =Atan(C$5/(B$7/2))*180/3.14

Figure 223 — Folding Basket

The thickness of the band saw blade and the thickness of the wood determine the taper.

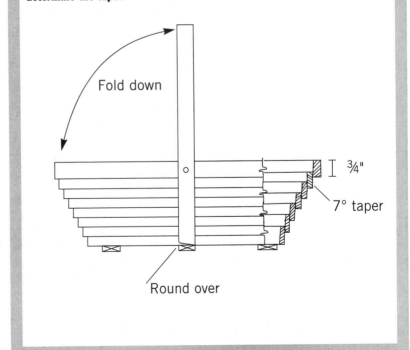

Fold down

¾"

7° taper

Round over

CHAPTER 20

Adjustable Shelving

When shelves are built into a cabinet, they are part of the structure — dadoed and glued at the ends and propped up by partitions and stiles. The strength of these shelves is not in question. Not all shelves, however, in a home or office, are built into casements. Probably a majority are adjustable and merely rest on end supports. Stand-alone shelving must gain its strength without being bound tightly at the ends and without help from the cabinet. Two structural characteristics of wood should be considered when designing free standing shelves. The first is compressive strength, that is, the ability of the shelf material to carry a load without crushing. The second is stiffness, that is, its ability to carry a load without too much deflection.

Until recently only the cheaper cabinets were made of plywood. Today, with the availability of veneered plywood and fiber boards, even high-end cabinets are being made of man-made materials and, if not the cabinet, at least the interior shelves. Because these man-made wood substitutes are so common, any discussion of shelving strength must also include plywood, fiber board and hardboard. When veneered, these boards are quite respectable although the veneer adds no strength.

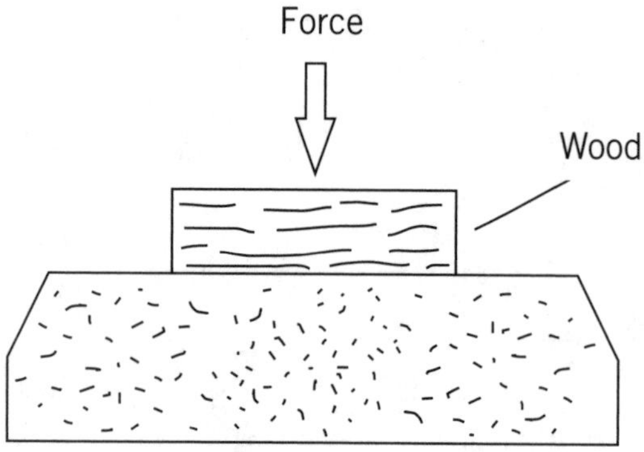

In most cases, with wood shelves, controlling the deflection is the more important consideration because, while a wooden shelf might sag, very seldom will it suddenly break. The fiber boards, tempered hard boards and particle boards are a different story. They will bend a little, and then break.

What do we do if, even after we choose what we think is the best material for a shelf, it still sags? There are seven different edge treatments here along with the math. You can decide which one suits you and how much strength it will add.

Wood Strength

A measure of wood strength is the ability of the fibers to resist applied stress, i.e. being able to hold a weight without crushing. The relative strength of different woods can be measured by

Figure 224 — Compressive Strength of Wood

Compression strength perpendicular to the grain.

applying weight and measuring the deformation. Engineers call the applied force 'stress' and the deformation 'strain'. The strength of the wood chosen for a project determines the design, how the pieces will be cut, machined, glued and fastened. Wood strength is an important factor in the mechanical performance of the finished piece and the load it can carry.

Stress

All wood species react to force in different ways and in fact sections of the same piece of wood will differ in their resistance because of varying growth ring size and position, grain direction, moisture content, physical defects and other conditions. When a weight is placed on the flat surface of a board, stress is applied perpendicular to the grain (**Figure 224**). As the weight increases, the fibers compact and each unit of force causes a proportional unit of compression but, once the weight is removed, the fibers spring back. At some point however, as more force is applied, there is no more compression and the fibers are crushed. Once the force is removed, the fibers do not spring back and we have compressive failure, i.e. breakage. This point is called the 'compressive proportional limit' of the wood and occurs just before the fibers are crushed.

Figure 225 — Compression Strength of Wood Perpendicular to the Grain

The Fiber Stress at Proportional Limit (FSPL) is the amount of load (weight) the material can withstand and still spring back i.e. retain its elasticity. Beyond this point the wood will be permanently deformed and is in danger of failure. The figures are in pounds per square inch (psi).

Wood Type	Parallel To The Grain FSPL (1)	Perpendicular To The Grain FSPL (2)
Alder	4530	540
Ash	5790	1410
Beech	4880	1250
Birch, Paper	3610	740
Birch, Yellow	6130	1190
Cherry	5960	850
Douglas Fir	5850	870
Elm	4030	850
Hickory	5180	2130
Maple, Sugar	5390	1810
Oak, Red	4580	1250
Oak, White	4760	1070
Pine, Eastern White	3670	440
Pine, Western White	4480	540
Poplar	3730	560
Walnut, Black	5780	1250
Average	**4897**	**1047**

(1) Fiber Stress at Proportional Limit (parallel to the grain)
(2) Fiber Stress at Proportional Limit (perpendicular to the grain)

When different wood species are subjected to such a test, a chart can be prepared comparing the compressive strength of woods, see **Figure 225**. There is a wide range from the weakest, eastern white pine at 440 psi, to the strongest, hickory at 2130 psi.

Problem 1: Occasionally we have friends over and a colleague's wife wears high-heeled shoes with spikes. We recently pulled up the old wall-

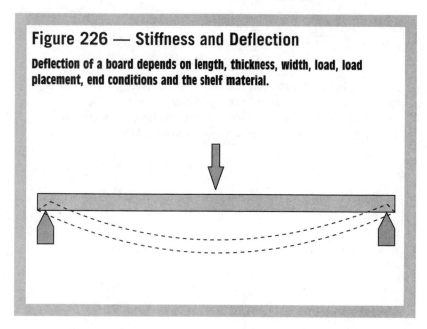

Figure 226 — Stiffness and Deflection

Deflection of a board depends on length, thickness, width, load, load placement, end conditions and the shelf material.

Wood Stiffness

It can be seen from **Figure 225** that a shelf is in no danger of failure from compression therefore the only other question is whether it will deflect under a load. Shelf stiffness, or its resistance to bending, depends on seven factors:

The first three, (1) length, (2) thickness and (3) width, define the size of the shelf. The next two, (4) load and (5) load placement are part of the usage — how much weight it will carry and whether the load is concentrated in the center or spread out along the length. The end conditions (6) affect the ability of the beam to rotate and flex and (7) the material the beam is made of (e.g. low density fiber board versus red oak) is a measure of the intrinsic strength of the material. All seven factors play their part in determining whether the shelf deflects under a weight (**Figure 226**).

To calculate the deflection of a wooden shelf, we need to examine these seven factors:

Length

The longer the shelf, the more it deflects under a weight. Length is important because in the deflection equation this value is cubed, therefore if you double the length of a beam (multiply by 2), the deflection increases eight times (2 x 2 x 2). For

to-wall carpet to reveal beautiful red oak, hard-wood floors. Is there any danger the lady will dent the floor? Should we ask her to leave her shoes in the entryway? I estimate her weight at 125 pounds and the size of the heel at about ½ inch x ½ inch.

> **Solution 1:** The area of force will be:
>
> Area = 0.5 x 0.5 = 0.25 sq. in.
>
> Therefore the weight is 125 lbs. per 0.25 sq. in.
>
> or
>
> 4 x 125 lbs.
>
> = 500 lbs. per sq. in. (psi).

The lady is applying 500 psi. to the floor. **Figure 225** shows that red oak has perpendicular compression strength of 1,250 psi. so the floor is probably safe. This would not have been true had the floor been made of eastern white pine (440 psi).

example, if a 48 inch shelf has sag of ¼ inch, other things being equal and with the same weight, a 96 inch shelf would deflect eight times as much or 8 x ¼ = 2 inches. In the equation, length is measured in inches.

Thickness

A thicker shelf can hold more weight. Like length, thickness is also cubed in the deflection formula. By doubling the thickness, for example using a 2 inch piece of pine instead of a 1 inch piece, the stiffness will increase by a factor of eight. Thickness is measured in inches.

Width

Width plays a role in shelf deflection but it is not as important as length or thickness. A wider shelf can hold more weight and all other things being equal, a shelf twice as wide will carry twice the load. The carrying capacity per square inch remains the same but, by doubling the width, you've doubled the square inches over which the load is distributed. Width is measured in inches.

Load

The main purpose of a shelf is to store or display something — whether it's knick-knacks or a set of the Encyclopedia Britannica. The weight of the former is negligible but books and magazines are quite heavy. A shelf, four foot long, filled with large 8 inch x 10 inch books, may have to carry 80 pounds or 20 pounds per foot of shelf length. In the deflection equations, we will use this weight (20 lbs./ft.), probably the largest weight that would normally be expected. Load is measured in pounds.

Load Placement

Weight on a shelf can be evenly distributed or centered. A shelf will deflect about two times as much if all the weight is placed mid-span rather than being distributed along the whole length. In general use, items are generally spread out along the length and not piled up in the center. In our equations we will assume the load is evenly distributed.

End conditions

If the shelf is attached securely at each end, it is stiffer and the deflection is less. A shelf fixed firmly at both ends is about five times stronger than a shelf merely resting on end brackets. Adjustable shelves, by their very nature, are not fixed therefore we will use a formula that calculates the stiffness of a shelf that just rests on the ends. Any end attachment that is added will make the shelf stronger.

Materials

The ability of wood to resist bending (deformation) is known as the 'modulus of elasticity'

Rule of Thumb
Shelf Strength

1. Length — Make a shelf one-half as long and it can carry eight times the weight.

2. Thickness — Make a shelf twice as thick and it can carry eight times the weight.

3. Width — A shelf twice as wide can carry twice the weight.

4. Load Placement — Distribute the weight evenly along the length of the shelf and the deflection will be one-half as much as when the load is centered.

5. End Conditions — The tighter the ends of the shelf are secured, the less it sags. A shelf firmly fixed at both ends will carry five times the weight of a shelf resting on brackets.

6. Materials — The higher the E-value of the material, the stiffer the shelf.

Figure 227 — E-Value Table, Various Materials

The E-Value can be used to calculate and compare deflection, the higher the E-Value, the stiffer the material. Note that wet plywood is 83–92% as strong as dry plywood.

Hardwoods	E-Value[1]		Plywoods	E-Value[1]	
Alder	1.38				
Ash	1.77		**Group 1 Plywood**	**Wet**	**Dry**
Beech	1.60		Beech, Amer.	1.50	1.80
Birch	1.80		Birch, Sweet		
Cherry	1.50		Douglas Fir 1[2]		
Chestnut	1.23		Maple, Sugar		
Elm	1.40		Pine		
Locust	2.00		Tanoak		
Maple	1.70				
Oaks	1.65		**Group 2 Plywood**	**Wet**	**Dry**
Polpar	1.58		Cedar, Pt. Orford	1.30	1.50
Walnut	1.68		Cypress		
Avg.	**1.61**		Douglas Fir 2[2]		
Softwoods			Fir, Balsam		
Balsam Fir	1.23		Fir, Calif. Red		
Cedar	1.19		Hemlock		
Douglas Fir	1.95		Lauan		
Hemlock	1.40		Maple, Black		
Pine	1.40		Pine, West. White		
Redwood (old)	1.34		Spruce		
Spruce	1.40		Poplar, Yellow		
Avg.	**1.42**				
Man Made Boards			**Group 3 Plywood**	**Wet**	**Dry**
High Density Fiberboard (HDF)	0.60		Alder, Red	1.10	1.20
Medium Density Fiberboard (MDF)	0.50		Birch, Paper		
Low Density Fiberboard (LDF)	0.20		Cedar, Alaska		
Tempered Hardboard	0.80		Hemlock, Eastern		
Particleboard	0.30		Pine, Ponderosa		
Oriented Strand Board (OSB)	0.40		Redwood		
Wheat Stalk	0.40		Spruce, White		
Avg.	**0.46**				
Marine Plywood			**Group 4 Plywood**	**Wet**	**Dry**
Keruing	2.35		Aspen	0.90	1.00
Fir	1.95		Cativo		
Khaya	1.48		Cedar, West. Red		
Meronti	1.63		Cottonwood		
Lauan	1.69		Pine, East. White		
Okoume	1.25		Pine, Sugar		
Avg.	**1.73**				
Metals					
Brass	9.00				
Aluminum	10.00				
Bronze	14.00				
Iron	28.00				
Steel	30.00				
Avg.	**18.20**				

(1) x 1,000,000 psi
(2) Douglas Fir 1 comes from the west coast, Douglas Fir 2 comes from NV, UT, CO, AZ & NM.

(MOE) which usually is written as 'E' and referred to as the 'E-Value'. (Note: modulus means measure).

Figure 227 shows a list of the E-Values of various materials. Specifically the modulus of elasticity is defined as stress divided by strain i.e., the amount of deflection divided by the applied weight. The E-Value is often abbreviated e.g. MOE 1,800,000 psi is written as E1.8. The higher the E-Value of the material, the more resistant it is to stress. White and red oak average about 1,650,000 psi or E1.65 while particle board is E0.30. This means the innate stiffness of oak is about 5.5 times that of particle board.

$$1.65 \div 0.30 = 5.5$$

Most natural woods are fairly similar in stiffness as measured by the Modulus of Elasticity — hardwoods average E1.6 while softwoods average E1.42. More and more we are using man-made materials for shelving i.e., plywood, fiberboard, hardboard, particle board and other materials. These materials differ widely in their stiffness and are more likely to break under load than natural woods.

Determining Deflection
Math

$$Y = (0.013 \times Wt. \times L^3) \div (E \times I)$$

Where Y = maximum deflection at mid-span measured in inches

0.013 = A special constant for a shelf that is non-fixed and with an evenly distributed load.

Wt = weight measured in pounds

L = length measured in inches

E = Modulus of Elasticity, psi

I = moment of inertia

Moment of Inertia

The moment of inertia (I) of a shelf depends on the cross section of the end. Because the ends of most shelves are rectangular, the I-Value is the horizontal width times the vertical thickness cubed and divided by 12. Width and thickness are measured in inches.

$$I = [(width \times (thickness^3)] \div 12$$

Note that thickness is cubed in the equation. Huge gains in the I-Value are achieved when we increase the thickness (vertical) number. This is why a 2 inch x 6 inch floor joist is so much stiffer on edge than when laid flat.

$$I = [(width \times (thickness^3)] \div 12$$
$$I = [2.0 \times (6.0^3)] \div 12$$
$$I = (2.0 \times 216) \div 12 = 36 \text{ (on edge)}$$
$$I = [6.0 \times (2.0^3)] \div 12$$
$$I = (6.0 \times 8.0) \div 12 = 4 \text{ (flat)}$$

The beam on edge is 9 times as stiff as the same beam laid flat.

$$36 \div 4 = 9$$

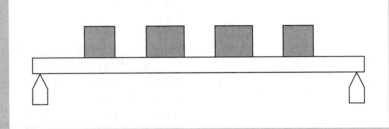

Figure 228 — A Free-Standing Shelf

The Free Standing shelf is supported at both ends, but not fixed, with an evenly distributed load. The equation for determining deflection is:
$$Y = (0.013 \times Wt. \times L^3) \div (E \times I)$$

Problem 2: What is the deflection at mid-span of a shelf that is ¾ inch thick x 6 inches wide x 48 inches long? The shelf will be filled with paperback books that weigh about 55 pounds and will be made of MDF which has an E-Value of 0.5×10^6 (see **Figure 227**).

Solution 2: First we have to find the end cross-sectional value:

$$I = [(width \times (thickness^3)] \div 12$$
$$I = (6 \times 0.75^3) \div 12 = 0.21$$

We'll use the equation for shelf deflection where the load is evenly distributed and the ends of the shelf are not fixed, merely resting on supports.

$$Y = (0.013 \times Wt. \times L^3) \div (E \times I)$$
$$Y = (0.013 \times 55 \times 48^3) \div (0.5 \times 10^6 \times 0.21)$$
$$Y = 0.079 \div 0.11$$
$$Y = 0.72 \text{ inches}$$

The deflection equation shows that the shelf will deflect about ¾ inch. If this little shelf is going

Rule of Thumb

In shelf calculations, figure about **25 pounds of load** per foot of shelving. This is the weight of vinyl record albums and large books printed on glossy paper, such as the Encyclopedia Britannica, the largest weight that you will commonly encounter.

(a) 1x8 shelf

(b) add solid edge

(c) add edge under

(d) add full edge

(e) front and back

(f) miter edge

(g) 1/8" steel screwed to front

(h) 1/8" steel front and back

(i) 3/16" steel screwed to front

(j) 3/16" steel front and back

(k) 1/4" steel screwed to front

(l) 1/4" steel front and back

Figure 229 — Making Shelves Stronger

If the stand-alone shelf (a) deflects excessively it can be strengthened with edge treatments. By adding a solid piece to the front horizontally (b), a small amount of strength is added. A thin piece under the front edge is better (c). More stiffness is gained with the front piece vertically (d), and still more by adding a second edge strip or ledger at the back (e). By turning the shelf under to hide the edge, some strength is gained (f). By adding thin strips of steel — ⅛ inch (g), ³⁄₁₆ inch (i) or ¼ inch (k) — rigidity is added. By doubling up the steel strips as in (h), (j) and (l) the shelves become very stiff.

to hold 55 pounds it needs help. It is in no danger of breaking from compression. The 55 pounds is spread over 288 sq. in. and exerts less that a pound per square inch of pressure.

$$6 \times 48 = 288\text{-in.}^2$$

$$55 \text{ lbs. } / 288 = 0.19 \text{ psi}$$

Cherry can withstand 850 psi before failing from compression force (**Figure 225**).

Comparative Shelf Strength

Once you've decided on the size of your shelf — width, length and thickness — then you pick the material — hardwood, softwood, plywood etc. Each material has a different E-Value and thus a different inherent stiffness or resistance to deflection. **Figure 227** lists some of the common shelf materials with E-Values, and the higher this number, the stiffer the shelf. This chart shows that only a few of the man-made fiber materials are as stiff as the natural hard- and soft-woods. Marine plywood and the Group 1 plywoods are the exception. See **Figure 227** for a breakdown of all materials.

Problem 3: We plan to make shelf ¾ inch thick x 8 inch wide x 60 inch long out of Douglas fir. It will be free-standing and it must hold a weight of 100 pounds, evenly distributed. What will be the deflection?

Solution 3: From **Figure 227** we find the E-value of Douglas fir is E1.95 psi. Because E-Value and deflection are directly proportional we can compare the Doug fir shelf to the generic hardwood shelf in **Figure 230**:

$1.60 \div 1.95 = 0.82$

$Y = 0.63 \times 0.82 = 0.52$ or ½ inch deflection at mid-span.

Making Shelves Stronger

Often the shelf size, the span and the material we choose leads to a shelf that will not hold the weight without excessive deflection.

Problem 4: We want to install a ¾ inch walnut shelf beside the fireplace in the den. We figure it will have to hold books, electronic equipment, speakers and collectables. The weight probably will be about 100 pounds distributed along the length. It will be 8 inches wide by 5 feet long. Will this shelf hold the weight without deflecting too much?

Solution 4: First we need to find the Moment of Inertia which depends on the cross section of the shelf.

$I = \text{Width} \times \text{Thickness}^3 \div 12$

$I = 8\text{-in.} \times .75\text{-in.}^3 \div 12$

$I = 8 \times 0.42 \div 12 = 0.28$

Next we use the deflection (Y) formula to find the amount of sag with 100 pounds of weight.

Figure 230 — Shelf Deflection, Comparison of Different Loads

Data are for a ¾ inch T x 8 inch W x 60 inch L shelf carrying weights of 100, 50 and 25 pounds evenly distributed.

w3/4T x 8W x 60L Shelf Type		100 lbs. Deflection (Inches)	75 lbs. Deflection (Inches)	50 lbs. Deflection (Inches)	25 lbs. Deflection (Inches)
a		5.0	3.8	2.5	1.3
b	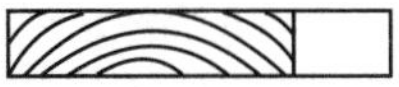	2.1	1.5	1.0	0.51
c		2.9	2.2	1.4	0.72
d		0.73	0.54	0.36	0.18
e		0.38	0.29	0.19	0.10
f		3.9	2.9	1.9	1.0
g		1.5	1.1	0.74	0.37
h		0.88	0.66	0.44	0.22
i		1.1	0.83	0.55	0.28
j		0.62	0.46	0.31	0.15
k		0.88	0.66	0.44	0.22
l		0.46	0.35	0.23	0.12

Y=0.013 x Wt. x 216,000 / (E1 x I1) + (E2 x I2)
I=W x T3 / 12

Figure 231 — Shelf Stiffeners

The added strength is about the same whether the 'helper' is put against the front edge of the shelf centered (a), flush with the bottom surface (b) or flush with the top surface (c). By moving the neutral axis off center, the math is a little more complicated but the effect is about the same.

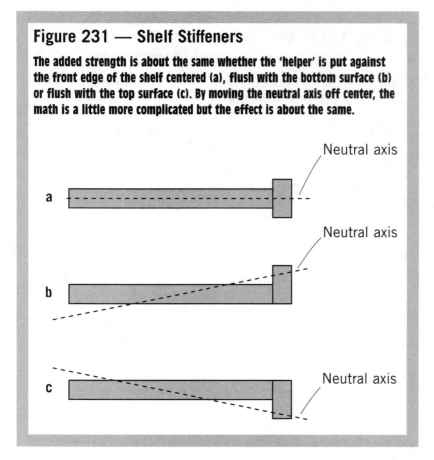

Neutral axis

a

Neutral axis

b

Neutral axis

c

The E-Value for walnut (**Figure 227**) is E1.68.

$$Y = (0.013 \times \text{Wt.} \times L^3) \div (E \times I)$$

$$Y = (0.013 \times 100\text{-lbs.} \times 60\text{-in.}^3) \div (.68 \times 10^6 \times 0.28)$$

$$Y = 0.28 \times 10^6 \div 0.47 \times 10^6 =$$
$$0.28 \div 0.47 = 0.60 \text{ or } \tfrac{5}{8}$$
inches.

We like the clean look of a long piece of wood extending across a space with no visible support but the ⅝ inch sag is too much. How do we build a nice-looking shelf and still make it strong enough to resist deflection? Over the years woodworkers have devised various means (**Figure 229**):

1. Ledger Boards

A board is cleated to the wall and the shelf rests on this board. This effectively creates a shelf with no span. The problem is that the 'fix' is obvious and the clean look of a shelf extending across the wall is lost. There's no mystery and it's pretty obvious what's holding it up. When a shelf is fastened to the wall in a toe-nail manner, the effect is the same — very strong with no span and no deflection but it's no longer adjustable.

2. Front Edge Treatment with Wood

By adding a wooden stretcher to the shelf, you can make the shelf stronger and cover up an unsightly edge at the same time, see **Figure 231**. When a shelf deflects it rotates around the neutral axis. In (a) this axis corresponds to the center-line of both the shelf and the front piece and figuring the deflection is pretty straight forward. In conditions (b) and (c) the center lines of the shelf do not coincide with the neutral axis and the math is a little more complicated. For our purposes we will treat all three conditions the same. The difference is strength is minimal.

3. Front Edge Treatments with Metal

At your local home supply hardware store you can purchase ¾ inch wide strips of steel in ⅛ inch, ³⁄₁₆ inch and ¼ inch thickness. These thin, seemingly weak pieces of metal can be used to stiffen a shelf. While they are small, their strength is deceptive. The basic way we determine stiffness in a material is by comparing E-values. **Figure 227** shows that most woods have E-values about 1.5 while steel has an E-value of 30. This means that steel is about 20 times stronger that most woods. The steel strip by itself would buckle and twist and the stiffness would be lost, however, by attaching the metal tightly to the edge of the wooden shelf, the metal strip will be held vertical and because of the high E-value will add strength to a shelf.

Drill holes about every 3 inches and attach the metal with epoxy and ¾ inch flat-head wood screws. The metal can be covered with a thin strip of wood molding as in **Figure 232**.

Math for Combination Shelf

A shelf composed of two different beams — the original shelf plus the stretcher — acts as one beam but the calculations are done as if each acts independently and the values are then added together. A beam rotates around the neutral axis and the calculation is more complicated but for our purposes, the I-Value will be a combination of them both, see **Figure 231**.

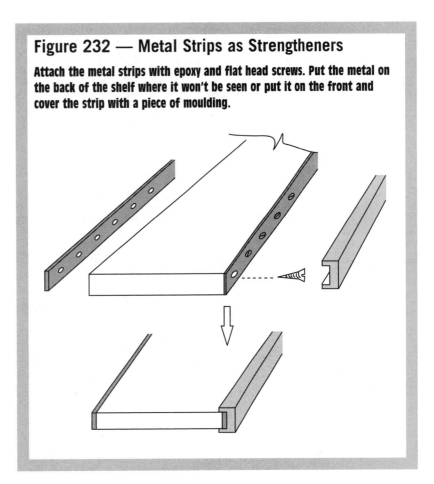

Figure 232 — Metal Strips as Strengtheners

Attach the metal strips with epoxy and flat head screws. Put the metal on the back of the shelf where it won't be seen or put it on the front and cover the strip with a piece of moulding.

Problem 5: We have determined that a ¾ inch x 8 inch x 60 inch walnut-veneered, MDF shelf deflects 0.5-inch with a load of 25 pounds (see **Figure 230**). This is too much sag. We could live with ¼ inch. Will a ⅛ inch steel strip do the job?

Solution 5: The end cross section of the wood is ¾ inch x 8 inch. The end cross section of the steel strip is ¾ inch x ⅛ inch.

$$I = \text{Width x Thickness}^3 \div 12$$

$$I \text{ (wood)} = 8 \times 0.75^3 \div 12 = 8 \times 0.42 \div 12 = 0.28$$

$$I \text{ (steel)} = 0.125 \times 0.75^3 \div 12 = 0.125 \times 0.42 \div 12 = 0.0044$$

The E-Value for MDF is 0.5; the E-value for steel is 30.

EI (total) = EI (wood) + EI (steel)

EI (total) = $(0.5 \times 10^6 \times 0.28)$ + $(30 \times 10^6 \times 0.0044)$

EI (total) = (0.14×10^6) + $(0.13 \times 10^6) = 0.27 \times 10^6$

The deflection equation is:

Y = $0.013 \times$ Wt. $\times L^3 \div$ EI (total)

Y = 0.013×25-lbs. $\times 60^3 \div 0.27 \times 10^6$

Y = $70,200 \div 270,000 = 0.26$ or ¼

From these figures, we see the shelf can hold 25 pounds with about ¼ inch deflection.

Problem 6: We want to make a shelf out of a veneered piece of HDF. The shelf will be ¾ inch thick x 7¼ inch wide x 60 inch long with a ¾ inch x 1½ inch hardwood stretcher attached to the front (See **Figure 229d**). The weight will be 100 pounds, evenly distributed. What will be the deflection?

Solution 6:

I = Width x Thickness$^3 \div 12$

I (HDF) = $7.25 \times 0.75^3 \div 12$ = $7.25 \times 0.42 \div 12 = 0.25$

I (wood) = $0.75 \times 1.53 \div 12$ = $0.75 \times 3.38 \div 12 = 0.21$

The E-Value for HDF is 0.6; the E-value for average hardwood is 1.6.

EI (total) = EI (HDF) + EI (wood)

EI (total) = $(0.6 \times 10^6 \times 0.25)$ + $(1.6 \times 10^6 \times 0.21)$

EI (total) = (0.15×10^6) + $(0.34 \times 106) = 0.49 \times 10^6$

The deflection equation is:

Y = $0.013 \times$ Wt. $\times L^3 \div$ EI (total)

Y = $(0.013 \times 100 \times 60^3)$ $\div (0.49 \times 10^6)$

Y = $280,800 \div 490,000$ = 0.57 or ⁹⁄₁₆

If this deflection (0.57-inch) is excessive, then a stronger wood can be used in place of MDF (E0.50) e.g. a piece of veneered, grade #1 plywood (E1.80). Because the deflection is directly proportional to the E-Values of the material:

1.8 (plywood) ÷ 0.5 (MDF) = 3.6

0.57 ÷ 3.6 = 0.16

By using a piece of #1 plywood, the deflection has been reduced from 0.57 inch to 0.16 inch.

Conclusion

Even a shelf made of a hardwood like oak deflects under heavy weight and often needs help. By using an edge facing you can eliminate sag or at least minimize it to an acceptable degree. The new man-made materials give shelves that are light, stable, flat and come in a variety of thicknesses. They can be covered with beautiful veneers. The one drawback is a lack of deflective strength. These fiberboard and particleboard

Figure 233 — Shelf Deflection with Edging

By using the edging shown in column 1, deflection is minimized e.g., with MDF (E0.50) plus hardwood edging (d), a 2 inch deflection is reduced to 0.6 inch. Because the deflection is linear, a 50 pound weight would deflect 1 inch as a stand-alone and with edging (d) would deflect 0.3 inch. The top row of figures show how a 3/4 inch H x 8 inch W x 60 inch L shelf with 100 pounds of load deflects with no help (No Edging) and with 11 different edgings.

Shelf = 3/4 T x 8 W x 60 L, Weight = 100 pounds.

E-Value	E1.60	E1.42	E0.20	E0.50	E0.60	E1.80	E1.50	E1.20	E1.00
Shelf	Hard	Soft	LDF +	MDF +	HDF +	PLY#1 +	PLY#2 +	PLY#3 +	PLY#4 +
Type	Wood	Wood	HdWd	HdWd	HdWd	HdWd	HdWd	HdWd	HdWd
	Deflection in Inches								

No Edging

		E1.60	E1.42	E0.20	E0.50	E0.60	E1.80	E1.50	E1.20	E1.00
a		0.60	0.70	5.00	2.00	1.70	0.60	0.70	0.80	1.00

Edging Type

		E1.60	E1.42	E0.20	E0.50	E0.60	E1.80	E1.50	E1.20	E1.00
b	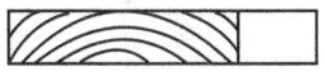	0.60	0.70	2.10	1.40	1.30	0.60	0.70	0.80	0.90
c	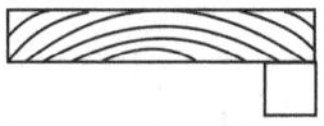	0.60	0.60	2.90	1.50	1.30	0.50	0.60	0.70	0.90
d	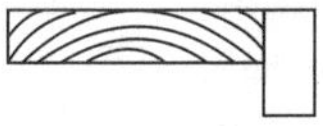	0.40	0.40	0.70	0.60	0.60	0.40	0.40	0.40	0.50
e		0.26	0.26	0.45	0.38	0.38	0.26	0.26	0.26	0.32
f	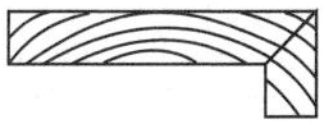	0.50	0.50	3.90	1.60	1.30	0.40	0.50	0.60	0.80
g		0.50	0.50	1.50	1.00	0.90	0.40	0.50	0.60	0.70
h		0.28	0.28	0.83	0.55	0.50	0.22	0.28	0.33	0.39
i		0.40	0.50	1.10	0.80	0.80	0.40	0.50	0.50	0.60
j		0.24	0.30	0.66	0.48	0.48	0.24	0.30	0.30	0.36
k		0.40	0.40	0.90	0.70	0.60	0.40	0.40	0.50	0.50
l		0.24	0.24	0.55	0.43	0.37	0.24	0.24	0.31	0.31

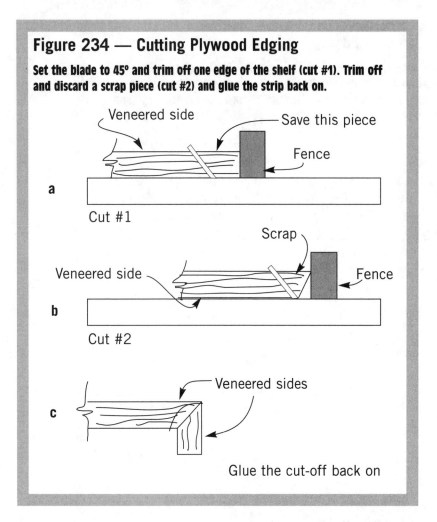

Figure 234 — Cutting Plywood Edging

Set the blade to 45° and trim off one edge of the shelf (cut #1). Trim off and discard a scrap piece (cut #2) and glue the strip back on.

Veneered side — Save this piece

Fence

a

Cut #1

Scrap

Veneered side

Fence

b

Cut #2

Veneered sides

c

Glue the cut-off back on

edge. This edging increases the stiffness of the weakest board (LDF) by a factor of seven.

By adding a thin strip of steel ($\frac{1}{8}$ inch, $\frac{3}{16}$ inch or $\frac{1}{4}$ inch) to a material with a low E-Value e.g. LDF (E0.20) and MDF (E0.50), a shelf of acceptable strength is made. The $\frac{1}{8}$ inch steel strip increases the stiffness of the LDF board by three times and the MDF by two. By using a thicker steel strip, such as $\frac{3}{16}$ inch, LDF is stiffened over fourfold. Using a $\frac{1}{4}$ inch steel strip increases the stiffness by a factor of five.

When the steel strips are added to a piece of LDF, the result is dramatic. **Figure 230** shows that a shelf ($\frac{3}{4}$ inch x 8 inches x 60 inches long) made of LDF will sag 5.0 inches under a weight of 100 pounds. In fact because the fiber boards break rather than deflect, the shelf would be broken. **Figure 230** shows that by adding a strip of $\frac{1}{8}$ inch steel the deflection changes from 5.0 inches to 1.5 inches, a gain in strength of 333%. A $\frac{3}{16}$ inch piece of steel added to the shelf drops the deflection to 1.1-in. — 4.5 times stronger. By adding a piece of $\frac{1}{4}$ inch steel, the deflection drops to 0.9-in.

Problem 7: A shelf ($\frac{3}{4}$ inch T x 8 inches W x 60 inches L) made of MDF (E0.50) deflects 0.75-inch under a load of 100 pounds. What edging can be used to

materials are not stiff, perhaps as much as one-third to one-quarter as stiff as a hardwood and they deflect alarmingly under normal weights. The stiffeners shown in **Figure 229** help all shelf materials but, percentage-wise, they help the weaker materials more.

In all instances the strongest addition is a solid piece of wood fastened vertically to the shelf (**Figure 229d**). This treatment makes the shelf appear thicker and can also cover an unsightly reduce the deflection to less than ¼ inch?

Solution 7: We need a strengthening value of at least 3.0:

0.75 ÷ 0.25 = 3.0

Shelf treatment #3 gives 3.33 extra stiffness:

0.75 ÷ 3.33 = 0.23 or ¼

Shelf treatment #7 gives 2.86 extra stiffness:

0.75 ÷ 2.86 = 0.23 or ¼

Figure 234 shows how to cut a piece of veneered plywood to make an edging piece.

Figure 235 shows nine examples of edging treatments for plywood.

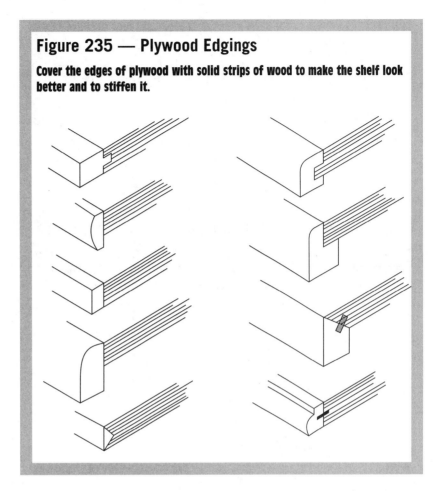

Figure 235 — Plywood Edgings

Cover the edges of plywood with solid strips of wood to make the shelf look better and to stiffen it.

References

Compression strength of wood comes from Hoadley's *Understanding Wood*, Taunton Press, 1980 and the USDA Forest Products Laboratory *Wood Handbook*, 2002.

CHAPTER 21

Coves on the Table Saw

Whether complex or simple, mouldings enhance the appearance of cabinetry, furniture, and interiors because of their ability to reflect light and create shadows. The ogees, fillets, and cyma rectas invite the eye to travel and explore along the surface and generate visual interest; the ovolos and bull noses lend aesthetic enhancement.

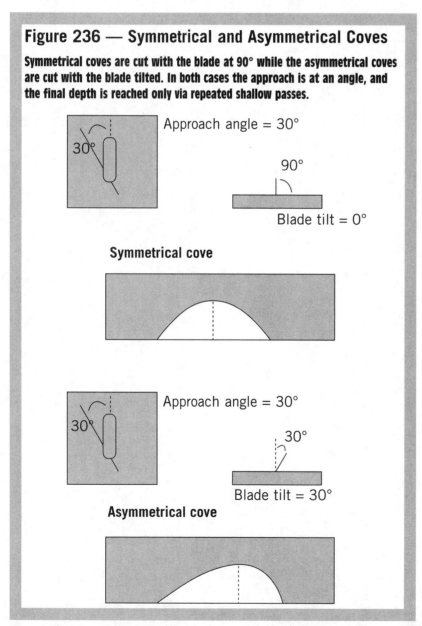

Figure 236 — Symmetrical and Asymmetrical Coves

Symmetrical coves are cut with the blade at 90° while the asymmetrical coves are cut with the blade tilted. In both cases the approach is at an angle, and the final depth is reached only via repeated shallow passes.

Approach angle = 30°
30°
90°
Blade tilt = 0°

Symmetrical cove

Approach angle = 30°
30°
30°
Blade tilt = 30°

Asymmetrical cove

Simply put, a moulding is a combination of profiles — convex curves (beads) and concave curves (coves) with a chamfer and a flat thrown in here and there. In industry, the easiest and fastest way to make moulding is with a shaper with mechanical feeds and strong hold-downs. For the woodworker these machines are quite expensive — and in the shop, a shaper with a 3 inch moulding head spinning at 6,000 rpm is one scary machine.

Even if you do have a shaper or router table, you should know just how easy it is to make coves on the table saw. And once you have a cove – the most common element in a crown moulding – you have the basic building block to be enhanced with straight cuts, rabbets, and hand-planed transitions. You can make not only crown mouldings, but also drawer pulls, fluted pilasters, and ogee bracket feet, as you'll see here.

Perhaps you cringe at the thought of passing a board sideways past a table saw blade. The usual result of pushing wood through a blade at an angle is burning, jamming, and kickback. Right! But let's call this a controlled angle cut, and one that's made with a number of shallow passes, not with a big all-at-once bite.

By setting up an auxiliary fence at an angle to the blade, using proper hold-downs and push sticks, and with the blade only ¹⁄₁₆ inch above the surface of the table, a cove can be cut safely — and predictably. The tilt and height of the blade and the workpiece angle of approach determine exactly the depth, width, and shape of the cove. It takes repeated passes, but the size of the coves! With a 10 inch blade it's possible to cut a cove 3 inches deep and 9 inches wide. How many shapers can do that?

Different Coves

Using a table saw we are able to make two types of coves — symmetrical and asymmetrical depending on whether the blade is tilted or upright, **Figure 236.**

Symmetrical Coves

Symmetrical coves have the same shape on either side of a vertical centerline. This type is cut by changing the angle of approach to the blade while leaving the blade perpendicular to the table.

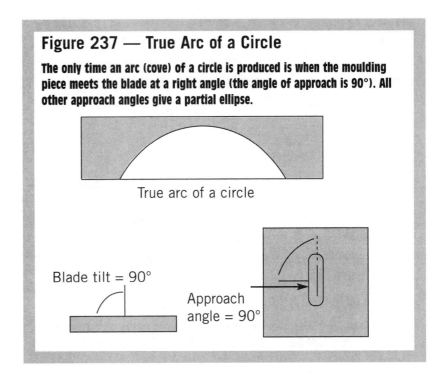

Figure 237 — True Arc of a Circle

The only time an arc (cove) of a circle is produced is when the moulding piece meets the blade at a right angle (the angle of approach is 90°). All other approach angles give a partial ellipse.

True arc of a circle

Blade tilt = 90°

Approach angle = 90°

The stock is pushed along a skewed fence and passes over the blade, removing an elliptical arc (**Figure 236**).

Asymmetrical Coves

In an asymmetrical cove the curve on one side, for example the left side is different than the curve on the right side. These coves are cut in much the same manner as the symmetrical coves except that the blade is tilted.

Semi-Circular Coves — Special Case

All coves cut on the table saw with the blade at 90° (0° tilt) are sections of an ellipse except one (**Figure 237**). When the wood approaches the blade at a right angle, the cove generated is a true arc of a circle.

Rule of Thumb

Mouldings not only cover gaps and unite furniture elements, they also enhance the appearance of the room by modulating light and shadow, and invite the eye to visit.

Figure 238 — Family of Symmetrical Coves

Choose the cove from this chart and set the fence at the angle shown. The depth of the cove will be the same as the blade height.

No blade tilt

0° 10°   30°   60° 90°

Approach angle

Figure 239 — Symmetrical Coves

Four different coves are shown with approach angles at 10°, 15°, 25° and 30°. In all cases the blade is at 90° to the table.

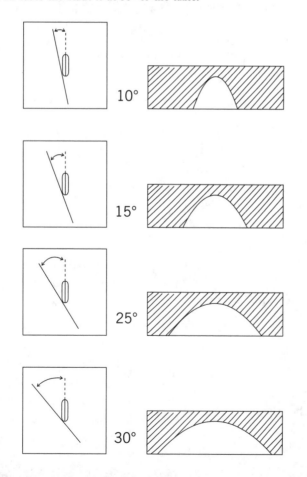

10°

15°

25°

30°

Math

In all the math that follows, we will assume a very thin blade. The effect of using a blade with non-zero thickness 'W' will be to widen the cove produced by a maximum of 'W'. The narrower the cove, the more the thickness of the blade comes into play. To find the cove width, use this formula:

Cove Width$=2 \sqrt{[D (10 - D)]}$

Where D = cove depth "10" assumes you are using a 10 inch blade.

Problem 1: We are using a 10 inch blade. The blade is at 90° and the approach is 90°. If the cove depth (D) is ⅜ inch what is the width of the cove?

Solution 1:

Cove Width$=2 \sqrt{[D (10 - D)]}$

Where D = 0.375

CW = $2 \sqrt{[0.375 (10 - 0.375)]}$

CW = $2 \sqrt{[0.375 (9.625)]}$

CW = $2 \sqrt{3.61}$

CW = 2 x 1.9 = 3.80
= $3\frac{13}{16}$ inch.

This tells us that if we want a semi-circular cove ⅜ inch deep, the cove will be $3\frac{13}{16}$ inch wide.

Symmetrical Coves – Elliptical Shape

Determine the shape of the cove you want by using the Chart of Coves in **Figure 238**.

Dimensions — The defining

measurements of the cove are its depth and its width. The measurements are not critical in many situations, but become so when you want to match an existing moulding where even a small variation would be apparent.

Find Blade Approach when Height and Width Are Given

Find the Cove Depth and Cove Width (columns 1 & 2) on the chart in **Figure 241** and read the Approach Angle in column 4. The Depth Factor in column 5 can be used to find the approach angle for any width cove with the depth in column 1. For example, if the cove isn't listed in the table in **Figure 241** but you know its width and depth, you can use the depth factor to find the approach angle as follows:

Problem 2: What is the approach angle for a cove ⅝ inch deep and 2¼ inch wide? Note this width is not listed in **Figure 241**. The depth factor for ⅝ inch coves is 4.84.

Solution 2:

Arcsine Angle = Cove Width ÷ Depth Factor

Arcsine Angle = CW ÷ DF

Where CW = 2.25 and DF = 4.84

Arcsin Angle = 2.25 ÷ 4.84 = 0.4649

ASin 0.4649 = 27.7° ≈ 28°

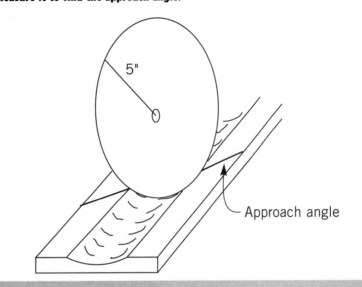

Figure 240 — Finding the Approach Angle

Wiggle a 10 inch disk in the cove until it fits snugly. Mark this position and measure it to find the approach angle.

5"

Approach angle

Therefore, we should set our auxiliary fence at 28° and cut the cove ⅝ inch deep by 2¼ inch wide in small bites.

Calculate the Approach Angle

If the cove you want isn't in the chart (**Figure 241**), you can draw your own cove and calculate the approach angle to cut the desired profile. The formula is:

Approach angle = Arcsine {W ÷ 2 √ [D (10 - D)]}

Where W = cove width, D = cove depth

Problem 3: Find the approach angle when cove depth = ⁷⁄₁₆ inch and cove width = 2¹⁄₃₂ inch.

Solution 3:

Angle=ASinW÷2√[D(10-D)]

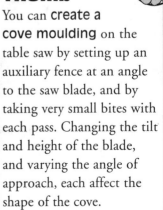

Rule of Thumb

You can **create a cove moulding** on the table saw by setting up an auxiliary fence at an angle to the saw blade, and by taking very small bites with each pass. Changing the tilt and height of the blade, and varying the angle of approach, each affect the shape of the cove.

Figure 241—Approach Angle for Symmetrical Coves

Find the Cove Depth and Cove Width on the chart and read the Approach Angle in column four. If you want the approach angle for a depth where the width is not on the chart, use the Depth Factor in Column 5. Because these numbers are linear you can also find angles using math ratios, for example, ¾ inch deep x ¾ inch wide will be ½ of 1 ½ inch wide. 16.5° ÷ 2 = 8.25°.

Cove Depth	Cove Width	Asin (1)	Approach Angle Deg. (2)	Depth Factor (3)
0.25	1	0.3205	18.7	3.12
(1/4")	1.5	0.4808	28.7	
	2	0.6411	39.9	
	2.5	0.8013	53.3	
0.375	1	0.2632	15.3	3.8
(3/8")	1.5	0.3947	23.2	
	2	0.5263	31.8	
	2.5	0.6579	41.1	
0.5	1.5	0.3441	20.1	4.36
(1/2")	1.75	0.4014	23.7	
	2	0.4587	27.3	
	2.5	0.5734	35.0	
0.625	1.5	0.3099	18.1	4.84
(5/8")	2	0.4132	24.4	
	2.5	0.5165	31.1	
	3	0.6198	38.3	
0.75	1.5	0.2846	16.5	5.27
(3/4")	2	0.3795	22.3	
	2.5	0.4744	28.3	
	3	0.5693	34.7	
0.875	1.5	0.2655	15.4	5.65
(7/8")	2	0.3540	20.7	
	2.5	0.4425	26.3	
	3	0.5310	32.1	
1	2	0.3333	19.5	6
	2.5	0.4167	24.6	
	3	0.5	30.0	
	3.5	0.5833	35.7	

(1) Asin = Cove Width / Depth Factor
(2) Approach angle = Asin x Cove Width / Depth Factor
(3) Depth Factor = 2 √ [D (10-D)]
*Cove Width / Depth Factor = ASin
Example 1.5 / 5.27 = 0.2846
and ASin 0.2846 = 16.5367

Figure 242 — Using a Calculator for Approach Angles

Make sure your calculator has a button for Asin.

	10
-	0.44
=	9.5600
x	0.44
=	4.2064
√x	2.0510
x	2
=	4.1019
	2.03
÷	4.09
=	0.4949
ASIN	29.66

Where D = 0.4375 and W = 2.0313. In the formula we'll round off the numbers and use D = 0.44 and W = 2.03.

= ASin 2.03 ÷ 2 √ [0.44 (10 - 0.44)]

= ASin 2.03 ÷ 2 √ [0.44 (9.56)]

= ASin 2.03 ÷ 2 √ 4.21

= ASin 2.03 ÷ 2 (2.05)

= ASin 2.03 ÷ 4.10

ASin 0.4951 = 29.7° ≈ 30°

To use a calculator to solve this problem, see **Figure 242**.

Problem 4: Find the approach angle when cove depth = 1 inch and cove width = 3 inches.

Solution 4:

= ASin W ÷ 2 √ [D (10 - D)]

Where D = 1 and W = 3

= ASin 3 ÷ 2 √ [1 (10 - 1)]

= ASin 3 ÷ 2 √ [1 (9)]

= ASin 3 ÷ 2 √ 9

= ASin 3 ÷ 2 x 3

= ASin 3 ÷ 6

ASin 0.5 = 30°

Asymmetrical Coves

The word asymmetrical means not symmetrical, that is, not having symmetry. When we talk about cove symmetry, we mean having equal parts on both sides of a vertical dividing line. When we made coves earlier in the chapter, we pushed the board at an angle through the saw with the blade at 0° tilt and a partial ellipse was cut having equal shape left and right. If the saw blade is tilted from perpendicular, the resulting cove is not equal on both sides of the vertical dividing line, thus it is asymmetrical.

Using the Cove Sets

The easiest way to set up the saw with the proper blade tilt and approach angle is to pick a curve off one of the cove sets in **Figure 243**. These give all necessary data to set up the saw.

Drawing Your Own Curve

We can draw the cove once we know the angle of approach and the tilt angle of the blade, but the math is complicated. Because the cove is not symmetrical, we plot both sides of the curve by determining numerous values of 'x' and 'y.' See **Figure 244**.

The Math

X = SinA x SinB + CosA x SinC

Y = CosA x CosC

A = Points on curve (they change from -90° through 0° to +90°).

B = Approach Angle

C = Blade Tilt Angle

R = Blade Radius (5 for a 10 inch blade).

Problem 5: Find the x,y coordinate for an asymmetric cove when the blade tilt is 45°,

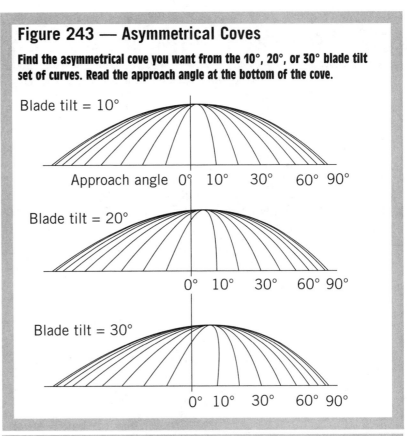

Figure 243 — Asymmetrical Coves

Find the asymmetrical cove you want from the 10°, 20°, or 30° blade tilt set of curves. Read the approach angle at the bottom of the cove.

Blade tilt = 10°

Approach angle 0° 10° 30° 60° 90°

Blade tilt = 20°

0° 10° 30° 60° 90°

Blade tilt = 30°

0° 10° 30° 60° 90°

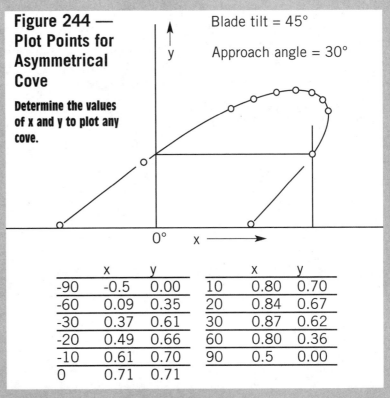

Figure 244 — Plot Points for Asymmetrical Cove

Blade tilt = 45°

Approach angle = 30°

Determine the values of x and y to plot any cove.

0°   x

	x	y		x	y
-90	-0.5	0.00	10	0.80	0.70
-60	0.09	0.35	20	0.84	0.67
-30	0.37	0.61	30	0.87	0.62
-20	0.49	0.66	60	0.80	0.36
-10	0.61	0.70	90	0.5	0.00
0	0.71	0.71			

Figure 245 — Sighting in a Cove

Draw the cove outline on the end of a board and sight across the blade until you find the right approach angle. Mark this spot and test cut a scrap.

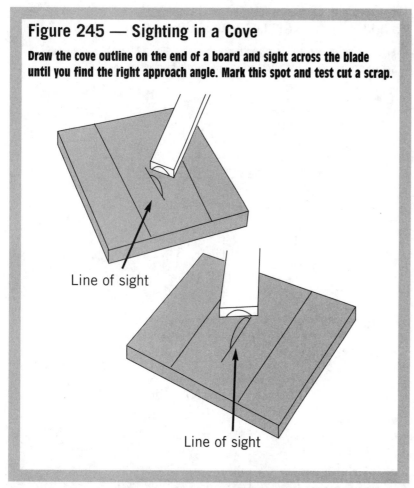

Line of sight

Line of sight

Figure 246 — Setting the Approach Angle

A miter gauge helps set the approach angle. Hold the miter gauge against the front edge (a) or put it in the miter slot (b).

Gauge set at 56°

Gauge set at 20°

a

Moulding blank against gauge sets 20° approach angle

b

Set fence against blade and clamp to table

---

the approach angle is 30° and the point on the curve is 60°.

Solution 5:

X=SinA x SinB+CosA x SinC

Where A = 60°, B = 30° and C = 45°.

X = Sin 60 x Sin 30 + Cos 60 x Sin 45

X = 0.87 x 0.50 + 0.50 x 0.71

X = 0.44 + 0.36 = 0.80

Y = CosA x CosC

Where A = 60° and C = 45°

Y = Cos 60 x Cos 45

Y = 0.5 x 0.71 = 0.36

On the graph we would locate the point x = 0.80 and y = 0.36. All of the other points are shown in the x,y box in **Figure 244**. This formula can be entered in a computer spreadsheet such as Excel and the points plotted from the resulting table, or the points can be entered directly onto the screen.

Setting the Approach Angle

The table saw miter gauge can be used to set the correct appproach angle. **Figure 246** shows a miter gauge set at 20° then snugged against the front of the saw table. A moulding blank is placed against the gauge and then clamped in place. The miter gauge can also be put into the miter slot and used to mark the correct approach angle.

Sighting In a Cove

1. Draw the cove on the end of a

piece of scrap about 2 feet long that is the exact width and thickness of the finished moulding piece.

2. **With the saw** turned off, lay the sample piece on the table with the moulded face down. Stand in front of the saw and put the stock behind the blade, as in **Figure 245**.

3. **Raise** the blade as high as the deepest section of the cove.

4. **Sight** along the top of the table, looking over the blade at the sample. Vary the angle of the sample relative to the blade until the blade obstructs your view of the entire cove. The top of the blade and the cove should match perfectly.

5. **Draw** pencil lines along each side of the sample onto the table. Remove the sample and extend the two lines to the front of the saw. Clamp fences along each line, making a chute for the stock to slide in.

Template Method

1. **The Cove Width** — Raise the saw blade to the final depth of the cove (½ inch for example) and place strips of masking tape where the teeth of the blade exit the table, see **Figure 247**. Note that the height of the blade is the depth of the cove.

2. **The Template** — To find the correct angle of approach, cut a template from a piece of poster board. The outside width of this template should be the same width as the moulding blank you

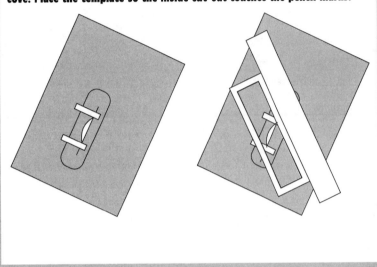

Figure 247 — Template for Angle of Approach

Raise the blade to the cove height and put pieces of tape on the throat plate. Make pencil marks on the tape to mark the blade tooth exit and entry points. Use poster board to make the template — the outside width will be the width of the board and the inner rectangle will be the width of the cove. Place the template so the inside cut-out touches the pencil marks.

plan to use. The inside cutout is equal in width to the width of the cove. The length doesn't matter so long as the template does not hang up on the saw blade. Angle the template on the table saw so its inside edges (the width of the cove) touch the marks. Tape the template in place, see **Figure 247**.

3. **The Fence** — Use two straight pieces of 1 x 4 clamped at both ends. This will position the fences on both sides of the blade and at the correct angle to make the cove.

To check the setting, draw the cove full size on the end of one of the pieces of stock you'll be cutting. Raise the blade to the

Rule of Thumb

Increasing the angle at which the stock crosses the blade makes the cove wider and more circular. Decreasing the angle makes the curve narrower and more elliptical.

Rule of Thumb

When the saw blade is **square to the saw table**, the cove will be a symmetrical section of an ellipse. When the saw blade is tilted, the cove will be asymmetrical.

Figure 248 — Hog out Wood before Cutting Coves

Use a dado (a) or your regular blade (b) with multiple saw cuts to remove the majority of the wood before you start cutting coves.

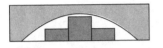

(a) Use dado cuts to remove waste

(b) Use multiple saw cuts to remove waste

Rule of Thumb

To make a cove that is a true **arc of a circle**, keep the saw blade square to the table, the tilt at zero, and the workpiece angle of approach at 90° to the face of the saw blade.

proper height. Set this piece behind the blade and sight it in. You can immediately tell if the set-up is correct.

4. Cut The Cove — Lower the blade and slide the workpiece through the fence chute. Make sure it glides smoothly with very little or no play. Raise the blade to ⅟16 inch and turn on the table saw. Use a hold down and push the workpiece slowly over the blade. If there is any burning, you should move the workpiece across the blade a little faster. Raise the blade another ⅟16 inch and do it again, until the cove is cut to almost the right depth. At this point the cove width should also be nearly correct.

5. Finishing The Cove — Make the last cut by taking off a very small amount of wood (⅟32 or less) and push the wood across the blade slowly. A curved cabinet scraper will smooth the surface nicely.

Safety

Use a dado set or a regular blade to remove the bulk of the waste wood before passing the pieces through the blade at an angle, see **Figure 248**.

1. If you're making narrow moulding, cut the cove in wider stock then rip to finished width. Always shape little pieces on the edge of big pieces, and then cut them off.

2. The saw exerts pressure upward and toward the rear of the workpiece. For safety and to keep the workpiece exactly in line, always use two parallel fences.

3. Raise the blade just a little bit after each pass. The job may take a few minutes longer, but it's safer. If you try to take a deep cut, the piece probably will ride up on the blade.

4. When cutting symmetrical coves, the approach angle can be from either the left or the right. For asymmetrical coves, the approach should be into the blade as it is tilted. If the blade tilts to the left, organize the setup so you can feed the workpiece from the left front of the table.

5. Use jointer-type push blocks so you can exert downward pressure over a wide area while keeping your hands safely out of the way.

6. If the design leaves the workpiece thin above the apex of the cove, downward force may cause the cove to crack at the apex. Using two fences will support the work as you bear down and will lessen the chance of the wood splitting directly above the blade.

7. **Listen** to the blade and the motor. If either are struggling, slow down the feed rate and take smaller cuts.

8. **Because you** can't see the blade, be especially careful. Never push the stock from the rear or hold it down over the blade with your hands. Use push blocks.

9. **Use the** table saw miter gauge to set the approach angle (see **Figure 246**).

Practical Uses for Table-Sawn Coves
1. Crown Moulding

By making your own crown moulding you won't be limited to the selection at the local wood yard. Red oak is common for staining or varnishing and pine or poplar for painting. Use your table saw and the wood of your choice to make your own moulding. Even if you plan to paint the moulding, it's important to select straight, clear material. Knots and twisting grain will be nasty to shape and difficult to install. Mouldings are show-pieces that always require clear, clean wood.

To make crown moulding 2 1/2 inches wide start with lengths of

wood 5/8 inch thick and 3 inches wide. Each piece should be made a few feet longer than needed and make a few extra pieces — just in case. **Figure 249** shows the table saw setup.

Raise the blade to the final height (5/16 inch) and position an auxiliary fence in front of the blade at the correct angle (30°), and clamp it in place. This fence should be 3/8 inch from the blade at its highest setting to account for the 3/8 inch shoulder on each side of the cove.

Lower the blade, lay the moulding against the fence, and clamp a second fence parallel to the first.

Raise the blade 1/16 inch and cut the cove in a series of light passes, raising the blade 1/16 inch each time until the full depth of 5/16 inch is reached.

A series of bevel cuts with the saw blade tilted 45° will finish up the crown moulding, see **Figure 249**. See *Woodworkers' Essential* Chapter 29, Miters, Bevels & Crown Moulding for advice on cutting and installing crown moulding.

2. Fluted Panels

Sometimes when you need long fluted panels such as column pilasters, it's easier to make them on a table saw than on a router table. The idea is the same as

Rule of Thumb
You can use drawings and calculations to precisely set the blade tilt and angle of approach, but you can also "sight" the cove you want to saw. Draw its outline on the end of a board and move your viewpoint around until the saw blade covers the outline. Then set up the auxiliary fence and make a series of test cuts.

Rule of Thumb
Going from 10 degrees angle of approach to 20 degrees about doubles the width of the cove and each additional 10 degrees up to 60 degrees increases the width by about the same amount.

Figure 249 — Fence Angle for Crown Moulding

Set the fence at a 30° angle to the saw blade and clamp at both ends. A second fence ensures the moulding will stay on track. Four cuts with the blade set at 45° will give you beautiful crown moulding.

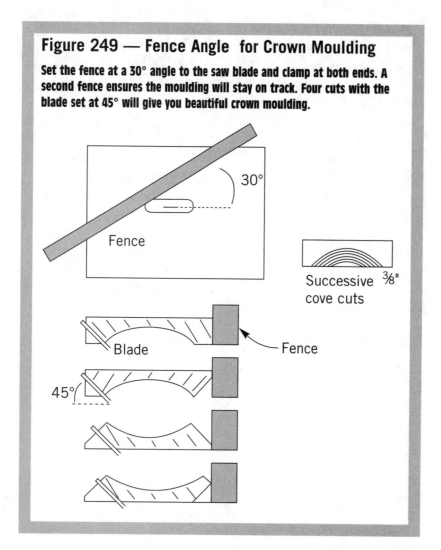

30°

Fence

Successive ⅜" cove cuts

Blade

Fence

45°

screwed to the rip fence. This setup allows easily moving the fence to make successive flutes. I determined that the flutes I wanted were ⅜ inch wide (W = 0.375) and 3/16 inch deep (D = 0.1875). I used a math equation to find the approach angle for the moulding piece, where W = 0.375 and D = 0.1875.

$$\text{Angle} = \text{ASin } W \div 2 \sqrt{[D(10 - D)]}$$

$$= \text{ASin } 0.375 \div 2 \sqrt{[0.1875(10 - 0.1875)]}$$

$$\text{Angle} = \text{ASin } 0.375 \div 2 \sqrt{[0.1875(9.8125)]}$$

$$= \text{ASin } 0.375 \div 2 \sqrt{1.84}$$

$$= \text{Asin } 0.375 \div 2 (1.36)$$

$$= \text{ASin } 0.375 \div 2.72$$

$$\text{Asin } 0.1379 = 8°$$

Cut the angled fence to 8°.

Fix the rip fence the proper distance from the blade and set the blade depth at 1/16 inch.

Pass the workpiece through and reverse the board to make a second pass near its opposite edge. Raise the blade 1/16 inch (or because the approach angle and therefore the cutting surface of the blade is so small, raise it perhaps ⅛ inch) and make another pass on each side.

Reset the fence to make additional flutes.

Note: Use the thinnest blade possible. At this shallow

before and the approach angle will determine the shape of the flutes but now the fence has to be moved without changing the approach angle. A small approach angle will produce deep, narrow flutes, while a larger angle will give shallow, wide flutes.

In this case, since the amount of wood to be removed is small, the angled fence is simply a single wedge-shaped piece of wood screwed to a plywood fence approach angle, the thickness of the blade will affect the width of the cove. For example, if the blade normally cuts a ⅛ inch kerf, then the actual width of the cove will be closer to one half inch:

⅜ inch + ⅛ inch = ½ inch.

Also at this shallow approach, the cove will tend to have a flat bottom.

3. Ogee Bracket Feet

Two hundred years ago ogee bracket feet were made with hand tools — perhaps a moulding plane with a curved blade, and a bow saw. We'll use a table saw to cut the coves and a band saw to cut the profiles and unless you spill the beans, no one will be the wiser. The results are the same; great looks and plenty of strength, without the hard hand-work.

Only the concave part of the ogee curve's S-shape is cut using the table saw cove method, starting with wood 1½ high x 5½ wide x 16 inches long for each leg

Raise the saw blade to the final depth of the cove (½ inch in this case) and place strips of masking tape where the teeth of the blade exit the table (see **Figure 247**).

Make a template of poster board with an inside cutout equal to the width of the cove (2 inches in this case), and an

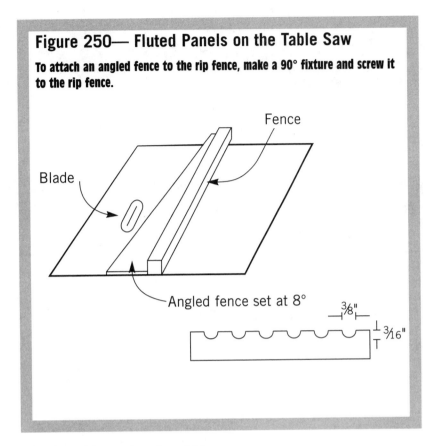

Figure 250— Fluted Panels on the Table Saw

To attach an angled fence to the rip fence, make a 90° fixture and screw it to the rip fence.

Fence

Blade

Angled fence set at 8°

⅜"

3/16"

outside width equal to the width of the wood stock (5½ inches). Angle the template so it's inside edges touch the marks, and tape it into place.

Clamp two fences in place just touching the edges of the template. Raise the blade ¹⁄₁₆ inch and make the first pass. Raise the blade in ¹⁄₁₆ inch increments until the full depth (½ inch) is reached.

Cut the concave portion of the ogee profile with a hand plane as shown in **Figure 251**.

Miter the piece at 45° to form the corner.

Rule of Thumb

Cove-cutting on the table saw is a great technique for creating the bevel and shoulder on a raised panel.

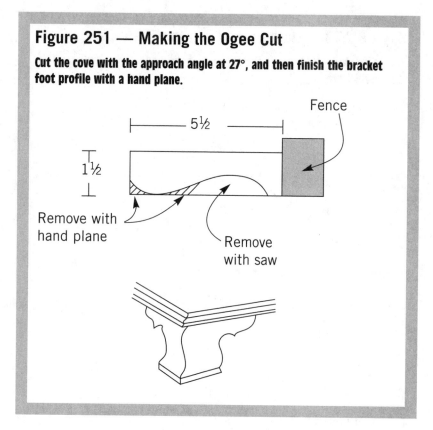

Figure 251 — Making the Ogee Cut

Cut the cove with the approach angle at 27°, and then finish the bracket foot profile with a hand plane.

Fence

5½

1½

Remove with hand plane

Remove with saw

Band saw the profile of the foot.

Glue two pieces together to form the foot. Glue and screw a backer block to the rear for stability.

To calculate the approach angle instead of making a template, use the following equation:

$$= ASin\ W \div 2 \sqrt{[D\,(10 - D)]}$$

Where $W = 2$ and $D = \frac{1}{2}$.

$$= ASin\ 2 \div 2 \sqrt{[0.5\,(10 - 0.5)]}$$

$$= ASin\ 2 \div 2 \sqrt{[0.5\,(9.5)]}$$

$$= ASin\ 2 \div 2 \sqrt{4.75}$$

$$= ASin\ 2 \div 2\,(2.18)$$

$$= ASin\ 2 \div 4.36$$

$$ASin\ 0.4587 = 27.3°$$

4. Drawer Pull

This flush, integral drawer pull can be made on the table saw. The profile seems to mirror gripping fingers, making it well suited to its task (**Figure 252**).

Tilt the blade to 42° and set the approach angle at 10°.

Reverse the workpiece each pass if the double coved grip is to be in the center of the drawer. If the grip is off-set, cut one cove to the final depth, and then reset the fence system to cut the other half of the grip.

5. Shaker Bench Seat

The Shakers, who invented the table saw, made the seat for this bench by hand, using scorps and in-shaves. The contoured seat can also be made on a table saw.

With the blade set at 0° tilt, set the fence to 56° approach angle with the help of a miter gauge (see **Figure 246**). The final height of the blade (depth of the cove) will be ¾ inch, see **Figure 253**.

Lower the saw blade and clamp a second guide fence to the other side of the workpiece. Position this fence parallel to the first so the distance between the two is equal to the width of the rear section of the bench seat (8¾ inch).

Cut the cove in multiple

passes. Start with the blade $\frac{1}{16}$ inch high and then raise the blade $\frac{1}{16}$ inch between passes. If the workpiece is long and heavy, use an out-feed table to support it after it passes over the blade. A temporary table can be made by clamping a piece of plywood between the two guide fences.

Glue the two seat sections together and make a template showing the final profile. The rest of the seat can be hogged out using a dado set. Tip the dado blades slightly and pass the seat blank over, using the profile template as a guide to set the dado height after each pass. The seat then can be smoothed with a plane and scraper. Avoid sandpaper if you want the seat to look authentic.

6. Moulding

Besides the blade height, the approach angle and the blade tilt, there is actually one more variable to be considered in making coves. Sometimes adjusting these three just isn't enough. It takes tilting the workpiece to get it just right. Begin by copying a profile onto the end of the workpiece as in **Figure 254**.

Set the approach angles at 30° and clamp the two fences as shown in **Figure 254**.

Set the blade tilt at 45°.

Figure 252 — Drawer Front with Built-In Pull

You don't have to worry about adding pulls to this drawer — the pulls are built in.

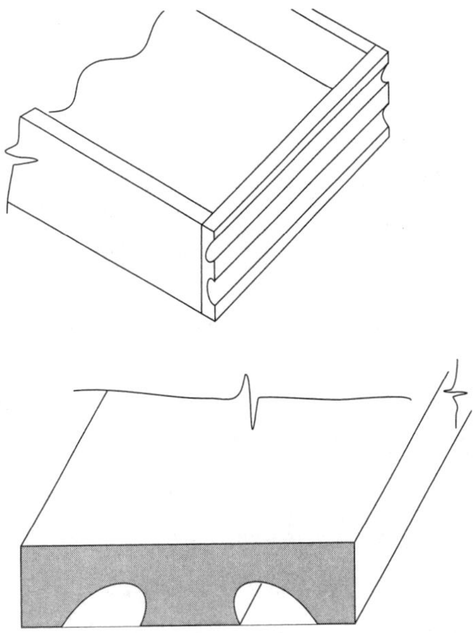

Figure 253 — Shaker Bench Seat

Only the cove portion of the seat is cut on the table saw. The rest of the material is removed with a dado set and hand plane. The seat is made by gluing together two 8¾ inch pieces of wood.

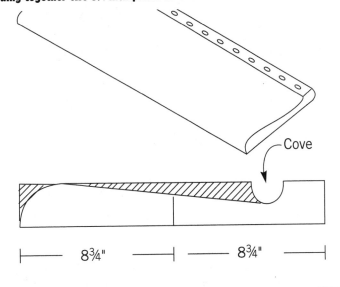

Cove

8¾"   8¾"

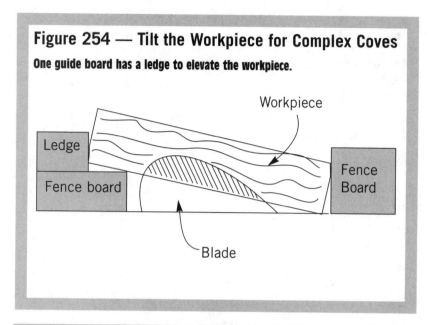

Figure 254 — Tilt the Workpiece for Complex Coves

One guide board has a ledge to elevate the workpiece.

Workpiece

Ledge

Fence board

Fence Board

Blade

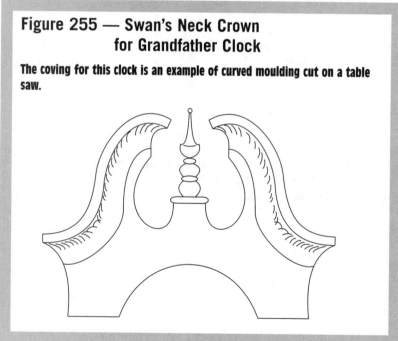

Figure 255 — Swan's Neck Crown for Grandfather Clock

The coving for this clock is an example of curved moulding cut on a table saw.

Cut the cove carefully, with multiple passes.

7. Curved Coves

When straight coves are cut, the wood is passed over the blade at an angle. With a curved piece of moulding, the workpiece must still pass over the blade at an angle — but because the desired moulding is curved, the piece must also pass over the blade in an arc.

To cut the swan's-neck moulding (see **Figure 255**) often seen on grandfather clocks, you need to rotate the workpiece through the blade in a circular fashion. **Figure 256** shows the setup.

Start with a fixed base that is big enough to be clamped to the saw table. Determine the required approach angle and mark this on the sub-base. Make a line perpendicular to this theoretical fence starting at the center of the blade. The pivot point will be located on this line at the correct radius for the cove.

On top of this base, mount a rotating top. The pivot point of the rotating top will be the radius of the required cove. Cut the radius on the pivoting top back just far enough so the saw blade at maximum height (for the depth of the cove) doesn't touch it.

Mount the workpiece onto the pivoting top with screws through the back and then attach the pivot to the sub-base with a carriage bolt with its head inset in a counter-bore coming from the bottom of the base. Raise the blade ⅙ inch above

Figure 256 — Finding the First Pivot Point

The first pivot point is on a line perpendicular to the approach angle. A second pivot point will be on the same line but on the opposite side of the blade, and it might be at a different radius.

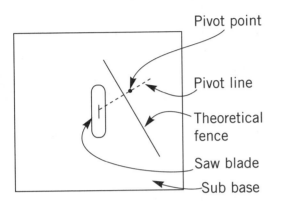
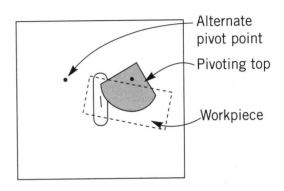

Figure 257 — Cutting Curved Coves

Use a pivoting top board to rotate the workpiece through the band saw blade to give goose-neck moulding.

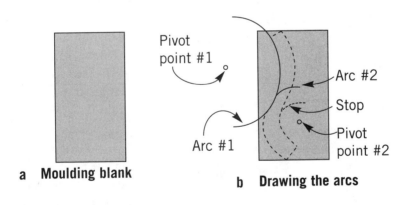

a   **Moulding blank**

b   **Drawing the arcs**

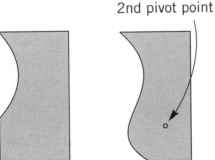
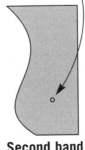
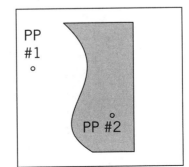

c   **First band saw cut**

d   **Second band saw cut**

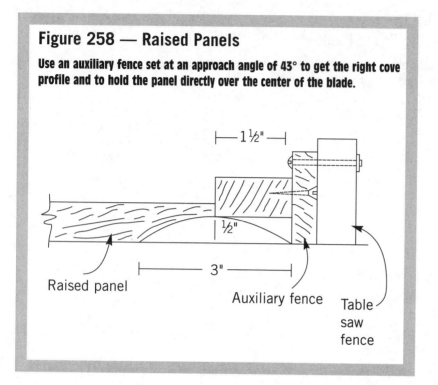

Figure 258 — Raised Panels

Use an auxiliary fence set at an approach angle of 43° to get the right cove profile and to hold the panel directly over the center of the blade.

— 1½" —

½"

— 3" —

Raised panel

Auxiliary fence

Table saw fence

or shaper and a bit with a pilot bearing to add the desired shapes on the inside and outside of the faces of the pieces to complete the desired profile.

8. Raised Panels

Raised panels fit better into the frame when they are cut concave instead of with a straight bevel. These cuts could be made by holding the panel on edge and moving it past a table saw blade. This would require that the panel be held tightly against a tall fence with the panel passing between the fence and the blade, and any small movement or bump by the panel would make a gouge in the bevel. The best jigs are designed so if the workpiece slips, the wood moves away from the cutters and not into them. Holding the workpiece on edge is unwieldy and does not produce great results.

It is safer and easier to lay the panel flat on the top of the saw table and to cut the cove just as we've cut the other coves discussed in this chapter.

Figure 258 shows the setup, it's straightforward except that we will use only one half of the blade. The auxiliary fence does double duty — it is set at 43° to control the approach angle and it also has a ledge to keep the edge of the panel directly over the center of the blade. Notice

the sub-base and slowly rotate the work through the blade. Make cuts about ⅛ inch on each pass until you get the required cove depth.

The mirror-image cove can be cut in a similar manner by using a pivot point on the opposite side of the blade. This point must have the same radius.

Locate the second pivot point to make the other part of the ogee or S-curve. Some hand work with a curved scraper will complete the transition between the two curved coves.

After the S-coves have been completed, cut the inside and outside radii on a band saw and sand smooth. Use a router table that the fence prevents the panel from slipping into the blade, and if the panel slips away from the fence, it does not damage the profile. Note also that this is one of those happy situations where the precise shape of the cove doesn't matter, so long as the thickness of the remaining wood matches the groove in the frame. But there will be cases where it needs to be precisely figured, as follows:

Math

Problem 6: Find the angle of approach for the raised panel cove in **Figure 258**. The cove is 3 inches wide and ½ inch deep.

Solution 6a: There are two ways to find the angle of approach. The first is by using **Figure 241** which shows the Depth Factor for ½ inch deep coves is 4.36.

ASin of Approach Angle = Cove Width ÷ Depth Factor

Where CW = 3
and DF = 4.36

Asin Angle = 3 ÷ 4.36
= 0.6881

Asin 0.6881 = 43.5°

Solution 6b: The other way to find the approach angle is with math.

Approach Angle = Asin W ÷ 2 $\sqrt{}$ [D x (10-D)]

Where Cove Width W = 3,
Cove Depth D = 0.5

Angle = Asin 3 ÷ 2 $\sqrt{}$ [0.5 x (10-0.5)]

Angle = Asin 3 ÷ 2 $\sqrt{}$ (4.75)

Angle = Asin 3 ÷ 4.36
= 0.6881

Asin 0.6881 = 43.49°

CHAPTER 22

Compound Butt Joints

As woodworkers, we often fail to consider a butt joint when we're casting about for the best joinery for a piece of fine furniture — and I plead guilty here. We consider the butt joint appropriate only for tool totes, saw horses, and heavy construction — mitered joints are so much more elegant. But then we come across a plan for a stylish serving tray, a cradle or a Shaker stool — all with handcut dove-tails. Now we have to reconsider because all these projects begin with the joints butted together — and if the sides and ends slope, then we have compound butt joints. I covered compound miter joints in Woodworkers' Essential, Chapter 29, *Miters, Bevels & Crown Molding*. I hadn't considered the butt joint important enough to include in that chapter or for a separate chapter. Recently a friend called about a project he was deep into that had compound butt joints. He asked how to figure the miter setting and the blade tilt. "I looked in your book and it wasn't there." Thus, this chapter.

A compound butt joint at first seems pretty simple, just one edge of a board nudged flat against the side of another board, but a little thought shows that this hopper joint is

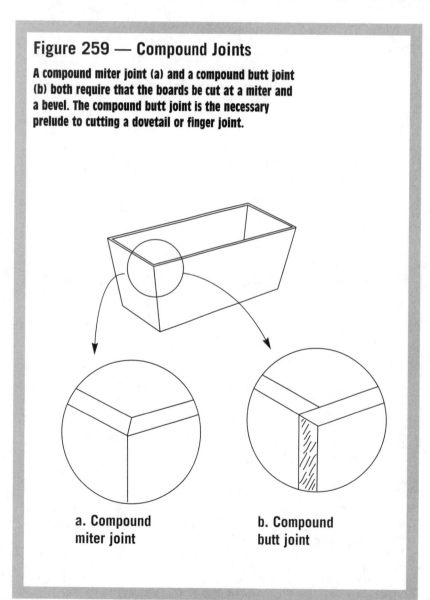

Figure 259 — Compound Joints

A compound miter joint (a) and a compound butt joint (b) both require that the boards be cut at a miter and a bevel. The compound butt joint is the necessary prelude to cutting a dovetail or finger joint.

a. Compound miter joint

b. Compound butt joint

every bit as complicated as a compound miter. In both instances we need to cut the boards at both a miter and a bevel so they fit tightly together. In the compound miter, each piece that makes up the joint is cut at one-half of the corner angle. With the compound butt joint, each piece of the joint is cut at 100% of the corner angle. See **Figure 259**.

Compound Butt Joint

A compound angle occurs whenever two sloped sides meet; the resulting joint can either to be mitered or butted. If the joint is to be dovetailed or joined with fingers, the sides must be butted together first before the specialized joinery is cut. At the sloped corner, there are two sets of angles — a miter to be set on the miter gauge and a bevel to be cut with the blade tilted. These angles must be exact or the boards will fit poorly. An error in the bevel and the two boards will not meet correctly — with a gap either inside or outside. An error in the miter and the end of one board will not be in the same plane as the flat side of the mating piece. **Figure 260** shows a cradle I made for my grand-daughter with compound butt joints.

To form a compound angle on a table saw or a radial-arm saw, both the blade and the miter

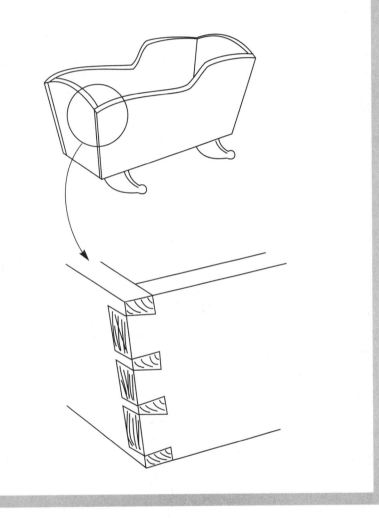

Figure 260 — Cradle

The cradle is first constructed with compound butt joints. If the joints are converted to dovetails, dimensions should be adjusted accordingly because the width (or length) will decrease by double the thickness of the stock.

must set at an angle, that is, the miter gauge or tracking arm moved to a setting other than 90° and the blade tilted to one side.

Determining the Correct Angles

It is standard practice to draw a project to scale and take size and

Figure 261 — Compound Butt Joints

In the side view (a) and the end view (b) the two slopes are apparent and measurable but the bevel angle and the miter angle are not apparent. In the top view (c) the bevels and miters are distorted.

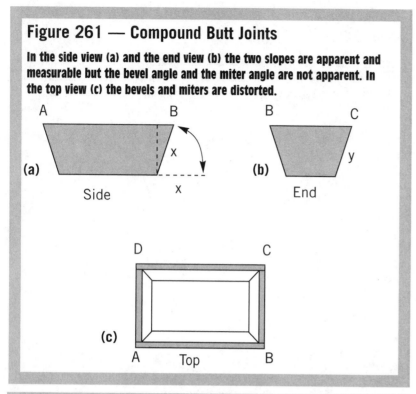

Figure 262 — Developing a Compound Shape

Compound shapes must be opened and flattened to one plane before they can be measured accurately. The values 'x' and 'y' came from Figure 261.

angle readings directly from the diagram. This works well when the corners are 90° and the sides, ends and top all align with the x, y and z axes. When a drawing has a surface that is not perpendicular to our line of sight, for example, the front side is not flat on the surface of the paper but slopes outward, then the drawing gives us a distorted sense of size and shape (see **Figure 261**). When the ends and the sides both slope, the front view of the drawing shows a shortened view of the front (a) and the end view shows a shortened view of the end (b). This makes measurements difficult. In addition, the top view (c) is distorted because we are not looking straight down on the top edges of the box, which means the bevel is apparent but not measurable. From the top view (c), the miter angle of the butt joint also is not apparent. The only angles that are measurable from the drawing are the slopes of the sides and the slopes of the ends. There are three methods for finding the correct blade tilt and miter setting to cut butt joints for sloped sides; first by mechanical drawing, second by using math, and third with a set-up block.

1. Mechanical Drawing

The first, and incidentally the most difficult to comprehend and to use, is by mechanical drawing. This drafting procedure starts with a plan drawing and then extends and rejoins the lines to create a corrected drawing that will show the true dimensions and angles. When compound shapes need to be measured accurately from a two-dimensional drawing of elevation and plan, they require development, that is, the parts need to be opened out and flattened onto one plane. **Figure 262** illustrates the top view of an object with both the ends and the sides splayed. It can be seen that the elevational outline is correct, but the given width of the sides and ends do not allow for the actual splay or leaning outward, which cannot be shown. To develop these true measurements:

1. **Draw the plan** ABCD. See **Figure 262a**.

2. **Extend** the outer dimensions as shown by the dotted lines. See **Figure 262b**.

3. **Draw lines** AB and DC parallel to the plan at a distance equal to 'x' from **Figure 261**.

4. **Draw lines** BC and AD parallel to the plan at a distance equal to 'y' from **Figure 261**.

5. **Complete** the drawing, **Figure 262c**.

6. **Measure** the drawing for dimensions.

2. Math

The second method of finding the miter angle and blade tilt for

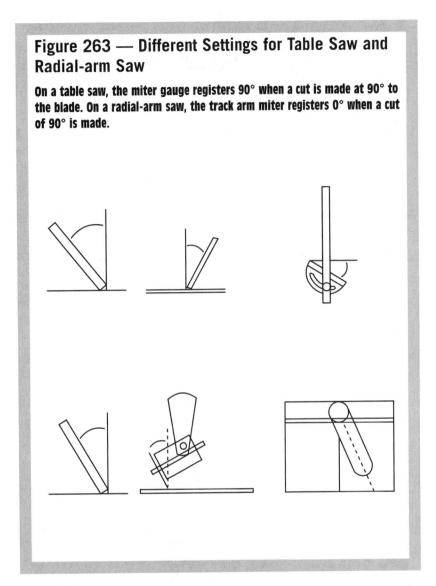

Figure 263 — Different Settings for Table Saw and Radial-arm Saw

On a table saw, the miter gauge registers 90° when a cut is made at 90° to the blade. On a radial-arm saw, the track arm miter registers 0° when a cut of 90° is made.

a compound butt joint is by using mathematics. Deriving the equation is complicated but afterwards, using the procedure is simple with the use of a small hand calculator (see **Figure 263**). I've also put together a chart (**Figure 264**) to use to set your saw blade tilt and miter gauge accordingly.

Table Saw versus Radial-arm Saw

Figure 264 — Using a Calculator for Compound Butt Miters

Both the ends and the sides are at 20°. Set the miter gauge at 90°-18.8° = 71°. Set the blade tilt at 7°.

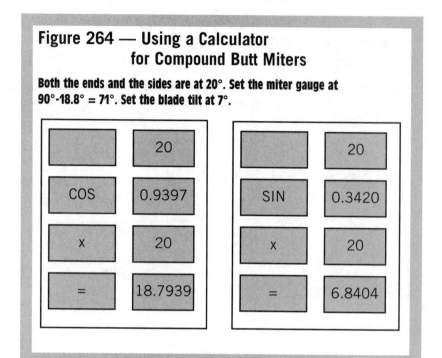

	20
COS	0.9397
x	20
=	18.7939

	20
SIN	0.3420
x	20
=	6.8404

Compound Butt Angles on the Table Saw

Miter — Miter Gauge = 90 – [(Side Angle α) x (Cos End Angle γ)]

Note: The '90' is to adjust for the setting of a table saw miter gauge.

Bevel — Blade Tilt = (End Angle γ) x (Sin Side Angle α)

To show how this works, let's figure the miter and bevel angles for the cradle in **Figure 260**.

Using a Calculator

Buy an inexpensive scientific calculator and the math will go a lot faster (**Figure 264**). Make sure the calculator has buttons for TAN, SIN and COS. You'll also need the inverse values — these keys are sometimes listed as INVTAN, INVSIN, INVCOS, or ATAN, ASIN, ACOS or ARCTAN, ARCSIN, ARCCOS. If you own a personal computer you can use a calculator on Microsoft Windows under Program/Accessories. Let's do a calculation step-by-step:

Problem 1: We want to make an early American cradle using compound butt joints, see **Figure 260**. The sides and ends both slope outward at 20°. What is the miter gauge setting and the blade tilt? Note that the height of the cradle is immaterial, as are the width of the ends

Whether you use a table saw, a chop saw or a radial-arm saw, a degree is a degree. But, because of the different way the radial-arm saw's tracking arm and the table saw's miter gauge are marked, you must be careful to use 0° or 90° as the starting reference. **Figure 262** shows the basic difference between the two saws. The starting point for a miter gauge is 90°, and the starting point for a tracking arm is 0°. For example, if we were to cut a 14° miter on the table saw using a miter gauge, we would set it at 76° (90°-14° = 76°). If we were to cut the same angle on a radial-arm saw we would set the tracking arm at 14° (0° + 14° = 14°). Keep in mind that in both cases the angle we want is a 14° offset from the normal 90° square setting.

and the length of the sides. We plan to cut the joints on a table saw.

Solution 1:

Miter Gauge = 90 − [(Side α) x (Cos End γ)]

Where the Side α = 20° and the End γ = 20°.

Miter Gauge = 90 − [20 x (Cos 20)]

Miter Gauge = 90 − [20 x 0.9397] = 90 - 18.79 = 71.21° ≈ 71°

Now we can figure the blade tilt.

Blade Tilt = (End γ) x (Sin Side α)

Where the Side α = 20° and the End γ = 20°.

Blade Tilt = 20 x Sin 20

Blade Tilt = 20 x 0.3420 = 6.84 ≈≈7°

We now can set the miter gauge of the table saw at 71° and tilt the blade to 7° and cut both the ends and the sides. **Figure 264** shows the steps using a calculator.

After cutting the miter and the bevel, the top and bottom edges of the sides and ends are still at 90° to the surface of the boards. Set the blade to 20° and rip the edges of all the pieces. Now when the box is put together, it will set flat and the top edges will be parallel to the floor.

The same settings can be found in **Figure 265**.

Compound Butt Angles on the Radial-arm Saw

Because angles are measured from 0° to 90° on the radial saw tracking arm, butt angles from **Figure 265** must be adjusted.

Problem 2: Find the miter gauge setting and the blade tilt for a compound butt joint where both the ends and the sides slope at 30°. We plan to use a radial-arm saw to cut the joints.

Solution 2: We will use the table in **Figure 265** to find the proper angle and miter settings. Find 30° in column 1 under "End Slope" and also 30° in column 2 under "Side Slope". Read 64° "Miter Gauge" and 15° "Blade Tilt." The radial-arm setting will be 90° - 64° = 26°. The blade tilt will be the same, 15°.

Making Complicated Boxes

When the sides and the ends are sloped at different angles, the miters and bevels become more complicated. The following formula will help calculate the correct saw settings. Note:

this is for the table saw and the '90' is to adjust the setting of a table saw miter gauge.

Miter Gauge = 90 − [(Side α) x (Cos End λ)]

Blade Tilt = (End λ) x (Sin Side α)

Figure 265 — Compound Butt Angles for Table Saw

Set the miter gauge to the setting under "Miter Gauge Setting" and tilt the blade to the angle under "Blade Tilt". To cut boards for a cradle with both the ends and the sides sloping 30°, set the miter gauge at 64° and tilt the blade to 15°.

End Slope	Side Slope	Miter Gauge	Blade Tilt
0	0	0.0	0.0
0	10	80.0	0.0
0	20	70.0	0.0
0	30	60.0	0.0
0	40	50.0	0.0
0	50	40.0	0.0
10	0	90.0	0.0
10	10	80.2	1.7
10	20	70.3	3.5
10	30	60.5	5.2
10	40	50.6	6.9
10	50	40.8	8.7
20	0	90.0	0.0
20	10	80.6	3.4
20	20	71.2	6.8
20	30	61.8	10.3
20	40	52.4	13.7
20	50	43.0	17.1
30	0	90.0	0.0
30	10	81.3	5.0
30	20	72.7	10.0
30	30	64.0	15.0
30	40	55.4	20.0
30	50	46.7	25.0
40	0	90.0	0.0
40	10	82.3	6.4
40	20	74.7	12.9
40	30	67.0	19.3
40	40	59.4	25.7
40	50	51.7	32.1
50	0	90.0	0.0
50	10	83.6	7.7
50	20	77.1	15.3
50	30	70.7	23.0
50	40	64.3	30.6
50	50	57.9	38.3

Figure 266 — Serving Tray with Sloped Sides and Ends

The complicated miters and bevels for these butt joints can be made using a set-up block.

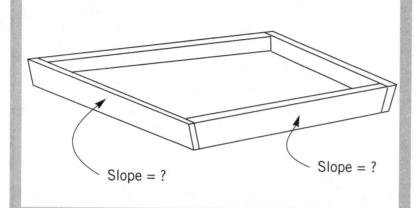

Slope = ?

Slope = ?

Figure 267 — Making the Set-Up Block

(a) Set the bevel gauge by using the slope from a drawing or a mock-up. (b) Transfer the slope to the saw blade. (c) Cross-cut the ends of the set-up block to the slope of the tray. (d) Rip the block on one side (viewed from the rear on a left-tilting blade). (e) The finished set-up block is a miniature model of the tray with one side and both ends cut at a miter.

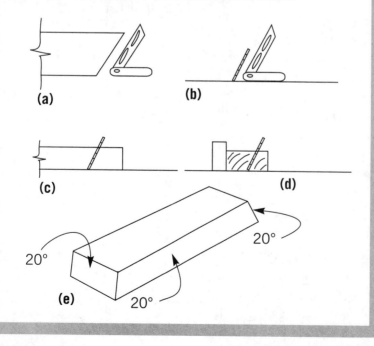

(a)

(b)

(c)

(d)

(e)

20°

20°

20°

20°

Problem 3: Let's assume we are building a flower box to go on the back deck. The ends will slope out at 10° and the sides will slope out at 20°. What are the miter gauge setting and the blade tilt? We plan to cut the joints on a table saw.

Solution 3:

Miter Gauge = 90 − [(Side α) x (Cos End λ)]

Where side α = 20°, end λ = 10°

Miter Gauge = 90 − (20 x Cos 10)

Miter Gauge = 90 − (20 x 0.9848) = 90 - 19.70 = 70.3 ≈ 70°

Blade Tilt = (End λ) x (Sin Side α)

Where side α = 20°, end λ = 10°

Blade Tilt = 10 x (Sin 20)

Blade Tilt = 10 x 0.3420 = 3.4°

Figure 265 for the table saw gives settings when the slopes of the sides and ends are different.

Set-Up Block – Compound Angles without Math

For years, craftsmen have been using set-up blocks to set the miter gauge and the blade tilt for compound butt joints. These blocks have the advantage of making a project reproducible. Woodworkers label their set-up blocks and store them away for future use. They can be reused to set the miter and tilt when another cradle just like the first is made. And they are simple to use. Another appealing feature is the blade and the miter are set without math and without knowing, or caring, what the degree of miter or the degree of bevel is.

To show how to use a miter-bevel block, let's make a serving tray as in **Figure 266**.

To Make a Set-Up Block

1. Prepare a block of wood about 2 inches thick x 3 inches wide x 12 inches long.

2. Set a bevel gauge against a prototype or against the drawing and set the arm to the slope of the side. See **Figure 267a**.

3. Use the bevel gauge to transfer the slope to the saw blade. See **Figure 267b**.

4. Lay the 2x3 block flat on the saw table and cross-cut both ends with the miter gauge set at 90° and the blade tilted. See **Figure 267c**.

5. Put the block against the fence and rip one edge with the saw blade at the same tilt (**Figure 267d**). You now have a representative model of your compound miter with the same slope at two ends and on one side. See **Figure 267e**.

6. Before the blade tilt is

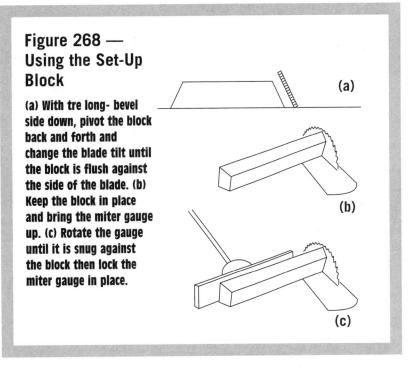

**Figure 268 —
Using the Set-Up
Block**

(a) With tre long- bevel side down, pivot the block back and forth and change the blade tilt until the block is flush against the side of the blade. (b) Keep the block in place and bring the miter gauge up. (c) Rotate the gauge until it is snug against the block then lock the miter gauge in place.

(a)

(b)

(c)

changed, rip both edges of the boards you'll be using to make the tray. It will look better if the top and bottom edges of the box are at the same angle as the slope of the sides.

To Use the Set-Up Block

1. Lay the set-up block on the saw table with the beveled (long) edge down and push the short end of the block up against the blade. Wiggle the block and change the saw blade tilt until the block fits flush against the surface of the blade. The reason the block is only 2 inches high is so it will fit under the teeth of the saw.

2. Hold the block in this position and loosen the miter gauge so it rotates freely. Bring the miter gauge up against the

Figure 269 — Cutting the Pieces

(a) Label all the pieces; use 'N' and 'O' for inside and outside. The arrow points to the top edge. (b) Cut one end of each piece with the gauge to the left of the blade. (c) Rotate the piece 180° and flip it over to cut the other end with the miter gauge on the right of the saw blade.

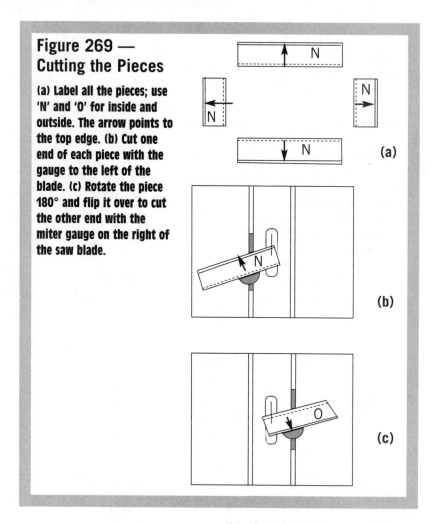

during the cutting so carefully label all the pieces. Lay all the pieces flat on the work bench and mark the inside and outside of each. I use 'N' for inside and 'O' for outside. Also draw an arrow on each surface pointing to its top edge. See **Figure 269a**.

2. Set the fence and bevel rip each board at the top and bottom edges, then remove the fence for the rest of the cuts.

3. Stack the pieces so all 'N' surfaces are up and the arrow faces away.

4. Cut the right end of each board with the gauge in the left-hand slot with the inside 'N' facing up and the arrow pointing away. See **Figure 269b**.

5. Put the miter gauge in the right hand slot. Don't change the setting of the miter gauge nor of the blade tilt.

6. Flip each piece so the outside face 'O' is up and the arrow is pointing towards you, and saw all four boards. See **Figure 269c**.

block and lock the gauge. The correct compound miter and bevel angles are now set to cut compound butt joints. See **Figure 268**.

Making the Cuts

Because the saw blade tilts only one way, one end of each board will be cut with the miter gauge in the left hand slot of the table and the other end of that same board will be cut using the miter gauge in the right hand slot.

1. It's easy to get confused

CHAPTER 23

Shaping Wood with Patterns and Templates

Templates are special fixtures used to shape duplicate pieces in the shop. They are like cookie cutters, allowing you to cut multiple pieces of wood that conform exactly to the original pattern. The most basic templates are stiff, thin plates of wood or metal that serve as a gauge or guide in mechanical work. Templates mimic the shape of the desired piece and provide a guide for trimming a rough-cut part to final size. More sophisticated templates allow perfect inlays or joints between irregularly shaped parts. Whether simple or complex, templates ensure consistent, precise results and should be part of every woodworker's repertoire.

Most woodworkers are familiar with router and shaper templates for duplicating complicated shapes where bits are used with bushings or guide bearings. Savvy woodworkers should know that they can also use templates with the table saw for straight cuts, the band saw for gently curving shapes, and the drum sander for straight or curved shapes. Disk sander templates are used for straight pieces or convex curves where only a little material is removed and lathe templates are used to duplicate intricate beads and coves using hand-held cutting units. Although templates can be used by themselves, it is often more convenient to incorporate them into some sort of fixture to align and clamp the part as it is being shaped.

Template Material

Templates should be made of a material that is strong, stiff, flat,

Figure 270 — Table Saw Template Cutting

The auxiliary fence is set ⅛ inch above the workpiece and attached to the table saw fence with clamps or screws. The saw fence is then moved so the outside of the saw blade is flush with the edge of the auxiliary fence. The template, which is the exact size of the finished piece, is attached to the workpiece with double-sided tape, brads, or sometimes screws. The template is then pushed along the auxiliary fence one side at a time. The hole in the fixture is to remove off-cuts before they get caught between the blade and the fence.

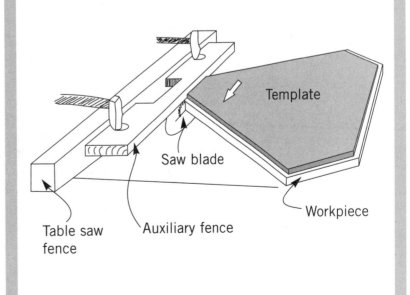

Template

Saw blade

Workpiece

Table saw fence

Auxiliary fence

Rule of Thumb

Templates can be used to **rout or shape** complex parts, and they can also be used with the table saw for duplicating straight parts, with the band saw for gentle curves, with the lathe for duplicating turnings, and with the drum sander for straight or curved shapes.

and dimensionally stable. It's best if it is also readily available and inexpensive. Templates have been made of plywood, fiberboard, hardboard, plastic, and metal, and each material has its good and bad points. Solid wood is usually avoided because of dimensional instability. Whatever material you use, make sure the working edges are smooth. A good sanding and then an application of paste wax will ensure that the template and the fence slide easily against each other. For permanent fixtures that you plan to use often, plastic or aluminum templates will hold up indefinitely.

Aluminum sheet can be purchased at most hardware stores and home supply stores. It's available in ⅛ inch sheets and can be cut easily on the band saw. Aluminum, either by itself or fastened to a piece of ¼ inch plywood, is the best material for long-lasting templates where the pattern and shape are intricate, such as for finger joints and dovetails.

Plastic, such as clear, high impact polystyrene, is great for templates because it's flat, stable and quite strong and you can see what's going on below. The 0.40 inch (approx. ⅜ inch) material costs about $5 for a 36 inch x 36 inch piece, large enough for more than one template guide. To cut the plastic, just score the

surface with a sharp knife and bend the plastic at the line. It will snap cleanly. Plastic can also be cut on the band saw. Use 320-grit sandpaper to feather the sharp edges.

High density fiberboard

(HDF, Masonite®, tempered hardboard) comes in ⅛ inch or ¼ inch thick sheets. HDF is ideal for making templates because it is hard, strong and will stand up to repeated use. It's also easier to cut and shape than aluminum or plastic.

Medium density fiberboard

(MDF) comes in sheets that are ¼ inch to 1 inch thick. It's stable and, like all the fiberboards, it stays flat as the humidity changes. MDF can be glued together face-to-face to make large blocks and rigid fences. All the fiberboards hold screws in the face but not in the edges.

Particleboard has similar characteristics to MDF and is sold in two grades — construction and industrial — with industrial having smoother faces and being made to higher specifications. Particleboard is only good for straight patterns because its edge is somewhat soft and uncertain.

Cabinet grade plywood

comes in sheets ¼ inch to 1 inch thick and has smooth surfaces and edges. It is strong, inexpensive and stable but frequently twists during manufacture and stays that way afterward. The small pieces used for templates are usually free of distortion. It is not strong enough for long-lasting use or intricate patterns.

Solid wood is a poor choice for permanent templates because it shrinks, expands and distorts with seasonal changes in humidity. Normal wood movement is more than enough to destroy the accuracy of most setups.

Table Saw Templates
Full size templates

You can produce exact duplicates from a master template using an overhanging fixture on your table saw (see **Figure 270**). To make the fixture, start with ¾ inch cabinet-grade plywood about 24 inches long. Drill two holes for the clamps and cut a peep hole along one side. Sand the working edge smooth and wax it. Clamp the fixture to the saw's rip fence and allow ⅛ inch clearance between the underside of the fixture and the top of the stock to be cut — the workpiece should slide freely beneath it. Move the rip fence and set the guide edge of the auxiliary fence directly over the outside of the saw blade (see **Figure 271**).

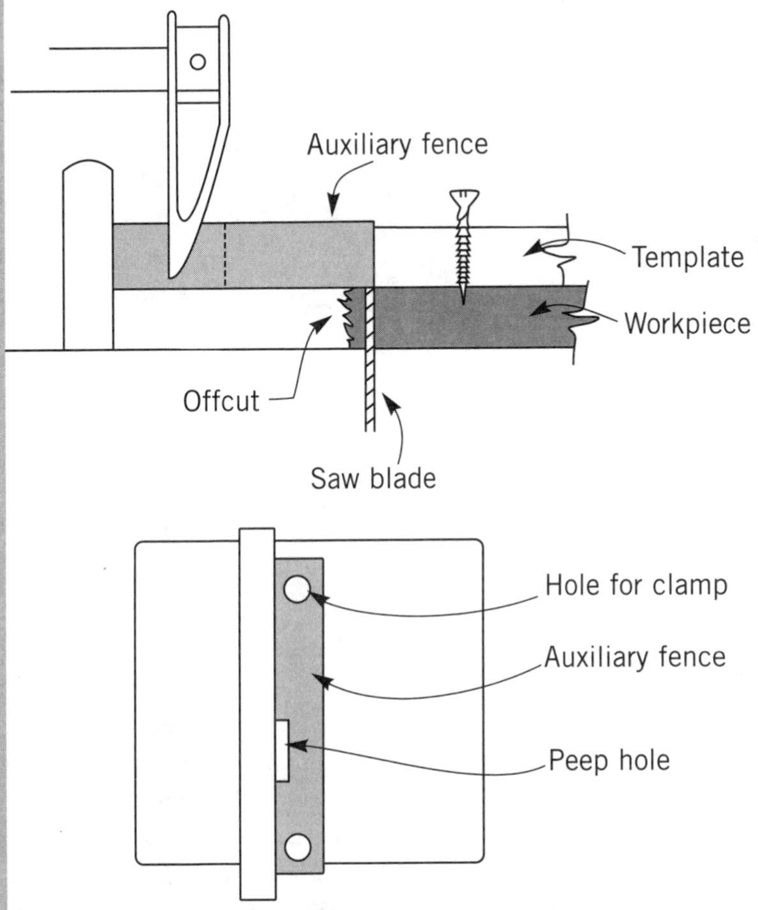

Cutting straight pieces with a template on the table saw is

Figure 271 — Table Saw Template Cutting

Set the outside of the auxiliary fence even with the outside of the saw blade and about ⅛ inch higher than the workpiece.

faster than using a router for two reasons. First, when roughing out the shape of the blank, you don't need to be as exact. Instead of cutting close to the line like you do before template routing, you only have to get within an inch or so.

Second, there is less clamping involved with the table saw method. You just screw or nail the template to the side of the

Rule of Thumb

The more intricate the pattern, the more chance there is that sharp points will become blurred and worn down with use. A general rule: the more complex the pattern, the harder should be the template material.

Figure 272 — To Cut Straight Lines on Odd-Shaped Pieces

Use a guide board to cut straight lines on the workpiece. Attach the guide with hot-melt glue or double-sided tape.

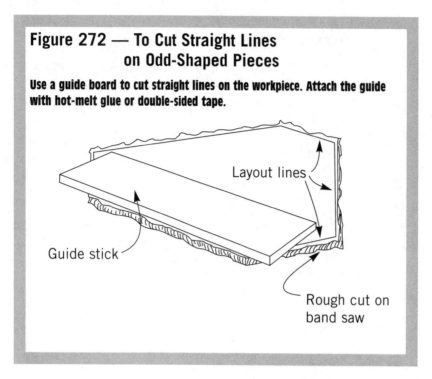

Layout lines

Guide stick

Rough cut on band saw

part that won't show (the underside of a shelf, for example) and go. Small parts and those where screws can't be used can be fastened to the template with hot-melt glue or double-sided tape. With a router, you have to clamp the workpiece and the template to the bench, make part of the cut, readjust the clamps, and then finish the cut. With the table saw, attach the template to the workpiece one time and cut all sides.

Cut a master template from ½ inch material to the exact size and shape of the part to be duplicated. To cut the duplicate parts, press the template against the guide edge of the auxiliary fence and push through the blade. Watch out for small pieces of cut-offs that may get caught

between the fence and the blade. For safety's sake, stand to one side of the line-of-cut. Shut the saw OFF and remove scraps under the fixture as you cut, and. With this simple fixture, you can use the table saw to cut duplicates of large odd-shaped parts of almost any size.

Straight Edges

Instead of using a full size template, it is possible to use the auxiliary fence and a guide stick to cut odd shaped but straight-edged pieces (see **Figure 272**). First cut the workpiece to rough dimensions on the band saw, staying outside the lines by anywhere from ⅛ inch to 1 inch. Prepare a guide stick of MDF or plywood long enough to grip the workpiece firmly then use hot-melt glue or double-sided tape to hold the piece. You can also use the tips of brads or the points of screws driven through until the points just protrude. Plant the guide stick directly on a layout line of the workpiece and make the cut by running the guide against the auxiliary fence.

This method is often used to prepare the original template, which will be used later to cut the workpieces.

Band Saw Templates
Straight Cuts

When the workpiece is small and it doesn't feel safe to cut it on the table saw, use the band saw. The secret is in making a template guide that mounts to the saw's table as shown (see **Figure 273**). Construct the fixture so that the inside cutting edge of the blade is a standard distance from the outer edge of the fixture — ½ inch in this case. This allows you to cut the hardboard template pieces a standard ½ inch smaller than the desired final dimensions of the workpiece. One important part of the fixture is a strip of plastic laminate held in place with double-sided tape, which provides a continuous surface against which the template can be run, avoiding any snags at the cutout around the saw blade. The plastic strip is attached after the fixture is in place. It's important to bring the top blade guides as close as possible to the surface of the fence to avoid the blade bowing. Any blade distortion will give uneven cuts and unsatisfactory results.

Curved Cuts

If you find yourself with a project that requires a large number of duplicate rounded cutout parts, the band saw is the perfect tool. To make curved pieces, make both the guide and the templates from ¼ inch hardboard (see **Figure 274**). Position the guide on the band saw so the tip surrounds the blade and so that its right edge is flush with the right side of the

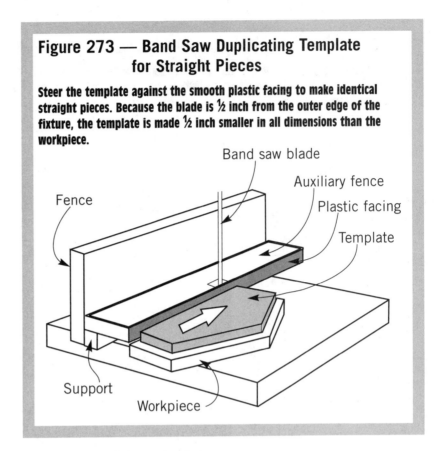

Figure 273 — Band Saw Duplicating Template for Straight Pieces

Steer the template against the smooth plastic facing to make identical straight pieces. Because the blade is ½ inch from the outer edge of the fixture, the template is made ½ inch smaller in all dimensions than the workpiece.

blade. A pair of clamps holds it in place.

To use the guide, fasten a template the exact size and shape of the desired final piece to the underside of the stock with double-sided tape then push it through the band saw, running the edge of the template against the nose of the guide.

This simple fixture lets you duplicate pieces quickly and accurately, as long as the curves are not too abrupt for the blade to follow. One advantage of this template guide is that it can be used with a variety of templates and shapes.

Figure 274 — Curved Pieces on the Band Saw

The template guide is clamped to the band saw table with the nose notch positioned so it surrounds the blade. The edge of the blade should be even with the outer edge of the guide. The workpiece is attached to the top of the template.

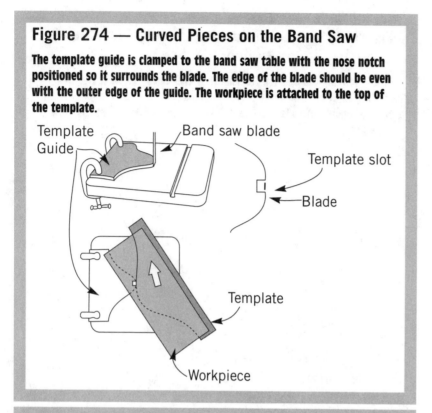

Template Guide

Band saw blade

Template slot

Blade

Template

Workpiece

Figure 275 — Cutting Odd Shapes on the Band Saw

The template is uniformly smaller than the finished piece and glides back and forth in the groove as the template rubs against the guide pin. The upper blade support (not shown) should be as close to the workpiece as possible.

Band saw blade

Workpiece

Pattern

Spacer

Sliding pivot

Guide pin

Auxiliary table

Oval and Round Cuts

This fixture evolved from the common circle cutting jig that uses an auxiliary table clamped to the band saw table. The fixture is simply a piece of ¾ inch plastic-covered plywood with a ¾ inch wide groove routed in the top. The center line of the groove should line up with the cutting edge of the blade. The rest of the fixture consists of a guide pin, a sliding pivot pin, and a spacer. The guide pin and the sliding pivot are both ¼ inch dowels pressed into small blocks sized to fit the groove (see **Figure 275**).

To use the fixture, first cut a template exactly one inch smaller than the finished size of the workpiece and drill a pivot hole near its center. Make sure the edges are smooth and polished with paste wax because this piece must rotate as it rubs against the guide pin. Next, place the guide pin in the groove at an appropriate distance from the blade, in this case ½ inch. Fix the guide pin at this distance by placing one or more spacer blocks between the guide and the end of the groove. The distance from the guide pin to the blade will determine the enlargement of the finished duplicate over the template.

Now, attach a blank to the template with brads, double-sided tape or hot-melt glue. Fit the blank and template assembly over the pivot pin and cut the duplicate by rotating it while applying gentle pressure toward the guide pin. The pivot pin will slide back and forth in the groove as the template follows the guide pin. Often, the stock is too large to allow the template to contact the guide pin at first. In this case, simply turn the template and feed the stock into the blade until the template touches the pin much as is done with a circle cutting fixture.

Drum Sander Templates
Drum Sander on the Drill Press

Use a drum sander instead of a shaper to prevent tear-out in heavily figured woods such as bird's-eye maple. Also, pieces that are too small to work on the shaper safely can be readily shaped with a drum sander.

To use a drum sanding template on a drill press, first build a bearing rub block. Cut the base from ¾ inch plywood or particle board and place it on the drill press table or drum sander table (see **Figure 276**), fastening it to the drill press base with carriage bolts or from underneath with large wood screws. Make a rubbing block out of ¼ inch hardboard with the circular end the same diameter as the sanding drum. Install the rubbing block and chuck up your sanding drum. Align the rubbing block

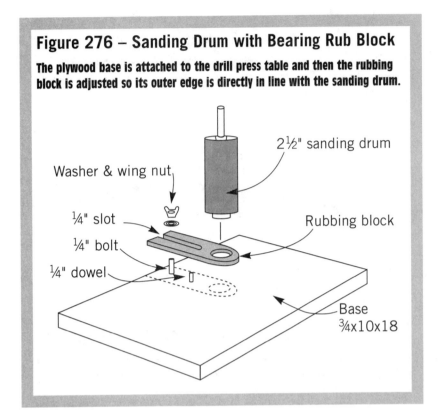

Figure 276 – Sanding Drum with Bearing Rub Block
The plywood base is attached to the drill press table and then the rubbing block is adjusted so its outer edge is directly in line with the sanding drum.

2½" sanding drum

Washer & wing nut

¼" slot

¼" bolt

¼" dowel

Rubbing block

Base ¾x10x18

side to side with the sanding drum and then lock the table in place. Slide the rub block on the dowel and locking bolt to align it front to back. Tighten the locking wing nut. Lower the sanding drum until the bottom of it is just above the rubbing block.

In use, make the template from ¼ inch material. Band saw your part to close but rough shape, and attach the template to it with double-sided tape. Move the workpiece against the spinning sanding drum until the template contacts the rub block. This method only works well when ⅛ inch or less of material is to be removed.

Rule of Thumb
When you're shaping **birds'-eye maple**, prevent tear-out by using a drum sander instead of a router.

Figure 277 — Bearing Guided Sanding Drum

The template is beneath the workpiece and rubs against the bearing mounted on the drum. This method works best when ⅛ inch or less material is to be removed.

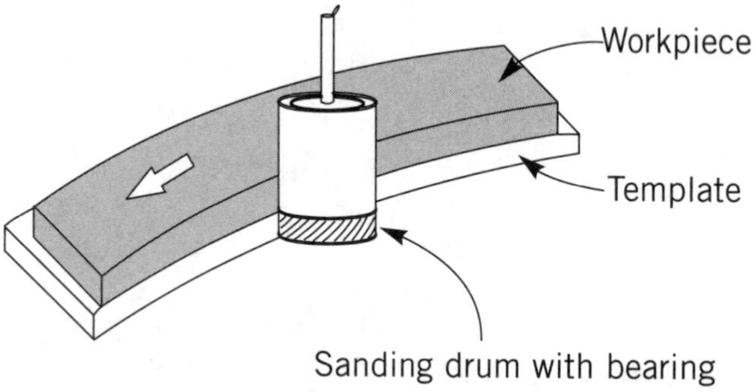

Workpiece

Template

Sanding drum with bearing

Figure 278 — Template Shaping with a Disk Sander

The workpiece is shaped as the template rubs against the metal fence. Make the template smaller than the finished size by the distance from the inside of the fence to the sanding disk.

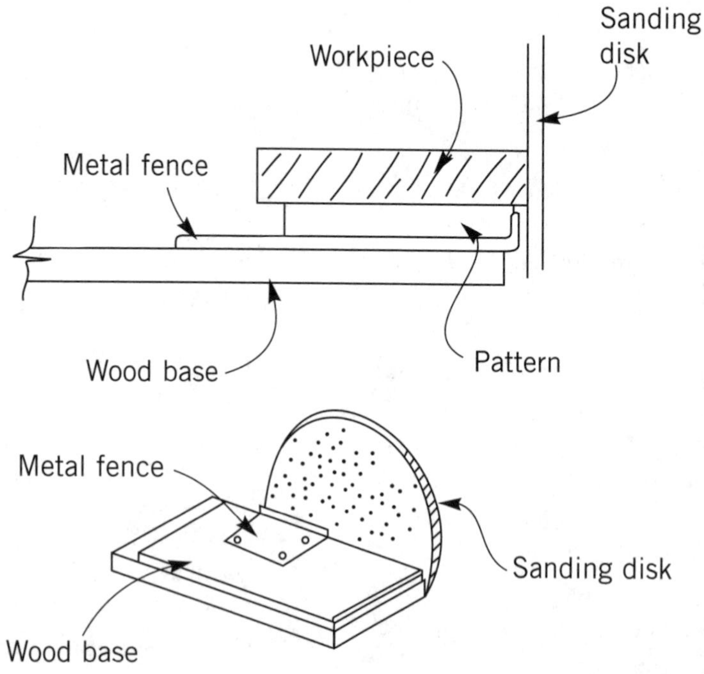

Sanding disk

Workpiece

Metal fence

Wood base

Pattern

Metal fence

Wood base

Sanding disk

Bearing-Guided Drum Sanding

Sanding drums with bearing guides are commercially available. Fasten a template of the same thickness as the bearing guide to the workpiece and go (see **Figure 277**). To avoid a lip on the workpiece the template can be slightly thicker than the bearing.

Disk Sander Templates
Straight Cuts

A 10 inch disk sander is just the tool to use when producing small items that are dangerous to do with a shaper. Only two parts are necessary — a template and a guide fence. The template is best made of ¼ inch thick plastic shaped and smoothed on the disk sander. Because the template rubs against the guide fence, it must be made smaller than the dimensions of the finished work. The guide fence is simply a 4 inch square of sheet metal with one edge bent up to form a ³⁄₁₆ inch lip. Attach the guide fence to a plywood base with countersunk screws so that the lip slightly overhangs one edge of the plywood. Now clamp the plywood to the disk sander table with the guide fence next to, but not touching, the disk (see **Figure 278**).

Fasten the slightly over-size workpiece to the plastic template with sandpaper, double-sided tape or protruding brad points. A sheet of sandpaper glued to the top of the template provides enough friction for most situations. Push the template against the sheet metal fence and slide it along to grind the workpiece to shape. With 100 grit sandpaper, fashioning one piece on all four sides takes less than a minute for a small, uncomplicated shape. The fixture shown may be used to form straight or convex shapes only. Concave shapes could be easily cut using a similar device that incorporated a curved guide fence and a small drum sander.

Circles

Those of you who make toys know that each one needs a different size wheel. By cutting the circles with a hole-saw and then smoothing the crude piece on the disk sander, duplicate wheels are a snap to make — and they're all the same size. A template, a fence and a dowel on which to rotate the workpiece is all you need. Place the rough-cut wheel on the dowel and use the appropriate side of the template. The metal fence attached to the sander table keeps the wheels equal distance from the sanding disk. **Figure 279** shows a template that can be used for 1, 2, 3, and 4 inch wheels.

In use, the rough-cut wheel made with a hole saw or a fly-

wheel cutter, is placed on the template. The template is pushed up to the fence and the workpiece is rotated against the disk until the piece is completely rounded.

Lathe Templates

We often must use a lathe to make duplicate parts such as furniture legs, posts, and spindles. Smaller pieces, such as candle holders or finials, also come to mind. Every wood turner knows that it's pretty easy to turn the first spindle — it's cutting that exact shape three more times that gives you trouble. And what about turning 50 or 60 balusters for the porch railing? Sometimes the pieces can be done by hand because they only have to be close — the eye readily detects turned features that are different heights and lengths, but is easily fooled by different diameters. Other times the pieces have to be exactly the same. Using a template and a hand-held cutting unit will increase accuracy and speed production when all the pieces have to be dead on (**Figure 280**).

Plan and lay out the template on a piece of heavy paper or light cardboard. Then glue the temporary pattern to a more substantial template surface and cut with a band saw — be sure to cut to the waste side of the layout line. Fine details are

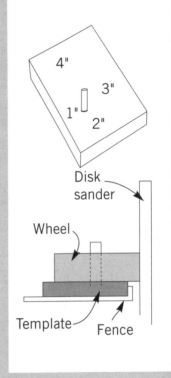

Figure 279 —Wheels

The dowel pin in the square block is placed so that wheels of different diameters can be shaped using different sides of the same template.

Rule of Thumb

Template-guided cuts work best when the amount of material removed is small. In general, use the band saw to rough out parts to within 1/8 inch of the layout line, before you use a template to shape, rout, or sand them to final shape and size.

Figure 280 — Lathe Duplicator

The duplicator table is attached with metal strapping to the tubular lathe bed, or with bolts to a flat bed, and lined up so the center-line of the template is directly under the center-line of the lathe. Use either the original turning as a pattern or make a flat template of plastic or tempered hardwood. The hand-held follower traces the template and cuts the workpiece.

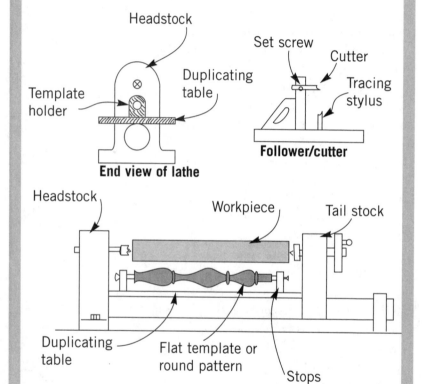

Headstock

Set screw

Cutter

Tracing stylus

Template holder

Duplicating table

End view of lathe

Follower/cutter

Headstock

Workpiece

Tail stock

Duplicating table

Flat template or round pattern

Stops

with each pass, steadily deteriorating the fine details. If the pattern doesn't have sharp beads and ridges, use ¼ inch tempered hardboard, it's fairly hard, durable, inexpensive, and provides a template that can be used 10 or 15 times.

Plastics, such as acrylic or polycarbonate, make excellent templates. They are harder than tempered hardboard, long wearing, cheap, readily available, and easy to work.

For more durability, or when the pattern is such that sharp points may become blurred with long use, use aluminum laminated to a piece of ¼ inch plywood. I found 0.25 inch aluminum sheet 6 inch x 24 inch at a local store for $6.50. If this is an original, it isn't critical that the pattern exactly match the drawing. The curves and beads and coves can be slightly different, as long as all the pieces are the same. If you are copying an existing turning, the template should be laid out with extreme care, because any error in the template measurements will be reproduced in the workpiece.

Duplicator

The duplicator consists of a table that is attached to the lathe bed and a hand-held follower that slides along the table and does the actual cutting. The uprights at each end of the table hold a

added with a file and sandpaper. The final template should include all details necessary for completing the final turning.

Lathe templates are always constructed full size. Template material should be hard enough to resist the pressure of the stylus rubbing against it because in time you'll create a flat strip down the length that gets wider flat template or the turning you want to duplicate. The follower that guides the cutting is made of hard wood or a workable metal such as brass or aluminum. The heavier this piece, the less vibration you will experience during the cutting. A cutter is mounted directly over the tracing stylus, **Figure 280**.

This set-up isn't robust enough to cut a part from a square blank but once the blank has been rounded to within ½ inch, this duplicator will finish the job nicely.

The duplicating table is made of any flat, stable material. I made mine of ¾ inch plywood topped with a plastic such as Melamine that allows the follower to slide easily. You'll have to make a new base for each duplication so keep it simple. The end uprights are screwed to the base and hold the template or the original turning, and can be saved and used again.

The cutting unit (**Figure 281**) consists of two pieces — the base and the upright. The base is 12 inches long and 4 inches wide. The upright is 5¼ inches long by 4 inches wide. Both are made of ¾ inch oak or similar hardwood.

First cut a dado into the base to hold the upright. The base has two handles made of 1 inch dowel set at 15° angles. Drill the holes with a 1 inch Forstner bit

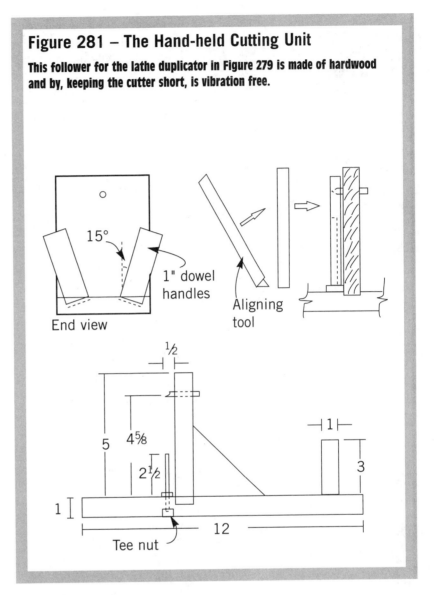

Figure 281 – The Hand-held Cutting Unit

This follower for the lathe duplicator in Figure 279 is made of hardwood and by, keeping the cutter short, is vibration free.

and attach the handles with glue and screws. Drill a ⅜ inch hole in the base and drive in a metal threaded insert from the bottom. The internal threads should be ¼ inch x 20 tpi. To make the tracing stylus, cut the head off a stainless steel carriage bolt, add a nut, and thread this into the insert.

Drill a ¼ inch hole for the cutter

Rule of Thumb

In most **template routing** applications, a bit with spiral (helical) flutes and a ball-bearing guide will produce smoother and more accurate results than a straight-flute bit with a solid steel pilot.

at the exact height so it will be at the center line of the lathe. Also drill and add a metal threaded insert for a set screw. Attach the upright to the base with glue and screws. Add two triangular braces and the unit will be sturdy enough to cut without vibration.

The cutter can be made from a ¼ inch drill bit or drill rod ground to a pencil-shaped cone and then ground flat on top. The end of the cutter should be the same diameter as the tracing stylus directly below it. Mount and adjust these parts so that when the edge of the tracer touches the template, the cutter cuts that diameter. Make an aligning tool from a piece of metal. This triangular piece, about 6 inches long, makes lining them up easy.

A lot of old turnings are out-of-round and bowed. If you position the original with the bow up or down, it shouldn't affect the reproduction; that's why the tracing stylus is fairly tall. If the original spindle is broken or if it flexes in the middle and you plan to make a lot of duplicates, make a template from it. Use the regular tool rest and rough out the new parts in the normal manner. You can get pretty close by just eying the old spindle.

In use, the old spindle or the

template is mounted between centers on the duplicator.

After the new parts have been roughed out, move the standard tool rest out of the way and install the duplicator table with the template attached. Line everything up and tighten the table down. Polish and wax the follower base to keep it sliding smoothly. Now, just guide the follower/cutter to trim the new turning to final size.

Note — The end pieces on the duplicator table act as stops so the tracing stylus does not drop off the end of the template, which would allow the cutter to dig into the workpiece or perhaps to contact the revolving drive center or tail center.

You'll have to decide when to use a lathe duplicator — when it's worth the effort to make a template and set it all up. For me, I figure it's about six turnings. Up to that number, I can use calipers, a cardboard pattern, and then eyeball each piece. I can get pretty close and, even when the pieces are installed side-by-side, they look good. More than six and it's hard to keep the quality high and each piece seems to get just a little further from the original. It's time for a duplicator.

Shaper Templates
Curved Pieces

The trick to making uniform curved pieces is to use a shaper with a flush-trim bit and a template. The template makes cutting out the pieces a simple one-two process — first on the band saw and then on the shaper — that produces pieces with the same shape, **Figure 282**.

Use ¼ inch Masonite to make the template. It's an inexpensive, hard material that doesn't have voids or knots and you can easily work the edges smooth. Start by laying it out full-size on a piece of paper. Glue it to the hardboard and cut the shape slightly oversize so you can carefully sand and file right up to the line.

Any notches or gouges on the edge of the template will be transmitted to the finished pieces so take time to work the edges smooth. After the template is made, securely attach it to the workpiece with double-sided tape or with wood screws. Then band saw the piece about ⅛ inch larger than the template. Be careful here to not saw into the template.

Using an Original as a Pattern

In many situations you can use an original part as a pattern for making duplicates. Mount a

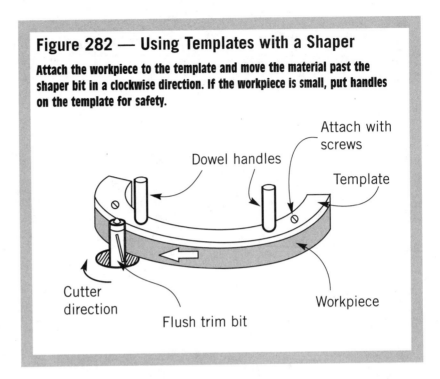

Figure 282 — Using Templates with a Shaper

Attach the workpiece to the template and move the material past the shaper bit in a clockwise direction. If the workpiece is small, put handles on the template for safety.

Attach with screws
Dowel handles
Template
Cutter direction
Flush trim bit
Workpiece

flush trim bit into the shaper and with the original part taped or screwed to the workpiece, raise the bit until the bearing rides on the edge of the pattern. Then rout in a clock-wise direction around the bit (see **Figure 283**).

Thick Pieces

If the workpiece is thicker than the cutting edge of the bit, lower the bit to make a second pass. The bearing will now rub against the freshly cut surface of the workpiece to cut off the remaining shoulder, **Figure 284.**

Shaping with a Pin Guide

Using a pin to guide the pattern on a shaper has the advantage that the template is quite easy to make and the setup can be used

Figure 283 — Duplicating Parts on the Shaper

Attach the original piece to the workpiece with double-sided tape or screws. The flush trim bit will remove up to ¼ inch of material.

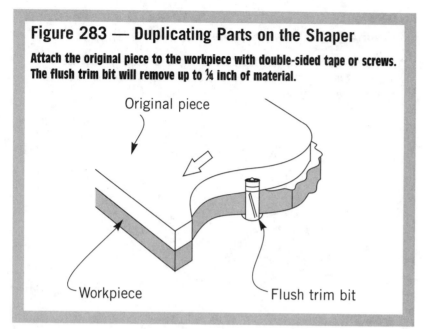

Original piece

Workpiece

Flush trim bit

Figure 284 — Material is Bigger than the Bit

If the workpiece is thicker than the cutting edge of the bit (a) make the first cut with the bearing on the template. Then lower the bit to make a second cut (b). The bearing will now ride against the freshly cut surface of the workpiece to cut off the remaining shoulder.

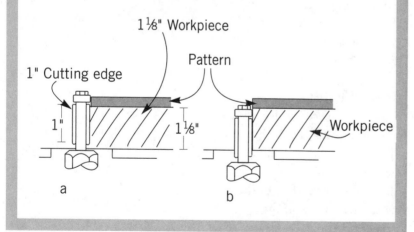

1⅛" Workpiece

Pattern

1" Cutting edge

1"

1⅛"

Workpiece

a   b

fussy, for any departure from a straight line is doubled when the pieces are placed face-to-face. The traditional solution is to use a shooting board where you clamp the veneers between cauls and hand-plane the exposed edges. This is tricky because the cauls do not always distribute pressure equally and the grain tends to split and run.

By using a form of pattern cutting on a shaper, with a piece of ground tool steel as the template, the precision cutting of veneer edges becomes routine. The ground metal stock is available at any tool-and-die supply house. It's somewhat expensive (about $32 for a ⅛ inch x 1½ inch x 32 inch piece). You don't want to buy thinner material because accuracy is based on the stiffness of the steel cross section. To avoid distortion, do not heat-treat the bar or machine it in any way — simply embed and bond it into the upper jig section. I used ⅞ inch red oak and cut the slot on a table saw with a thin-kerf blade. Use polyurethane adhesive to hold the steel piece in place and let about ¼ inch metal protrude. See **Figure 285a**. Cut a rabbet ⁵⁄₁₆ inch wide x ¼ inch deep along the edge of the bottom board and push in a length of ⅜ inch OD rubber or plastic tubing. This will provide support along the protruding bottom edge of the veneer.

many times. In the example here, we'll be cutting a straight edge on veneer pieces.

Joining long edges of veneer requires a truly straight cut. Book matching is particularly

Clamp the wavy veneers between the upper jig member and the lower member. It's important that the veneers be supported top and bottom - unsupported veneer will chip away. As the veneers are cut, the sides of the template will push against the guide pin. If either the pin or the pin's support arm moves, there will be a bump in the routed edge. To eliminate any movement, the guide pin should be clamped in a thick support arm which is attached firmly to the fence. See **Figure 285b**.

In use, install a straight spiral bit the same size as the pin. Attach the metal pin, equal in diameter to that of the cutter, to the fence so that the pin is centered over the cutter about ½ inch above it. Great precision is not required; eyeballing the pin location is adequate. With the pin guiding the steel bar, the cutter usually will generate a perfect edge on the veneers in one pass. The newer spiral bits cut a lot smoother than a straight flute bit. Even such hard and brittle materials as bird's-eye maple are easily cut with this technique.

Router Templates

The hand-held router is one of the most versatile tools in the shop and has changed the way we do woodworking. With modern bits, it can make clean, tear-free cuts. It is fast and it does not require a lot of skill to

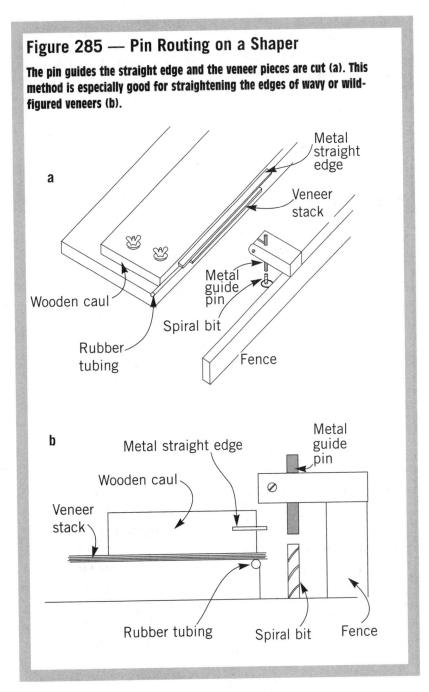

Figure 285 — Pin Routing on a Shaper

The pin guides the straight edge and the veneer pieces are cut (a). This method is especially good for straightening the edges of wavy or wild-figured veneers (b).

operate. Probably it takes more skill to make an accurate template to guide the router than it does to complete the actual routing. The router's strong suit is its potential for truly accurate work. The machine's shaft and

Figure 286 — Bits with Tip- and Shank-Mounted Pilots

Flush trimming bits with pilots at the tip (a) can be guided by the shaped portion of the workpiece edge or they can follow a template. Pattern bits with the pilot on the shank (b) must be guided by a template fastened to the workpiece.

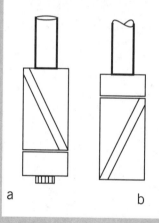

a   b

Rule of Thumb

There are **four ways** to guide a hand-held router using templates. They are:

- The router base is guided by a fence attached to the workpiece,

- An edge guide attached to the base follows workpiece edge,

- Pilot on router bit rides template,

- Guide collar on router base rides template.

collet whirl the cutter in near-perfect rotation, the base drops the cutter to precise depth, and the machine moves smoothly along a guided path.

There are four ways to guide a hand-held router — with the router guided by a fence attached to the workpiece, with the router guided by the edge of the workpiece, with a pilot on the router bit riding the template and with a guide collar on the router base riding the template.

Pilot Bearing

The simplest way to reproduce a piece with a pattern or a template is with a straight bit that has a pilot bearing either at the end of the bit or mounted between the bit and its shank, see **Figure 286**. This free-spinning ball-bearing pilot will not burn the workpiece and, if the bearing freezes, it's usually replaceable by removing the center screw. When the pilot bearing is the same size as the bit, the part will be an exact match. When the pilot bearing is larger or smaller, the piece will be enlarged or reduced. Remember that the router is a finishing tool, not the best tool for rough cutting. Before routing, trace the template onto the blank and band saw the bulk of the waste away.

Following a Pattern

Figure 287 shows three ways to duplicate patterns with a hand-held router. A shank-mounted bearing (**Figure 287a**) is used to guide the bit against a template on top of the workpiece. Glue the pattern to a piece of ¼ inch hardboard and band-saw the piece to rough size. Using files and sandpaper shape the template to final size. The template is then fastened to the workpiece with double-sided tape or screws and the assembly is clamped to the edge of the work bench. Use a straight bit with a shank-mounted pilot bearing and guide the router around the template, cutting in a counter-clockwise direction. If there are other sides of the workpiece to be shaped, the assembly will have to be unclamped, repositioned and clamped again before the rest of the routing can be done.

In **Figure 287b** the router base is held against a template that is clamped or fastened to the workpiece. Rotate the router base so one handle is firmly planted on top of the workpiece. Because the router bit is seldom in the exact center of the router base, the distance from the router bit to the edge of the router base is not the same in all directions. Make a mark on the router base and always keep this point against the fence.

In **Figure 287c** a tip-mounted bearing guides the router against the template that's under the workpiece. By using different sized bearings, the final piece can be made different in size from the pattern. An offset base plate, sometimes called an outrigger, will help stabilize the router as it hangs out in space. Orient the wood so you are cutting with the grain to reduce tear-out. If you still get small chips take light cuts and wet the wood before the final pass.

Straightening Veneer

Straighten and trim veneers between a straight-edge template and a second clamping board. The tip-mounted pilot bearing that rides on the edge of the pattern. Clamp the whole assembly so it hangs over the edge of the bench. An out-rigger on the router improves stability. See **Figure 288**.

Guide Collars

A guide collar, as in **Figure 289**, can be thought of as a much reduced router base. The collar runs against a template and can reproduce the shape of a pattern. The result is a piece enlarged by the offset distance between the outside of the guide collar and the bit's cutting circle. To rout parts that fit precisely together, use guide collars in matched pairs as discussed below.

Figure 287 — Duplicating with a Hand-Held Router

Fasten the pattern to the workpiece with double-sided tape and clamp the assembly to the edge of the work bench. The pilot bearing follows the pattern to cut a duplicate workpiece. Guide a shank-mounted bearing against a fence that's on top of the workpiece. An offset base plate (outrigger) stabilizes the router (a). Guide the router base against the pattern clamped to the workpiece. Rotate the machine to put one handle firmly over the contact between the base and fence (b). Guide a tip-mounted bearing against the pattern that's under the workpiece. An offset base plate will help stabilize the router (c).

(a) Shank-mounted bearing against a pattern

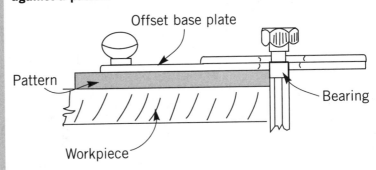

(b) Router base against a pattern

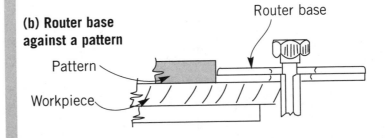

(c) Tip-mounted bearing against a pattern

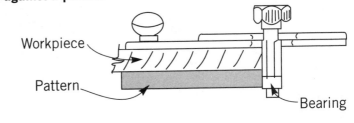

Figure 288 — Straightening Veneers

Capture the veneer pack between a straight template board and a second clamping board. The template must be dead-on straight if long pieces of veneer are to be joined together. The out-rigger, or off-set base plate, provides stability for the router as it hangs out into space.

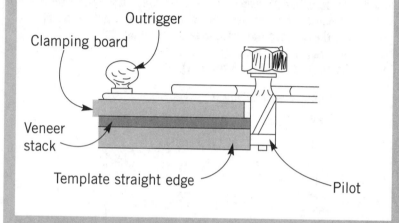

Outrigger

Clamping board

Veneer stack

Template straight edge

Pilot

Figure 289 — Routing the Recess and the Inlay

Using the same template, the large collar allows you to rout the recess (a). Use the small collar to rout the inlay (b).

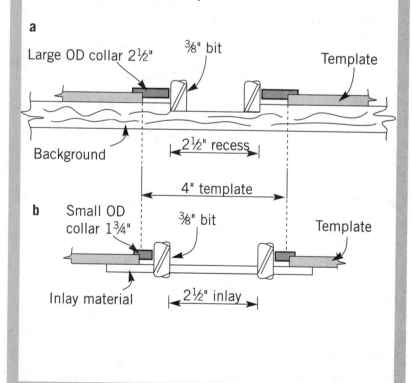

a

Large OD collar 2½"

⅜" bit

Template

Background

2½" recess

4" template

b Small OD collar 1¾"

⅜" bit

Template

Inlay material

2½" inlay

Inlay Work

Figure 289 shows how you can use a single pattern and the same router bit to cut both the recess in the background and the inlay piece. Use different sized collars — a large collar for the recess cut and a small collar for the inlay piece.

When you use guide collars with a shaped template, the diameter of the bit and the diameters of the collars must match. In **Figure 289** we use the same bit and the same template to cut both the 2½ inch recess and the 2½ inch inlay. Adding and subtracting offsets is a source of much confusion and most people have to experiment before they understand how it works. Nevertheless, it's often the only way to rout a recess that will exactly fit an inlay.

Math for Routing an Inlay

For the inlay to fit exactly into the recess, the size relationship of the large and small collars is:

Outside Diameter of Large Collar minus two times the Bit Diameter = Outside Diameter of Small Collar

$$LC - 2BD = SC$$

Where LC = Large collar, BD = Bit diameter, SC = Small collar.

Problem 1: We have a 2 inch collar and a ½ inch bit. What size small collar should we use?

Solution 1:

$$LC - 2BD = SC$$

Where LC = 2,

BD = 0.5, SC =?

$$2 - 2(0.5) = SC$$

$$SC = 2 - 1 = 1$$

Therefore we would use a ½ inch bit, a 2 inch large guide collar and a 1 inch small collar for the inlay job.

The table in **Figure 290** shows matching guide collar sizes to use when doing inlay work. To illustrate the use of the table take the following example:

Problem 2: We have a set of router guide collars (bushings) and different sized bits. We want to inlay a butterfly across a table joint. The inlay will be approximately 3 inches long and 2 inches wide with ½ inch radius corners. What bit should be used and what set of guide collars?

Solution 2: For the ½ inch radius corners, we probably should use a small bit – say ¼ inch. From the chart in **Figure 290** we see five bushing sets for a ¼ inch bit from 2 inch - 1½ inch through 1 inch - ½ inch. Our first choice will be the set of 1 inch and ½ inch guide collars because of the tight corners. If the 1 inch OD bushing doesn't seat in the template corners, you could instead use the ⅛ inch bit and the ½ inch and ¼ inch set of guide collars.

Figure 290 — Inlay Guide Collar Pairs

Use the guide collar pairs listed in this table with the bit size indicated to rout a recess and to cut out an inlay piece that fits it. The same pattern will be used for both inlay and recess.

Bit Diameter (English)	OD Large Bushing (English)	OD Small Bushing (English)	Bit Diameter (Decimal)	OD Large Bushing (Decimal)	OD Small Bushing (Decimal)
1/8	1	3/4	0.125	1	0.75
	3/4	1/2		0.75	0.5
	1/2	1/4		0.5	0.25
1/4	2	1-1/2	0.25	2	1.5
	1-3/4	1-1/4		1.75	1.25
	1-1/2	1		1.5	1
	1-1/4	3/4		1.25	0.75
	1	1/2		1	0.5
5/16	2	1-3/8	0.3125	2	1.375
	1-3/4	1-1/8		1.75	1.125
	1-1/2	7/8		1.5	0.875
	1-1/4	5/8		1.25	0.625
3/8	2-1/2	1-3/4	0.375	2.5	1.75
	2	1-1/4	0.375	2	1.25
	1-3/4	1		1.75	1
	1-1/2	3/4		1.5	0.75
	1-1/4	1/2		1.25	0.5
1/2	3	2	0.5	3	2
	2-3/4	1-3/4		2.75	1.75
	2-1/2	1-1/2		2.5	1.5
	2	1		2	1
	1-3/4	3/4		1.75	0.75

Index

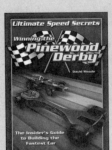